PREFACE TO WILLS, TRUSTS AND ADMINISTRATION

By

PAUL G. HASKELL
William Rand Kenan, Jr. Professor of Law
University of North Carolina School of Law

SECOND EDITION

Westbury, New York
THE FOUNDATION PRESS, INC.
1994

Library of Congress Cataloging-in-Publication Data
Haskell, Paul G.
   Preface to wills, trusts, and administration / by Paul G. Haskell.
  — 2nd ed.
     p.   cm. — (University textbook series)
   Includes index.
   ISBN 1-56662-148-8
    1. Wills—United States. 2. Trusts and trustees—United States.
  3. Executors and administrators—United States. I. Title.
  II. Series.
KF755.H27 1994
346.7305'4—dc20
[347.30654]   94–7713

 TEXT IS PRINTED ON 10% POST CONSUMER RECYCLED PAPER

Haskell-Wills, Trusts & Admin. 2nd Ed. UTS
2nd Reprint–2001

PREFACE TO THE SECOND EDITION

There are several reasons for a new edition at this time. In 1990 substantial changes were made in the Uniform Probate Code which require explanation and discussion. The prudent person rule for trustee investment was replaced by modern portfolio theory in the Restatement of Trusts in 1990, a most significant change. I have included a section which explains the economics of modern portfolio theory in terms that the uninitiated can understand. Finally, estates and trusts lawyers are now focusing on problems of professional responsibility much more than in the past. I have added a chapter in which some basic issues are discussed. I teach professional responsibility, and it is apparent to me that trusts and estates instruction usually does not deal with this area adequately.

I have experimented recently by assigning my texts and distributing problems and old exam questions. This is not a new idea, of course, but I have found it to be a good one; the classroom is livelier than it has been in previous years. A steady diet of cases, many of them poorly constructed, for two or three years may not be pedagogically effective.

Karin Dovey and Debra Pittman of the class of 1992 at the University of North Carolina Law School did research for me on this edition. I am very grateful to them for their able and conscientious efforts.

PAUL G. HASKELL

October 1993

*

iii

PREFACE TO THE FIRST EDITION

This is a textbook intended primarily for use by law students. The purpose is to present a brief, readable statement of the legal framework of wills, trusts and administration which the law student can understand without any assistance from the classroom.

In the past several decades there has been a great expansion of private and public law, but the semester hours of legal education have not been increased. This has resulted in the reduction of the number of hours allocated to many basic subjects such as trusts and estates. The trusts and estates instructor often has insufficient time to deal adequately with sophisticated cases, estate planning problems, policy considerations or law reform. If the students have read the appropriate sections of this book before class, the instructor should be better able to treat the subject as he would like.

I have always found it difficult to deal with the administration of the decedent's estate in the classroom. I have an extensive chapter on estate administration which uses the Uniform Probate Code as the thread with comparative references to non–UPC statutes and rules. This approach illustrates the statutory nature of the subject and familiarizes the reader with the usual procedural steps and alternatives.

An earlier book of mine, Preface To The Law Of Trusts, has been incorporated into this book. Portions of it have been integrated with the wills materials, and the rest has been updated to reflect the broader adoption of uniform legislation and recent case law.

Several University of North Carolina Law School students did research for me. Ronald Rogers of the class of 1986 assisted me for about a year, and among other chores, plowed through a great deal of difficult statutory material. Chalk Broughton, class of 1988, Beth Ann Falk, class of 1988, and Judith Siegel, class of 1986, assisted me during summer months. I am very grateful to them for their able and conscientious efforts.

PAUL G. HASKELL

April 1987

*

v

SUMMARY OF CONTENTS

TABLE OF CONTENTS

TABLE OF CONTENTS

x

TABLE OF CONTENTS

PREFACE TO WILLS, TRUSTS AND ADMINISTRATION

*

Chapter 1

A LISTING OF THE PRINCIPAL AREAS OF THE LAW CONCERNED WITH WEALTH TRANSMISSION

People accumulate property in a variety of forms, such as furniture, jewelry, bank accounts, land, government and corporate bonds, corporate stock, and gold. This book describes the law that is concerned with the donative disposition of such property at death and in some instances during life.

The law permits one to designate who are to become the owners of one's property after death, subject to a qualification or two. This is done by a will. Since the donor of the property is no longer around to confirm the authenticity of the document which purports to dispose of the property, it is important that precautions be taken to assure its genuineness. This accounts for the ritualistic procedure for the signing of the will. The person who dies leaving a will is called a "testator," and is described as having died "testate." Matters pertaining to wills are referred to as "testamentary." The gift of real property in a will is a "devise," and the recipient is a "devisee;" the gift of personal property in a will is a "bequest" or "legacy," and the recipient is a "legatee." Because the rules governing testamentary gifts of real property and personal property are substantially the same today, it is common practice to use the words "devise" and "devisee" with respect to testamentary gifts of both categories of property.

Some people do not deem it necessary to have a will, for one reason or another, or neglect to make one. In this event a statute designates who the successors to the property are to be. The statutes vary, but they give first priority to the spouse and descendants of the decedent, and in their absence provide for more remote relations in a stated order of priority. The passing of property at death by statute rather than will is called "intestacy," and the decedent is said to have died "intestate." Those who take real property in intestacy are "heirs," and those who take personal property are sometimes called "next of kin," or "distributees." In the past real property and personal property passed differently in intestacy, but in most states today both forms of property pass to the same persons in the same shares. There is consequently little reason to differentiate between the takers of the different forms of property, and the word "heirs" is generally used to describe those who take in intestacy regardless of the nature of the property.

Here are a few problems that may arise when a person attempts to dispose of her property by will. Can a person validly execute a will if she is senile, or schizophrenic? Is there a legal problem if a competent but elderly and infirm widow leaves a will disposing of her property to her housekeeper upon whom she has been wholly dependent physically, and leaves nothing to her children? Is it legally permissible for a testator to leave a substantial portion of her property to the lawyer who prepares the will and is not related to the testator? Can a person disinherit her spouse in her will, or her minor or disabled children?

Suppose a person executes a will in 1982. Can she tear it up and execute a new will with different provisions in 1985? And then do the same thing again in 1986? Can a person legally contract to leave a will containing certain provisions?

Suppose a person validly executes a will in his lawyer's office, and takes it home with him. At his death six months later the will cannot be found. An unsigned copy was retained by the lawyer in her file. Does the person die with a will or does his property pass by intestacy?

What happens if Blackacre is left to Jones in the decedent's will and Jones predeceases the decedent? What happens if Jones survives the decedent but the decedent gave Blackacre away to Smith, or sold it to Brown, after he executed the will and never changed his will?

Suppose a person executes a will leaving $25,000 to his sister. Later he makes a gift of $25,000 to his sister, sends her a note stating that the gift is in lieu of the provision for her in his will, and never changes his will before his death. Is sister entitled to the $25,000 in the will?

When the property owner dies there is a need to wind up his affairs in an orderly fashion and distribute the net assets in accordance with the terms of the will or to those who take in intestacy. This process is called estate administration. A person or a bank is appointed by the appropriate court to collect the decedent's assets, to pay his debts, taxes and administrative expenses, and to distribute what is left to those entitled. If the decedent leaves a will, the party to perform this function is usually designated in the will and is called an "executor." In the case of a will the first step in the administration of the estate is the judicial determination that the will is valid and the appointment of the executor by the court. The judicial establishment of the will as the legally dispositive document is called the "probate" of the will. If there is no will, the first step is the appointment by the court of a party to administer the estate, who is called the "administrator." The generic term for the party who administers an estate, testate or intestate, is the "personal representative." The specific individuals who take in intestacy are usually determined by the court in the course of administration.

Now that we have referred to wills, intestacy and estate administration, the reader should know promptly that a good deal of accumulated wealth does not pass through estate administration and is not distributed to those who take under the will or the intestacy statute. For example, a person purchases land or stocks and has title placed in the names of himself and his wife as joint tenants with right of survivorship. If nothing is done to sever the joint tenancy while both are living, and the donor dies, his share passes by operation of law to his wife by virtue of the nature of the joint tenancy. The passing of his interest is unaffected by the terms of his will or the intestacy statute, and his interest is not subject to estate administration. Another example is life insurance payable to a specified beneficiary, such as a spouse or a child; upon the death of the insured the proceeds pass directly by contract to the designated beneficiary unaffected by the will or intestacy and do not pass through estate administration. Other transactions having similar characteristics are revocable trusts (to be described in a succeeding paragraph) and bank accounts payable on death to a designated person. All these devices which allow for the passing of property at death outside of estate administration and without regard to the will or intestacy are frequently referred to collectively as "will substitutes." Needless to say, a substantial amount of wealth at death is held in these forms.

If a person holds title to stocks or bank accounts or chattels in his name, its disposition at death is controlled by his formally executed will or the intestacy statute, and the asset passes through estate administration which protects creditors and the tax collector and assures that the net estate passes to the right people. If the decedent owned "will substitutes," these safeguards are not applicable. Why do we have two systems of wealth transmission, one of which involves delay and expense but offers protection, the other of which is expeditious but less protective? The answer is that it simply evolved. Lawmakers did not deliberately plan it that way. There is, however, no evidence that the informal, expeditious transmission by will substitute has substantially disadvantaged creditors or the tax collector, or that the relatively informal designation of the recipients of the decedent's wealth by will substitute is subject to more chicanery than the designation by the formally executed will. If this is so, then one wonders whether the will and estate administration process is worth the expense and trouble.

Wills questions, intestate distribution, estate administration, and will substitutes constitute a substantial portion of the contents of this book.

The person who has substantial wealth frequently has some reservations about leaving large amounts outright to his or her spouse or to the children, for one reason or another. Significant considerations may be the lack of confidence that the wealth will be invested competently, concern that the wealth may be dissipated, or concern that the wealth may be diverted from the family line. The person of wealth may wish to designate and control who are to have the benefit of his wealth successively, e.g., his spouse, then his children, then his grandchildren. / Concerns and considerations such as these may move a wealthy person to establish a trust rather than dispose of his property outright.

The trust separates the responsibility of ownership of specific property from the benefit of ownership. The party having the responsibility is called a "trustee" and holds legal title to the specific property in the trust. The persons having the benefit are called the "beneficiaries" and hold the equitable title to the specific property in the trust. The trustee is a fiduciary who holds his title and manages the property exclusively for the benefit of the beneficiaries. The power of management of the trust property is vested in the trustee free of any control by the beneficiaries as long as the trustee is not in violation of his fiduciary obligation. The trustee derives no benefit from his position except the compensation he receives for performing the trustee function.

To understand the functioning of the trust it is necessary to understand the meaning of principal and income. Wealth may be invested in land, government and corporate bonds, corporate stock, and bank accounts. The investment in land produces a return in the form of rent, in stocks a return in the form of dividends, in bonds and bank accounts a return in the form of interest. Invested wealth is called principal; the return which the principal earns, whether in the form of rent, dividends, or interest, is called income. The rate of return varies with the nature of the investment and economic circumstances. It would not be unusual for the return on an annual basis to be as high as 8% or as low as 5% of the value of the principal. This would mean that $300,000 of principal placed in trust would earn from $15,000 to $24,000 per year.

A person with substantial wealth may leave $300,000 in his will to First National Bank, as trustee, whose duty under the terms of the will is to pay the income each year to the decedent's wife for her life, and upon her death, to pay the income each year to the decedent's two children for their lives, and upon their deaths, to distribute the principal to the decedent's grandchildren outright, thereby terminating the trust. In this fashion the decedent property owner has assured that the principal will be professionally managed, that his spouse and children will obtain the benefit of the wealth for their lives, and that the wealth will also benefit his grandchildren. One may ask why the decedent did not continue the trust for the lives of his grandchildren, his great-grandchildren, and so on; he couldn't do that even if he wanted to because of the rule against perpetuities which, in effect, imposes limits upon the duration of trusts.

The trust described in the preceding paragraph is a very much simplified one, but it conveys the fundamental usefulness of the trust as a method of donative disposition to achieve certain objectives. In our example the trust was created by the will of the property owner and it would come into being following his death. This type of trust is called a "testamentary trust." A person may create a trust during his life by transferring assets to a person or bank as trustee for the benefit of himself or others, or both; the trust becomes operative immediately upon the transfer of the property to the trustee. This trust is called a "living trust," or "inter vivos trust." The person creating the trust is called a "settlor." The living trust may provide that it is amendable and revocable by the settlor—that is to say, the settlor reserves the right to change the beneficiaries, or to change his mind at any time and take back the property transferred in trust, thereby terminating the trust.

An example of a revocable and amendable living trust would be one in which the trustee would be obligated to pay the income to the person creating the trust for his life, and upon his death, to pay the income to his children for their lives, and upon their deaths, to pay the principal to his grandchildren, thereby terminating the trust. If the creator of the trust does not revoke during his life, the trust continues after his death in accordance with its terms, and the trust assets do not pass through estate administration. The revocable trust is a type of "will substitute."

The trust is usually intended as a protective device for the family, which raises certain questions. Can the creditors of the beneficiaries levy upon or attach the equitable interests of the beneficiaries? Can the settlor of the trust include provisions in the trust which would deny creditors access to the interests of the beneficiaries? Can the settlor include terms which would give the trustee discretion with respect to the making of payments to the beneficiaries? If it turns out that the dispositive terms of the trust are inadequate to meet the support needs of a beneficiary, can the trust terms be modified by the court? Can the settlor include terms in the trust which condition the payment of benefits upon certain personal conduct, such as marrying within a particular faith, divorcing a particular spouse, or remaining single? Can all the beneficiaries get together and require the trustee to terminate the trust and pay them the principal in the trustee's hands?

The executor or administrator of a decedent's estate is as much a fiduciary as a trustee, but his function is a short-term one; he is required, as expeditiously as possible, to collect assets, pay claims, and distribute to those entitled. This may be done within a year, or it may take several years, depending upon the complexity of the estate and the resolution of death tax liability. The trust, on the other hand, is a long-term function, frequently lasting the lives of several people. The basic principles of fiduciary administration are applicable to both the personal representative of the estate and the trustee, but the trustee is likely to run into more legal questions because of the greater duration of his responsibility. As examples, under what circumstances is a trustee personally liable for a decline in the value of an investment held in trust? If a trustee is empowered to exercise discretion in the making of payments to beneficiaries, what considerations are permissible in arriving at a decision? What are the consequences if a trustee sells trust property to a corporation in which he has a substantial interest?

The law of trusts and trust administration is a substantial portion of the contents of this book.

There is another substantial component of succession law, namely, future interests. Most trusts create a life estate in one person or class of persons, and a remainder in another person or class. Frequently someone holds a power of appointment over all or some part of the assets in the trust. There are sometimes questions concerning whether a future interest holder must survive to the time of the scheduled distribution to her. The rule against perpetuities must always be kept in mind in the preparation of any trust or the exercise of a power of appointment. In sum, the donative trust raises future interest issues involving the law of conditions of survivorship, class gifts, powers of appointment, and the rule against perpetuities. The law of these areas is not dealt with in this book systematically, although from time to time certain elements are alluded to and explained. The reader is directed to another text co-authored by the writer for a treatment of that subject written in the same style as this book.[1]

A wealthy person sometimes disposes of substantial wealth during her lifetime by outright gift free of trust. The donor reserves no life income or power to recall what she has given. The making of such outright gifts does not usually involve significant

---

1. Bergin and Haskell, Preface To   121–238 (2d ed.1984).
Estates In Land And Future Interests

legal questions. Such outright "living" gifts, frequently referred to as "inter vivos" gifts, are not dealt with in this book. The reader is referred to another text for a treatment of the subject.[2]

Then there is the taxation of transfers at death and living transfers. There is a federal estate tax and a federal gift tax, but only the wealthy are affected by these taxes. First of all, the gift tax wholly excludes from consideration any gift by a donor of $10,000 or less to any person in any one year. This means that one donor can make a gift of $10,000 to his daughter in every year without any gift tax consequences. If the donor has five children, he can make gifts of $10,000 to each of his five children every year without any gift tax consequence. Furthermore, the $10,000 per donee per year exclusion can be doubled to $20,000 per donee per year if the donor is married and his or her spouse agrees that the gift shall be deemed to be made one-half ($10,000) by each of them; this is called marital gift-splitting. In addition, gifts of property to one's spouse can be made without gift tax consequences. An enormous amount of wealth can be disposed of by gift over a lifetime without any gift tax consequence. Also, anything given to the spouse at death by will or intestacy passes free of any federal estate tax.

The property owner also has the benefit of an exemption (credit equivalent) of $600,000 for his combined living gifts and property transferred at death. This exemption is over and above the per donee per year exclusion of $10,000 ($20,000 under gift-splitting) and the deduction for living gifts and transfers at death to the spouse. The person of modest wealth is not likely to be touched by federal gift and estate taxes. The person of substantial wealth can minimize the tax impact.

Only a few states have gift taxes. Many states have no estate or inheritance tax except an amount equal to the credit that is allowed under the federal law against the federal estate tax for state death taxes paid. This means that if there is no federal estate tax, there is no state death tax. Other states have estate or inheritance taxes, many with complete exclusion for property passing to the spouse. The state death tax rates tend to be modest.

Since 1986 the federal law has included a "generation-skipping" transfer tax, for the purpose of closing an old and obvious gap in the estate tax system. Assume a donor at his death bequeaths and devises his wealth in trust to pay the income to his spouse for her life, then to pay the income to his children for their lives, and upon their deaths, to pay the principal outright to the grandchildren. Prior to the generation-skipping transfer tax, there would be no tax on account of the principal of the trust at the death

2. Brown, Law of Personal Property
154–188 (3d Ed.1975).

of the wife or at the deaths of the children. They only had life estates; at their deaths they owned nothing that would be subject to the estate tax because their interests terminated at their deaths. The generation-skipping transfer tax is not imposed at the death of the spouse because she is deemed to be in the same generation as the decedent donor who was subjected to the estate tax at his death on the principal of the trust; there is no skipping of a generation at that point. But the generation-skipping tax is imposed at the deaths of the children because the benefit does move from one generation to the next at that time without any estate tax imposed. There is, however, a substantial exemption applicable to this situation which means that the generation-skipping transfer tax applies only to those of considerable wealth. It should be noted that if the decedent left property outright, or in trust, directly to his grandchildren without any prior interest in his living children, the generation-skipping transfer tax would apply. The generation-skipping transfer tax is a very complex system. The purpose here is to let the reader know of its existence.

Gift, estate and generation-skipping taxation is beyond the scope of this text. The reader is referred to another text for a treatment of the subject.[3]

3. McNulty, Federal Estate And Gift Taxation In A Nutshell (4th ed.1989).

Chapter 2

INTESTACY

The Uniform Probate Code was promulgated in 1969. Uniform laws are legislative recommendations to the states. The Uniform Probate Code has been legislated in a minority of states, but individual sections have been legislated in many states.

There have been piecemeal amendments to the Code from time to time. In 1990, however, there was a substantial revision of Article 2 of the Code dealing with intestacy, will execution, will revocation, will construction, will substitutes, spouse's elective share, and related matters. These topics are dealt with in Chapters 2, 3, 4, 6, 7 and 8 of this book. In 1989 Article 6 of the Code dealing with certain will substitutes was substantially revised; Chapter 7 of this book deals with these matters. Whether or not these substantial revisions will receive acceptance by the states remains to be seen.

In this Chapter 2 there are references to the pre–1990 Uniform Probate Code (or pre–1990 Code) and to the 1990 Uniform Probate Code (or 1990 Code). There are also references to the Uniform Probate Code (or the Code) in instances in which no substantial change has been made by the 1990 revision.

SECTION 1. GENERAL STRUCTURE

If a person dies without a will his property passes to those specified in the intestacy statute. In order to be an heir one must survive the decedent. If the decedent and the would-be heir die in a common disaster so that it is impossible to determine the order of their deaths, the Uniform Simultaneous Death Act,[1] which has been legislated in most jurisdictions, provides that the decedent is deemed to have been the survivor. This avoids having the decedent's property pass through two estates in immediate succession. In 1991 the Uniform Simultaneous Death Act was revised to require that an heir survive the decedent by 120 hours.[2] The Uniform Probate Code[3] also requires that to be an heir one must survive the decedent by 120 hours.[4]

1. 8A U.L.A. 557 (1983).

2. 8A U.L.A. 315 (Supp.1992).

3. Pre-1990 U.P.C.: 8 U.L.A. 1 (1983); 1990 U.P.C.: 8 U.L.A. 66 (Supp. 1992).

4. U.P.C. § 2–104 (both versions).

It should be noted that the heirs take what is left over after the payment of debts, taxes, and the expenses of administration. It should also be noted that joint tenancy property, life insurance payable to beneficiaries other than the estate, bank accounts payable on death to specified individuals, and other will substitutes pass in accordance with their terms and not to the heirs, as discussed in Chapter 7.

A person may die with a will but it may not dispose of all his property. In that event what is not disposed of by the will passes under the terms of the intestacy statute. For example, the will may bequeath $25,000 to Jones, and devise Blackacre, a specific parcel of land, to Smith; this was the property the testator owned at the time he executed his will. At the testator's death his net estate consisted of $50,000, Blackacre, and another parcel of land, Whiteacre. $25,000 and Whiteacre pass by intestacy. The testator has died partially testate and partially intestate. Partial intestacy is generally avoided by the inclusion of a catch-all concluding "residuary clause" which reads, "All the rest and residue of my property, real and personal, I bequeath and devise to Brown." This clause disposes of all property not disposed of by means of bequests or devises of specific property or bequests of dollar amounts. The will at the time of execution is obviously prospective in its application; it controls the disposition of the property the testator owns at his death which may be more or less than or different from what he owns when he executes his will. A professionally drafted will invariably includes a residuary clause to cover changes in the nature of the property from the time of the execution of the will to the time when the will takes effect.

Even with a residuary clause a testator may die partially intestate. This may occur if Brown is the residuary legatee and devisee, as in our preceding example, and Brown predeceases the testator. This raises the subject of lapse, discussed in Chapter 6, Section 7. Sound drafting would provide for alternative residuary legatees and devisees should Brown predecease the testator, in order to avoid intestacy.

A testator may leave nothing in her will to a relation who would take in intestacy, and may wish to provide in her will that such person is not to receive anything in the event partial or total intestacy occurs. The common law rule is that a provision in a will which purports to deny a person a share of the estate in the event of intestacy is ineffective. The will cannot affect intestate distribution which is a statutory direction. 1990 Uniform Probate Code § 2–101(b) contains an unusual provision which changes the common law by permitting a testator in her will to exclude a person from succeeding to her property by intestate succession; that person's intestate share passes as if he had disclaimed (renounced) his share. Disclaimer is discussed in Section 7 of this chapter.

The intestacy statutes of the states vary in a number of respects, but there are several generalizations that can be made. If the decedent is survived by a spouse and descendants, they usually share in designated proportions. If the decedent is survived by descendants, and no spouse, the descendants take all. If the decedent is survived by a spouse and a parent, but no descendants, the spouse and parent may share in designated proportions or the spouse may take all. If there is a surviving parent but no surviving spouse or descendant, the parent usually takes all. If there is a surviving sibling or issue of a sibling, but no spouse, descendant or parent, the sibling or issue usually take all. If there is no surviving spouse, descendant, parent, sibling or issue of a sibling, then a surviving grandparent or descendant of a grandparent may take. It is reiterated that there are numerous variations in this order, and a few states pass real property somewhat differently from personal property. If none of the specifically enumerated persons survives, the Uniform Probate Code and the statutes in many states provide that the estate escheats to the state, whereas the statutes in other states provide that the estate passes to the decedent's "next of kin," determined as described in Section 3 of this chapter.

An example of an intestacy statute is Ohio Rev. Code Ann. § 2105.06, the principal provisions of which are as follows:

(A) If there is no surviving spouse, to the children of the intestate or their lineal descendants, per stirpes;

(B) If there is a spouse and one child or his lineal descendants surviving, the first sixty thousand dollars if the spouse is the natural or adoptive parent of the child, or the first twenty thousand dollars if the spouse is not the natural or adoptive parent of the child, plus one-half of the balance of the intestate estate to the spouse and the remainder to the child or his lineal descendants, per stirpes;

(C) If there is a spouse and more than one child or their lineal descendants surviving, the first sixty thousand dollars, if the spouse is the natural or adoptive parent of one of the children, or the first twenty thousand dollars if the spouse is the natural or adoptive parent of none of the children, plus one-third of the balance of the intestate estate to the spouse and the remainder to the children equally, or to the lineal descendants of any deceased child, per stirpes;

(D) If there are no children or their lineal descendants, then the whole to the surviving spouse;

(E) If there is no spouse and no children or their lineal descendants, to the parents of the intestate equally, or to the surviving parent;

(F) If there is no spouse, no children or their lineal descendants, and no parent surviving, to the brothers and sisters, whether of the whole or of the half blood of the intestate, or their lineal descendants, per stirpes;

(G) If there are no brothers or sisters or their lineal descendants, one half to the paternal grandparents of the intestate equally, or to the survivor of them, and one half to the maternal grandparents of the intestate equally, or to the survivor of them;

(H) If there is no paternal grandparent or no maternal grandparent, one half to the lineal descendants of the deceased grandparents, per stirpes; if there are no such lineal descendants, then to the surviving grandparents or their lineal descendants, per stirpes; if there are no surviving grandparents or their lineal descendants, then to the next of kin of the intestate, provided there shall be no representation among such next of kin;

(I) If there are no next of kin, to stepchildren or their lineal descendants, per stirpes;

(J) If there are no stepchildren or their lineal descendants, escheat to the state.

The principal intestacy provisions of the pre-1990 Uniform Probate Code are as follows:

Section 2–102.   [Share of the Spouse.]

The intestate share of the surviving spouse is:

(1) if there is no surviving issue or parent of the decedent, the entire intestate estate;

(2) if there is no surviving issue but the decedent is survived by a parent or parents, the first [$50,000], plus one-half of the balance of the intestate estate;

(3) if there are surviving issue all of whom are issue of the surviving spouse also, the first [$50,000], plus one-half of the balance of the intestate estate;

(4) if there are surviving issue one or more of whom are not issue of the surviving spouse, one-half of the intestate estate.

Section 2–103. [Shares of Heirs Other Than Surviving Spouse.]

The part of the intestate estate not passing to the surviving spouse under Section 2–102, or the entire intestate estate if there is no surviving spouse, passes as follows:

(1) to the issue of the decedent; if they are all of the same degree of kinship to the decedent they take equally, but if of unequal degree, then those of more remote degree take by representation;

(2) if there is no surviving issue, to his parent or parents equally;

(3) if there is no surviving issue or parent, to the issue of the parents or either of them by representation;

(4) if there is no surviving issue, parent or issue of a parent, but the decedent is survived by one or more grandparents or issue of grandparents, half of the estate passes to the paternal grandparents if both survive, or to the surviving paternal grandparent, or to the issue of the paternal grandparents if both are deceased, the issue taking equally if they are all of the same degree of kinship to the decedent, but if of unequal degree those of more remote degree take by representation; and the other half passes to the maternal relatives in the same manner; but if there be no surviving grandparent or issue of grandparent on either the paternal or the maternal side, the entire estate passes to the relatives on the other side in the same manner as the half.

Section 2–105. [No Taker.]

If there is no taker under the provisions of this Article, the intestate estate passes to the [state].

1990 Uniform Probate Code § 2–102 changes the intestacy provisions of the pre–1990 Code substantially in the circumstance of the survival of the spouse. (1) First of all, it provides that if the decedent is survived by a spouse and descendants, and all of the descendants are also descendants of the surviving spouse, and there is no other descendant of the surviving spouse who survives the decedent, the surviving spouse takes the entire estate. (2) Next, it provides that if the decedent is survived by a spouse, and the decedent is not survived by a descendant, but is survived by a parent, the surviving spouse receives the first $200,000, plus three-fourths of the balance, and the surviving parents receive the rest. (3) Next, if the decedent is survived by a spouse, and the decedent has surviving descendants all of whom are descendants of the surviving spouse, and the surviving spouse also has survivng descendants who are not descendants of the decedent, the surviving spouse receives the first $150,000 plus one-half of the balance, and decedent's surviving descendants receive the rest. (4) Next, it provides that if the decedent is survived by a spouse, and the decedent has a surviving descendant who is not a descendant of the surviving spouse, the surviving spouse receives the first $100,000 plus one-half of the balance, and the surviving descendants of the decedent receive the rest. (5) Finally, if the decedent is not survived by a descendant or a parent, the surviving spouse takes the entire estate.

The 1990 Code breaks radically with tradition in its provision for distribution of the entire estate to the surviving spouse when the decedent is survived by descendants in the specific circumstance set forth in part (1) of the preceding paragraph.

SECTION 2. DESCENDANTS (ISSUE)

Close to decedent
letter off you are !

"Descendants" and "issue" are synonymous. The descendants of the decedent take a certain portion or the whole in intestacy, depending upon whether the decedent's spouse survives. But the term is not to be taken literally. If the decedent dies intestate and is survived by two children, C1 and C2, and five grandchildren, of whom GC1 and GC2 are children of C1, and GC3, GC4 and GC5 are children of C2, all are descendants of the decedent but they do not all share in his estate. A grandchild or more remote descendant does not take if a parent or more distant ancestor who is also a descendant of the decedent is living. This means that C1 and C2 would each take one-half.

Suppose C1 predeceased the decedent and all the rest survived. C2 would take one-half, and GC1 and GC2 each take one-fourth. GC1 and GC2 take the share their parent would have taken had he survived. GC1 and GC2 are often said to take "by representation;" GC1 and GC2 are sometimes described as the "representatives" of C1 in these circumstances. It is also often said that in this situation GC1 and GC2 take "per stirpes." Per stirpes is Latin meaning "by roots," and C1 is the "root." "By representation" and "per stirpes" are interchangeable.

If both C1 and C2 predecease the decedent, and all the grandchildren survive, states differ on the distribution of the property. Some states adopt a strict representational or per stirpital position, using the children generation as the base or root, and give GC1 and

tor to the claimant. The total number of generational steps is the degree of relationship. The person or persons in the closest relationship (least number of steps) are the intestate takers.[13]

As an example, a first cousin is in the fourth degree of relationship to the decedent. The nearest common ancestor of the decedent and first cousin is grandparent. Counting up from the decedent, the first generational step is parent of decedent, the second step is grandparent; counting down from grandparent, the third step is parent of the first cousin (uncle or aunt of decedent), and the fourth step is first cousin. Another example is second cousin who is in the sixth degree of relationship to the decedent. The nearest common ancestor of decedent and second cousin is great-grandparent. There are three generational steps counting from decedent to great-grandparent. There are three generational steps counting down from great-grandparent to second cousin: great-uncle or aunt; first cousin of decedent's parent (first cousin once removed of decedent); and second cousin.

In some states the civil law method is modified by providing that if two claimants are in the same degree of relationship to the decedent but one claims through a common ancestor with the decedent that is nearer than the ancestor through whom the other claims, the claimant with the nearer common ancestor prevails.[14]

It should be noted that the representational principle is not used in the determination of next of kin in the degree of relationship method of computation; each claimant is measured by her own position, not her parent's.[15]

In a few states next of kin are determined in an entirely different manner. After the specific listing of intestate takers which ends, let us say, at grandparents and their issue, there is unlimited heirship by provision for the "nearest ancestors and their descendants." In other words, great-grandparents and their issue are next in order of priority, and if there are none, great-great-grandparents and their issue are next, and so on. There is no computation of degrees of relationship; those in the great-grandparent line take before those in the great-great-grandparent line. This method of determining next of kin is known as the parentelic method.[16]

13. Toomey v. Turner, 184 Miss. 831, 186 So. 301 (1939); Simonton v. Edmunds, 202 S.C. 397, 25 S.E.2d 284 (1943).

14. E.g., Cal.Prob.Code § 6402; Mass.Gen.Laws Ann. ch. 190, § 3; Minn.Stat.Ann. § 524.2–103; Nev.Rev. Stat. § 134.070.

15. See Ill.Ann.Stat. ch. 110½, § 2–1; Miss.Code Ann. § 91–1–3; Ohio Rev. Code Ann. § 2105.06; Vt.Stat.Ann. tit. 14, § 551.

16. Colo.Rev.Stat. § 15–11–103; Ky. Rev.Stat.Ann. § 391.010; R.I.Gen.Laws § 33–1–2; Tex.Prob.Code Ann. § 38; Va.Code § 64.1–1.

It is apparent that heirs of a decedent fall into several categories. There is the spouse, ancestors (parents and grandparents), descendants (children and grandchildren), and others who are related through a common ancestor with the decedent, such as siblings and cousins. Those who are in this last category are often referred to collectively as "collaterals," a word commonly used by trusts and estates lawyers.

SECTION 4. ADOPTED CHILDREN

In all states the adopted child is the child of the adoptive parents for purposes of intestate taking from her adoptive parents. In most states the adopted child also inherits "through" her adoptive parents; that is to say, the adopted child is the child of the adoptive parents for purposes of inheritance from relatives of the adoptive parents, such as parents and siblings of the adoptive parents. In most states the adoptive parents and those related to them inherit from the adopted child and through the adopted child.[17]

In most states the adopted child is cut off from her natural parents and their kindred with respect to inheritance, except that usually the relationship of heirship between the adopted child and the natural parent remains when the spouse of the natural parent adopts the child.[18] That is to say, if father dies and mother remarries, and the new husband adopts the child, the relationship of heirship between the child and the mother and her kindred is unchanged. Pre-1990 Uniform Probate Code § 2–109, and a few states, go one step further to provide that when the spouse of a natural parent adopts the child, the relationship of heirship remains unchanged with respect to the child and both natural parents and their kindred.[19]

1990 Uniform Probate Code § 2–114 continues to provide that when the spouse of the natural parent adopts the child, the relationship of heirship between the child and that natural parent is unchanged. The child also continues to inherit from and through the other natural parent. The other natural parent, however, does not inherit from or through the child.

In a few states, the adopted child continues to inherit from and through her natural parents in all circumstances, as well as her

---

17. E.g., Del.Code Ann. tit. 12, § 508, tit. 13, § 920; D.C.Code Ann. § 16–312; Ind.Code Ann. § 29–1–2–8; N.Y.Dom.Rel.Law § 117; N.C.Gen.Stat. § 29–17; Ohio Rev.Code Ann. § 3107.-15; S.C.Code Ann. § 20–7–1770; Wash. Rev.Code Ann. § 26.33.260; W.Va.Code § 48–4–11; Wis.Stat.Ann. § 851.51.

18. E.g., Ariz.Rev.Stat.Ann. § 8–117; Hawaii Rev.Stat. § 578–16; La.Civ.Code Ann. art. 214; N.M.Stat.Ann. § 45–2–109; Utah Code Ann. § 75–2–109.

19. E.g., Me.Rev.Stat.Ann. tit. 18A, § 2–109; Alaska Stat. § 13.11.045.

adoptive parents, but the natural parents do not inherit from or through the adopted child.[20]

SECTION 5. CHILDREN BORN OUT OF WEDLOCK

The common law view was that the child born out of wedlock did not inherit from his parents and they did not inherit from him. For inheritance purposes the nonmarital child had neither ancestors nor collateral relatives. The nonmarital child was the innocent legal victim of his parents' indiscretion. If the nonmarital child married, he had a relationship of heirship only with his spouse and descendants.

It then came about by statute that the nonmarital child was the heir of the mother. If the statute provided that the child might be the heir of the father, the right of inheritance would be severely conditioned; the former statutes of Louisiana and Illinois described in succeeding paragraphs of this section are examples.

Today by statute in most states the nonmarital child has the same relationship of heirship with the mother as the legitimate child.[21] The former harsh treatment of the nonmarital child with respect to inheritance from the father produced several United States Supreme Court decisions, the net effect of which is to require constitutionally that the nonmarital child be permitted to establish heirship from the father by proof of parentage, subject to reasonable regulation.

In Labine v. Vincent, 401 U.S. 532, 91 S.Ct. 1017, 28 L.Ed.2d 288 (1971), the Supreme Court in a 5 to 4 decision held that the Louisiana statute which barred intestate succession from the father by illegitimate children unless the decedent father had no spouse, legitimate descendants, ancestors, or collaterals, was not violative of the due process or equal protection clauses of the Fourteenth Amendment. The Court reasoned that the state was empowered to legislate to protect and strengthen family life and to regulate the disposition of property at death.

Six years later in Trimble v. Gordon, 430 U.S. 762, 97 S.Ct. 1459, 52 L.Ed.2d 31 (1977), the Supreme Court in a 5 to 4 decision effectively, but not explicitly, overruled the Labine case. The Court held unconstitutional as violative of the equal protection clause of the Fourteenth Amendment the Illinois statute which barred intestate succession from the father unless the illegitimate child was

---

20. E.g., R.I.Gen.Laws § 15–7–17; Tex.Prob.Code Ann. § 40; Vt.Stat.Ann. tit. 15, § 448; Wyo.Stat. § 2–4–107.

21. E.g., Fla.Stat.Ann. § 732.108; Ga.Code Ann. §§ 53–4–4, 53–4–5; Md. Est. & Trusts Code Ann. § 1–208; Mass. Gen.Laws Ann. ch. 190, §§ 5, 6; Ohio Rev.Code Ann. § 2105.17; Wash.Rev. Code Ann. § 11.04.081; Wis.Stat.Ann. § 852.05.

legitimated by the marriage of the mother and father and was acknowledged by the father. The Court stated that the only permissible basis for differential treatment of nonmarital children for intestate purposes is certainty of parentage. Legitimation through subsequent marriage and acknowledgment of the child are not essential to the accurate and orderly determination of intestate rights. A judicial determination of paternity alone would achieve the permissible purpose. The Court stated that it is constitutionally impermissible to penalize the child as a means of attempting to influence parental conduct.

One year later, the Supreme Court in Lalli v. Lalli, 439 U.S. 259, 99 S.Ct. 518, 58 L.Ed.2d 503 (1978), another 5 to 4 decision, upheld as constitutional a New York statute which allowed intestate succession from the father if a court had entered an order declaring paternity during the father's lifetime. The plurality opinion of Justice Powell reasoned that this statute was related to the permissible objective of the accurate and orderly disposition of the decedent's estate, as required under the Trimble case.

The Uniform Parentage Act provides that a person is a child of her parents for all purposes regardless of the marital status of her parents; pre–1990 Uniform Probate Code § 2–109 adopts this position with respect to heirship for states which have adopted that Act. For states which do not have such a statute, the pre–1990 Code deals with the question of the nonmarital child's inheritance status as follows:

> If, for purposes of intestate succession, a relationship of parent and child must be established to determine succession by, through, or from a person,
>
>   * * *
>
> (2) ... a person born out of wedlock is a child of the mother. That person is also a child of the father, if:
>
> > (i) the natural parents participated in a marriage ceremony before or after the birth of the child, even though the attempted marriage is void; or
> >
> > (ii) the paternity is established by an adjudication before the death of the father or is established thereafter by clear and convincing proof, but the paternity established under this subparagraph is ineffective to qualify the father or his kindred to inherit from or through the child unless the father has openly treated the child as his, and has not refused to support the child.

Most states impose conditions to the nonmarital child's inheritance from the father, many using the language of the Uniform Probate Code.[22]

1990 Uniform Probate Code § 2–114 modifies the pre–1990 Code by providing simply that a person is the child of her natural parents for heirship purposes regardless of their marital status, with the qualification that inheritance from or through a child by either natural parent is precluded unless that natural parent has openly treated the child as his or her own and has not refused to support the child.

SECTION 6. ADVANCEMENTS

A decedent dies intestate with a net estate of $100,000, and his heirs are his two children. One year before his death the decedent made an outright gift of $50,000 to one of his two children, with the intention expressed in writing that the gift was to be an advance upon the child's inheritance. The distribution of the intestate estate is adjusted to take into account the living gift. The $100,000 estate is distributed $25,000 to the child who received the living gift and $75,000 to the other child. This result derives from the doctrine of advancements. Statutes in almost all states provide that in certain circumstances the distribution of an intestate estate may be adjusted on account of living gifts made by the decedent to those who are his heirs if that is the donor's intention when he made the gift. There are, however, substantial variations among the statutes. It should be emphasized that the living gift remains an absolute transfer; the adjustment in the distribution of the intestate estate of the donor does not affect the finality of the living gift.

The statutes in a number of states provide that the doctrine applies only in the event of total intestacy.[23] There are, however, statutes in several states which expressly apply the doctrine in the case of partial intestacy, i.e., the situation in which there is a will which does not dispose of the entire estate.[24] In some states the statute is not explicit on the question of whether the doctrine applies only to total intestacy.[25]

22. E.g., Ark.Code Ann. § 28–9–209; Ind.Code Ann. § 29–1–2–7; Mo.Ann. Stat. § 474.060; N.J.Stat.Ann. § 3B:5–10; N.C.Gen.Stat. § 29.19; Pa.Stat. Ann. tit. 20, § 2107; Vt.Stat.Ann. tit. 14, §§ 553, 554; Va.Code § 64.1–5.1.

23. E.g., Del.Code Ann. tit. 12, § 509; Ind.Code Ann. § 29–1–2–10; Mo. Ann.Stat. § 474.090; N.C.Gen.Stat. § 29–23; Or.Rev.Stat. § 112.135.

24. Colo.Rev.Stat. § 15–11–110; Md. Est. & Trusts Code Ann. § 3–106; Pa. Stat.Ann. tit. 20, § 2109.1; Va.Code § 64.1–17; W.Va.Code § 42–4–1.

25. E.g., Iowa Code Ann. § 633.224; Mass.Gen.Laws Ann. ch. 196, § 3; N.H.Rev.Stat.Ann. § 561.13; Ohio Rev. Code Ann. § 2105.05.1.

Most statutes provide that the doctrine applies to advances to any heir of the decedent,[26] but a small number of states limit the application of the doctrine to children or other descendants of the decedent.[27]

In the past there was considerable authority to the effect that a substantial living gift to a child or other descendant was rebuttably presumed to be an advancement; the donee had the burden of establishing that the donor did not intend that his intestate share be reduced in the amount of the living gift. Many statutes today, however, require a writing by the decedent that the gift is intended as an advancement or an acknowledgment in writing by the donee that the gift is an advancement.[28] The requirement of a writing obviously does away with the presumption. Some statutes that do not have the requirement of a writing provide that a gift is rebuttably presumed not to be an advancement.[29] The presumption of an advancement in the case of a gift to a descendant can exist only in a small minority of states.[30] In most states the person who wishes to establish that a living gift is an advancement must produce a writing to that effect or other evidence that the donor intended the gift as an advancement.

Let us examine the operation of the doctrine. The donor has two children, C1 and C2, makes a living gift of $50,000 to C1 which is stated in writing by the donor to be an advancement, and dies intestate with a net estate of $100,000. The two children are her only heirs. As we have pointed out above, the $100,000 is divided $25,000 to C1 and $75,000 to C2. How is this arrived at? Bear in mind that the $50,000 was an absolutely valid living gift, and belongs to C1 in all events. For computational purposes only, the $50,000 is added to the $100,000, as if it were part of the estate, the total is divided by two, and C1 is then credited with the amount of his living gift.[31]

26. E.g., Colo.Rev.Stat. § 15–11–110; Iowa Code Ann. § 633.224; Kan.Stat. Ann. § 59–510; N.H.Rev.Stat.Ann. § 561.13; N.C.Gen.Stat. § 29–2.

27. E.g., Ga.Code Ann. § 53–4–50; Mass.Gen.Laws Ann. ch. 196, § 3; Okla. Stat.Ann. tit. 84, § 223; R.I.Gen.Laws § 33–1–11; Va.Code § 64.1–17.

28. E.g., Del.Code Ann. tit. 12, § 509; Ill.Ann.Stat. ch. 110½, § 2–5; Md.Est. & Trusts Code Ann. § 3–106; N.Y.Est.Powers & Trusts Law § 2–1.5; Ohio Rev.Code Ann. § 2105.05.1; Pa. Stat.Ann. tit. 20, § 2109.1.

29. E.g., Ind.Code Ann. § 29–1–2–10; Iowa Code Ann. § 633.224;

N.C.Gen.Stat. § 29–24; Tex.Prob.Code Ann. § 44.

30. Watt v. Lee, 238 Ala. 451, 191 So. 628 (1939); Bowen v. Holland, 184 Ga. 718, 193 S.E. 233 (1937); Cravens v. Cravens, 56 Tenn.App. 619, 410 S.W.2d 424 (1966); Trotman v. Trotman, 148 Va. 860, 139 S.E. 490 (1927); In re Boggs' Estate, 135 W.Va. 288, 63 S.E.2d 497 (1951).

31. See D.C.Code Ann. § 19–319; Ind.Code Ann. § 21–1–2–10; Mass.Gen. Laws Ann. ch. 196, § 3; N.Y.Est.Powers & Trusts Law § 2–1.5.

That the absolute nature of the living gift which is intended as an advancement is not affected by the doctrine can be illustrated by a modification of the above example. Suppose the $50,000 living gift was intended to be and qualified as an advancement, but the donor suffered financial reverses thereafter and died with a net estate of only $40,000. Add $50,000 to $40,000, divide by two, credit C1 with his $50,000 gift, and it is apparent that C1 has already received more than the formula provides for him. In this circumstance C2 gets the $40,000 estate, and C1 keeps his $50,-000.[32]

Suppose the donor makes an advancement to one child, C1, who predeceases the donor, and the donor dies intestate survived by a second child, C2, and a grandchild by C1. The donor's heirs are C2 and the grandchild by C1. The statutes of some states provide that the living gift is charged against the grandchild's share of the intestate estate. There is no inquiry as to whether the grandchild in fact obtained the benefit of the living gift to C1. If an advancee predeceases the donor, those issue of the advancee who replace him as heirs of the donor are charged with the advancement.[33] Other states do not charge the living gift against the grandchild's intestate share, unless the writing evidencing the advancement provides that it is to be so charged.[34]

The doctrine of advancements is unusual because it allows for the distribution of a decedent's estate assets on the basis of an informal writing or an oral statement. As a general rule intestate distribution can be changed only by the terms of a will executed in accordance with certain procedural safeguards.

An example of an advancement statute is pre–1990 Uniform Probate Code § 2–110, which has been enacted in a number of states:

If a person dies intestate as to all his estate, property which he gave in his lifetime to an heir is treated as an advancement against the latter's share of the estate only if declared in a contemporaneous writing by the decedent or acknowledged in writing by the heir to be an advancement. For this purpose the property advanced is valued as of the time the heir came into possession or enjoyment of the property or as of the time of the death of the decedent,

32. See Iowa Code Ann. § 633.224; Kan.Stat.Ann. § 59–510; N.C.Gen.Stat. § 29–25; Or.Rev.Stat. § 112.145; Vt. Stat.Ann. tit. 14, § 1724.

33. E.g., Ill.Ann.Stat. ch. 110½, § 2–5; Mass.Gen.Laws Ann. ch. 196, § 7; N.C.Gen.Stat. § 29–27; Okla.Stat.Ann. tit. 84, § 227; Or.Rev.Stat. § 112.155.

34. E.g., Alaska Stat. § 13.11.050; Ariz.Rev.Stat.Ann. § 14–2110; Fla.Stat. Ann. § 733.806; Hawaii Rev.Stat. § 560:2–110; Me.Rev.Stat.Ann. tit. 18A, § 2–110.

whichever first occurs. If the recipient of the property fails to survive the decedent, the property is not taken into account in computing the intestate share to be received by the recipient's issue, unless the declaration or acknowledgment provides otherwise.

1990 Uniform Probate Code § 2–109 changes the pre–1990 Code with respect to advancements by providing that the doctrine applies to partially intestate estates as well as wholly intestate estates. The Comment to the 1990 Code § 2–109 states that an advancement can be in the form of a will substitute such as designation as a beneficiary of a life insurance policy or beneficiary of the remainder interest in a revocable living trust. There is no reason why a will substitute should be treated differently from an outright living gift for advancement purposes.

If the jurisdiction applies the doctrine of advancements to a partially intestate estate, the adjustment is made only with respect to the intestate portion. In Chapter 6, Section 9, we discuss the doctrine of satisfaction, the testate counterpart of the doctrine of advancements, whereby bequests and devises are reduced in the amount of living gifts to the same person in certain circumstances.

SECTION 7. RENUNCIATION (DISCLAIMER)

A donor cannot force a living gift on a person who chooses not to accept it, nor can the testator force a bequest or devise on a person. The gift, living or testamentary, is a volitional transaction, and one need not accept the title. The common law rule is different with respect to the intestate transfer of title. Title vests in the heir by operation of law rather than volitionally, and the heir cannot prevent that from occurring. If the heir wishes to have the property pass to the person who would take the property if he did not exist, he must transfer it. This means that title comes to the heir first, subjecting it to the rights of creditors,[35] and then he must make a transfer which may be subject to gift taxation. If the heir could renounce, he would avoid creditors' claims and he could avoid gift taxation, as the legatee and devisee can. If an heir purports to renounce, the attempted but ineffective renunciation could be construed to be a gift to the person who would take if the heir did not exist, with creditor and gift tax consequences.[36]

---

35. The unsatisfied judgment creditor may have a lien by operation of law upon real property acquired by the debtor. Also, a transfer without adequate consideration by one who is in financial difficulty may be treated as fraudulent as to creditors, which enables them to reach the property in the hands of the transferee.

36. Hardenbergh v. Commissioner, 198 F.2d 63 (8th Cir.1952), cert. denied, 344 U.S. 836, 73 S.Ct. 45, 97 L.Ed. 650 (1952).

These problems are now eliminated for the heir. Most states have in the recent past enacted legislation permitting heirs as well as legatees and devisees to renounce. There is uniform legislation on the subject of intestate and testate renunciation, or, as it is often called, disclaimer: Uniform Disclaimer of Transfers by Will, Intestacy or Appointment Act,[37] and pre–1990 Uniform Probate Code § 2–801, which contain the same provisions. The state statutes frequently follow the terms of the uniform legislation.[38] The uniform acts and the statutes set forth the time limits for renunciation and certain filing requirements for the instrument of renunciation. The uniform acts and the statutes also provide for renunciation (disclaimer) of part of the intestate or testamentary gift, as well as the entire gift. The uniform acts and usually the statutes provide that the renounced interest passes as if the renouncing party predeceased the decedent.

Pre–1990 Uniform Probate Code § 2–801, entitled Renunciation of Succession, reads in part as follows:

(a) A person ... who is an heir, devisee, person succeeding to a renounced interest, beneficiary under a testamentary instrument, or appointee under a power of appointment exercised by a testamentary instrument, may renounce in whole or in part the right of succession to any property or interest therein, including a future interest, by filing a written renunciation under this Section....

(b)(1) An instrument renouncing a present interest shall be filed not later than 9 months after the death of the decedent or the donee of the power.

(2) An instrument renouncing a future interest may be filed not later than 9 months after the event determining that the taker of the property or interest is finally ascertained and his interest is indefeasibly vested.

(3) The renunciation shall be filed in the probate court of the county in which proceedings have been commenced for the administration of the estate of the deceased owner or deceased donee of the power.... If real property ... is renounced, a copy of the renunciation may be recorded in the office of the Recorder of

---

37. 8A U.L.A. 93 (1983). There is also the Uniform Disclaimer of Transfers Under Nontestamentary Instruments Act, 8A U.L.A. 111 (1983), which applies to interests other than those acquired by will or intestate succession; and there is the Uniform Disclaimer of Property Interests Act, 8A U.L.A. 85 (1983), which embraces the renunciation of all the interests included in the other uniform acts.

38. E.g., Del.Code Ann. tit. 12, § 601; Ky.Rev.Stat.Ann. § 394.610; Minn.Stat.Ann. § 525.532; Utah Code Ann. § 75–2–801; Wis.Stat.Ann. § 853.-40.

Deeds of the county in which the real estate is situated.

(c) Unless the decedent or donee of the power has otherwise provided, the property or interest renounced devolves as though the person renouncing had predeceased the decedent or, if the person renouncing is designated to take under a power of appointment exercised by a testamentary instrument, as though the person renouncing had predeceased the donee of the power. A future interest that takes effect in possession or enjoyment after the termination of the estate or interest renounced takes effect as though the person renouncing had predeceased the decedent or the donee of the power.

Suppose a testator creates a trust in his will to pay the income to A for life, principal at A's death to A's children who survive her. A renounces her life estate. A has one child. A is deemed to have predeceased the testator. The child then living receives the principal; later children would take nothing.

1990 Uniform Probate Code § 2–801 has replaced the pre–1990 Code § 2–801; the new section incorporates the Uniform Disclaimer of Property Interests Act which covers disclaimers of nontestamentary transfers, such as will substitutes, as well as testamentary and intestate transfers. With respect to the provision that the disclaimed interest passes as if the disclaimant predeceased the decedent, the new section expressly states that the interest passes to the disclaimant's descendants if the intestacy statute or the antilapse statute so provides.

The Internal Revenue Code has provisions dealing with renunciations ("disclaimers" in the Code) which must be complied with in order for the renunciation to be effective for federal gift and estate tax purposes, such as the time within which the renunciation must be made.[39]

It should be noted that a few courts have held that renunciation made for the purpose of keeping the property from creditors of the legatee, devisee or heir is ineffective as to creditors.[40]

SECTION 8. AFTER–BORN HEIRS; HALF–BLOODS; MISCREANTS; ALIENS

In a majority of states any relative of the decedent conceived at his death but born thereafter inherits in intestacy as if she had

---

39. I.R.C. §§ 2518, 2045.

40. In re Kalt's Estate, 16 Cal.2d 807, 108 P.2d 401 (1940); Stein v. Brown, 18 Ohio St.3d 305, 480 N.E.2d 1121 (1985); In re Estate of Reed, 566 P.2d 587 (Wyo.1977). See In re Betz, 84 B.R. 470 (Bkrtcy.Ohio 1987). There are also several statutes to this effect: e.g., Fla.Stat.Ann. §§ 689.21(6), 732.801(6); N.J. Stat.Ann. § 3A:25–46.

been living at the decedent's death.[41] 1990 Uniform Probate Code § 2–108 requires that the after-born heir live for at least 120 hours. In some states only children or other descendants conceived at the decedent's death and born thereafter are entitled to inherit as if they had been living at his death; other relatives do not inherit unless living at the decedent's death.[43]

If the decedent was a child of his father and his father's first wife, and his brother was a child of his father and his father's second wife, the latter is a half-brother of the decedent. If the decedent is related to a collateral heir through one common ancestor (parent, grandparent), instead of two, he is a relative of the half-blood.

An ancestor or a descendant cannot be of the half-blood. The decedent's parents are his parents, and a later marriage of a parent does not change that relationship. The decedent's child by his first marriage is his child as is the decedent's child by a later marriage; the two children are, of course, of the half-blood in relation to each other.

Under old English law, half-bloods did not inherit land. That exclusion did not exist in this country. In most states today the half-blood inherits the same as the collateral heir of the whole blood,[43] but in a minority of states distinctions are made. In a few states the half-blood takes one-half the portion that a person of the whole blood of the same category of relationship takes; if there are only half-bloods in that category they take it all.[44] In a few states, the half-blood takes only if there are no persons of the whole blood in that particular category of relationship.[45]

Most states now have statutes which bar a person who feloniously kills another from receiving anything from the victim's estate.[46] In the absence of statute courts have come to the same result in the case of the felonious killing,[47] although there is

---

41. E.g., Fla.Stat.Ann. § 732.106; Iowa Code Ann. § 633.220; N.J.Stat. Ann. 3B:5–8; N.C.Gen.Stat. § 29–9; Or. Rev.Stat. § 112.075; Va.Code § 64.1-8.1.

42. E.g., Ark.Code Ann. § 28–9–210; D.C.Code Ann. § 19–314; Ind.Code Ann. § 29–1–2–6; Mo.Ann.Stat. § 474.050.

43. E.g., Idaho Code § 15–2–107; Ill. Ann.Stat. ch. 110½, § 2–1; Mich.Stat. Ann. § 27.5109; N.J.Stat.Ann. § 3B:5–7; Tenn.Code Ann. § 31–2–107.

44. Fla.Stat.Ann. § 732.105; Ky. Rev.Stat.Ann. § 391.050; Tex.Prob. Code Ann. § 41; Va.Code § 64.1-2.

45. Conn.Gen.Stat.Ann. § 45–276; Miss.Code Ann. § 91–1–5.

46. E.g., Ill.Ann.Stat. ch. 110½, § 2–6; Mich.Stat.Ann. § 27.5251; N.M.Stat. Ann. § 30–2–9; Pa.Stat.Ann. tit. 20, §§ 2106, 8803; Tenn.Code Ann. § 31–1–106.

47. Perry v. Strawbridge, 209 Mo. 621, 108 S.W. 641 (1908); Riggs v. Palmer, 115 N.Y. 506, 22 N.E. 188

authority to the contrary.[48]

There are some statutes which bar a parent from inheriting from a child that he has abandoned,[49] or bar an adulterous or abandoning spouse from inheriting from the victimized spouse.[50]

A handful of states have statutes which prohibit inheritance by a nonresident alien if a United States citizen could not inherit under the law of the alien's country.[51] There may be problems with respect to the constitutionality of such statutes.[52]

(1889); Parks v. Dumas, 321 S.W.2d 653 (Tex.Civ.App.1959).

48. Kelley v. New Hampshire, 105 N.H. 240, 196 A.2d 68 (1963).

49. E.g., N.Y.Est.Powers & Trusts Law § 4-1.4; N.C.Gen.Stat. § 31A-2; Pa.Stat.Ann. tit. 20, § 2106.

50. E.g., Ind.Code Ann. §§ 29-1-2-14, 29-1-2-15; N.Y.Est.Powers &

Trusts Law § 5-1.2; Pa.Stat.Ann. tit. 20, § 2106.

51. E.g., Mont.Code Ann. § 72-2-214; Neb.Rev.Stat. § 4-107; N.C.Gen. Stat. § 64-3; Wyo.Stat. § 34-15-101.

52. See Zschernig v. Miller, 389 U.S. 429, 88 S.Ct. 664, 19 L.Ed.2d 683 (1968). For a discussion of the problems of inheritance by aliens, see Ritchie, Alford, Effland and Dobris, Decedents' Estates and Trusts 148 (8th ed. 1993).

Chapter 3

EXECUTION AND VALIDITY OF WILLS

In 1990 changes were made in certain sections of the Uniform Probate Code dealing with execution of wills. In this chapter there are references to the pre–1990 Uniform Probate Code (or pre–1990 Code) and to the 1990 Uniform Probate Code (or 1990 Code). There are also references to the Uniform Probate Code in instances in which no substantial change has been made by the 1990 revision. The reader is referred to the introduction to Chapter 2 for further information on the development of the Uniform Probate Code.

SECTION 1. FORMALITIES OF EXECUTION

In some jurisdictions the holographic will is recognized, i.e., one in the handwriting of the testator which need not be witnessed. In some states oral wills are recognized in special circumstances and subject to strict conditions, often for the limited purpose of disposing of small amounts of personalty. These are discussed in the following section. Here we deal with the formalities of the standard witnessed will which is always employed by lawyers even where the other types of wills are permitted.

The essence of the formalities is that the testator must sign the will, or make a subsequent acknowledgment of such signing, in the presence of two witnesses [1] who also sign their names as witnesses. The purpose of the procedure is to assure the genuineness of the document. The presence of the witnesses presumably assures that the instrument was signed by the person whose will it purports to be, and that the testator did not act under any coercion. It has also been maintained that the ritualistic nature of the procedure serves the purpose of impressing upon the testator the seriousness of the action he is taking.

The signing almost invariably is at the end of the will, but many statutes do not expressly provide for the location of the signature. Under such statutes signing in the margin or at the top may suffice.[2] Some statutes require that the will be signed by the

1. Vt.Stat. tit. 14 § 5 requires three witnesses.

2. Plemons v. Tarpey, 262 Ala. 209, 78 So.2d 385 (1955); In re Thomas' Estate, 243 Mich. 566, 220 N.W. 764 (1928); In re Williams' Will, 234 N.C. 228, 66 S.E.2d 902 (1951); In re Lagershausen's Estate, 224 Wis. 479, 272 N.W. 469 (1937).

testator at the end,[3] or be "subscribed" by the testator, which has been construed to mean the same thing.[4] Under such statutes, if there are dispositive provisions of the will in existence at the time of signing which are below the signature, the entire will is probably invalid because it is improperly executed.[5]

In almost all states the statute allows for signing by another on behalf of the testator, at the testator's request and in his presence.[6] This means of execution would be used in the case of the physically disabled testator.

The testator's signing must be done in the presence of two witnesses,[7] or if the witnesses are not present at the testator's signing, the testator must subsequently make an acknowledgment of his signature or of the will, depending on the statute, before the witnesses. The Uniform Probate Code § 2–502 and the statutes of a number of states provide that the acknowledgment may be of the signature or of the will.[8] Some states provide only for the acknowledgment of the signature,[9] and several provide only for the acknowledgment of the will.[10] If the acknowledgment is of the signature, it must be seen on the will by the witnesses at the time of the acknowledgment.[11] If the acknowledgment is of the will rather than the signature, the will must be present and visible at the time of the acknowledgment, but it has usually been held that the testator's signature need not be seen.[12]

In a few states the testator must sign or acknowledge in the

---

3. E.g., Ark.Code Ann. § 28–25–103; Cal.Prob.Code § 50; N.Y.Est. Powers & Trusts Law § 3–2.1; Ohio Rev.Code Ann. § 2107.03; Pa.Stat.Ann. tit. 20, § 2502.

4. See French v. Beville, 191 Va. 842, 62 S.E.2d 883 (1951); 2 Page, Law of Wills § 19.65 (Bowe-Parker Rev.1960).

5. In re Jordan's Estate, 81 Cal. App.2d 419, 184 P.2d 165 (1947); Irwin v. Jacques, 71 Ohio St. 395, 73 N.E. 683 (1905). See 2 Page, Law of Wills § 19.72 (Bowe-Parker Rev.1960). See N.Y.Est. Powers & Trusts Law § 3–2.1 and Pa.Stat.Ann. tit. 20, § 2502, validating language above the signature.

6. E.g., Ariz.Rev.Stat.Ann. § 14–2502; D.C.Code Ann. § 18–103; Ill.Ann. Stat. ch. 110½, § 4–3; Wis.Stat.Ann. § 853.03.

7. See note 1 supra.

8. E.g., Idaho Code § 15–2–502; Me. Rev.Stat.Ann. tit. 18–A, § 2–502; Minn. Stat.Ann. § 524.2–502; N.J.Stat.Ann. § 3B:3–2.

9. E.g., Ind.Code Ann. § 29–1–5–3; N.C.Gen.Stat. § 31–3.3; Ohio Rev.Code Ann. § 2107.03; R.I.Gen.Laws § 33–5–5.

10. Ky.Rev.Stat.Ann. § 394.040; Va. Code § 64.1–49; W.Va.Code § 41–1–3.

11. In re Abbey's Estate, 183 Cal. 524, 191 P. 893 (1920); Appeal of Pope, 93 Conn. 53, 104 A. 241 (1918); In re Sage's Will, 90 N.J.Eq. 209, 107 A. 151 (1919), aff'd 90 N.J.Eq. 580, 107 A. 445 (1919); In re Redway's Will, 238 App. Div. 653, 265 N.Y.S. 848 (1933).

12. Conway v. Conway, 14 Ill.2d 461, 153 N.E.2d 11 (1958); Wersich v. Phelps, 186 Ind. 290, 116 N.E. 49 (1917); Robertson v. Robertson, 232 Ky. 572, 24 S.W.2d 282 (1930). There is, however, some authority that acknowledgement of the will requires that the witnesses see the testator's signature. See 2 Page, Law of Wills § 19.116 (Bowe-Parker Rev.1960).

presence of both witnesses at the same time.[13] In most states the testator may sign in the presence of one witness and acknowledge in the presence of the other at different times, or acknowledge to the witnesses separately.[14]

All statutes require that the witnesses sign their names on the will. Almost invariably the witnesses sign below the testator's signature or to the left of it. Some statutes require witnesses to sign at the end of the will,[15] but under others it is permissible for the witnesses to sign anywhere on the will.[16] Some statutes require the witnesses to "subscribe" the will,[17] but this has usually been construed to mean only that they write their names but not necessarily at the end.[18]

The testator should sign before the witnesses do. If the order is reversed, but the signing by all is part of one contemporaneous transaction with all parties present, the execution is usually held to be valid.[19]

Some statutes require that the witnesses sign in the presence of the testator,[20] and some in addition, require that the witnesses also sign in the presence of each other.[21] Other statutes, and the Uniform Probate Code § 2–502, have neither requirement.[22]

The statutes of a few states require that the testator request the witnesses to serve as such.[23] In the absence of an express statutory requirement, some courts have held that such a request is

13. E.g., Cal.Prob.Code § 6110; R.I.Gen.Laws § 33–5–5; Va.Code § 64.1–49; W.Va.Code § 41–1–3.

14. E.g., Alaska Stat. § 13.11.155; Colo Rev.Stat. § 15–11–502; N.J.Stat. Ann. § 3B:3–2; N.Y.Est. Powers & Trust Law § 3–2.1; N.C.Gen.Stat. § 31–3.3.

15. E.g., N.Y.Est. Powers & Trusts Law § 3–2.1; Okla.Stat.Ann. tit. 84, § 55; S.D.Comp.Laws Ann. § 29–2–6.

16. In re Estate of Charry, 359 So.2d 544 (Fla.App.1978); In re Bybee's Estate, 179 Iowa 1089, 160 N.W. 900 (1917).

17. E.g., Conn.Gen.Stat.Ann. § 45–161; Del.Code Ann. tit. 12, § 202; D.C.Code Ann. § 18–103; Ohio Rev. Code Ann. § 2107.03.

18. Plemons v. Tarpey, 262 Ala. 209, 78 So.2d 385 (1955); In re Kobrinsky's Will, 51 Misc.2d 222, 273 N.Y.S.2d 156 (1966); Mossler v. Johnson, 565 S.W.2d 952 (Tex.Civ.App.1978). See 2 Page,

Law of Wills § 19.137 (Bowe-Parker Rev.1960).

19. Billings v. Woody, 167 F.2d 756 (D.C.Cir.1948); Waldrep v. Goodwin, 230 Ga. 1, 195 S.E.2d 432 (1973); Hopson v. Ewing, 353 S.W.2d 203 (Ky.1961); Sellers v. Hayden, 154 Md. 117, 140 A. 56 (1928); Wilkinson v. White, 8 Utah 2d 336, 334 P.2d 564 (1959).

20. E.g., Conn.Gen.Stat.Ann. § 45–161; Mass.Gen.Laws Ann. ch. 191, § 1; Mo.Ann.Stat. § 474.320; Tex.Prob.Code Ann. § 59; Va.Code § 64.1–49.

21. E.g., Fla.Stat.Ann. § 732.502; Ind.Code Ann. § 29–1–5–3; Iowa Code Ann. § 633.279; Ky.Rev.Stat.Ann. § 394.040.

22. E.g., Ala.Code § 43–8–131; Ariz. Rev.Stat.Ann. § 14–2502; Colo.Rev. Stat. § 15–11–502; Hawaii Rev.Stat. § 560.2–502; Idaho Code § 15–2–502.

23. E.g., Ark.Code Ann. § 28–25–103; Iowa Code Ann. § 633.279; Okla. Stat.Ann. tit. 84, § 55.

required.[24] The request may, however, be implied from conduct where the witnesses serve with the testator's approval without any explicit request.[25] The statutes of a small number of states require that the testator declare to the witnesses that the instrument is his will;[26] this is sometimes referred to as "publication" of the will. If the statute does not expressly require such a declaration, it is usually not required.[27] If it is a requirement, it may be satisfied by a statement by the lawyer presiding at the execution, or by another, to which the testator impliedly acquiesces, or by actions of the testator which imply that the instrument is his will.[28]

If a declaration is required, obviously the witnesses are required to know that the instrument is a will.[29] If a declaration is not required, it is not necessary that the witnesses know that the instrument is a will.[30] It is necessary, however, that the witnesses intend to be witnesses to the testator's signing, whatever it is that they may think he has signed. In other words, it is not a proper execution if the witnesses think they are merely signing something, whatever it may be, after it has been signed by the testator.[31]

Pre–1990 Uniform Probate Code § 2–502 does not require many of the technical formalities of execution:

Section 2–502. [Execution.]

Except as provided for holographic wills, writings within Section 2–513, and wills within Section 2–506, every will

24. In re Estate of Watkins, 75 So.2d 194 (Fla.1954); In re Calo's Estate, 1 Ill.2d 376, 115 N.E.2d 778 (1953); Moore v. Sanders, 202 Ky. 286, 259 S.W. 361 (1924); In re Gates' Estate, 149 Minn. 391, 183 N.W. 958 (1921).

25. Hollingsworth v. Hollingsworth, 240 Ark. 582, 401 S.W.2d 555 (1966); Estate of Bearbower, 426 N.W.2d 392 (Iowa 1988); Moyer v. Walker, 771 S.W.2d 363 (Mo.App.1989); Howard v. Estate of Smith, 344 P.2d 260 (Okl. 1959).

26. E.g., Ark.Code Ann. § 28–25–103; Ind.Code Ann. § 29–1–5–3; N.Y.Est. Powers & Trusts Law § 3–2.1.

27. Weaver v. Grant, 394 So.2d 15 (Ala.1981); In re Beakes Estate, 306 So.2d 99 (Fla.1974); Taliaferro v. King, 279 S.W.2d 793 (Ky.1955); In re Estate of Brantlinger, 418 Pa. 236, 210 A.2d 246 (1965).

28. Arnold v. Parry, 173 Ind.App. 300, 363 N.E.2d 1055 (1977); Estate of Eckert, 93 Misc.2d 677, 403 N.Y.S.2d 633 (1978); In re Estate of Samochee,

542 P.2d 498 (Okl.1975); In re Estate of Walsh, 89 S.D. 342, 232 N.W.2d 850 (1975).

29. In re Norswing's Estate, 47 Cal. App.2d 730, 118 P.2d 858 (1941); In re Matter of Sheehan's Will, 51 A.D.2d 645, 378 N.Y.S.2d 141 (1976); Lawrence v. Lawrence, 35 Tenn.App. 648, 250 S.W.2d 781 (1951).

30. In re Estate of Beakes, 306 So.2d 99 (Fla.1974); In re Elkerton's Estate, 380 Ill. 394, 44 N.E.2d 148 (1942); In re Koellen's Estate, 162 Kan. 395, 176 P.2d 544 (1947); Casson v. Swogell, 304 Md. 641, 500 A.2d 1031 (1985); In re Estate of Brantlinger, 418 Pa. 236, 210 A.2d 246 (1965).

31. See Weaver v. Grant, 394 So.2d 15 (Ala.1981); In re Montgomery's Estate, 89 Cal.App.2d 664, 201 P.2d 569 (1949); Williams v. Springfield Marine Bank, 131 Ill.App.3d 417, 86 Ill.Dec. 743, 475 N.E.2d 1122 (1985); Darnaby v. Halley's Executor, 306 Ky. 697, 208 S.W.2d 299 (1947); Tilton v. Daniels, 79 N.H. 368, 109 A. 145 (1920).

shall be in writing signed by the testator or in the testator's name by some other person in the testator's presence and by his direction, and shall be signed by at least 2 persons each of whom witnessed either the signing or the testator's acknowledgment of the signature or of the will.

The 1990 Code § 2–502 also requires that the witnesses sign the will within a reasonable time after they witness the testator's signing or acknowledgement.

It is standard practice to comply with all the formal requirements that exist in this country, although they may exceed in certain respects those that obtain in the jurisdiction in which the execution takes place. At the time of execution it cannot be known which state or states will have jurisdiction over probate at the testator's death, a matter which is discussed in Chapter 9, Section 8. Many states, however, have statutes which provide that the will is valid although not executed in accordance with the statutory formalities of the state in which the will is being probated if it was executed in accordance with the formalities required by the state in which it was executed at the time of execution, or by the law of the state in which the testator was domiciled at the time of execution.[32] Uniform Probate Code § 2–506 is as follows:

Section 2–506. [Choice of Law as to Execution.]

A written will is valid if executed in compliance with Section 2–502 or 2–503 or if its execution complies with the law at the time of execution of the place where the will is executed, or of the law of the place where at the time of execution or at the time of death the testator is domiciled, has a place of abode or is a national.

It is also standard practice to include immediately below the testator's signature and above the witnesses' signatures an attestation clause which recites the observance of the testamentary formalities as follows:

"On the 5th day of February, 1986, John Jones published and declared to us, the undersigned, that the foregoing instrument was his last will, and he requested us to act as witnesses to it and to his signature thereon. He then signed the will in our presence, we being present at the same time. We now, at his request, in his presence, and in the presence of each other, hereunto subscribe our names as witnesses, and each of us declares that in his or her opinion this testator is of sound mind.

32. E.g., Ark.Code Ann. § 28–25–105; Conn.Gen.Stat.Ann. § 45–161; Hawaii Rev.Stat. § 560:2–506; Neb.Rev. Stat. § 30–2331; Or.Rev.Stat. § 112.255.

The attestation clause should be read aloud by one of the witnesses immediately following the testator's signing and before the signing by the witnesses.

The attestation clause is not required. It does, however, create a prima facie case or presumption that the formalities were complied with,[33] serves to refresh the recollection of the witnesses when they testify at the time of probate, and can be used to impeach the credibility of a witness who testifies incorrectly at probate that the formal requirements were not met.

The 1990 Code has made a significant change in wills law by the inclusion of a new § 2–503 as follows:

Section 2–503. Writings Intended as Wills, Etc.

> Although a document or writing added upon a document was not executed in compliance with Section 2–502, the document or writing is treated as if it had been executed in compliance with that section if the proponent of the document or writing establishes by clear and convincing evidence that the decedent intended the document or writing to constitute (i) the decedent's will, (ii) a partial or complete revocation of the will, (iii) an addition to or an alteration of the will, or (iv) a partial or complete revival of his (or her) formerly revoked will or of a formerly revoked portion of the will.

In other words, under the 1990 Code, a writing is valid as a will without compliance with the formalities of execution if the decedent clearly intended the writing to be his will. The Comment to the Section uses as an illustration the situation of the execution in which, due to misunderstanding, there is only one witness or no witness. Another illustration is the testator's crossing out of a provision in a will and replacement with a different provision, without compliance with the statutory formalities. The power of the court to validate writings in such circumstances as wills or codicils has been referred to as a "dispensing power." This power has been legislated in several Australian and Canadian jurisdictions.

The pre–1990 Uniform Probate Code introduced the practice of combining the signing by the testator and the witnesses with an affidavit by them stating that the formalities were complied with, as follows:

---

33. In re Estate of Chlebos, 194 Ill. App.3d 46, 141 Ill.Dec. 23, 550 N.E.2d 1069 (1990); In re Will of Felson, 206 Misc. 988, 135 N.Y.S.2d 737 (1954); Jones v. Whiteley, 533 S.W.2d 881 (Tex. Civ.App.1976); In re Estate of Campbell, 47 Wash.2d 610, 288 P.2d 852 (1955).

Section 2–504. [Self-proved Will.]

(a) Any will may be simultaneously executed, attested, and made self-proved, by acknowledgment thereof by the testator and affidavits of the witnesses, each made before an officer authorized to administer oaths under the laws of the state where execution occurs and evidenced by the officer's certificate, under official seal, in substantially the following form:

I, _____, the testator, sign my name to this instrument this _____ day of _____, 19__, and being first duly sworn, do hereby declare to the undersigned authority that I sign and execute this instrument as my last will and that I sign it willingly (or willingly direct another to sign for me), that I execute it as my free and voluntary act for the purposes therein expressed, and that I am eighteen years of age or older, of sound mind, and under no constraint or undue influence.

_____
Testator

We, _____, _____, the witnesses, sign our names to this instrument, being first duly sworn, and do hereby declare to the undersigned authority that the testator signs and executes this instrument as his last will and that he signs it willingly (or willingly directs another to sign for him), and that each of us, in the presence and hearing of the testator, hereby signs this will as witness to the testator's signing, and that to the best of our knowledge the testator is eighteen years of age or older, of sound mind, and under no constraint or undue influence.

_____
Witness

_____
Witness

The State of _____
County of _____

Subscribed, sworn to and acknowledged before me by _____, the testator, and subscribed and sworn to before me by _____, and _____, witnesses, this _____ day of _____.

(Seal)

(Signed) _____
_____

(Official capacity
of officer)

Pre–1990 Uniform Probate Code § 2–504(b) also provides, in the alternative, for conventional execution followed by a separate affidavit to the same effect as the affidavit quoted above.

1990 Code § 2–504 is substantially the same as the pre–1990 Code provision, with the significant addition of a subsection (c) as follows:

(c) A signature affixed to a self-proving affidavit attached to a will is considered a signature affixed to the will, if necessary to prove the will's due execution.

The subsection corrects for the following mistake: The will provides for conventional execution, followed by a self-proving affidavit, and the testator or the witnesses or both sign only the affidavit.

The will with such an affidavit is referred to as a "self-proved" will. Uniform Probate Code § 3–406 provides that an affidavit in this form creates a conclusive presumption that the formalities of execution were complied with, i.e., the will cannot be contested on these grounds, and there is no need for the witnesses to testify at probate on the question of the formalities of execution. The will can, however, be contested on substantive grounds such as testamentary capacity, undue influence, and the like. Most states have legislated the "self-proved" will concept in one form or another,[34] but many do not provide that it creates a conclusive presumption of compliance with the formal requirements of execution.[35] In such jurisdictions the self-proved will does dispense with the need for the witnesses to testify at the time of probate in the case of the uncontested will; the affidavit takes the place of testimony. The matter of proof required at probate is discussed generally in Chapter 9, Section 3.

SECTION 2. HOLOGRAPHIC AND ORAL WILLS

About half the states have statutes which provide that a will in the handwriting of the testator and signed by her is valid without witnesses or other formal requirements. This is called a holographic will. The function of witnesses in the conventional will is

---

34. E.g., Ala.Code § 43–8–132; Alaska Stat. §§ 13.11.165, 13.16.165; Ariz. Rev.Stat.Ann. § 14–2504; Idaho Code § 15–2–504; Va.Code § 64.1–87.1; Wyo. Stat. § 2–6–114.

35. E.g., Colo.Rev.Stat. §§ 15–11–504, 15–12–406; Ga.Code Ann. § 53–2–40.1; Kan Stat.Ann. § 59–606; Ky.Rev. Stat.Ann. § 394.225; Okla.Stat.Ann. tit. 84, § 55; Tex.Prob.Code Ann. § 59.

to protect against forgery and coercion of the testator. It seems that the handwriting requirement of the unattested will protects only against forgery.

About half the statutes allowing holographic wills provide that it must be "wholly" or "entirely" in the handwriting of the testator.[36] If this is taken literally, it means that any typed words in the will invalidate it, but some courts have held that typed words in the will which are not essential to its meaning do not invalidate it if the essential language is handwritten.[37] The statutes of a few of these states add the requirement that the will be dated in the handwriting of the testator.[38] Pre–1990 Uniform Probate Code § 2–503, 1990 Code § 2–502(b), and the statutes of about half the states allowing the holographic will provide that it is valid if the "material provisions" are in the handwriting of the testator.[39] The Comment to the 1990 Code states, as an example, that if a will form is used which contains printed language such as, "I give, devise and bequeath to _____," and the testator fills out the remaining portion of the dispositive provision in his own handwriting and signs the will, the requirements for a holographic will are complied with.

A minority of states have statutes which provide that an oral will, often referred to as a nuncupative will, may be probated if it complies with several conditions of which the following are examples: It must be made in the testator's last illness; it must be made before a specified number of witnesses, such as two or three; it must be probated within a specified period such as six months.[40] In some states the oral will can dispose only of personalty.[41] Some statutes place a limit on the value that can be disposed of, such as $1,000.[42]

Some states have statutes recognizing oral wills for people in

36. E.g., Ark.Code Ann. § 28–25–104; Ky.Rev.Stat.Ann. § 394.040; Tex. Prob.Code Ann. § 60; Va.Code § 64.1–49; W.Va.Code § 41–1–3; Wyo.Stat. § 2–6–113.

37. Fairweather v. Nord, 388 S.W.2d 122 (Ky.1965); Watkins v. Boykin, 536 S.W.2d 400 (Tex.Civ.App.1976); In re Estate of Teubert, 171 W.Va. 226, 298 S.E.2d 456 (1982).

38. Nev.Rev.Stat. § 133.090; Okla. Stat.Ann. tit. 84, § 54; S.D.Comp. Laws Ann. § 29–2–8.

39. E.g., Ariz.Rev.Stat.Ann. § 14–2503; Colo.Rev.Stat. § 15–11–503; Me. Rev.Stat.Ann. tit. 18–A, § 2–503;

N.J.Stat.Ann. § 3B:3–3; Utah Code Ann. § 75–2–503.

40. E.g., Kan.Stat.Ann. § 59–608; Mo.Ann.Stat. § 474.340; Miss.Code Ann. § 91–5–15; N.H.Rev.Stat.Ann. § 551:16; Ohio Rev.Code Ann. § 2107.-60.

41. Kan.Stat.Ann. § 59–608; Ohio Rev.Code Ann. § 2107.60; Tenn.Code Ann. § 32–1–106; Tex.Prob.Code Ann. § 64.

42. Nev.Rev.Stat. § 133.100; Okla. Stat.Ann. tit. 84, § 46; S.D.Comp.Laws Ann. § 29–2–9; Tenn.Code Ann. § 32–1–106.

the military service.[43]

SECTION 3.   THE WITNESS–LEGATEE

At the time of execution of the will the witness must be mentally competent to serve as a witness in litigation.   If the witness who was competent at that time is not competent at the time of probate, he is a valid witness for purposes of the will although he cannot testify at probate.[44]   The law requires the witnessing of execution by competent persons; it does not require that those witnesses testify at probate on the matter of the execution of the will.   The validity of execution may be proved by means other than the testimony of the formal witnesses to the will.

There has been an unusual development in the law of will attestation concerning the witness who is a legatee or devisee under the will.   Historically a mentally competent person who was financially interested in a law suit was deemed not to be competent to be a witness in the suit because of bias.   Applying that principle to wills, the witness who was a legatee was not a valid witness. Although long ago the law changed to permit the interested witness to testify in litigation generally, the vestiges of the old rule remain in many of our statutes with respect to witnesses to wills.   In a majority of states there are statutes which provide that if a witness is a legatee or devisee, the bequest or devise is made void.[45]   The witness becomes a valid witness by depriving him of his interest. Uniform Probate Code § 2–505 and the statutes of a number of states reject this approach by providing that a witness may take under the will.[46]   These statutes do away with the anachronism of interest as a disqualification.

The statutes which invalidate testamentary gifts to witnesses usually are qualified to provide that if the witness is an heir (intestate taker) of the testator, the testamentary gift is invalid only to the extent that the value of the gift exceeds the value of the share of the estate she would have taken had the testator died intestate.[47]   Also, if there are three witnesses to a will, of whom

---

43. E.g., Alaska Stat. § 13.11.158; Mass.Gen.Laws.Ann. ch. 191, § 6; N.Y.Est. Powers & Trust Law § 3–2.2.

44. Ala.Code § 43–8–163; Kan.Stat. Ann. § 59–607; Mass.Gen.Laws Ann. ch. 191, § 3; Wis.Stat.Ann. § 853.07; Wyo.Stat. § 2–6–112; Berndtson v. Heuberger, 21 Ill.2d 557, 173 N.E.2d 460 (1961); Ferguson v. Ferguson, 187 Va. 581, 47 S.E.2d 346 (1948).

45. E.g., Cal.Prob.Code § 51; Ill. Ann.Stat. ch. 110½, § 4–6; Miss.Code Ann. § 91–5–9; Mo.Ann.Stat. § 474.330;

N.C.Gen.Stat. § 31–10; Ohio Rev.Code Ann. § 2107.15.

46. E.g., Colo.Rev.Stat. § 15–11–505; Del.Code Ann. tit. 12, § 203; Fla.Stat. Ann. § 732.504; Hawaii Rev.Stat. § 560:2–505; N.J.Stat.Ann. § 3B:3–8; N.M.Stat.Ann. § 45–2–505.

47. E.g., Ark.Code Ann. § 28–25–102; Kan.Stat.Ann. § 59–604; Ky.Rev. Stat.Ann. § 394.210; Neb.Rev.Stat. § 30–2330; S.C.Code Ann. § 62–2–504; Utah Code Ann. § 75–2–505.

one is a legatee, and the jurisdiction requires only two witnesses, most of these states provide that the interested witness may retain her gift because she is not essential to the validity of the will.[48] It should be noted that a minority of these statutes void the testamentary gift to a spouse of a witness in the same fashion and subject to the same qualifications as a gift to the witness.[49]

In states which void gifts to interested witnesses, the executor or trustee under the will can serve as a witness and retain the executorship or trusteeship because she earns what she is paid by virtue of her designation as fiduciary under the will.[50] Clearly the lawyer who prepares the will and presides at its execution is a valid witness.[51]

The law of many states is anachronistic and capable of producing the unfortunate result of voiding gifts where there is no dispute about the validity of the execution of the will. It is a trap for the unsuspecting layperson who arranges her own will execution, and it punishes the testator and legatee for the error of the lawyer. It is a rule of deterrence which probably does more damage than the situation it is supposed to discourage. The Uniform Probate Code provision makes much more sense.

SECTION 4. TESTAMENTARY CAPACITY

For a will to be admissible to probate, not only must the statutory formalities of execution be complied with, but the testator must have the capacity to execute a will. First of all, the testator must be of a certain age when he executes the will; in most states that age is 18.[52] In addition, testamentary capacity requires that the testator meet a standard of mental competence. The standard is a low one. This is illustrated by the line of authority that holds that a person may have testamentary capacity although a conservator has been appointed to manage his property because of his

48. E.g., Cal.Prob.Code § 51; Ill. Ann.Stat. ch. 110½, § 4–6; Mass.Gen. Laws Ann. ch. 191, § 2; N.C.Gen.Stat. § 31–10; Tenn.Code Ann. § 32–1–103; Vt.Stat.Ann. tit. 14, § 10.

49. E.g., S.C.Code Ann. § 62–2–504; Vt.Stat.Ann. tit. 14, § 10; W.Va.Code § 41–2–1; Wis.Stat.Ann. § 853.07.

50. Ind.Code Ann. § 29–1–5–2; Mo. Ann.Stat. § 474.330; Wis.Stat.Ann. § 853.07; In re Estate of Giacomini, 4 Kan.App.2d 126, 603 P.2d 218 (1979); In re Longworth, 222 A.2d 561 (Me. 1966); Estate of Fracht, 94 Misc.2d 664, 405 N.Y.S.2d 222 (1978); Blankner v.

Lathrop, 169 Ohio St. 229, 159 N.E.2d 229 (1959).

51. Rosenbaum v. Cahn, 234 Ark. 290, 351 S.W.2d 857 (1961); Wilburn v. Williams, 193 Miss. 831, 11 So.2d 306 (1943); Pavletich v. Pavletich, 78 N.M. 93, 428 P.2d 632 (1967); Blankner v. Lathrop, 169 Ohio St. 229, 159 N.E.2d 229 (1959); In re Andersen's Estate, 192 Or. 441, 235 P.2d 869 (1951).

52. E.g., Ariz.Rev.Stat.Ann. § 14–2501; Conn.Gen.Stat.Ann. § 45–160; Fla.Stat.Ann. § 732.501; Hawaii Rev. Stat. § 560:2–501; Ill.Ann.Stat. ch. 110½, § 4–1.

inability to do so.[53]

Why this difference between the standard for managing one's property and for making a will? The management of property requires dealing with other people at arm's length, whereas a will is a unilateral act involving no bargaining or dealings with other people. In addition, a person's ability to support himself can be jeopardized by mismanagement of his property, whereas there is no such danger in the making of a will.

The requirements for testamentary capacity have usually been expressed as follows: The testator must have the mental capacity to (a) know the nature of his property, (b) know the natural objects of his bounty, (c) form an orderly plan of disposition, and (d) understand the disposition made by his will.[54] The failure of any one of these requirements deprives the testator of testamentary capacity. It is reiterated that the standard of capacity is a modest one, and accordingly the testator is required to know the nature of his property only in a general way, and is required to understand the disposition in the will only in a general way. One's property may be extensive, the definition of one's ownership may be legally technical, the provisions of one's will may be detailed and technical; the testator is not required to know the details or the technicalities.[55]

A testator may fail to meet the standard of capacity because he is mentally deficient, or because he is mentally ill but not mentally deficient. Mental deficiency may be congenital, as in the case of an imbecile or an idiot. It may be the result of the deterioration of the brain as a consequence of age, or disease such as syphilis, or physical damage. It may also be the result of very serious mental illness. A person whose mental deficiency prevents him from satisfying one of the requirements for testamentary capacity is incapable of making a valid will.

The will of a person who is mentally ill but not mentally deficient may or may not be valid, depending on circumstances. Here we are speaking of a person whose mental illness does not

53. Estate of Raney, 247 Kan. 359, 799 P.2d 986 (1990); Estate of Congdon, 309 N.W.2d 261 (Minn.1981); In re Estate of Hastings, 479 Pa. 122, 387 A.2d 865 (1978); Matter of Estate of Hastings, 347 N.W.2d 347 (S.D.1984); Matter of Estate of Kesler, 702 P.2d 86 (Utah 1985); Estate of Roosa, 753 P.2d 1028 (Wyo.1988).

54. Estate of Wrigley, 104 Ill.App.3d 1008, 60 Ill.Dec. 757, 433 N.E.2d 995 (1982); Hodges v. Hodges, 692 S.W.2d 361 (Mo.App.1985); In re Estate of Peterson, 232 Neb. 105, 439 N.W.2d 516

(1989); In re Will of Shute, 251 N.C. 697, 111 S.E.2d 851 (1960); Matter of Estate of Kesler, 702 P.2d 86 (Utah 1985); Gibbs v. Gibbs, 239 Va. 197, 387 S.E.2d 499 (1990); In re Will of Wicker, 15 Wis.2d 86, 112 N.W.2d 137 (1961).

55. Shulman v. Shulman, 150 Conn. 651, 193 A.2d 525 (1963); In re Estate of Edwards, 433 So.2d 1349 (Fla.Dist.Ct. App.1983); Estate of Rosen, 447 A.2d 1220 (Me.1982); Matter of Estate of Evans, 83 Wis.2d 259, 265 N.W.2d 529 (1978).

wholly interfere with his mental processes. His mind functions normally in some or most respects, but he is divorced from reality in one or more respects. He suffers from an insane delusion or delusions, but the effect upon his mind is not so pervasive that it renders him mentally deficient. A person in this condition can make a valid will if the insane delusion does not affect the provisions of the will. For example, a person may believe that his neighbors are stealing from him and damaging his property. He attributes various forms of natural damage to his property to them, without any basis whatever, and accuses them of stealing from his mailbox, without any basis whatever. He is insanely delusional with respect to his neighbors' conduct. In other respects he is a normal, albeit rather neurotic person, and functions well as a husband, father, and insurance salesman. He executes a will disposing of his entire estate to his wife, and dies suddenly of a heart attack several months thereafter. The insane delusion was unrelated to his will. He met the standard for testamentary capacity, and the will is valid.[56]

On the other hand, a person who functions normally in the business world as an insurance salesman may believe without any basis in fact that his wife is unfaithful and is trying to poison him. He is insanely delusional in this respect, but is healthy in all other respects. He has no children. He executes a will in which he leaves his entire estate to his brother, and dies suddenly three months thereafter. He is not mentally deficient, but the insane delusion undoubtedly affected the disposition in his will. There is no question that the will is invalid because he lacked testamentary capacity. Are any of the enumerated requirements for capacity missing? It appears not. The testator knew his property, knew the natural objects of his bounty, understood his disposition, and was capable of forming an orderly dispositive plan. These requirements apply to testamentary capacity in general; that is to say, a mentally deficient person who does not satisfy one of them cannot make a valid will of any kind. For the person who is not mentally deficient but suffers from an insane delusion, the definition must be supplemented to the effect that an insane delusion that materially affects any of those factors or materially affects the disposition made by the will renders that person incompetent insofar as the affected disposition is concerned.[57]

56. Kelley v. Reed, 265 Ark. 581, 580 S.W.2d 682 (1979); Matter of Estate of Bonjean, 90 Ill.App.3d 582, 45 Ill.Dec. 872, 413 N.E.2d 205 (1980); Benjamin v. Woodring, 268 Md. 593, 303 A.2d 779 (1973); Flaherty v. Feldner, 419 N.W.2d 908 (N.D.1988); Estate of Roosa, 753 P.2d 1028 (Wyo.1988).

57. Velez v. Metropolitan Life Ins. Co., 723 F.2d 7 (10th Cir. 1983); In re Estate of Weil, 21 Ariz.App. 278, 518 P.2d 995 (1974); Spruance v. Northway, 601 S.W.2d 153 (Tex.Civ.App.1980); Matter of Estate of Kesler, 702 P.2d 86 (Utah 1985); In re Will of Wicker, 15 Wis.2d 86, 112 N.W.2d 137 (1961); Mat-

The testator's misperception of reality which affects the will raises the issue of the difference between an insane delusion and a sane mistake. If the dispositive provisions of the will are the product of a mistaken perception rather than an insane delusion, the will is valid. Except in very unusual circumstances, the law does not correct for mistaken motivation in the making of a will.[58] How are insanity and mistake distinguished? An insane delusion has been described as a belief that is the product of the imagination and is held tenaciously against all evidence and reason to the contrary. A mistaken belief is one for which there is some basis in fact, however unreasonable the belief based on such information may be.[59]

The determination of what constitutes testamentary capacity is said to be a legal conclusion, not a medical conclusion. This means that capacity is defined by the law and that the determination is to be made by the judicial process. Psychiatric testimony is admissible and influential, but sometimes the experts disagree. Even if the psychiatric testimony is presented only by one side, it is not conclusive; the finder of fact may believe it or not as he sees fit. There is also the rule of evidence in this area that the opinion of a lay witness on a question of capacity is admissible.[60]

Suppose a husband believes that his wife is unfaithful, and that this belief is an insane delusion. His wife owns considerable property. They have no children. The husband executes a will in which he disposes of his property to his brother who is struggling financially. Husband dies. His wife contests the will on the ground that it is the product of an insane delusion. The proponent of the will responds that the will left the property to the brother rather than the wife because the brother was poor and the wife was rich. What is the standard for determining validity where the testator may have been motivated by an insane delusion or another consideration, or both? It appears that the prevailing rule is that the gift is the product of the delusion if, except for the delusion, it

ter of Estate of Meagher, 60 Wash.2d 691, 375 P.2d 148 (1962).

58. See discussion infra p. 49.

59. Huffman v. Dawkins, 273 Ark. 520, 622 S.W.2d 159 (1981); In re Estate of Edwards, 433 So.2d 1349 (Fla. Dist.Ct.App.1983); Hammett v. Reynolds, 243 Ga. 669, 256 S.E.2d 354 (1979); Matter of Estate of Bonjean, 90 Ill. App.3d 582, 45 Ill.Dec. 872, 413 N.E.2d 205 (1980); Estate of Raney, 247 Kan. 359, 799 P.2d 986 (1990); Matter of Estate of Kesler, 702 P.2d 86 (Utah 1985). There is limited authority for the position that an insane delusion may

exist where there is a factual basis if the conclusion drawn from the fact is not rational. Estate of Flaherty, 446 N.W.2d 760 (N.D.1989); In re Wicker, 15 Wis.2d 86, 112 N.W.2d 137 (1961).

60. In re Estate of Hammermann, 387 So.2d 409 (Fla.Dist.Ct.App.1980); Bailey v. Clark, 203 Ill.App.3d 1017, 149 Ill.Dec. 89, 561 N.E.2d 367 (1990); Matter of Estate of Carothers, 220 Kan. 437, 552 P.2d 1354 (1976); Estate of Rosen, 447 A.2d 1220 (Me.1982); Estate of Thompson, 225 Neb. 643, 407 N.W.2d 738 (1987); Estate of Elam, 738 S.W.2d 169 (Tenn.1987).

would not have been made.[61]   There is also authority that the gift is invalid if it "might have been" the product of the delusion.[62]

If the will is invalid because of the testator's mental deficiency, the will is necessarily invalid in toto.   If the testator is not mentally deficient but is suffering from an insane delusion which affects provisions of the will, it is possible for the will to be partially invalid and partially valid.   One dispositive provision may be the product of the insane delusion, and the remaining provisions may not be.   The affected portion is denied probate for lack of capacity but the remainder is admissible to probate,[63] unless the affected and unaffected portions are related in such a manner that intestacy would be a more sensible disposition than the unaffected portion standing alone.

The standard of capacity for the execution of a will is also applicable to the revocation of a will.[64]   Assuming the testator has capacity, he may execute a will one day, revoke it the next by tearing it up, execute a new will the following day, revoke it the next by tearing it up, and so on day after day.   The last validly executed and unrevoked will at the time of his death disposes of his property.   What happens if a testator executes a will when he has the requisite capacity, and subsequently ceases to have testamentary capacity, which condition continues to the time of his death?   His validly executed will cannot be revoked because he lacks capacity.   Any purported revocation would be ineffective.   His will may become obsolete, but it remains his last will.   It is necessary that revocation should require testamentary capacity because it is a testamentary act, i.e., it changes the disposition from the provisions of the will to intestate distribution.

If a will is contested on the ground of lack of capacity, there is the question of which side has the burden of proof, the proponent of the will or the contestant.   The courts and statutes are divided

61. In re Estate of Martin, 270 Cal. App.2d 506, 75 Cal.Rptr. 911 (1969); Newman v. Smith, 77 Fla. 633, 82 So. 236 (1918); Kingdon v. Sybrant, 158 N.W.2d 863 (N.D.1968); Matter of Estate of Evans, 83 Wis.2d 259, 265 N.W.2d 529 (1978).

62. In re Honigman's Will, 8 N.Y.2d 244, 203 N.Y.S.2d 859, 168 N.E.2d 676 (1960).   One court has stated that the gift is invalid if the insane delusion "probably" affected it.   Campbell v. Campbell, 215 S.W. 134 (Tex.Civ.App. 1919).

63. In re Hart's Estate, 107 Cal. App.2d 60, 236 P.2d 884 (1951); In re City Nat. Bank and Trust Co. of Dan-bury, 145 Conn. 518, 144 A.2d 338 (1958); Holmes v. Campbell College, 87 Kan. 597, 125 P. 25 (1912).   There is some authority to the contrary: Irvine v. Greenway, 220 Ky. 388, 295 S.W. 445 (1927); Moore v. Jackson, 247 Miss. 854, 157 So.2d 785 (1963).   For a discussion of this issue, see Annot., 64 A.L.R.3d 261, 320 (1975).

64. Matter of Will of Nassano, 199 N.J.Super. 414, 489 A.2d 1189 (1985); Matter of Davis, 154 A.D.2d 461, 546 N.Y.S.2d 23 (1989); Matter of Will of Maynard, 64 N.C.App. 211, 307 S.E.2d 416 (1983); In re Hunter's Estate, 416 Pa. 127, 205 A.2d 97 (1964); Dean v. Garcia, 795 S.W.2d 763 (Tex.App. 1989).

on this issue.[65] Uniform Probate Code § 3–407 places the burden of proof on the contestant.

The definition of testamentary capacity and the distinction between the insane delusion and the sane mistake are obviously imprecise, and as a consequence the finder of fact often has a great deal of discretion as to the existence of capacity. In such circumstances it is to be expected that the determination of validity or invalidity may turn on the question of the fairness of the challenged testamentary disposition or the perceived injustice to those family members who are disinherited by it.

SECTION 5.   UNDUE INFLUENCE

If a person signs a will while another holds a loaded pistol to her head, the will is invalid. Action taken by a person under duress of this nature is not binding upon her. The law recognizes only those commitments and obligations undertaken freely.

A person under hypnosis is subject to the psychological control of another. If the subjected person executes a will pursuant to the direction of the hypnotist, the will is not valid because the execution is not the free act of the subjected person. Obviously duress and hypnosis are very different but they share the characteristic of coercion.

Undue influence is not duress or hypnotism, but in theory it shares the characteristic of coercion and consequent loss of free agency. Undue influence over a person exists if he is subject to such psychological domination by another that he cannot help but to do what the other wishes.[66] The will signed by one under undue influence of another is not valid because it is not the free act of the signer.

The references to duress and hypnotism are for the purpose of elucidating the theory of undue influence. Will contests are rarely based on duress, and hypnotism as a ground for contest is unheard

65. On proponent: Duchesneau v. Jaskoviak, 360 Mass. 730, 277 N.E.2d 507 (1972); Matter of Estate of Kumstar, 66 N.Y.2d 691, 496 N.Y.S.2d 414, 487 N.E.2d 271 (1985); Matter of Estate of Hastings, 347 N.W.2d 347 (S.D.1984); Croucher v. Croucher, 660 S.W.2d 55 (Tex.1983). On contestant: Sessions v. Handley, 470 So.2d 1164 (Ala.1985); Baerlocker v. Highsmith, 292 Ark. 373, 730 S.W.2d 237 (1987); Matter of Estate of Polda, 349 N.W.2d 11 (N.D.1984); In re Estate of Kuzma, 487 Pa. 91, 408 A.2d 1369 (1979); In re Will of Smoak, 286 S.C. 419, 334 S.E.2d 806 (1985).

66. Estate of Baker, 131 Cal.App.3d 471, 182 Cal.Rptr. 550 (1982); Ableman v. Katz, 481 A.2d 1114 (Del.1984); Burke v. Burke, 801 S.W.2d 691 (Ky. App. 1990); Moore v. Smith, 321 Md. 347, 582 A.2d 1237 (1990); Matter of Will of Fields, 75 N.C.App. 649, 331 S.E.2d 193 (1985); Okken v. Okken Estate, 348 N.W.2d 447 (N.D.1984); In re Will of Smoak, 286 S.C. 419, 334 S.E.2d 806 (1985).

of. Undue influence as a ground for contest is very common. The difficulty with undue influence is that its existence, as a practical matter, cannot be established objectively, i.e., by direct evidence. That an individual may come under such influence of another that he cannot resist what the other wishes him to do is plausible, but proving such psychological domination directly is virtually impossible.

It should be emphasized that it is commonplace for a person who has a close relationship with another to do all manner of things, including the making of gifts, that are beneficial and pleasing to the other. The making of gifts to the other may also follow certain importuning and appeals to obligation. It is only when the making of the gift is considered not to have been freely done because of psychological domination that the law intercedes. The crossing of the line can only be established by inference from circumstances. If the party contesting the will proves that certain circumstances existed, a rebuttable presumption of undue influence arises.[67] The setting for a challenge of undue influence often involves a testamentary disposition to one child who is close to the testator and unfavorable treatment of other children,[68] or to a friend of long-standing and unfavorable treatment of family,[69] or to one who cares for the testator in his last days,[70] or to a lover.[71]

It should be noted parenthetically that the definition of undue influence set forth above, i.e., the loss of free agency through psychological domination, is the traditional one, and the courts for the most part continue to honor it, at least verbally. A few courts, however, have defined it differently as unethical conduct in relation to a testator to obtain an advantage which the law will not

67. Blades v. Ward, 475 So.2d 935 (Fla.Dist.Ct.App.1985); Estate of Jessman, 197 Ill.App.3d 414, 143 Ill.Dec. 783, 554 N.E.2d 718 (1990); Haynes v. First Nat. State Bank of N.J., 87 N.J. 163, 432 A.2d 890 (1981); Estate of Till, 458 N.W.2d 521 (S.D.1990); In re Estate of Rotax, 139 Vt. 390, 429 A.2d 1304 (1981); In re Estate of Kamesar, 81 Wis.2d 151, 259 N.W.2d 733 (1977).

68. Matter of Estate of Davenport, 346 N.W.2d 530 (Iowa 1984); Estate of Langley, 586 A.2d 1270 (Me.1991): Estate of Vick, 557 So.2d 760 (Miss.1989); Haynes v. First Nat. State Bank of N.J., 87 N.J. 163, 432 A.2d 890 (1981); Okken v. Okken Estate, 348 N.W.2d 447 (N.D.1984); In re Estate of Kamesar, 81 Wis.2d 151, 259 N.W.2d 733 (1977).

69. Estate of Baker, 131 Cal.App.3d 471, 182 Cal.Rptr. 550 (1982); Estate of Kern, 239 Kan. 8, 716 P.2d 528 (1986); Matter of Estate of Borsch, 353 N.W.2d 346 (S.D.1984); Estate of Obra, 749 P.2d 272 (Wyo.1988).

70. In re Estate of Lamberson, 407 So.2d 358 (Fla.Dist.Ct.App.1981); Moore v. Smith, 321 Md. 347, 582 A.2d 1237 (1990); Matter of Estate of Swenson, 48 Or.App. 497, 617 P.2d 305 (1980); Mitchell v. Smith, 779 S.W.2d 384 (Tenn.App. 1989).

71. Parrisella v. Fotopulos, 111 Ariz. 4, 522 P.2d 1081 (1974); In re Dilios' Will, 156 Me. 508, 167 A.2d 571 (1960); Matter of Will of Moses, 227 So.2d 829 (Miss.1969); In re Kelly's Estate, 150 Or. 598, 46 P.2d 84 (1935); In re Kaufmann's Will, 20 A.D.2d 464, 247 N.Y.S.2d 664 (1964), aff'd 15 N.Y.2d 825, 257 N.Y.S.2d 941, 205 N.E.2d 864 (1965).

countenance.[72]

Assuming the traditional definition, what are the circumstances which raise the presumption? The cases vary in their description of the circumstances. Some cases require the following circumstances: (a) A testator susceptible to undue influence; (b) a confidential relationship between the testator and the person allegedly exercising the influence; and (c) a testamentary gift to the confidant, or to someone in whom he has an interest, which is unusual or unnatural.[73] Some cases have also required that the confidant of the testator play some role, however indirect, in the formulation, preparation or execution of the will.[74] Some cases have not required susceptibility to influence but have required participation in the making of the will by the confidant.[75]

Other courts have described the circumstances which raise the presumption in a somewhat different but similar manner, as follows: (a) A testator who is susceptible to undue influence; (b) an opportunity for the person allegedly exercising undue influence to do so; (c) a disposition on the part of the influencer to exercise influence over the testator; and (d) a testamentary gift to the influencer or someone in whom he has an interest, which is unusual or unnatural.[76] The reference in (b) to the opportunity to influence certainly includes the confidential relationship. The reference in (c) to the disposition to influence certainly includes participation by the influencer in the preparation, formulation or execution of the will, as well as other manifestations of a desire to obtain a benefit.

There is yet another judicial position on the question of what the contestant must establish to create a presumption of undue influence. Some courts have held that the existence of a confidential relationship, a will containing an unusual gift to the confidant, and "suspicious circumstances" surrounding the making of the will, create the presumption.[77] What may the "suspicious circum-

---

72. Morris v. Morris, 192 Miss. 518, 6 So.2d 311 (1942); Matter of Estate of Hogan, 218 Mont. 428, 708 P.2d 1018 (1985); Matter of Estate of Swenson, 48 Or.App. 497, 617 P.2d 305 (1980).

73. In re Hull's Estate, 63 Cal. App.2d 135, 146 P.2d 242 (1944); In re Estate of Fickert, 461 Pa. 653, 337 A.2d 592 (1975).

74. Evans v. Liston, 116 Ariz. 218, 568 P.2d 1116 (1977); Estate of Henke, 203 Ill.App.3d 975, 149 Ill.Dec. 36, 561 N.E.2d 314 (1990); Folsom v. Folsom, 601 S.W.2d 79 (Tex.Civ.App.1980).

75. Estate of Baker, 131 Cal.App.3d 471, 182 Cal.Rptr. 550 (1982); In re

Estate of Lamberson, 407 So.2d 358 (Fla.Dist.Ct.App.1981); Monaco v. Cecconi, 180 Mont. 111, 589 P.2d 156 (1979); Peters v. Skalman, 27 Wash. App. 247, 617 P.2d 448 (1980).

76. Ableman v. Katz, 481 A.2d 1114 (Del.1984); Estate of Novak, 235 Neb. 939, 458 N.W.2d 221 (1990); Estate of Herr, 460 N.W.2d 699 (N.D.1990); Rich v. Quinn, 13 Ohio App.3d 102, 468 N.E.2d 365 (1983); In re Estate of Kamesar, 81 Wis.2d 151, 259 N.W.2d 733 (1977).

77. Estate of Lawler v. Weston, 451 So.2d 739 (Miss.1984); Matter of Will of Ferrill, 97 N.M. 383, 640 P.2d 489

stances" be? Activity of the confidant in connection with the will, an unexplained change in the testator's attitudes towards others, an unexplained change in the testator's testamentary plan, susceptibility of the testator to influence, secrecy and haste in the execution of the will, and absence of independent advice to the testator, have been mentioned as suspicious circumstances.[78] This approach includes some of the same considerations as the other formulas set forth above.

The burden of proof of undue influence is usually on the contestant;[79] Uniform Probate Code § 3–407 so provides. If the circumstances described above are established by the contestant the courts speak of their raising a rebuttable presumption of undue influence, although occasionally a court will speak in terms of a permissible inference.

It was mentioned above that there are courts which have defined undue influence as improper conduct in relation to the testator for the purpose of obtaining a benefit, rather than as the psychological domination of the testator by another causing the testator to lose his free agency. A court which adopts this position considers the same factors as in the proof of undue influence defined as psychological domination.[80] There are also courts which define undue influence as psychological domination but purport to deal with it as a matter to be proved directly rather than by use of a presumption; such courts also speak of confidential relationship, susceptible testator, unusual benefit, as elements in the proof.[81] Courts frequently do not discuss undue influence in a structured or systematic manner, but the essence of the matter seems to be the exploitation of a confidential relationship with a susceptible person to obtain an unusual benefit.

The confidential relationship which is central to the case of undue influence may take various forms. A child who establishes an especially close relationship with a testator who has other

---

(1981); Matter of Estate of Dejmal, 95 Wis.2d 141, 289 N.W.2d 813 (1980).

78. Matter of Will of Ferrill, 97 N.M. 383, 640 P.2d 489 (App. 1981); McKee v. Stoddard, 98 Or.App. 514, 780 P.2d 736 (1989); In re Estate of Kamesar, 81 Wis.2d 151, 259 N.W.2d 733 (1977); Estate of Laitinen, 145 Vt. 153, 483 A.2d 265 (1984).

79. Cushman v. Nichols, 20 Mass. App.Ct. 980, 482 N.E.2d 862 (1985); Matter of Estate of Hogan, 218 Mont. 428, 708 P.2d 1018 (1985); In re Will of Smoak, 286 S.C. 419, 334 S.E.2d 806 (1985); Estate of Raedel, 152 Vt. 478, 568 A.2d 331 (1989); Estate of Loomis, 810 P.2d 126 (Wyo.1991).

80. Matter of Estate of Hogan, 218 Mont. 428, 708 P.2d 1018 (1985); Matter of Estate of Reddaway, 214 Or. 410, 329 P.2d 886 (1958); Matter of Estate of Swenson, 48 Or.App. 497, 617 P.2d 305 (1980).

81. Estate of Dankbar, 430 N.W.2d 124 (Iowa 1988); In re Dilios' Will, 156 Me. 508, 167 A.2d 571 (1960); In re Kaufmann's Will, 20 A.D.2d 464, 247 N.Y.S.2d 664 (1964), aff'd 15 N.Y.2d 825, 257 N.Y.S.2d 941, 205 N.E.2d 864 (1965); Lipper v. Weslow, 369 S.W.2d 698 (Tex.Civ.App.1963).

children,[82] a friend upon whom the testator becomes unusually dependent,[83] a lover upon whom the testator becomes dependent,[84] are examples. Confidential relationships are also found between attorney and testator-client,[85] guardian and testator-ward,[86] clergyman and testator,[87] and physician and testator-patient.[88] It should be reiterated that it is essential to a finding of undue influence that the gift to the confidant, or someone in whom he is interested, be unusual or unnatural.

A spouse's influence may be very great, but it is generally not the stuff of undue influence because it is considered to be normal conduct, and a testamentary gift to the spouse is obviously the norm.[89] There is, nevertheless, authority for undue influence in cases involving a surviving spouse in which he or she has engaged in extremely improper conduct.[90]

The proponent's defense to the contestant's case of undue influence may take several forms. Obviously the proponent may present evidence that contradicts the contestant's evidence of a confidential relationship, testator's susceptibility, and so on. In addition, the proponent may present evidence that the testator received advice and counsel from an independent source concerning

---

82. In re Estate of Gelonese, 36 Cal. App.3d 854, 111 Cal.Rptr. 833 (1974); In re Estate of Carpenter, 253 So.2d 697 (Fla.1971); Estate of Larson, 394 N.W.2d 617 (Minn.App. 1986); Haynes v. First Nat. State Bank of N.J., 87 N.J. 163, 432 A.2d 890 (1981); Matter of Estate of Reddaway, 214 Or. 410, 329 P.2d 886 (1958).

83. Matter of Will of Ferrill, 97 N.M. 383, 640 P.2d 489 (App.1981); Matter of Estate of Swenson, 48 Or.App. 497, 617 P.2d 305 (1980); Matter of Estate of Borsch, 353 N.W.2d 346 (S.D.1984); Matter of Estate of Vorel, 105 Wis.2d 112, 312 N.W.2d 850 (App.1981).

84. In re Dilios' Will, 156 Me. 508, 167 A.2d 571 (1960); In re Will of Moses, 227 So.2d 829 (Miss.1969); In re Kaufmann's Will, 20 A.D.2d 464, 247 N.Y.S.2d 664 (1964), aff'd 15 N.Y.2d 825, 257 N.Y.S.2d 941, 205 N.E.2d 864 (1965); In re Kelly's Estate, 150 Or. 598, 46 P.2d 84 (1935).

85. Estate of Novak, 235 Neb. 939, 458 N.E.2d 221 (1990); Matter of Estate of Lawson, 75 A.D.2d 20, 428 N.Y.S.2d 106 (1980); Estate of Younger, 314 Pa.Super. 480, 461 A.2d 259 (1983); Matter of Estate of Nelson, 274 N.W.2d 584 (S.D.1978); In re Estate of Komarr, 46 Wis.2d 230, 175 N.W.2d 473 (1970).

86 Birch v. Coleman, 15 Ark.App. 215, 691 S.W.2d 875 (1985); Estate of Clegg, 87 Cal.App.3d 594, 151 Cal.Rptr. 158 (1978); Pepin v. Ryan, 133 Conn. 12, 47 A.2d 846 (1946); Estate of Beal, 769 P.2d 150 (Okla.1989).

87. In re Estate of Cox, 383 Mich. 108, 174 N.W.2d 558 (1970); In re Hartlerode's Will, 183 Mich. 51, 148 N.W. 774 (1914).

88. In re Bucher's Estate, 56 Cal. App.2d 135, 132 P.2d 257 (1942); Matter of Estate of Hendricks, 110 N.W.2d 417 (N.D.1961); Foster v. Brady, 198 Wash. 13, 86 P.2d 760 (1939).

89. Matter of Estate of Robinson, 231 Kan. 300, 644 P.2d 420 (1982); Genna v. Harrington, 254 So.2d 525 (Miss.1971); Matter of Will of Rasnick, 77 N.J.Super. 380, 186 A.2d 527 (1962); In re Detsch's Estate, 191 Or. 161, 229 P.2d 264 (1951).

90. Blits v. Blits, 468 So.2d 320 (Fla. Dist.Ct.App.1985); Burke v. Burke, 801 S.W.2d 691 (Ky.App. 1990); Hodges v. Hodges, 692 S.W.2d 361 (Mo.App.1985); Matter of Will of Andrews, 299 N.C. 52, 261 S.E.2d 198 (1980); Green v. Green, 679 S.W.2d 640 (Tex.App.1984); Matter of Estate of Waters, 629 P.2d 470 (Wyo. 1981).

his will.[91] For example, the lawyer who prepared the will may have
questioned the testator concerning the unusual nature of the provisions of the will; such contact does not necessarily establish that
the testator's decision was not the product of undue influence, but
it has some probative value to that effect. The proponent may also
present evidence that although the gift was unusual, there was a
good reason for it.[92] For example, the family members who would
be expected beneficiaries of the testator's bounty were wealthy, and
the friend accused of undue influence was a person who was very
helpful to the testator in his declining years and was in need. It is
reiterated that the burden of proof is usually on the contestant,
although he does have the benefit of the presumption resulting
from the proof of relevant circumstances.

After all is said and done about the theory of undue influence,
the circumstances which raise the presumption, and so on, it should
be kept in mind that findings of undue influence often reflect a
sense of offense at what has occurred, i.e., the disinheritance of
family members and the benefit to someone who appears to have
improperly exploited his relationship with the testator. When the
legal principles are as nebulous as they are in this area, it is to be
expected that the success of the challenge is likely to turn on
notions of what is unfair or unethical.

SECTION 6. MISTAKE

The subject of mistake with respect to wills arises in two
contexts. First, there is the type of mistake which raises the
question of whether the will, or some part of it, is to be admitted to
probate. Second, assuming the will is admitted to probate, there is
the mistake in the description of property or a beneficiary which
presents a constructional issue. Here we are dealing with the
former; the latter is discussed in Chapter 6, Section 6.

Mistakes which relate to probate are of two basic types. First,
there is the mistake in the inducement to the making of the will.
Testator mistakenly believes that his son is dead, and disposes of
his entire estate to his daughter; or testator mistakenly believes
that his son has substantial wealth, and disposes of his entire estate
to his daughter. The rule is that probate will not be denied

91. In re Teller's Estate, 288 Mich.
193, 284 N.W. 696 (1939); Kelly v. Shoe-
make, 460 So.2d 811 (Miss.1984); White
v. Palmer, 498 P.2d 1401 (Okla.1971);
Matter of Estate of Swenson, 48 Or.App.
497, 617 P.2d 305 (1980); Askew v. Askew, 619 S.W.2d 384 (Tenn.App.1981).

92. Matter of Estate of Ross, 316
Pa.Super. 36, 462 A.2d 780 (1983); Matter of Estate of Weickum, 317 N.W.2d
142 (S.D.1982); Lipper v. Weslow, 369
S.W.2d 698 (Tex.Civ.App.1963); Small-
wood v. Jones, 794 S.W.2d 114 (Tex.App.
1990).

because of a mistake in the inducement to the making of a will.[93] Some cases, however, contain the dictum that if the mistake appears on the face of the will, and if the will evidences what the disposition would have been in the absence of the mistake, the will which is the product of the mistake is to be denied probate.[94] It should be emphasized that the application of this dictum would result in intestacy; the will would not be reformed to reflect what the testator would have done in the absence of the mistake.

Pre–1990 Uniform Probate Code § 2–302 and the statutes of a minority of states have modified the law with respect to mistake in the inducement in the limited situation of the will which omits any provision for the child of a testator because the testator mistakenly believes that the child is dead, by providing such child with the right to his intestate share of the estate.[95] 1990 Code § 2–302(c) has a similar but qualified provision which gives the child a share equal to what she would receive if she were an omitted afterborn child, as discussed in Chapter 8, Section 6, which share may be more or less than her intestate share, or nothing, depending upon the circumstances.

In mistake in the inducement to the making of the will the testator knows what the will contains. Another type of probate mistake has to do with a misperception of the contents of the will. Suppose the testator is not aware of the inclusion of a particular dispositive clause in the will. The clause was in the first draft of the will at testator's direction. The testator then changed his mind and told the lawyer to remove it, but through inadvertence it was not removed in the execution copy and the testator executed the will believing that it had been removed. Testator dies with that will. The mistakenly included clause will probably be denied probate, and the rest of the will is admitted to probate.[96] It is not apparent why the mistakenly induced will should be treated differently from the situation of mistaken contents.

93. Thompson v. Estate of Orr, 252 Ark. 377, 479 S.W.2d 229 (1972); York v. Smith, 385 So.2d 1110 (Fla.Dist.Ct. App.1980); Estate of Henrich, 389 N.W.2d 78 (Iowa App. 1986); Estate of Vick, 557 So.2d 760 (Miss. 1989); Estate of Angier, 381 Pa.Super 114, 552 A.2d 1121 (1989); Union Planters Nat. Bank v. Inman, 588 S.W.2d 757 (Tenn.App. 1979); Kaufhold v. McIver, 682 S.W.2d 660 (Tex.App.1984).

94. In re Goettel's Will, 184 Misc. 155, 55 N.Y.S.2d 61 (1945); Gifford v. Dyer, 2 R.I. 99, 57 Am.Dec. 708 (1852); Union Planters Nat. Bank v. Inman, 588 S.W.2d 757 (Tenn.App.1979).

95. E.g., Hawaii Rev.Stat. § 560:2–302; Me.Rev.Stat.Ann. tit. 18–A, § 2–302; N.M.Stat.Ann. § 45–2–302; Utah Code Ann. § 75–2–302.

96. Fuller v. Nazal, 259 Ala. 598, 67 So.2d 806 (1953); Hill v. Burger, 10 How.Pr. (N.Y.) 264 (1854); Christman v. Roesch, 132 App.Div. 22, 116 N.Y.S. 348 (1909), aff'd mem. 198 N.Y. 538, 92 N.E. 1080 (1910). See O'Connell v. Dow, 182 Mass. 541, 66 N.E. 788 (1903). A contrary position was adopted in Connecticut Junior Republic v. Sharon Hospital, 188 Conn. 1, 448 A.2d 190 (1982), in which extrinsic evidence of mistaken inclusion was inadmissible.

There have been cases of mistake in which reciprocal wills have been prepared for husband and wife. Reciprocal wills provide for disposition to the other if the other survives, or if the other does not survive, the estate passes to designated beneficiaries who are the same or similar in both wills. They go to the lawyer's office to execute the wills together, and each mistakenly signs the other's will. One dies with that will. It has been held that the wills are not admissible to probate.[97] This situation is a mistake as to the instrument itself, which is a form of mistake as to contents. One court, however, has admitted the husband's will to probate in these circumstances by reforming the will to substitute the husband's name for the wife's name wherever the latter appeared, and vice-versa.[98] This case is unusual because it is traditional probate doctrine that a court will not reform a will.

Finally, there is the issue of the clause that is omitted from the will by mistake. Testator instructs the lawyer to include a certain dispositive provision. Through inadvertence the clause is not included, and testator executes the will believing that it was included. Testator dies with the will. It is highly unlikely that the court will reform the will to include the omitted clause.[99] It is not easy to explain why the court is likely to strike what is included by mistake, but is not likely to include what is omitted by mistake.

It should be emphasized that this section is limited to mistake, i.e., misperceptions which are self-induced or are the result of innocent or negligent misrepresentation of others. If fraud is involved, i.e., misperceptions induced by the misrepresentation of others made with the intent to deceive, the results are different, as described in the following section.

SECTION 7. FRAUD

Mistake denotes an inaccurate perception which has been self-induced or induced by the innocent or negligent misrepresentation of another. Fraud denotes an inaccurate perception which has been induced by another with the intention to deceive. With respect to wills, fraud falls into two basic categories. In one category, the testator has been deceived with respect to the contents of the instrument. This is called fraud in the execution. In the other category, the testator knows the contents of the instru-

---

97. In re Pavlinko's Estate, 394 Pa. 564, 148 A.2d 528 (1959). See dictum in In re Gluckman's Will, 87 N.J.Eq. 638, 101 A. 295 (1917).

98. Matter of Snide, 52 N.Y.2d 193, 437 N.Y.S.2d 63, 418 N.E.2d 656 (1981).

99. In re Estate of Townsend, 221 Cal.App.2d 25, 34 Cal.Rptr. 275 (1963); Matter of Kronen, 114 A.D.2d 1033, 495 N.Y.S.2d 471 (1985); Farmers & Merchants Bank of Keyser v. Farmers & Merchants Bank of Keyser, 158 W.Va. 1012, 216 S.E.2d 769 (1975).

ment but has been deceived concerning certain facts which relate directly to the provisions of the will. This is called fraud in the inducement.

The following is an example of fraud in the execution. Testator, an elderly person who has no will, asks Lawyer to prepare a will devising Blackacre to X and Whiteacre to Y, X and Y being friends of the testator. Blackacre and Whiteacre constitute all the property of the testator. Lawyer's wife is the testator's sole heir (intestate taker). Lawyer prepares a will which devises Blackacre to X and makes no disposition of Whiteacre. This omission was done deliberately by Lawyer for the purpose of benefiting Lawyer's wife as the testator's heir. The testator executes the will believing that it is in accordance with her instructions. Testator dies with this will; she is intestate as to Whiteacre. Lawyer's wife had no knowledge that the fraud was being committed. The will is entitled to probate as far as it goes, but what is to be done about the omitted clause?

As a starting point, probate will not be granted to a clause which was omitted from the will due to fraud upon the testator. The court will not write a will for a testator, even for one who has been the victim of fraud.[1] As far as the question of will or no will is concerned, there is a will for Blackacre because that was not affected by the fraud, and intestacy as to Whiteacre, thereby passing legal title to Whiteacre to Lawyer's wife. But Y, the intended devisee, should not be without a remedy. The prevailing position is that on facts of this nature a constructive trust is imposed upon Whiteacre,[2] which means that Lawyer's wife holds mere legal title and is required to convey that title to the intended devisee, Y, who is deemed to have equitable title. There is also limited authority that on facts of this nature no constructive trust is imposed upon Whiteacre because Lawyer's wife was not a participant in the fraud;[3] if she had participated in the fraud, the constructive trust remedy would have been imposed. If the constructive trust remedy is not available, the only remedy available to Y, the defrauded devisee, is a tort action for damages against Lawyer.

The constructive trust is an equitable restitutional remedy that is employed in various circumstances of which fraud is one. If one

1. Dye v. Parker, 108 Kan. 304, 194 P. 640 (1921). See Henderson, Mistake and Fraud in Wills, 47 B.U.L.Rev. 303, 382–403 (1967); 1 Page, Law of Wills § 14.8 at 706 (Bowe-Parker Rev.1960).

2. In re Holmes' Estate, 98 Colo. 360, 56 P.2d 1333 (1936); White v. Mulvania, 575 S.W.2d 184 (Mo.1978); Bohannon v. Trotman, 214 N.C. 706, 200 S.E. 852 (1939). See Pope v. Garrett, 147 Tex. 18, 211 S.W.2d 559 (1948). See Restatement of Restitution § 184 comment j (1937).

3. Dye v. Parker, 108 Kan. 304, 194 P. 640 (1921); Powell v. Yearance, 73 N.J.Eq. 117, 67 A. 892 (1907).

party has been unjustly enriched by the fraudulent receipt of title to property, the unjustly deprived party may be entitled to recover the legal title to that property by the imposition of a constructive trust upon that property for the benefit of the unjustly deprived party who is viewed as holding the equitable title. Obviously there is no true trust here, but equity uses the fiction of a trust to effect the remedy of taking property from one person and giving it to another. The unjustly enriched person is called a trustee of the property for the benefit of the unjustly deprived person, and under the fictitious trust is required to transfer the legal title to the unjustly deprived person.

The hypothetical situation described above and the remedy, if any, may raise certain jurisdictional issues. The court with probate jurisdiction makes the decision as to the existence or non-existence of a valid will. The will was valid as far as it went. The court, however, cannot insert a clause omitted because of fraud. In this case partial intestacy results because there was no residuary clause. In some states the court with probate jurisdiction does not have general legal and equitable jurisdiction, and is limited to matters of probate, estate administration, and guardianship. Other remedies which may be appropriate, such as the imposition of a constructive trust, must be sought in the court having general jurisdiction. In such a state the probate court could not correct for the fraud; the defrauded party would have to bring an action in the court of general jurisdiction to impose a constructive trust or to obtain damages. In some states the court of general jurisdiction has probate jurisdiction as well, and the nonprobate relief could be obtained in the same proceeding.

If a testator intends to dispose of his entire estate to Y, but the lawyer who drafts his will fraudulently substitutes X for Y in the will, it is denied probate because of the fraud. If Y is the sole intestate taker of the testator, there is no need for a constructive trust remedy. If Y is not the sole intestate taker, then the constructive trust remedy is appropriate. If the probate process itself passes the property to the defrauded party, no recourse to the constructive trust remedy is necessary; if the probate process passes the property to someone other than the defrauded party, the constructive trust remedy is necessary.

The limits of the probate process should be noted. The probate court will deny probate to a will which is the product of fraud, but it will not probate a will which was not executed because of fraud. The probate court will probate a will which was revoked because of fraud, but it will not deny probate to a will which was not revoked because of fraud. Probate will undo what was done because of fraud, but it will not do what was not done because of fraud.[4] To the extent that the operative probate process does not compensate the defrauded party, the constructive trust remedy is employed.

Now an example of fraud in the inducement. C1 and C2, the two children of the testator, are his sole heirs. Testator has no will. C1 tells the testator lies about C2 with the intention of inducing the testator to execute a will leaving all his property to C1. Testator proceeds to execute a will leaving all his property to C1. Testator dies leaving that will. Probate of the will is challenged by C2 on the basis of fraud in the inducement. C2 prevails, resulting in the intestate division of the property between C1 and C2.[5] There is no need for the constructive trust remedy.

Suppose the testator has a will in which he disposes of his entire estate to X. Testator decides to execute a new will in which he will leave one-fourth of his property to Y, and three-fourths to X. Testator informs X of his intention. X tells the testator that there is no need to change the will because he will pay Y one-fourth of what he receives from the testator's estate. X has no intention of doing this; the testator has been fraudulently induced not to revoke his existing will and to refrain from executing a new will. The testator dies with the existing will. The existing will is admissible to probate because it was not fraudulently executed and it was not revoked. The court will not effect a revocation that did not occur, or probate a will that was not executed. A constructive trust will be imposed upon what X receives to the extent of what Y would have received had the revocation of the existing will and execution of its replacement occurred.[6]

One final example which raises the question of the causal relationship between the fraud and the provisions of the will in cases of fraud in the inducement. Testator and Mary went through a wedding ceremony three years before Testator made his will, but Mary was married to another at the time of the ceremony. Testator never learned of this. Testator made his will leaving all his property to Mary, and he died shortly thereafter, leaving that will. Testator and Mary had a very happy relationship. The will is challenged by Testator's heirs for fraud. Testator was induced to make the will both by the fraud and by the happy relationship. In

---

4. See Henderson, Mistake and Fraud in Wills, 47 B.U.L.Rev. 303, 382–403 (1967); Wellman, Waggoner and Browder, Palmer's Cases and Materials on Trusts and Succession 239–243 (4th ed. 1983).

5. In re Newhall's Estate, 190 Cal. 709, 214 P. 231 (1923); Estate of Holmes, 98 Colo. 360, 56 P.2d 1333 (1936); In re Rosenberg's Estate, 196 Or. 219, 246 P.2d 858 (1952); Holcomb v. Holcomb, 803 S.W.2d 411 (Tex.App. 1991); In re Dand's Estate, 41 Wash.2d 158, 247 P.2d 1016 (1952).

6. Monach v. Koslowski, 322 Mass. 466, 78 N.E.2d 4 (1948); White v. Mulvania, 575 S.W.2d 184 (Mo.1978); Latham v. Father Divine, 299 N.Y. 22, 85 N.E.2d 168 (1949); Barone v. Barone, 170 W.Va. 407, 294 S.E.2d 260 (1982).

such circumstances, is the will invalid for fraud? It has been held that the will is invalid if Testator would not have made it had he known the truth.[7] Applied to these facts, would Testator have left all to Mary if he had known the truth when he executed the will? Although he was happily "married," he may not have done so if he knew the marriage was fraudulent. It is a close question. It should be emphasized that the relationship of the fraud to the provisions of the will must be determined as of the time of the execution of the will; it is either fraudulently induced or valid at that time. In theory at least, the state of mind of a testator immediately before death is irrelevant.

It may occur that one clause of a will is the product of fraud and the rest is not. The probate court may deny probate to a part of the will for fraud in the execution or in the inducement, and admit the rest of the will to probate.[8]

The burden of proof with respect to fraud is on the contestant.[9]

SECTION 8. CONTRACTS TO MAKE WILLS

Let us assume that Jones, an elderly person, promises his Housekeeper in writing that he will leave her $50,000 in his will if she agrees to remain in his employ until his death. Housekeeper agrees, and Jones executes a new will containing a bequest to her in that amount. One year later Jones revokes that will and executes another will in which the bequest to Housekeeper is deliberately omitted. No disclosure of this change is made to Housekeeper. Three years later Jones dies leaving as his last will the one which omits the bequest to Housekeeper. Housekeeper performs her part of the agreement. Will that last will be admitted to probate without modification? If so, does Housekeeper have a cause of action against the estate?

It should be noted that a person can execute a will one day, revoke it the next day, execute another will the next, revoke it a day later, and so on indefinitely. The last validly executed and unrevoked will disposes of the testator's property at death. A will has no legal effect while the testator lives; at testator's death his

---

7. In re Carson's Estate, 184 Cal. 437, 194 P. 5 (1920); Knox v. Perkins, 86 N.H. 66, 163 A. 497 (1932); In re Dand's Estate, 41 Wash.2d 158, 247 P.2d 1016 (1952).

8. Arrington v. Working Woman's Home, 368 So.2d 851 (Ala.1979); Estate of Holmes, 98 Colo. 360, 56 P.2d 1333 (1936); Williams v. Crickman, 81 Ill.2d 105, 39 Ill.Dec. 820, 405 N.E.2d 799 (1980); In re Hollis' Estate, 234 Iowa 761, 12 N.W.2d 576 (1944); West v. Fi-

delity-Baltimore Nat. Bank, 219 Md. 258, 147 A.2d 859 (1959).

9. Hiler v. Cude, 248 Ark. 1065, 455 S.W.2d 891 (1970); Yribar v. Fitzpatrick, 91 Idaho 105, 416 P.2d 164 (1966); Kuenne v. Kuenne, 219 Md. 101, 148 A.2d 448 (1959); Tarricone v. Cummings, 340 Mass. 758, 166 N.E.2d 737 (1960); In re Estate of Elias, 429 Pa. 314, 239 A.2d 393 (1968).

last will is admissible to probate and disposes of his property. The subject of revocation is discussed in Chapter 4. Briefly and broadly stated, revocation of a will can be effected by its destruction with intent to revoke, or by a statement of revocation in a subsequent will, or by a subsequent will which is inconsistent with the prior will; this is a gross oversimplification of the subject but it suffices for present purposes.

A contract between a testator and another in which the testator promises to leave a will benefiting that person in a specified manner is valid.[10] A number of states have statutes requiring that the contract be evidenced by a writing.[11] The Uniform Probate Code requires a writing or reference to the contract in the will, as follows:

Section 2–701.   [Contracts Concerning Succession.]

A contract to make a will or devise, or not to revoke a will or devise, or to die intestate, if executed after the effective date of this Act, can be established only by (1) provisions of a will stating material provisions of the contract; (2) an express reference in a will to a contract and extrinsic evidence proving the terms of the contract; or (3) a writing signed by the decedent evidencing the contract. The execution of a joint will or mutual wills does not create a presumption of a contract not to revoke the will or wills.[12]

The hypothetical situation set forth above presents the issue of the relationship between revocability and the contract. The courts uphold both principles in these circumstances. The testator is entitled to revoke the will which complies with his contractual obligation, and the subsequent will which does not comply is admissible to probate.[13] The contract does not interfere with the principles of law which govern the revocation, execution, and probate of wills. The promisee, however, is entitled to enforce the

10. Apple v. Cooper, 263 Ark. 467, 565 S.W.2d 436 (1978); Wyrick v. Wyrick, 256 Ga. 408, 349 S.E.2d 705 (1986); Shimp v. Shimp, 287 Md. 372, 412 A.2d 1228 (1980); Klockner v. Green, 54 N.J. 230, 254 A.2d 782 (1969).

11. E.g., Ariz.Rev.Stat.Ann. § 14–2701; Cal.Civ.Code § 1624(6); Fla.Stat. Ann. § 732.701; Hawaii Rev.Stat. § 560:2–701; Mass.Gen.Laws Ann. ch. 259, §§ 5, 5A; N.Y.Est. Powers & Trusts Law § 13–2.1; Ohio Rev.Code Ann. § 2107.04.

12. 1990 Code § 2–514 is substantially the same.

13. Lewis v. Tanner, 252 Ga. 252, 312 S.E.2d 798 (1984); Matter of Estate of Isaacson, 77 Idaho 12, 285 P.2d 1061 (1955); Matter of Estate of Chapman, 239 N.W.2d 869 (Iowa 1976); Moats v. Schoch, 24 Md.App. 453, 332 A.2d 43 (1975); Olive v. Biggs, 276 N.C. 445, 173 S.E.2d 301 (1970). There is limited authority that a contractual will is irrevocable: Somogyi v. Marosites, 389 So.2d 244 (Fla.Dist.Ct.App.1980); Helms v. Darmstatter, 34 Ill.2d 295, 215 N.E.2d 245 (1966).

contract against the testator's estate; in our case Housekeeper has an action at law for damages in the amount of $50,000 against the estate of the testator.[14] Housekeeper in effect receives the legacy by enforcement of the contract. If the contract between Housekeeper and the testator was oral, and for that reason unenforceable in the jurisdiction, Housekeeper's only remedy may be an action in quasi-contract for the value of her services.[15]

If the contract between Housekeeper and the testator provided that he would devise Blackacre, a parcel of land, to Housekeeper, the contract would have to be evidenced by a writing because it is a contract to transfer land which invariably requires a writing,[16] regardless of whether there is a statute requiring a writing for a contract to make a will. Assuming an enforceable contract, if testator does not devise Blackacre to Housekeeper in his will admitted to probate, Housekeeper would have an action at law for damages, and also an action in equity for specific performance to acquire title to Blackacre, as contracts for land are invariably specifically enforceable.[17]

Frequently the contract to make a will provides that the promisor will leave his entire estate, or a fraction of his estate, to the promisee. If the promisor dies without such a provision in his will, the promisee has an action at law for damages, but this remedy is seldom employed in this circumstance. It is established that the promisee is entitled to specific performance of the contract, and that is the form of relief that is almost invariably given. The court either imposes a constructive trust on estate assets for the benefit of the promisee, or orders the executor or takers under the will to transfer title to estate assets to the promisee.[18] The courts

14. Regan v. Lenkowsky, 137 F.Supp. 133 (D.N.J.1956); Farrington v. Richardson, 153 Fla. 907, 16 So.2d 158 (1944); Wyrick v. Wyrick, 256 Ga. 408, 349 S.E.2d 705 (1986); Estate of Stratmann, 248 Kan. 197, 806 P.2d 459 (1991); Halsey v. Snell, 214 N.C. 209, 198 S.E. 633 (1938); In re Elwood's Estate, 309 Pa. 505, 164 A. 617 (1932).

15. Hastoupis v. Gargas, 9 Mass. App.Ct. 27, 398 N.E.2d 745 (1980); Williams v. Mason, 556 So.2d 1045 (Miss.1990); Humiston v. Bushnell, 118 N.H. 759, 394 A.2d 844 (1978); Peters v. Morse, 96 A.D.2d 662, 466 N.Y.S.2d 504 (1983); Gibson v. McCraw, 175 W.Va. 256, 332 S.E.2d 269 (1985).

16. Somerville v. Epps, 36 Conn.Sup. 323, 419 A.2d 909 (1980); Gable v. Miller, 104 So.2d 358 (Fla.1958); Unitas v. Temple, 74 Md.App. 506, 538 A.2d 1201 (1988), reversed 314 Md. 689, 552 A.2d

1285 (1989); Foster v. Barton, 365 P.2d 714 (Okl.1961); Benson v. Williams, 174 Or. 404, 149 P.2d 549 (1944).

17. Shepherd v. Mazzetti, 545 A.2d 621 (Del.1988); Anson v. Haywood, 397 Ill. 370, 74 N.E.2d 489 (1947); McDonald v. Scheifler, 323 Mich. 117, 34 N.W.2d 573 (1948); Adams v. Moberg, 356 Mo. 1175, 205 S.W.2d 553 (1947).

18. Ludwicki v. Guerin, 57 Cal.2d 127, 17 Cal.Rptr. 823, 367 P.2d 415 (1961); Stahmer v. Schley, 96 Cal. App.3d 200, 157 Cal.Rptr 756 (1979); Scham v. Besse, 397 Ill. 309, 74 N.E.2d 517 (1947); Matter of Estate of Maloney v. Carsten, 178 Ind.App. 191, 381 N.E.2d 1263 (1978); Matter of Estate of Chapman, 239 N.W.2d 869 (Iowa 1976); Jannetta v. Jannetta, 205 Minn. 266, 285 N.W. 619 (1939); Godwin v. Wachovia Bank and Trust Co., 259 N.C. 520, 131 S.E.2d 456 (1963).

often do not articulate the basis for equitable relief.[19]

The issue of the existence of a will contract arises from time to time in connection with mutual wills, which are also referred to as reciprocal wills. Mutual or reciprocal wills are those in which A leaves all to B if B survives, and if not, to C; and B leaves all to A if A survives, and if not, to C. In real life terms, A and B are likely to be husband and wife, and C may be the descendants of A and B. Sometimes the mutual or reciprocal wills do not have identical ultimate beneficiaries.

Invariably the testators of mutual wills have an understanding with respect to their provisions. It is one thing, however, for the testators to have an understanding, and quite another for them to be contractually bound to those wills. If one dies leaving all to the survivor, it becomes very important whether or not the survivor is contractually bound. A number of states have statutes which provide that the existence of mutual wills does not by itself create a presumption that they are the product of contract,[20] and pre–1990 Uniform Probate Code § 2–701 and 1990 Code § 2–514 so provide. The cases also have generally adopted this position.[21] The parties executing mutual wills may, of course, have expressly contracted with respect to them, or a contract may be inferred by the court from circumstances and statements.[22]

Husband and wife sometimes execute a joint will containing mutual provisions. A joint will is one document which contains the testamentary dispositions of both parties. It is two wills contained in one document, and each duly executes at the end of the document. At the death of the first to die, the instrument is probated as that person's will. At the death of the survivor, the instrument is probated as that person's will. Each will can be separately revoked. It is a very awkward and undesirable method of testamentary disposition. The execution of joint and mutual wills does not by itself create a contract. There is some evidence in the cases, however, that the courts are more likely to infer a contract from

---

19. See Sparks, Contracts To Make Wills 149 (1956).

20. E.g., Ky.Rev.Stat. § 394.540; Me.Rev.Stat.Ann. tit. 18–A, § 2–701; Mo.Ann.Stat. § 474.155; N.J.Stat.Ann. § 3B:1–4; Or.Rev.Stat. § 112.270; Tex. Prob.Code Ann. § 59A.

21. Proctor v. Handke, 116 Ill. App.3d 742, 72 Ill.Dec. 489, 452 N.E.2d 742 (1983); Johansen v. Davenport Bank & Trust Co., 242 Iowa 172, 46 N.W.2d 48 (1951); Oursler v. Armstrong, 10 N.Y.2d 385, 223 N.Y.S.2d 477, 179 N.E.2d 489 (1961); Paull v. Earlywine, 195 Okl. 486, 159 P.2d 556 (1945);

Estate of Kester, 477 Pa. 243, 383 A.2d 914 (1978); Sievers v. Barton, 775 P.2d 489 (Wyo.1989).

22. Lawrence v. Ashba, 115 Ind.App. 485, 59 N.E.2d 568 (1945); Wimp v. Collett, 414 S.W.2d 65 (Mo.1967); Woelke v. Calfee, 45 Or.App. 459, 608 P.2d 606 (1980); Pruitt v. Moss, 271 S.C. 305, 247 S.E.2d 324 (1978); O'Connor v. Immele, 77 N.D. 346, 43 N.W.2d 649 (1950). See Reznik v. McKee, 216 Kan. 659, 534 P.2d 243 (1975), dealing with a contract concerning a revocable trust.

circumstances in the case of the joint and mutual wills than they are in the case of separate and mutual wills.[23]

Mutual wills, joint or separate, are sometimes executed pursuant to contract. The ultimate takers under the contract can enforce its terms against the survivor as third party beneficiaries. It should be noted, however, that there is an anomalous line of authority in this area which runs counter to standard contract doctrine. These cases provide that while both parties are living, if one of them advises the other that he is revoking his will and does not intend to be bound, the contract is terminated.[24] This termination is effective without any explicit provision for such unilateral termination in the contract. It should be emphasized that if the option to terminate is not exercised by either while both are living, the estate of the first to die and the survivor are contractually bound. There is also contrary authority that there is no right of unilateral termination of the contract while both parties are living.[25]

Let us assume that the mutual wills are made pursuant to contract, and wife has died leaving all to husband in her will as she was bound to do. Husband now owns what his deceased wife owned as well as the property which he has owned all along, and he has a will in which he leaves all of it to the ultimate contractual beneficiaries. Let us assume that the marriage was a second marriage for husband and wife, each had children by the first marriage, there were no children by their marriage, and the ultimate contract takers are their children by the first marriages in equal shares. Husband now decides to avoid the objective of the contract by making substantial inter vivos gifts to his children, thereby reducing his estate that will pass to the children of the previous marriages equally. His contractual will remains. The contract requires that he leave that will, but makes no reference to inter vivos gifts. Can husband legally circumvent his contractual obligations by this means? There is authority that substantial inter vivos gifts which have the effect of defeating the purpose of the contract may be recovered from the donees by those who are

23. See In re Edwards' Estate, 3 Ill.2d 116, 120 N.E.2d 10 (1954); Matter of Estate of Chronister, 203 Kan. 366, 454 P.2d 438 (1969); Atkins v. Oppio, 105 Nev. 34, 769 P.2d 62 (1989); Glass v. Battista, 43 N.Y.2d 620, 403 N.Y.S.2d 204, 374 N.E.2d 116 (1978); Fisher v. Capp, 597 S.W.2d 393 (Tex.Civ.App. 1980).

24. Duhme v. Duhme, 260 N.W.2d 415 (Iowa 1977); Wright v. Wright, 215 Ky. 394, 285 S.W. 188 (1926); Allen v. Dillard, 15 Wash.2d 35, 129 P.2d 813 (1942). This view is criticized in Sparks, Contracts To Make Wills 121, 195 (1956).

25. Trindle v. Zimmerman, 115 Colo. 323, 172 P.2d 676 (1946); Estate of Jud, 238 Kan. 268, 710 P.2d 1241 (1985); Brown v. Webster, 90 Neb. 591, 134 N.W. 185 (1912).

the beneficiaries of the contract.[26] In effect the courts have recognized an implied provision in the contract against substantial inter vivos gifts to others.

Another problem area is the relationship of the will contract to the surviving spouse's forced share. Let us assume that husband and wife contract that each will leave his or her property by will to the survivor, and the survivor will leave all to the children of the marriage, and they execute wills accordingly. Wife dies first, and her will leaves all to husband. Several years later husband remarries. Several years after that husband dies leaving his contractual will which leaves all to the children. The jurisdiction has a forced share statute, as most do, i.e., one that entitles the disinherited wife to a certain fraction of the estate, which is usually the fraction she would receive on intestacy or sometimes a smaller fraction. The surviving spouse's forced share is discussed in Chapter 8, Section 2. Husband's surviving wife claims her forced share which in this instance is one-third of the estate. The children claim the entire estate under the will and contract. Who prevails?

There have been a number of cases dealing with this question which have arrived at different results. If one ignores all policy considerations and applies legal concepts mechanically, the children should prevail. The spouse's forced share is defined as a fraction of the net estate after creditors' claims; if the estate is insolvent, the forced share is worthless. Creditors come first. The function of the forced share is to place the spouse in about the position she would have in intestacy; intestate takers take what is left after creditors have been paid. The children are third party beneficiaries of a contractual obligation; they are contract creditors and take all. There is some authority for this position.[27]

Other cases have ignored this analysis. Some have held that the surviving spouse is entitled to the forced share if she did not know of the contract at the time she married the decedent spouse; if she knew of the contract at the time of the marriage the children prevail.[28] Still other cases have held for the surviving spouse on

26. Humphries v. Whiteley, 565 So.2d 96 (Ala.1990); Lawrence v. Ashba, 115 Ind.App. 485, 59 N.E.2d 568 (1945); Schwartz v. Horn, 31 N.Y.2d 275, 338 N.Y.S.2d 613, 290 N.E.2d 816 (1972); Robison v. Graham, 799 P.2d 610 (Okl. 1990); In re Estate of Chayka, 47 Wis.2d 102, 176 N.W.2d 561 (1970); Flohr v. Walker, 520 P.2d 833 (Wyo. 1974).

27. Lewis v. Lewis, 104 Kan. 269, 178 P. 421 (1919); Brindisi v. Stallone, 259 App.Div. 1080, 21 N.Y.S.2d 29 (1940); In re Estate of Beeruk, 429 Pa. 415, 241 A.2d 755 (1968). See Rubenstein v. Mueller, 19 N.Y.2d 228, 278 N.Y.S.2d 845, 225 N.E.2d 540 (1967).

28. Barkley v. Barkley, 314 F.2d 188 (5th Cir.1963); Mayfield v. Cook, 201 Ala. 187, 77 So. 713 (1918); Ver Standig v. St. Louis Union Trust Co., 344 Mo. 880, 129 S.W.2d 905 (1939); Patecky v. Friend, 220 Or. 612, 350 P.2d 170 (1960).

the ground that the protective aspect of the forced share statute should prevail in this circumstance.[29]

29. Wides v. Wides' Executor, 299 Ky. 103, 184 S.W.2d 579 (1944); Shimp v. Hutt, 315 Md. 624, 556 A.2d 252 (1989); Budde v. Pierce, 135 Vt. 152, 375 A.2d 984 (1977). See Simpson v. Dodge, 220 Ga. 705, 141 S.E.2d 532 (1965). For discussion of this issue, see Annot. 85 A.L.R. 4th 418 (1991).

Chapter 4

REVOCATION OF WILLS

In 1990 changes were made in certain sections of the Uniform Probate Code dealing with revocation of wills. In this chapter there are references to the pre–1990 Uniform Probate Code (or pre–1990 Code) and to the 1990 Uniform Probate Code (or 1990 Code). There are also references to the Uniform Probate Code in instances in which no substantial change has been made by the 1990 revision. The reader is referred to the introduction to Chapter 2 for further information on the development of the Uniform Probate Code.

SECTION 1. INTRODUCTION

In the language of the law, the will is said to be "ambulatory." This means that it can be changed or revoked prior to death. One can execute a will one day, revoke it the next day, execute another the following day, revoke that and execute another, and so on. The last validly executed, unrevoked will is admitted to probate and determines the disposition of the testator's property. A will has no legal effect until the death of the testator.

Revocation of a will can occur in three different ways, as provided by statute. One way is by physical act, such as tearing up the will or drawing lines through it, with the intention to revoke. Another way is by the execution of a later will in which the testator states that the prior will is revoked, or by a later will which is inconsistent with the prior will. The third way is by a change in the circumstances of the testator of such significance that the law deems the will to be revoked in whole or in part without any statement or action by the testator. The last method is referred to as revocation by operation of law. An example is divorce which in most states has the effect of revoking any testamentary gift to the former spouse in the will. The pre–1990 Uniform Probate Code provisions dealing with revocation are as follows:

Section 2–507. [Revocation by Writing or by Act.]

A will or any part thereof is revoked

(1) by a subsequent will which revokes the prior will or part expressly or by inconsistency; or

(2) by being burned, torn, canceled, obliterated, or destroyed, with the intent and for the purpose of revoking it

by the testator or by another person in his presence and by his direction.

Section 2–508. [Revocation by Divorce; No Revocation by Other Changes of Circumstances.]

If after executing a will the testator is divorced or his marriage annulled, the divorce or annulment revokes any disposition or appointment of property made by the will to the former spouse, any provision conferring a general or special power of appointment on the former spouse, and any nomination of the former spouse as executor, trustee, conservator, or guardian, unless the will expressly provides otherwise. Property prevented from passing to a former spouse because of revocation by divorce or annulment passes as if the former spouse failed to survive the decedent, and other provisions conferring some power or office on the former spouse are interpreted as if the spouse failed to survive the decedent. If provisions are revoked solely by this section, they are revived by testator's remarriage to the former spouse. For purposes of this section, divorce or annulment means any divorce or annulment which would exclude the spouse as a surviving spouse within the meaning of Section 2–802(b). A decree of separation which does not terminate the status of husband and wife is not a divorce for purposes of this section. No change of circumstances other than as described in this section revokes a will.

It should be pointed out that volitional revocation, i.e., by physical act or subsequent testamentary instrument, requires the same testamentary capacity as the execution of a will. Revocation is as much a testamentary act as the execution of a will. If a person becomes incompetent, he cannot revoke an existing will that was executed when he was competent. A person executes a will at age 60 when he was competent; he becomes incompetent 10 years later without having previously revoked that will; if he remains incompetent until his death the existing will controls the disposition of his property at death. The testator could not revoke it by a subsequent will because he lacked testamentary capacity. He could not revoke it by physical act because he did not possess the testamentary capacity for the requisite intent. The will may be unsuited for the later circumstances of his family but there is nothing that can be done.

SECTION 2. REVOCATION BY PHYSICAL ACT

Revocation can be accomplished by the destruction, cancellation, or obliteration of the will with the intent to revoke. The physical act may consist of tearing the document, or burning it, or drawing lines across the face of it. It should be noted that if the will is in a bureau drawer in a house and is destroyed when the entire house burns to the ground, there is no revocation because destruction was not accompanied by an intention to revoke. A will which has been accidentally destroyed or lost may be probated although there is the problem of proof of its contents. There is limited authority that an accidentally destroyed or lost will is deemed revoked if the testator, subsequent to the destruction or loss, clearly manifests an intention to revoke it,[1] but there is also authority that revocation cannot be accomplished by the subsequent ratification of the loss or destruction.[2]

In a large majority of states partial revocation by physical act is permitted by statute.[3] This is likely to occur by the drawing of lines through a dispositive provision of the will. There are some statutes which do not permit partial revocation by physical act.[4]

Suppose a testator has executed a will and a codicil to it. A codicil is an instrument executed in compliance with testamentary formalities which amends a will. Testator tears up the will with the manifested intention of revoking the will and the codicil, but the codicil is not touched. In this circumstance both the will and the codicil are deemed to be revoked. If, however, the intention to revoke the codicil is not clear, the codicil will be deemed to be revoked only if it is closely interrelated with the will; if that is not the case, it is deemed not to be revoked.[5] Revocation of the codicil in these circumstances is not literally consistent with the statute because the codicil is physically intact, but the result is sensible.

 If the codicil is destroyed with the intention to revoke it, or to revoke it and the will, but the will is not touched, only the codicil is deemed to be revoked.[6]

1. In re Will of Roman, 80 N.J.Super. 481, 194 A.2d 40 (1963); Cutler v. Cutler, 130 N.C. 1, 40 S.E. 689 (1902); Davis v. Davis, 214 S.C. 247, 52 S.E.2d 192 (1949); In re Murphy's Estate, 217 Wis. 472, 259 N.W. 430 (1935).

2. Miller v. Harrell, 175 Ky. 578, 194 S.W. 782 (1917); In re Estate of McCaffrey, 453 Pa. 416, 309 A.2d 539 (1973).

3. E.g., Cal.Prob.Code § 6120; D.C.Code Ann. § 18–109; Iowa Code Ann. § 633.284; Minn.Stat.Ann. § 524.2–507; Mo.Ann.Stat. § 474.400; N.J.Stat.Ann. § 3B:3–13.

4. E.g., Colo.Rev.Stat. § 15–11–507; Fla.Stat.Ann. § 732.506; Ind.Code Ann. § 29–1–5–6; N.Y.Est.Powers & Trusts Law § 3–4.1.

5. In re Estate of Cuneo, 60 Cal.2d 196, 32 Cal.Rptr. 409, 384 P.2d 1 (1963); Youse v. Forman, 68 Ky. (5 Bush) 337 (1869); Matter of Estate of Sapery, 28 N.J. 599, 147 A.2d 777 (1959); In re Halpern's Estate, 32 Misc.2d 808, 224 N.Y.S.2d 58 (1962); In re Francis' Will, 73 Misc. 148, 132 N.Y.S. 695 (1911); In re Ayres' Will, 36 Ohio L.Abs. 267, 43 N.E.2d 918 (1940); O'Neill's Estate, 58 Pa.D. & C. 351 (1947); Annot., 7 A.L.R.3d 1143 (1966).

6. Estate of Ivancovich, 151 Ariz. 442, 728 P.2d 661 (App. 1986); Matter of Estate of Hering, 108 Cal.App.3d 88, 166 Cal.Rptr. 298 (1980); In re Diament's Estate, 88 N.J.Eq. 552, 103 A. 199 (1918); In re Hargrove's Will, 262 App.Div. 202, 28 N.Y.S.2d 571 (1941),

The person who revokes his will by destruction is likely to execute a new one. Let us assume, however, that a testator revokes his will privately by destruction, never tells anyone, and never executes a new one. His lawyer and members of his family knew of his will but knew nothing about its destruction. The will obviously cannot be found at his death. As we indicated, a lost will can be probated, albeit with difficulty. To deal with this problem the courts have established a rebuttable presumption that if a will was known to be in the possession of the testator and cannot be found at his death, it has been revoked by destruction.[7] On the other hand, if the will was not in the possession of the testator and cannot be found at his death, no presumption of revocation arises and the will can be probated as a lost will.[8]

Sometimes a testator executes two copies of his will. One copy is left with the lawyer, and the other is retained by the testator. There are two instruments, both of which can serve as a will, but it is conceptually one will. The testator privately destroys his copy with the intention to revoke and never tells anybody. The will has been revoked.[9] There is no need to destroy both copies. At testator's death his copy obviously cannot be found. The lawyer presents the other copy. Nevertheless the presumption of revocation by destruction applies here as well as in the circumstance described in the preceding paragraph.

Many states have statutes which provide that a testator may leave his will with the clerk of the probate court for safe-keeping.[10] This has no legal significance as such; the probate court is simply a repository. The problem at the testator's death of not being able to find a will which in fact was not destroyed, and the risks of post-mortem destruction by disappointed parties, can be avoided by the use of the repository.

aff'd 288 N.Y. 604, 42 N.E.2d 608 (1942).

7. Matter of Estate of Travers, 121 Ariz. 282, 589 P.2d 1314 (1978); Gee v. Stephens, 562 N.E.2d 772 (Ind.App. 1990); Matter of Estate of Crozier, 232 N.W.2d 554 (Iowa 1975); Estate of Richard, 556 A.2d 1091 (Me.1989); In re Estate of Wasco, 444 Pa. 184, 281 A.2d 877 (1971).

8. Matter of Estate of Killgore, 86 Idaho 386, 387 P.2d 16 (1963); Matter of Estate of Fisher, 173 Neb. 510, 113 N.W.2d 625 (1962); In re Suarez's Estate, 131 N.Y.S.2d 419 (Sur.1953), aff'd 283 App.Div. 774, 128 N.Y.S.2d 594

(1954); Estate of Haynes, 25 Ohio St.3d 101, 495 N.E.2d 23 (1986).

9. Stiles v. Brown, 380 So.2d 792 (Ala.1980); Matter of Estate of Travers, 121 Ariz. 282, 589 P.2d 1314 (1978); In re Estate of Tong, 619 P.2d 91 (Colo. App.1980); Estate of Mettee, 10 Kan. App.2d 184, 694 P.2d 1325 (1985); In re Estate of Millsap, 55 Ill.App.3d 749, 13 Ill.Dec. 490, 371 N.E.2d 185 (1977); Miniter v. Irwin, 331 Mass. 8, 116 N.E.2d 567 (1954). There is authority that the presumption of revocation does not apply in this situation. Estate of Shaw, 572 P.2d 229 (Okl.1977).

10. E.g., Mass.Gen. Laws Ann. ch. 191, § 10; N.C.Gen.Stat. § 31–11; Ohio Rev.Code Ann. § 2107.07.

SECTION 3. REVOCATION BY SUBSEQUENT INSTRUMENT

A will may be revoked, in whole or in part, by a subsequent instrument executed in accordance with testamentary formalities. In the usual situation the subsequent instrument contains a clause which expressly revokes all prior wills, and goes on to dispose completely of the testator's property. It may be, however, that the subsequent instrument executed in accordance with the testamentary formalities contains only a clause revoking the entire prior will and no dispositive provisions. Sometimes a codicil will be duly executed for the sole purpose of revoking a specific dispositive provision of the will, leaving all else as it was. A codicil is an amendment to a will.

Occasionally the subsequent will contains no revocatory clause, but its dispositive provisions are wholly inconsistent with the prior will. Revocation may be by inconsistency as well as by an express revocatory clause. The first will disposes of the entire estate to A; the subsequent will contains no revocatory clause and disposes of the entire estate to B. The first will is deemed to be revoked because of the inconsistency. Suppose, however, that the first will bequeathed $10,000 to A, and disposed of the residue to B; the second will contains no revocatory clause, bequeaths $20,000 to C, and disposes of the residue to D. Obviously the residuary gift to B is revoked by inconsistency. Is the $10,000 bequest to A revoked by inconsistency? Probably so, because the second will is wholly dispositive and appears to be a different testamentary plan.[11]

1990 Uniform Probate Code §§ 2–507(b), (c) and (d) deal expressly with the constructional issue of inconsistency:

> (b) If a subsequent will does not expressly revoke a previous will, the execution of the subsequent will wholly revokes the previous will by inconsistency if the testator intended the subsequent will to replace rather than supplement the previous will.

> (c) The testator is presumed to have intended a subsequent will to replace rather than supplement a previous will if the subsequent will makes a complete disposition of the testator's estate. If this presumption arises and is not rebutted by clear and convincing evidence, the previous

---

11. In re Danford's Estate, 196 Cal. 339, 238 P. 76 (1925); Matter of Estate of Wiemer, 209 Cal.App.2d 7, 25 Cal. Rptr. 693 (1962); In re Reycraft's Estate, 260 Mich. 40, 244 N.W. 221 (1932); Neibling v. Methodist Orphans' Home Ass'n, 315 Mo. 578, 286 S.W. 58 (1926); Matter of the Will of Wiltberger, 70 A.D.2d 963, 417 N.Y.S.2d 325 (1979); In re Estate of Crooks, 388 Pa. 125, 130 A.2d 185 (1957).

will is revoked; only the subsequent will is operative on the testator's death.

(d) The testator is presumed to have intended a subsequent will to supplement rather than replace a previous will if the subsequent will does not make a complete disposition of the testator's estate. If this presumption arises and is not rebutted by clear and convincing evidence, the subsequent will revokes the previous will only to the extent the subsequent will is inconsistent with the previous will; each will is fully operative on the testator's death to the extent they are not inconsistent.[12]

SECTION 4. REVOCATION BY OPERATION OF LAW

In most states today revocation by operation of law is statutory. Here revocation is deemed to occur because of changed circumstances without any action by the testator. In almost all states divorce automatically revokes any provision for the divorced spouse in the will, unless the will provides otherwise.[13] In about ten states the will is automatically revoked in its entirety if the testator marries after she has executed the will, unless the will anticipates the subsequent marriage in some fashion.[14] In a few states if a testator marries and has children after the execution of the will, it is deemed revoked in its entirety.[15]

The apparent purpose of revocation as a consequence of changed family circumstances is to avoid the probate of a will which was not modified due to the testator's oversight. As stated above, the statutes usually provide that revocation does not occur if the will indicates that the testator anticipated the changed circumstances.

1990 Uniform Probate Code § 2–804(b) provides that divorce not only revokes the provision in the will for the former spouse, but also for a relative of the former spouse. "Relative" is defined as an individual related to the former spouse by blood, adoption or affinity, and who after the divorce is not related to the testator by blood, adoption or affinity.

Some states have statutes which provide that in the event a testator marries after the execution of the will which makes no

---

12. See In re Salmonski's Estate, 38 Cal.2d 199, 238 P.2d 966 (1951); In re Estate of Delany, 226 Cal.App.2d 473, 38 Cal.Rptr. 83 (1964); Jackman v. Kasper, 393 Ill. 496, 66 N.E.2d 678 (1946).

13. E.g., Cal.Prob.Code § 6122; Fla. Stat.Ann. § 732.507; Iowa Code Ann. § 633.271; Mass.Gen. Laws Ann. ch. 191, § 9; N.Y.Est. Powers & Trusts Law § 5–1.4; Tex.Prob.Code Ann. § 69.

14. E.g., Conn.Gen.Stat.Ann. § 45–162; Ky.Rev.Stat.Ann. § 394.090; R.I.Gen. Laws § 33–5–9.

15. E.g., Kan.Stat.Ann. § 59–610; S.D.Comp. Laws Ann. § 29–3–8.

provision for the spouse, the spouse is entitled to take his or her intestate share of the estate unless the will indicates that the absence of any provision was intentional.[16] Note that the will is not revoked; rather, the will remains effective but the spouse takes his or her intestate share of the estate. This type of statute is different from the surviving spouse's forced share statute which is discussed in Chapter 8, Section 2.

SECTION 5. DEPENDENT RELATIVE REVOCATION

Testator validly executes a will. Some months later the testator executes another instrument which she thinks is a will but it isn't because the formalities of execution are not complied with. At the same time the testator draws lines through the validly executed will intending to revoke it because she believes she has no more need for it. She is, of course, mistaken, and under the doctrine of dependent relative revocation, the revocation may be nullified because of the mistake. This doctrine is basically one which permits mistaken revocation to be undone.

Where did the phrase "dependent relative revocation" come from? It comes from the fiction that the revocation in our example was dependent (conditional) upon a related event, namely, the effectiveness of the subsequent instrument. To describe the testator's state of mind in this fashion is unrealistic, but that is the source of the title of the doctrine. The state of mind is invariably mistaken, not conditional. Why this fiction? It may be because of the traditional judicial reluctance to use mistake as a ground for changing testamentary dispositions. For the most part courts continue to give lip service to the idea of the fictitious conditional revocation rather than to describe what happens as mistakenly induced revocation, although unquestionably the courts are aware that mistake is actually involved. In any event, the purpose of the doctrine is to effect the intention of the testator who would presumably want his mistakenly revoked will to be admitted to probate. Most cases decided on the basis of this doctrine involve a revocation of a valid will and the substantially simultaneous attempt at a new will which fails because of noncompliance with the testamentary formalities or because the dispositive provisions are invalid for some reason.

In the case of the revocation of a valid will and the simultaneous execution of an invalidly executed instrument, the new invalid instrument may involve only minor changes from the prior valid will. In such case it obviously makes good sense to undo the

---

16. E.g., Ariz.Rev.Stat.Ann. § 14–2301; Colo.Rev.Stat. § 15–11–301; Minn.Stat.Ann. § 524.2–301; N.J.Stat. Ann. § 3B:5–15; N.M.Stat.Ann. § 45-2–301. See discussion of this type of statute in Chapter 8, Section 2.

mistaken revocation because the testator clearly would have preferred the prior will to no will. Suppose, however, the new invalid instrument contained an entirely different dispositive plan from the validly executed will. Although the testator believed the subsequent invalid instrument was valid when she revoked the valid will, she might well have preferred to die intestate rather than to have her property disposed of in accordance with the validly executed will. In other words, a mistake was made but it was not the primary inducement for the revocation of the valid will. Most courts do not mechanically resurrect the revoked will without examining the circumstances. Instead they hear evidence and consider the circumstances to determine whether the undoing of the revocation and consequent probate of the valid will, or revocation and consequent intestacy, would better effect the intention of the testator.[17]

The doctrine has applicability to the situation of partial revocation by physical act. Assume a validly executed will contains, among other gifts, a legacy of $25,000 to Jones. Testator decides later to increase the legacy to $30,000; she draws a line through "$25,000," and writes above it, "$30,000." Testator dies leaving the will in that condition. The partial revocation, without regard to the question of mistake, is valid, but the substituted figure can have no testamentary effect because it was not a properly executed codicil. It was merely the writing of "$30,000" which has no testamentary validity. The revocation was made on the basis of the mistaken assumption that the substituted figure would be valid. The partial revocation should be nullified on the basis of the testator's intent because she clearly would have preferred a $25,000 legacy to no legacy. Suppose, however, the amount written above the stricken amount was $5,000. In this circumstance the revocation probably should stand because the very substantial intended reduction indicates that the testator would have preferred no legacy to a legacy of $25,000.[18]

We have been discussing the doctrine of dependent relative revocation as it applies to mistaken revocation by physical act. Parol evidence of the testator's intent is admissible to show the mistaken state of mind and the consequent invalidity of the revocation. The doctrine runs into trouble, however, when applied to

---

17. In re Estate of Jones, 352 So.2d 1182 (Fla.Dist.Ct.App.1977); Carter v. First United Methodist Church, 246 Ga. 352, 271 S.E.2d 493 (1980); In re Heazle's Estate, 72 Idaho 307, 240 P.2d 821 (1952); Matter of Estate of McKay, 347 Mich. 153, 79 N.W.2d 597 (1956); Watson v. Landvatter, 517 S.W.2d 117 (Mo. 1974); Matter of Estate of Patten, 179 Mont. 299, 587 P.2d 1307 (1978).

18. Schneider v. Harrington, 320 Mass. 723, 71 N.E.2d 242 (1947); Woodson v. Woodson, 363 Mo. 978, 255 S.W.2d 771 (1953); Ruel v. Hardy, 90 N.H. 240, 6 A.2d 753 (1939); Matter of Will of Shuler, 45 N.J.Super. 209, 132 A.2d 33 (1957).

revocation by subsequent instrument. It should be recalled that a will cannot be challenged for mistake in the inducement to its execution, although there is dictum in some cases that a will can be challenged for mistake in the inducement if the mistake appears in the will and what the disposition would have been in the absence of the mistake also appears in the will. Does the same rule apply to a mistakenly induced revocatory clause in a subsequent testamentary instrument which is validly executed? This issue can best be considered by the use of illustrations.

Testator, unmarried and childless, has a will in which she leaves her entire estate to her Brother. Testator has not seen Brother for a number of years. She is later mistakenly informed that Brother has died. Testator then executes a new will in which she expressly revokes all prior wills and leaves her entire estate to her Friend. Testator then dies without having learned of her mistake. Brother survives the testator and challenges the later will on the ground of mistake. Clearly the later will is admissible to probate. The mistake in the inducement does not appear in the will, and consequently its dispositive provision is valid. That the revocatory clause also is the product of mistake is irrelevant because there is no basis for challenging the dispositive clause.

Suppose the testator executes a will in which she leaves her entire estate to her Friend, and names First Bank as executor. Subsequently the testator executes another will in which she expressly revokes all prior wills, leaves her entire estate to the same Friend, and designates Second Bank as executor. One of the two witnesses to the second will is Friend, which invalidates the gift to Friend. Testator then dies. A mistake of law invalidates the dispositive clause of the second will, and the revocatory clause of the second will was induced by the mistake of law. Can the revocatory clause be undone? Do the mistake and what the disposition would have been in the absence of mistake, appear in the second will? It seems so. But without bothering to use that rationale, it has simply been held by some courts that a mistaken revocation in a subsequent will can be undone where the dispositive provisions are invalid, thereby making the first will admissible to probate.[19]

Suppose the testator executes a will leaving her entire estate to her sister. Testator later executes another will in which she expressly revokes the first will, and leaves her entire estate in trust in perpetuity for a noncharitable purpose; the trust is void in toto. Assume that it can be established that the testator would have preferred the first will to intestacy. The revocatory clause was

19. La Croix v. Senecal, 140 Conn. 311, 99 A.2d 115 (1953); In re Estate of Jones, 352 So.2d 1182 (Fla.Dist.Ct.App. 1977). See Blackford v. Anderson, 226 Iowa 1138, 286 N.W. 735 (1939).

induced by the mistake of law. Can the revocation be undone? Was the mistake apparent on the face of the will? It was. Was it apparent on the face of the will what the disposition would have been in the absence of mistake? It was not. Without discussing these factors, some courts have simply held that the mistaken revocation can be undone if the dispositive provisions are invalid.[20]

There is also authority in situations similar to the ones discussed above, that the doctrine of dependent relative revocation is not applicable to the mistakenly induced revocatory clause executed in accordance with testamentary formalities. Such courts are not inclined to examine the mistaken inducement where revocation is involved any more than they would examine mistaken inducement where dispositive provisions are involved.[21]

SECTION 6. REVIVAL OF REVOKED WILL BY REVOCATION OF REVOKING WILL

Testator executes Will # 1. Later testator executes Will # 2 which expressly revokes Will # 1 and disposes of his property. Next, testator revokes Will # 2 by destruction; Will # 1 remains physically intact and is not revoked by physical act. Testator dies. Is Will # 1 admissible to probate? In most states this issue is resolved by statute.

Some statutes provide that Will # 1 was revoked for good when Will # 2 was executed and cannot come back to life when Will # 2 is revoked.[22] Other statutes provide that Will # 1 is "revived" when Will # 2 is revoked if that is the testator's intention at the time.[23] This is the position of Uniform Probate Code § 2–509.

1990 Code § 2–509 modifies the pre–1990 Code where Will # 2 only partially revokes Will # 1. In such case, the revocation of Will # 2 by physical act is deemed to revive the revoked portion of Will # 1 unless it is shown that the testator did not intend the revoked portion of Will # 1 to be effective. Pre–1990 Code § 2–509 made no distinction between the situation of total revocation and partial revocation of Will # 1.

20. In re Kaufman's Estate, 25 Cal.2d 854, 155 P.2d 831 (1945); Linkins v. Protestant Episcopal Cathedral Foundation, 87 U.S.App.D.C. 351, 187 F.2d 357 (1950); In re Estate of Jones, 352 So.2d 1182 (Fla.Dist.Ct.App. 1977); Charleston Library Society v. Citizens & Southern Nat. Bank, 200 S.C. 96, 20 S.E.2d 623 (1942).

21. In re Estate of Barker, 448 So.2d 28 (Fla.Dist.Ct.App.1984); Matter of Estate of Fairley, 159 N.W.2d 286 (Iowa 1968); Crosby v. Alton Ochsner Medical Foundation, 276 So.2d 661 (Miss.1973); Ely v. Megie, 219 N.Y. 112, 113 N.E. 800 (1916); Newman v. Newman, 28 Ohio Op.2d 154, 199 N.E.2d 904 (1964).

22. E.g., Ark.Stat.Ann. § 60–408; Md.Est. & Trusts Code Ann. § 4–106; N.C.Gen.Stat. § 31–5.8; Va.Code § 64.1–60.

23. E.g., Cal.Prob.Code § 6123; Ind. Code Ann. § 29–1–5–6; Mo.Ann.Stat. § 474.410; Ohio Rev.Code Ann. § 2107.-38.

It should be emphasized in connection with the above analysis that Will # 1 remains physically intact and has not been revoked by physical act. If Will # 1 was also revoked by physical act when Will # 2 was executed, Will # 1 is revoked for good everywhere. Those jurisdictions which revive Will # 1 when Will # 2 is revoked by destruction do so only because the revocatory effect of Will # 2 is problematical when it is revoked; if Will # 1 has been revoked by physical act, that is definitive. In most cases, when Will # 2 is executed, Will # 1 is simultaneously destroyed, so the issue presented by this section does not arise frequently.

Assume Will # 1 is revoked by Will # 2. Will # 2 is later revoked by Will # 3 which entirely disposes of the testator's estate. Will # 1 has not been revoked by physical act. Assume a jurisdiction in which Will # 1 is revived when Will # 2 is revoked if that is the testator's intention. Uniform Probate Code § 2–509 and the statutes of a number of states provide that in this circumstance Will # 1 is revoked for good because of the implicit intention in Will # 3 to that effect.[24]

There is a situation which combines this doctrine with dependent relative revocation. Testator has Will # 1, and later executes Will # 2 which revokes Will # 1 but Will # 1 is not also revoked by physical act. Testator later revokes Will # 2 by destruction, and at the time expresses her understanding that Will # 1 is now her valid will. Testator then dies with Will # 1. The jurisdiction has a statute that provides that Will # 1 is revoked for good by the execution of Will # 2. At the time the testator revoked Will # 2 she was mistaken as to its effect with respect to Will # 1. In this circumstance the doctrine of dependent relative revocation has been applied to undo the revocation of Will # 2 and admit it to probate.[25]

The subject of republication by codicil is discussed below, but it should be mentioned briefly here. Assume that Will # 1 has been revoked by Will # 2, Will # 2 has been revoked by destruction, Will # 1 cannot be revived by the revocation of Will # 2 in this jurisdiction, and Will # 1 remains in existence. Testator then validly executes what purports to be a codicil to Will # 1. Testator's will is now deemed to consist of Will # 1 and the codicil. The execution of the codicil is said to republish Will # 1. The codicil brings back to life the will which had been revoked.

24. E.g., Colo.Rev.Stat. § 15–11–509; Me.Rev.Stat.Ann. tit. 18–A, § 2–509; Mont.Code Ann. § 72–2–323; N.D.Cent. Code § 30.1–08–09; Utah Code Ann. § 75–2–509.

25. In re Estate of Alburn, 18 Wis.2d 340, 118 N.W.2d 919 (1963).

Chapter 5

FUNDAMENTALS OF THE TRUST

SECTION 1. INTRODUCTION

The trust is one of the most useful concepts in property law. In essence, it separates the responsibility of ownership of specific property from the benefit of ownership. The person who has the responsibility of ownership is called the trustee and holds the legal title to the specific property; the person who has the benefit of ownership is called the beneficiary and holds the equitable title. The specific property which is the subject of this divided ownership is called the trust res or the trust property. The trustee is a fiduciary who holds the legal title to the trust property exclusively for the benefit of the beneficiary. The power of management of the trust property is vested in the trustee free of any control by the beneficiary as long as the trustee is not in violation of his fiduciary obligation. The trustee derives no benefit from his legal title except whatever compensation he may receive for performing the trustee function.

The most common use of the trust is with respect to the donative disposition of wealth. An individual who has accumulated substantial wealth may wish to assure, after his death, the financial security of his wife and his children and possibly other relatives. He may not be confident, however, that they will be capable of properly managing substantial wealth in the form of land, corporate stocks, and corporate and government bonds. The management of investments requires special training and experience. One way of assuring proper management is to have the assets placed in trust with a professional trustee, usually a bank, for the benefit of his surviving relatives.

In addition to sound management, the individual who has accumulated substantial wealth may wish to assure that the wealth will be preserved to benefit more than one individual, or more than one class of individuals, successively. That is to say, he may wish to assure the financial security of his wife after his death, and then upon her death, to assure the financial security of his children, and upon their deaths, to have the wealth benefit his grandchildren. If the owner of property leaves his assets outright in fee to his wife, she may invest prudently and spend sparingly, and at her death,

73

she may leave the assets outright in fee to the children who may also invest prudently and spend sparingly, and at their deaths, they may leave the assets outright in fee to the grandchildren. On the other hand, the assets may be dissipated by the wife or the children. By the use of the trust, the objective of protecting the wife, children and grandchildren successively can be assured.

To appreciate how this objective is achieved by means of the trust, it is necessary to understand the meaning of principal and income. Wealth may be invested in land, in corporate stocks, in corporate and government bonds, and in bank certificates of deposit, among other things. The investment in land produces a return in the form of rent, in stocks a return in the form of dividends, and in bonds and bank deposits a return in the form of interest. Invested wealth is called principal; the money which the principal earns, whether in the form of rent, dividends, or interest, is called income. The rate of return on investment varies with the economy. In a stable economy, a 5% annual rate of return has been typical; principal of $400,000 would yield an annual income of $20,000. Year after year this income is produced and the $400,000 principal remains intact. The assets that are initially placed in trust constitute the principal of the trust, and what is earned by those assets constitutes the trust income. The principal of a trust is sometimes referred to as the corpus of a trust.

The person who has accumulated substantial wealth, such as $400,000, and wishes to provide a degree of financial security successively for his wife, his two children and his grandchildren, may bequeath his assets to a bank as trustee with directions that the trustee pay the income to his wife during her life, and after her death pay the income one-half to one child and one-half to the other, and upon the death of each child, to pay one-half the principal to the children of the deceased child. Note that the principal is retained by the trustee until the death of the children. By the use of the trust the original owner of the wealth obtains the skilled investment management of the bank and the assurance of a financial cushion for his wife, children and grandchildren. Of course, if the assets are left outright in fee to the wife, she may invest prudently, live off the income, and leave the principal to her children in fee; the children then may invest prudently, spend only the income, and at their deaths leave the principal to their children. On the other hand, the principal may be consumed by the wife or the children, or otherwise diverted from the family line. By means of the trust, these possibilities of consumption or diversion are avoided.

The trust is employed primarily in connection with the donative disposition of wealth. It is, however, used in various other contexts where it is necessary or desirable to vest control and responsibility of property in one party as a fiduciary for the benefit of others. Banks frequently hold corporate mortgages in trust for the benefit of the bondholders of the corporation. Assets accumulated for pension purposes are usually held in trust. The "business trust" is sometimes used instead of a corporation as a means of conducting a business enterprise with limited liability for the investor "beneficiary." In the case of insolvency, the trust device may be employed to protect assets of a debtor for the benefit of creditors. There are also situations which call for the vesting of title in one as fiduciary for another which are not referred to as trusts; for example, the executor or administrator of a decedent's estate manages the property as fiduciary for the creditors, legatees, and heirs of the decedent.

This book deals in part with the law concerning the trust as it is employed in connection with the donative disposition of wealth to achieve the preservation of value over an extended period of time for the benefit of individuals, usually relatives. This kind of trust is called a private trust. Chapter 12 of this book deals with the donative trust for purely charitable purposes, which is called a charitable trust. The resulting trust, which is discussed in Chapter 15, arises by implication of law in certain circumstances, and the constructive trust, which is discussed in Chapter 15 and in Section 7 of Chapter 3, is not really a trust at all, but rather a restitutional remedy.

SECTION 2.   CREATION OF THE LIVING TRUST

The basic characteristics of a trust are (i) the division of legal and equitable title, and (ii) the fiduciary responsibility of the holder of the legal title to the holder of the equitable title. The person owning absolute title to property creates the trust by a special type of transfer which separates the equitable title from the legal title and imposes fiduciary responsibility upon the legal title holder. The trust, then, is the product of a property transfer, and we shall now examine the rules which govern the creation of this unique property relationship.

A trust may be created by a property owner during his life or at his death by means of his will. The trust which is created by a person during his life is called an inter vivos trust, or a living trust. A trust which is created under the will of a decedent is called a testamentary trust. Here the creation of the living trust is discussed.

The living trust may be created by a declaration of trust or a transfer in trust. The person who creates a living trust is called a settlor or trustor. The settlor makes a declaration of trust by declaring himself trustee of specific property to pay the income to A for A's life, and upon A's death, to pay the principal of the trust to B. The settlor has retained the legal title, imposed fiduciary duties upon himself, and conveyed the equitable title to A and B. The settlor makes a transfer in trust by transferring legal title to T, in trust, to pay the income to A for A's life, and upon A's death, to pay the principal of the trust to B. The settlor has conveyed legal title subject to fiduciary duties to one person and equitable title to others.[1]

The formal requirements for the creation of the living trust vary depending upon whether the trust property is realty or personalty, and whether it is a declaration of trust or a transfer in trust. In the case of the declaration of trust, the only property interest conveyed is the equitable interest. If the declaration of trust involves only personal property, in most states the equitable interest can be created by the mere oral expression of the present intention to create the interest, and there is no need for any memorandum or other writing evidencing the creation of the trust.[2]

In the case of the transfer in trust, there is a conveyance of the legal title and a conveyance of the equitable title. If the transfer in trust involves only personal property, what are the requisite formalities? It is not possible to make a donative transfer of legal title to personalty by the mere oral expression of an intention to do so. In addition to the intention to transfer the legal title, there must be either physical delivery of the property itself, or some form of constructive delivery such as the execution and delivery of a writing of the donor stating that a gift is being made,[3] or in the case of certain intangible personalty such as stocks, bonds, and bank accounts, the registration of the property in the name of the donee (in this case, the trustee).[4] As stated in the preceding paragraph,

---

1. It is generally accepted today that title to trust property is divided as described. Some scholars have maintained, however, that the beneficiary does not have a property interest, an "in rem" interest, in the assets held in trust, but rather only a claim against the trustee. For a discussion, see 2 Scott, Law of Trusts § 130 (4th ed. Fratcher, 1987).

The example we have used is repeated at various times in this book. It should be noted that B has a vested remainder; B (or his estate) takes regardless of whether or not B survives A. The general rule is that there is no implied condition that a holder of a future interest must survive to the time his interest becomes possessory.

2. Estate of Pearce, 481 So.2d 69 (Fla.Dist.Ct.App. 1985); Estate of Trbo-

vich v. Pavlovich, 488 Pa. 583, 413 A.2d 379 (1980). See 1 Scott, Law of Trusts §§ 28, 52 (4th ed., Fratcher, 1987); Restatement (Second) of Trusts § 52 (1959).

3. Lawson v. Lowengart, 251 Cal. App.2d 98, 59 Cal.Rptr. 186 (1967); Gardella v. Santini, 65 Nev. 215, 193 P.2d 702 (1948); Whitehead v. Bishop, 23 Ohio App. 315, 155 N.E. 565 (1925); Burbridge v. First National Bank and Trust Co., 415 P.2d 591 (Okl.1965).

4. Wilmington Trust Co. v. General Motors Corp., 29 Del.Ch. 572, 51 A.2d 584 (1947); Chicago Title & Trust Co. v. Ward, 332 Ill. 126, 163 N.E. 319 (1928); In re Estate of Paulson, 219 N.W.2d 132 (N.D.1974); Simonton v. Dwyer, 167 Or. 50, 115 P.2d 316 (1941).

the creation of the equitable interest can be accomplished by the mere oral expression of the settlor to that effect, and that is as true with respect to the transfer in trust as it is with respect to the declaration of trust. In the vast majority of situations, of course, the trust of personalty is created by the execution of a formal written instrument by the settlor and the trustee (or the settlor alone if it is a declaration of trust) which sets forth the terms of the trust and the transfer of the trust property.

If in the case of the transfer in trust of personal property, the conveyance of the legal title is by means of a writing which makes no reference to the fact that a trust is intended, and the purported creation of the equitable interest is wholly oral, a problem involving the parol evidence rule is presented. Is evidence of the creation of the trust by oral statements admissible in view of the writing which states that legal title is transferred but makes no reference to its being subject to an equitable interest? There is authority that the oral evidence is admissible to establish the existence of a trust unless the instrument transferring legal title explicitly states that the transferee is to hold the property for his own benefit. In other words, if the instrument contains merely a statement of the transfer of title, parol evidence is admissible to establish that a trust was intended. Under this view it is virtually necessary that the instrument negate the existence of a trust in order for parol evidence of a trust to be inadmissible.[5]

The rules with respect to the formalities for the creation of a trust of land are different from those applicable to the creation of a trust of personalty. First of all, the transfer of legal title to land, which, of course, is an element of the transfer in trust, can only be accomplished by the execution of an instrument by the transferor which states that the title is thereby being transferred. It appears that there probably no longer is any requirement that the instrument, usually called a deed, be delivered to the transferee or someone on his behalf; the piece of paper and the requisite intent to convey title usually suffice.[6] In the declaration of trust of land, legal title, of course, does not move.

In most states it is required that the creation of an equitable interest in real property be in writing or be evidenced by a writing,

---

5. 1 Scott, Law of Trusts § 38 (4th ed., Fratcher, 1987); Restatement (Second) Trusts § 38 (1959); Carrillo v. Taylor, 81 Ariz. 14, 299 P.2d 188 (1956). There are cases involving oral trusts of real property superimposed on deeds conveying the legal fee, in which apparently there was no applicable statute of frauds requiring a writing for trusts of land, and the parol evidence rule was held not to bar proof of the oral trust.

See Levin v. Smith, 513 A.2d 1292 (Del. 1986); Brantley v. Brantley, 198 Tenn. 670, 281 S.W.2d 668 (1955); Peterson v. Peterson, 105 Utah 133, 141 P.2d 882 (1943).

6. Ferrell v. Stinson, 233 Iowa 1331, 11 N.W.2d 701 (1943); McMahon v. Dorsey, 353 Mich. 623, 91 N.W.2d 893 (1958).

but the statutes on this point vary. Some states have statutes which specifically provide that an equitable interest in land must be created by a writing of the settlor or trustee, just as a conveyance of a legal interest in land can only be effected by a written instrument.[7] Some states have no statute which specifically requires that an equitable interest in land be created in writing, but the statute which requires conveyances of interests in land to be in writing has been construed to be applicable to the creation of the equitable interest in land.[8] Other states require that a trust of land be "proved" by a writing of the settlor or trustee; that is to say, the writing is not the operative act of transfer but is necessary from an evidentiary standpoint.[9] It should be noted that there is a conceptual difference between the writing as the act of transfer and the writing as necessary evidence of the transfer otherwise effected by the expression of intention, but this difference among the statutes does not appear to have been of any substantial significance in the development of the law in this area.

The writing must adequately describe the trust property and the beneficiaries and their interests. There is no requirement that the writing be delivered to the beneficiary. In the vast majority of situations, of course, the trust is created by the execution of a formal written instrument by the settlor and the trustee (or the settlor alone if it is a declaration of trust) which sets forth the terms of the trust and the transfer of the trust property. The living trust of land is seldom created casually and informally, but when it is there is the possibility of formal inadequacy. For example, the settlor may execute a deed to land which purports to convey the fee to Jones absolutely, but the settlor has an understanding with Jones that he is to hold in trust for Smith. If there is no writing with respect to the trust, then the express trust is unenforceable.[10] If, however, the settlor signs the appropriate writing prior to or contemporaneous with the transfer of the legal title, the trust is enforceable, but the writing does not satisfy the statute if the settlor signs it after the transfer of legal title.[11] If Jones, the intended trustee, alone signs the appropriate writing

7. E.g., Cal.Prob.Code § 15206; Me. Rev.Stat.Ann. tit. 33, § 851; Mass.Gen. Laws Ann. ch. 203, § 1; N.D.Cent.Code 59–03–03.

8. E.g., Iowa Code Ann. § 622.32; McMains v. Tullis, 213 Iowa 1360, 241 N.W. 472 (1932).

9. E.g., Fla.Stat.Ann. § 689.05; Mo. Ann.Stat. § 456.010; N.J.Stat.Ann. 25:1–3; Pa.Stat.Ann. tit. 33, § 2.

10. Jones may not be permitted to keep the land, however. It is possible

that a constructive trust will be imposed upon the land held by Jones. See discussion in Chapter 15, Section 3.

11. Reagh v. Kelley, 10 Cal.App.3d 1082, 89 Cal.Rptr. 425 (1970); Phillips v. South Park Commissioners, 119 Ill. 626, 10 N.E. 230 (1887); Brackenbury v. Hodgkin, 116 Me. 399, 102 A. 106 (1917); Trustees of Presbytery of Willamette v. Hammer, 235 Or. 564, 385 P.2d 1013 (1963).

prior to, contemporaneous with, or even subsequent to the transfer of legal title, it has been held that the statute is satisfied and the trust is enforceable.[12]   In this latter circumstance, Jones in a sense can be considered the "settlor" because without his writing (or that of the true settlor), there would be no enforceable express trust.

What is the result if the settlor purports to create a trust consisting in part of personalty and in part of realty, and complies with the formal requirements for a trust of personalty but does not comply with the formal requirements for a trust of realty?   It seems that the trust is valid as far as the personalty is concerned. However, if it appears that the settlor would not have created the trust had he known that the realty portion would be ineffective, it is very possible that a court of equity would permit the rescission of the trust of personalty on the ground that the trust was created under a mistake of law.[13]

A word should be said about the capacity of a settlor to create a trust.   The general principle is that a settlor has the capacity to make a declaration of trust of property or a transfer in trust of property if he has the capacity to make a transfer of the same property without regard to a trust.[14]   Mental deficiency, mental derangement, and being a minor are factors which can render a person incapable of creating a living trust.

The living trust is irrevocable unless the settlor makes it revocable by the inclusion of a clause to that effect in the trust instrument.   The revocable trust is in all respects a valid property transfer but it can be terminated and the property taken back at any time by the settlor.   Title passes, subject to recall.   If the settlor never revokes, the trust continues in accordance with its terms after his death.   This power to make a donative transfer of title which is revocable is a quality peculiar to the trust.   If a property owner purports to make a nontrust gift of personalty but reserves the power to revoke, the transferee does not receive title. If a property owner purports to make a nontrust gift of land but reserves the power to revoke, the transferee probably does not receive title, although there is authority that title passes as in the

12. Wiggs v. Winn, 127 Ala. 621, 29 So. 96 (1900); Cashion v. Bank of Arizona, 30 Ariz. 172, 245 P. 360 (1926); Vogt v. Miller, 285 N.W.2d 1 (Iowa 1979); McCaffrey v. Laursen, 215 Mont. 305, 697 P.2d 103 (1985).

13. The courts have allowed rescission or reformation of trusts where a mistake has been made with respect to the purposes for which the trust was created.   For example, there is consider-able authority permitting rescission or reformation where the tax consequences of a trust are not what they were thought to be. 4 Scott, Law of Trusts § 333.4 (4th ed., Fratcher, 1989).

14. Rose v. Dunn, 284 Ark. 42, 679 S.W.2d 180 (1984); In re Estate of Granberry, 30 Colo.App. 590, 498 P.2d 960 (1972); In re Swartwood's Estate, 198 Wash. 557, 89 P.2d 203 (1939); Ind. Code Ann. § 30–4–2–10.

case of the revocable trust.[15] The revocable trust is discussed further in Section 7 of this chapter and in Chapter 7, Section 5.

SECTION 3.   CREATION OF THE TESTAMENTARY TRUST

The testamentary trust is one created under a validly executed will of a testator. It is a property transfer that takes effect at death by virtue of judicial action admitting the will to probate. This contrasts with the living trust which is a property transfer without judicial participation. For obvious reasons there is no testamentary counterpart to the living declaration of trust; every testamentary trust is analogous to the living transfer in trust. The testator may bequeath or devise her property absolutely to a legatee or devisee, or she may bequeath or devise legal title to one party as trustee, and equitable title to others as beneficiaries. Obviously the formal requirements for the creation of the testamentary trust are the formal requirements for the execution of a will, and the required capacity to create a testamentary trust is the same as the capacity required for the execution of a will. The trustee and beneficiaries of the testamentary trust are legatees and devisees under the will, and the assets which are bequeathed and devised in trust are first subject to estate administration in the same fashion as assets which are bequeathed or devised absolutely. If the testator's estate is insolvent, the trust never comes into existence.

The trust may be of specific property: "I bequeath my 5,000 shares of IBM common stock to Bank, in trust ..." The trust may consist of assets to be obtained from the estate generally: "I bequeath $200,000 to Bank, in trust ..." The trust may consist of assets not otherwise disposed of: "I bequeath and devise all the rest and residue of my estate, real and personal, to Bank, in trust ..." The classification of testamentary gifts (specific, general, residuary) is discussed in Chapter 6, Section 1.

SECTION 4.   TRUSTEE

The living trust comes into being without any judicial action. It is the product of a private transfer of property. The trustee performs his function by virtue of his legal title and fiduciary responsibility, both of which he has voluntarily assumed. The court having general equity jurisdiction usually has jurisdiction with respect to the relationship between the trustee and the beneficiaries of the living trust. The testamentary trust, on the other

---

15. See Garvey, Revocable Gifts of Legal Interests In Land, 54 Ky.L.J. 19 (1965).

hand, comes into being as a result of judicial action; the trustee and beneficiary are a category of legatee or devisee under the will which derives its legal effect from a judgment of the probate court. In addition, the testamentary trustee designated in the will in many states is required to file an oath that he will perform his duties and sometimes a bond with the probate court, and be approved by the court before he can perform the fiduciary function. If the probate court does not consider the designated individual fit to be a trustee, the trust does not fail, but rather the court will appoint another to serve as trustee. The probate court usually has continuing jurisdiction over the testamentary trust.

The trustee may be an individual possessing the capacity to manage property, or a bank corporation authorized by its charter and state or federal law to act as trustee.

A person cannot have legal title forced upon him, nor can he have a trusteeship forced upon him.[16] If the settlor tenders legal title and fiduciary responsibility to the prospective trustee of a living trust, and he declines to accept, no trust arises; the settlor is going to have to try again with somebody else. On the other hand, if the person designated in a will to be trustee declines to accept at the testator's death, the probate court will not permit the trust to fail, and will appoint another to serve as trustee. This, of course, makes good sense; the testator is dead and cannot correct the situation, whereas the settlor of the living trust can make the necessary adjustment himself.

Once the trusteeship is accepted, the trustee, whether testamentary or inter vivos, is usually not free to resign, that is, divest himself of his title and fiduciary obligation, at his pleasure. In most circumstances he cannot resign except with permission of the court. The court granting permission will, of course, see to it that there is someone to serve as trustee following the resignation.[17]

If two parties are co-trustees, they are considered to hold title as joint tenants.[18] Consequently, if one of them dies, the survivor

16. An intended inter vivos donee does not have to accept a gift. A legatee or devisee under a will can renounce the legacy or devise, and an intestate taker can renounce also.

17. In the case of a living trust, if the trust instrument authorizes the trustee to resign at his pleasure, he may do so without court authorization if there is someone who remains or succeeds as trustee under the terms of the trust. It seems that it would not be permissible so to resign if there was no such person to continue the trusteeship.

If all the beneficiaries agree to permit the trustee to resign he may do so. This follows from the fact that if all the beneficiaries and the trustee agree, they may terminate the trust or modify it as they see fit. This is discussed in Chapter 11, Section 1.

18. Bank of Delaware v. Bancroft, 269 A.2d 254 (Del.Ch.1970); Abbale v. Lopez, 511 So.2d 340 (Fla.Dist.Ct.App. 1987); Reichert v. Missouri & Illinois Coal Co., 231 Ill. 238, 83 N.E. 166 (1907); In re Will of Labold, 148 Ohio St. 332, 74 N.E.2d 251 (1947). There

succeeds to the share of the title previously held by the deceased trustee. The survivor will act as sole trustee until another replaces the deceased trustee if a replacement is appropriate. If the two trustees are a bank and a person, they hold as joint tenants even though only one of them can die. If a sole trustee dies, at common law his legal title is considered to pass to his heirs, devisees, administrator or executor, depending upon the circumstances, subject, of course, to the equitable interests, but the fiduciary function does not pass to such holder of legal title. The court will appoint a successor trustee who will succeed to the title and the fiduciary responsibility. The temporary holding of legal title by the nontrustee is merely a conceptual technicality. In many states this has been changed by statutes which provide that upon the death of a sole trustee legal title is vested in the court or is suspended until a successor trustee is appointed.[19]

The trust instrument, living or testamentary, frequently provides for a successor trustee, should the trustee die or be permitted to resign. In the case of the living trust, the successor, if he accepts, would assume the trusteeship without court action; in the case of the testamentary trust, usually the successor would have to be approved by the probate court.

It is common to have two or more parties as co-trustees. Frequently one of the trustees will be a bank and the other will be a family member or a friend or financial advisor. The bank offers continuity (it doesn't die), solvency, administrative capacity, and investment skill, but it is sometimes an impersonal institution; the individual offers the personal relationship to the settlor or the beneficiaries, and keeps an eye on the impersonal institution. If a co-trustee should die or be permitted to resign, and the trust instrument does not designate a successor, then it is a constructional question for the court whether the settlor intended that there should be a replacement or that the surviving trustee should act as sole trustee.

It should be emphasized that the trustee performs his management function independent of any control by the beneficiaries as long as the trustee does not commit any breach of his fiduciary duty. The trustee manages; the beneficiary benefits. The trustee is a fiduciary; this requires that he manage in the interest exclusively of the beneficiaries and with due care. If the trustee should violate his fiduciary duty in any respect, he may be liable, enjoined

may, of course, be more than two co-trustees who hold as joint tenants.

19. E.g., Kan.Stat.Ann. 58–2410; Minn.Stat.Ann. § 501B.08; N.Y.Est. Powers & Trusts Law § 7–2.3; Utah Code Ann. 22–2–1.

When a court appoints a trustee following the death, resignation or removal of a prior trustee, title is usually deemed to be vested in the new trustee without any conveyance from the prior trustee or his estate.

or removed in an action brought by the beneficiary, and in that respect the beneficiary controls the trustee.[20]

The trustee is entitled to compensation, which often is determined by agreement between the settlor and the trustee, and if not, it is determined by statute or by the court.

SECTION 5. BENEFICIARIES

A trust, living or testamentary, may be created without the knowledge of the beneficiary. Whether the beneficiary's interest is created by the settlor's oral expression, as may be the case in the living trust of personalty, or is evidenced by a writing of the settlor or the trustee, or is created by will, there is no requirement that the existence of the trust be communicated to the beneficiary or that the instrument be delivered to the beneficiary.[21] A property interest cannot, however, be forced upon one who is unwilling to receive it. If upon being informed of the purported creation of the equitable interest, the beneficiary declines to accept it, it is considered never to have come into being. Acceptance by the donee is a requirement for the donative transfer of property, but acceptance is presumed prior to notification to the donee, subject to disclaimer by the donee.[22]

The disclaimer may leave the trustee with legal title and no beneficiary. Does this mean that the trustee holds both legal and equitable title, and is absolute owner of the property for all purposes? Such a result was never intended by the settlor. In such a situation it is considered that the equitable interest is in the settlor (or his estate). Since the purpose of the trustee's legal title and fiduciary responsibility cannot be fulfilled, the trustee must reconvey his legal title to the settlor. In this situation there is said to be a resulting trust for the settlor. A resulting trust is one for the benefit of the settlor which arises when there is a failure of beneficial interests. It is presumed that the settlor did not intend that the trustee should have any beneficial interest unless it is expressly provided that he is to have such an interest.

20. Trust instruments sometimes provide that the settlor or a particular beneficiary shall direct the trustee with respect to an aspect of trust administration, such as investments, and such provisions are valid. See p. 310 below.

21. Mucha v. Jackson, 119 N.J.Eq. 348, 182 A. 827 (1936); Cassata v. Cassata, 148 A.D.2d 944, 538 N.Y.S.2d 960 (1989); First Federal Savings and Loan Assoc. v. Great Northern Development Corp., 282 Pa.Super. 337, 422 A.2d 1145

(1980); Green v. Green, 559 A.2d 1047 (R.I.1989).

22. Matter of Estate of Ramsey, 229 Kan. 7, 622 P.2d 626 (1981); Citizens Nat. Bank v. Parsons, 167 Md. 631, 175 A. 852 (1934); In re Grote's Estate, 390 Pa. 261, 135 A.2d 383 (1957); Aberg v. First Nat. Bank, 450 S.W.2d 403 (Tex. Civ.App.1970). See Chapter 2, Section 7 for uniform legislation dealing with disclaimers.

The resulting trust is discussed in Chapter 15, but another example may be useful at this point. The settlor transfers property to T, in trust, to pay the income to A for life, and upon A's death, to pay the principal to A's children who survive A. At A's death there are no surviving children. At A's death T holds title on resulting trust for the settlor. The remainder interest has failed, and the trustee is obligated to reconvey to the settlor.

The legal capacity to be a trust beneficiary presents no serious problem. If a person has the capacity to hold legal title, he has the capacity to hold equitable title. A minor and an adult incompetent have the capacity to hold legal title, and therefore can be trust beneficiaries.[23] The minor and the adult incompetent cannot manage property, but the beneficiary does no managing. It may be necessary to have a guardian appointed for the incompetent to receive the income or the principal to which the incompetent becomes entitled, but the equitable interest in the trust, and the legal title to the income and principal distributed, are held by the incompetent.

An unborn person can be a trust beneficiary and therefore an owner of property. In fact, future interests under a trust are frequently held by unborn beneficiaries. For example, the settlor transfers to T, in trust, to pay the income to A for life, and upon A's death, to pay the principal to the children of A; A is childless at the creation of the trust. The potential children of A are considered to have an equitable remainder. Although there may be some theoretical difficulty with the idea of ownership in nonexistent persons, there is no doubt that such ownership is recognized in trust law. The interests of the unborn are enforceable by court appointed guardians ad litem. If, in the example given, A dies without having any children, the unborn children's remainder, which was contingent in nature because no children were in existence, fails and the trustee holds on resulting trust for the settlor.

There is no reason why there cannot be a trust in which all the beneficiaries are unborn at the time it is created. For example, the settlor transfers to T, in trust, to distribute income among the children of A, and twenty-one years after the death of A, to distribute the principal equally among the children of A then living; A has no children at the creation of the trust. A trust of this nature is likely to provide that until the first child is born, the income is to be added to the principal, and that during the minority of a child, the trustee is to have discretion to retain the child's

23. Turner v. Barber, 131 Ga. 444,   Utah 468, 175 P.2d 470 (1946).
62 S.E. 587 (1908); Capps v. Capps, 110

income for his account or to expend it for the support of the child.[24]

There is a rule that the beneficiaries of a private trust, as distinguished from a charitable trust, must be definite. This means that the beneficiaries must be persons who are ascertainable at the creation of the trust, or if not, they must be ascertainable within the period of the rule against perpetuities. Clearly the beneficiaries need not be designated by name; a class designation will suffice if membership in the class can be precisely determined. If the class is such that membership cannot be precisely determined, the interests of the purported beneficiaries fail.

If a testator creates a trust in his will for his "children," the class designation meets the test because its membership can be precisely determined at his death. If the testamentary trust provides for the payment of income to the testator's children for their lives, and upon their deaths, payment of principal to testator's grandchildren, the class designation of grandchildren meets the test because its membership can be determined within the period of the rule against perpetuities. Other typical class designations are "brothers," "sisters," "nieces," "nephews," "employees." Beneficiaries may be designated by descriptions other than class descriptions, such as "wife," "husband," "widow," and the like; since the person is identifiable from the description, he or she is a valid beneficiary.

"Friends" as a class designation has been held to be invalid for indefiniteness; it is extremely difficult to determine membership in the class.[25] "Relatives" of the settlor or another person would also appear to be invalid for indefiniteness, because of the virtually limitless nature of the membership in the class.[26] However, there is considerable authority to the effect that "relatives" is intended to mean intestate takers; if this is the construction, then the class is identifiable.[27] The situation has arisen in which the trustee is directed to make distribution among such "relatives" of the settlor

---

24. The flexible trust for the period of the beneficiary's minority is very practical, because in the absence of such a provision there would have to be a guardianship of the property of the minor which involves judicial action and control, and some expense and considerable inflexibility.

It has been held that a declaration of trust (not a transfer in trust) for beneficiaries none of whom is then living does not create a trust. Morsman v. Commissioner of Internal Revenue, 90 F.2d 18 (8th Cir.1937), cert. denied 302 U.S. 701, 58 S.Ct. 20, 82 L.Ed. 542 (1937).

This result is not sound and is probably anomalous.

25. Clark v. Campbell, 82 N.H. 281, 133 A. 166 (1926); Early v. Arnold, 119 Va. 500, 89 S.E. 900 (1916).

26. Binns v. Vick, 260 Ark. 111, 538 S.W.2d 283 (1976); In re Bernheim's Estate, 82 Mont. 198, 266 P. 378 (1928).

27. Reagh v. Kelley, 10 Cal.App.3d 1082, 89 Cal.Rptr. 425 (1970); Thompson v. Thornton, 197 Mass. 273, 83 N.E. 880 (1908); In re Lawrence's Estate, 104 N.H. 457, 189 A.2d 491 (1963); American Nat. Bank v. Meaders, 161 Tenn. 184, 30 S.W.2d 246 (1930).

or of a third person, as the trustee shall select. On these facts, it has been held that the beneficiary designation does not fail for indefiniteness, that "relatives" is not confined to intestate takers, and that the trustee may select among those who clearly come within the class designation.[28] If the trustee is directed to make distribution among such "friends" of the settlor as the trustee shall select, the provision may be ineffective because of the peculiarly imprecise nature of the group.[29]

SECTION 6. TRUST PROPERTY

The trust is a relationship between the trustee and the beneficiary with respect to specific property. There is no trust unless there is specific property to which this relationship pertains.

For trust purposes, property is defined very broadly to include almost all tangible and intangible forms generally recognized as property in the law: land, chattels, stocks, bonds, bank accounts, cash, patents, copyrights, debts, contract rights, and enforceable claims of all kinds. Certain recognized forms of property, however, may not be trust property because they are not transferable. For instance, under the terms of a contract the rights of one of the parties may not be assignable for any purpose. In such case, the owner of the contract rights cannot transfer these rights in trust or make a declaration of trust of such rights, since the creation of the trust constitutes a transfer. Often the terms of a pension provide that the rights thereunder are not transferable, in which case the pension rights cannot be placed in trust.[30]

The expectancy that one will inherit by intestacy or under a will from a person now living is not property; it is not land, chattel or chose in action, but rather the hope of owning such in the future. Once the person from whom the inheritance is expected has died, the interest an heir or legatee has in the estate prior to distribution of the estate can be trust property, because it is a claim against the estate. Existing property, such as land or stocks, which a person does not now own but which he expects to own in the future, cannot be trust property. Obviously when he becomes owner, it can be trust property. If a person purports to create a trust the property of which consists of an expectancy of an inheritance or property he does not then own, there is no trust.

28. In re Lawrence, 104 N.H. 457, 189 A.2d 491 (1963); Zweig v. Zweig, 275 S.W.2d 201 (Tex.Civ.App.1955).

29. Clark v. Campbell, 82 N.H. 281, 133 A. 166 (1926). It has been maintained that such a provision should be valid as a power of appointment. See Restatement (Second) Trusts § 122

(1959); Restatement (Second) Property, Donative Transfers § 12.1, Comment e (1986).

30. Hatfield v. Buck, 193 Misc. 1041, 85 N.Y.S.2d 613 (Sup.Ct.1948). See Restatement (Second) of Trusts § 79 (1959).

The trust is normally created by donative declaration or transfer in trust, or by will which is donative in nature. If a person gratuitously promises to create a trust of certain property in the future, the promise is unenforceable. But if a person makes a promise to create a trust in the future, which promise is supported by adequate consideration, the promise may be specifically enforceable and the trust comes into being pursuant to such enforcement.

SECTION 7. SETTLOR

The settlor of the living trust is a transferor of property. Unless he retains, expressly or by implication, some interest in the trust, he ceases to have any legal relationship to the trust. This means that in the transfer in trust, if the trustee violates his fiduciary duty, the settlor can do nothing about it, and if the trustee and the beneficiaries change the terms of the trust, the settlor can do nothing about it. The terms of the trust do not constitute a contract among the settlor, the trustee and the beneficiaries which the settlor can enforce. The trust property belongs to the trustee and the beneficiaries, and the settlor has no standing to challenge what they do with their property, unless the settlor retains some interest in the trust.[31] The same is true of the estate of the testator who creates a trust under his will.

There are several ways in which the settlor of the living trust can retain an interest in the trust. First of all, the settlor can make himself a beneficiary under the trust. For example, the settlor transfers to T, in trust, to pay the income to the settlor for life, and upon the settlor's death, to pay the principal to the settlor's issue then living per stirpes. It is quite common for a property owner to make a living trust in which he is a life income beneficiary.

The settlor may be a beneficiary by resulting trust. For example, the settlor transfers to T, in trust, to pay the income to A for life. There is no provision for an equitable interest after the life estate, and therefore upon the death of A, T holds on resulting trust for the settlor, which means that T must reconvey to the settlor. The settlor is a beneficiary by implication. In the case of a

31. Ex parte Ingalls, 266 Ala. 45, 93 So.2d 753 (1957); Edmondson v. Edmondson, 303 Minn. 157, 226 N.W.2d 615 (1975); In re Reynolds Estate, 131 Neb. 557, 268 N.W. 480 (1936); Werbelovsky v. Manufacturers Trust Co., 12 A.D.2d 793, 209 N.Y.S.2d 564 (1961); Barrette v. Dooly, 21 Utah 81, 59 P. 718 (1899). Restatement (Second) of Trusts § 200 (1959), 3 Scott, Law of Trusts § 200.1 (4th ed., Fratcher, 1988), and Bogert, Trusts and Trustees § 42 (2d ed. 1960), also support this view. But see Wilmington Trust Co. v. Carpenter, 39 Del.Ch. 528, 168 A.2d 306 (1961); Carr v. Carr, 185 Iowa 1205, 171 N.W. 785 (1919); Abbott v. Gregory, 39 Mich. 68 (1878).

testamentary trust, the trustee would hold on resulting trust for the estate of the testator.[32]

The settlor may provide in the trust instrument that he retains the power to revoke the trust any time he pleases. This means that he has the right to retake the trust assets for himself and terminate the trust and all interests thereunder. A trust is deemed to be irrevocable unless the power to revoke is expressly reserved by the settlor.[33] Prior to the exercise of the power of revocation, the trust is in all respects valid and the rights and duties thereunder are in most respects the same as in the trust which is irrevocable. The settlor who retains a power of revocation but is not a beneficiary in the technical sense has substantially the rights of a beneficiary, since upon exercise of the power of revocation he can hold the trustee liable for any loss resulting from a breach of trust. It is generally held that if a person purports to make a gift of property free of trust but reserves the right to revoke the gift at his pleasure, title does not pass. The law is different with respect to the trust; legal and equitable title pass despite the right of revocation.

Finally, the settlor may reserve in the trust instrument the power to control the trustee with respect to certain administrative functions without retaining the power to revoke. For instance, the trust instrument may provide that all investments made by the trustee must be approved by the settlor. The trustee is bound by such controls.

SECTION 8. LEGAL AND EQUITABLE TITLE

In the description of the title to property held in trust, it is necessary to describe separately the equitable present and future interests and the legal present and future interests. For example, Testator bequeaths to T, in trust, to pay the income to A for life, and upon A's death, to transfer principal to St. Luke's Hospital; T has the legal fee simple absolute, A has an equitable life estate, and St. Luke's Hospital has an equitable vested remainder in fee. Upon the death of A, the trustee has the legal fee and St. Luke's Hospital has the equitable fee, and it is the duty of the trustee to convey the legal fee to St. Luke's Hospital, thereby giving it the absolute title free of trust.

---

32. Chapter 15 deals with resulting trusts.

33. Mortimer v. Mortimer, 6 Ill. App.3d 217, 285 N.E.2d 542 (1972); Young v. Young-Wishard, 227 Iowa 431, 288 N.W. 420 (1939); Peterson v. Peterson, 10 Kan.App.2d 437, 700 P.2d 585 (1985); Russell v. Russell, 18 Mass.App. Ct. 957, 468 N.E.2d 1104 (1984); Clay-ton v. Behle, 565 P.2d 1132 (Utah 1977). There are statutes in a few states which provide that a trust is revocable unless it is expressly made irrevocable: E.g., Cal.Prob.Code § 15400; Mont.Code Ann. § 72–33–401; Okl.Stat.Ann. tit. 60, § 175.41; Tex.Trusts Code Ann. § 112.051.

Another example: Settlor transfers to T, in trust, to pay the income to A for life, and upon A's death, to transfer the principal to the children of A who survive A; T has the legal fee simple absolute, A has an equitable life estate, the children of A have an equitable contingent remainder in fee, and the settlor has an equitable reversion in fee. The settlor's equitable reversion results from the fact that if there are no children of A alive at A's death, the trustee must reconvey the legal fee to the remaining equitable interest holder, the settlor; the equitable reversionary interest is the future interest owned by the beneficiary of the resulting trust, namely, the settlor.

The interests of the remaindermen in the above examples are fee interests although they were not expressly described as such, because it is presumed that a transferee gets a fee interest unless it appears to have been the settlor's intention that he receive a lesser interest. The same rule is applicable with respect to the trustee's title as far as the trust of personalty is concerned; the trustee of personalty virtually always is considered to have the legal fee interest where it is not expressly so provided.[34] With respect to the trustee's title to real property, the rule is that the trustee holds only such title as is necessary to perform his trustee function if it is not expressly provided that he holds the fee.[35] Nevertheless the trustee of real property usually holds the legal fee because whenever the trustee is directed to convey the principal to the remainderman after a prior life estate, it is intended that he is to convey the legal fee to the remainderman, and most trusts contain such a direction.[36] As a practical matter, in most trusts the trustee holds the legal fee, whether the trust consists of personalty or realty.

SECTION 9.   TRUSTEE AS BENEFICIARY

We have seen that the settlor can be a beneficiary, and that the settlor can also be a trustee. A trustee who is not the settlor can

34. Backer v. Levy, 82 F.2d 270 (2d Cir.1936); Hanson v. Worthington, 12 Md. 418 (1858). See Brown v. Richter, 25 App.Div. 239, 49 N.Y.S. 368 (1898). Restatement (Second) of Trusts § 88 (1959) supports this position.

35. Seymour v. Heubaum, 65 Ill. App.2d 89, 211 N.E.2d 897 (1965); Bourbon Agricultural Bank & Trust Co. v. Miller, 205 Ky. 297, 265 S.W. 790 (1924); Jones v. Endslow, 23 Md.App. 578, 328 A.2d 339 (1974); Fay v. Taft, 66 Mass. 448 (1853).

36. Hubbard v. Buddemeier, 328 Ill. 76, 159 N.E. 229 (1927); City Bank & Trust Co. v. Morrissey, 118 Ill.App.3d 640, 73 Ill.Dec. 946, 454 N.E.2d 1195 (1983); Harrison v. Marcus, 396 Mass. 424, 486 N.E.2d 710 (1985).

Restatement (Second) of Trusts § 88 (1959) also provides that the trustee holds the fee if the trust instrument gives him the power to sell the fee in the land, and most trusts so provide.

A trust may be created in which it is expressly provided that the trustee has a legal life estate for the life of A, A has an equitable life estate, and B has a legal remainder in fee. When A dies, the trust ends automatically and B has the absolute fee.

also be a beneficiary. But if the entire legal title in trust and the entire equitable title are in the same person, the trust ceases to be; the legal and equitable interests merge and that person holds the complete title free of trust. It makes no sense to consider that a trust exists in such a situation; one cannot be a fiduciary for himself. A person would not create a trust in which the sole trustee and the sole beneficiary were the same person, but after the trust is otherwise created, that identity of interests could come about. For example, the testator bequeaths to T, in trust, to pay the income to A for life, and at A's death, to transfer the principal to B. B dies intestate and T is B's sole heir. Subsequently A transfers his life interest to T. T now holds the entire legal interest and the entire equitable interest; these interests merge and T owns free of trust the property which theretofore had been held in trust.

The sole trustee, however, can be one of several beneficiaries,[37] and one of several trustees can be the sole beneficiary.[38] There is also authority that the several trustees can be the same persons as the several beneficiaries;[39] that is to say, the trust remains despite this identity of legal and equitable interests. As an example of the first situation mentioned, testator bequeaths to T, in trust, to pay the income to T for life, and upon T's death, to transfer the principal to A. T cannot be a fiduciary for himself, but he is a fiduciary for A. T must manage the trust property to protect and preserve A's future interest. In this situation, the generally accepted definition of title is legal fee in T, equitable life estate in T, and equitable vested remainder in fee in A. This definition indicates a fiduciary duty owing from T to himself for life, which, of course, cannot be. Nevertheless, there may be legal consequences to the separation of T's equitable life interest from his legal fee.[40]

The sole beneficiary can be one of several trustees. For example, testator bequeaths to A and B, in trust, to pay the income to A until he reaches age 35, and then to transfer the principal to A at age 35, or if A dies before age 35, to transfer the principal to A's

---

37. Black v. Black, 286 Ala. 233, 238 So.2d 861 (1970); Sieling v. Sieling, 151 Md. 536, 135 A. 376 (1926); Estate of Kagan, 118 Misc.2d 1084, 462 N.Y.S.2d 128 (1983); Moody v. Pitts, 708 S.W.2d 930 (Tex.App. 1986); Lamb v. First Huntington Nat. Bank, 122 W.Va. 88, 7 S.E.2d 441 (1940).

38. Tippett v. Tippett, 24 Del.Ch. 115, 7 A.2d 612 (1939); In re Brown's Will, 93 N.Y.S.2d 881 (Sur.Ct.1949).

39. First Alabama Bank of Tuscaloosa v. Webb, 373 So.2d 631 (Ala.1979); Cahill v. Armatys, 185 Neb. 539, 177

N.W.2d 277 (1970); Blades v. Norfolk Southern Railway Co., 224 N.C. 32, 29 S.E.2d 148 (1944); Miller v. Miller, 202 Tenn. 249, 304 S.W.2d 74 (1957); Horlick v. Sidley, 241 Wis. 81, 3 N.W.2d 710 (1942).

40. For example, T's equitable life interest may be protected against creditors by a spendthrift provision. If T is considered to have only a legal interest, such a disabling restraint would be ineffective. See Sections 1 and 2 of Chapter 10.

estate at his death. The title is described as legal fee in A and B as joint tenants, equitable estate for years determinable in A, and equitable vested remainder in A. A cannot be a fiduciary for himself, but B is a fiduciary for A.

There is authority that the several trustees may be the same persons as the several beneficiaries. For example, the settlor transfers to A and B, in trust, to pay one-third of the income to A and two-thirds of the income to B while both are living, and upon the death of the first of them to die, to transfer the principal to the survivor. The title is described as legal fee in A and B as joint tenants, equitable life estates in A and B for their joint lives, and equitable remainder in fee in the survivor of A and B. Once again, A cannot be a fiduciary for himself, and B cannot be a fiduciary for himself, but A can be a fiduciary for B, and vice-versa. This is an unusual situation, but it is theoretically possible.

SECTION 10. PASSIVE TRUST

If an owner transfers property in such a way that legal title and equitable title are in different parties but the holder of legal title has no active duties to perform, by operation of law the holder of equitable title is deemed to hold absolute title and the erstwhile holder of legal title has nothing. O transfers legal title in fee to A, without duties, for the benefit of B, in fee; B has absolute title by operation of law. This circumstance is referred to as a passive, or dry, trust, which ceases to be because there is no reason for it to be. Obviously this does not happen very often. If it happens, the parties have some devious objective such as the concealment of the interest of the holder of equitable title.

Suppose settlor transfers land to T, as trustee, in fee, to pay the income to A for life, and upon A's death, equitable remainder in fee in B, without any reference to T's conveying his legal interest to B. The trust becomes passive at A's death and B will have the absolute fee by operation of law. If, as is usually the case, the trust instrument provides that T is to convey to B at A's death, it has been generally held that the trust is not passive at A's death because of T's duty to convey. The practical significance of this distinction is not great.

Chapter 6

CONTENT AND CONSTRUCTION OF WILLS

In 1990 changes were made in certain sections of the Uniform Probate Code dealing with the content and construction of wills. In this chapter there are references to the pre–1990 Uniform Probate Code (or pre–1990 Code) and to the 1990 Uniform Probate Code (or 1990 Code). There are also references to the Uniform Probate Code in instances in which no substantial change has been made by the 1990 revision. The reader is referred to the introduction to Chapter 2 for further information on the development of the Uniform Probate Code.

SECTION 1. CLASSIFICATION OF BEQUESTS AND DEVISES

The dispositive provisions of a will are applicable to circumstances which cannot be defined with precision at the time the will is executed because the testator does not know what he will own or what his debts will be at his death. The prospective applicability of the will makes for different categories of bequests and devises. By way of contrast, there is only one category of living gift; when one makes a gift right now one hands over specific property to the donee. The will often contains such specific gifts, on the assumption that the specific property owned at the time of execution of the will is going to be owned at death, but other forms or classifications of testamentary gifts are also used. The basic testamentary gift classifications are specific, general and residuary. There is also the demonstrative form which is a mix of specific and general.

First, the specific bequest or devise. This is a gift of an identifiable thing or fund or chose in action or parcel of land. A bequest of "my diamond necklace," "my certificate of deposit dated May 1, 1985 with North Carolina National Bank in the amount of $10,000," are specific bequests. A devise of "my residence and lot at 120 Elm Street, Lakewood, Ohio," "my 310 acres of farm land in Aroostook County, Maine," are specific devises. When a testator makes a specific gift of this kind in his will he obviously anticipates that he will own that property at his death. If he does not own that property at his death, because he has sold it or given it away, or spent it during his life, the specific gift usually fails under the doctrine of ademption discussed in Section 8 of this chapter.

The specific testamentary gift may be different from the ones described in the preceding paragraph; it may be a gift of identifiable property owned at the time of death and not necessarily at the time of the execution of the will. A gift of "the furniture I own at my death," "all corporate stocks I own at my death," or "the residence I own at my death," are specific testamentary gifts. Suppose, however, that it is a bequest of "my furniture," or "my residence," without any indication of whether it is intended as a gift of property of that description owned at the execution of the will or owned at death. How is it to be construed? If the date of execution construction is used, and the property answering that description has been disposed of during the testator's life and replaced with other property of that description, which replacement is owned at death, the gift may fail under the doctrine of ademption discussed below in this chapter. If, however, the date of death construction is used, the gift is effective. Courts are likely to apply a date of death construction in such a situation, and there are some statutes to this effect.[1] This construction has the effect of preserving the benefit to the legatee, because if the property owned at execution is also owned at death, the gift is effective, and if the property has been replaced by other property of that description owned at death, the gift is effective.

Sometimes the specific gift changes its form from the date of execution of the will to the date of death. Suppose there is a specific bequest of ABC Corp. stock owned by the testator at the time of execution of the will, and after execution ABC Corp. is merged into XYZ Corp. As a result of the merger the testator receives one share of XYZ Corp. stock for each share of ABC Corp. he owned, but he does not change his will and dies owning the XYZ Corp. stock. Or suppose the testator makes a bequest of a specific certificate of deposit with First Bank which is owned at execution, and later closes out that deposit and transfers the funds into a certificate of deposit with Second Bank. The testator does not change his will and dies owning the Second Bank certificate. Do the bequests cover the later-acquired property? They probably do, because these are in the nature of changes in form only; this is discussed below under the heading of ademption.

The general bequest is one which is payable out of the assets of the estate generally, and does not require the delivery to the legatee or devisee of any specific item of property of the estate. Almost invariably the general bequest takes the form of a gift of a sum of money, e.g., "I bequeath $10,000 to my niece, Mary." The execu-

1. In re Cooper's Estate, 107 Cal. App.2d 592, 237 P.2d 699 (1951); Milton v. Milton, 193 Miss. 563, 10 So.2d 175 (1942); Waldo v. Hayes, 96 App.Div. 454, 89 N.Y.S. 69 (1904); In re Lusk's Estate, 336 Pa. 465, 9 A.2d 363 (1939); N.C.Gen.Stat. § 31–41; R.I.Gen.Laws § 33–6–6; W.Va.Code § 41–3–1.

tor is obligated to sell estate property, if necessary, to produce the cash to pay the legatee. This general legacy is to be distinguished from the specific bequest of "my certificate of deposit dated May 1, 1985 with First Bank in the amount of $10,000." If the testator closes out that account and buys a car with the money, the specific bequest is a nullity. In the case of the general bequest, the testator is saying that he wants the legatee to receive a certain quantum of value rather than a specific item of property, and it makes no difference what specific assets are owned by the testator at his death.

In rare instances the general bequest is of something other than money. Testator bequeaths "1,000 shares of General Electric common stock to my niece, Mary." Testator never owned any General Electric stock. There is no intention to make a specific bequest. It was her intention that the bequest was to be a general bequest payable in shares of General Electric stock rather than cash. The executor's duty is to produce sufficient cash from estate assets to buy 1,000 shares of General Electric for distribution to the legatee. This is just as much a general bequest as a gift of $25,000; only the form of payment differs.

Let us change the facts of the immediately preceding example by assuming that testator owned 1,000 shares of General Electric stock when she executed the will, but owned no General Electric stock at her death. Note that there was no reference to "my" General Electric stock in the bequest; it was a bequest merely of "1,000 shares of General Electric common stock." Is it a specific bequest, in which case the gift fails, or is it a general bequest, in which case the gift is good? It may be construed as a general bequest; once again this is discussed below under the heading of ademption.

It is theoretically possible for there to be a general testamentary gift of land, in the same fashion as a general bequest of stock, but this is very unusual. For example, the will contains a devise of "100 acres of farm land in Boone County." Testator never owned any such land. The executor's duty is to use estate funds to buy the land and convey it to the devisee.

Why would anyone use a general bequest of stock or land rather than cash? It's unusual to do so, but it may make sense. The will is executed years before death. Inflation erodes the value of the dollar. The bequest of a dollar amount declines in real value, i.e., purchasing power, each year at the rate of inflation. Stock or land may increase in dollar value at the rate of inflation. The general bequest of such property affords an opportunity to pass on a quantum of value which may remain constant or close to it; the monetary bequest does not provide that opportunity. Also, a monetary bequest may be readily squandered by the recipient; the bequest of stock or land may make the recipient investment-conscious.

The residuary testamentary gift is of what remains after debts, administration expenses, and specific and general gifts have been paid, and by its nature the identity and value of the property within it cannot be determined at the time of the execution of the will. The residuary clause reads, "I bequeath and devise all the rest and residue of my property, real and personal, to my son, Bill." Frequently a will contains no specific or general bequest or devise, and has only a residuary provision. A will which has only specific and general gifts and no residuary clause may be inadequate because the assets may exceed what is disposed of under those clauses. The residuary disposition is used because the will applies to circumstances which cannot be known with precision at the time of the execution of the will. Usually, but not necessarily, the residuary legatees and devisees are the primary objects of the testator's largesse, normally close family, and most of the estate passes under the residuary clause.

A word about the rarely used demonstrative legacy, which is a combination of the specific and general bequest. Testator bequeaths "$10,000 to my sister, to be paid from my account at First National Bank, or if the funds are inadequate or the account is closed at my death, from the general assets of my estate." This is a demonstrative legacy, primarily specific in nature because payable initially from a specific fund, and secondarily general in nature because payable out of other assets of the estate. If the language is "$10,000 to my sister, to be paid from my deposit account at First National Bank," it is not clear whether it is a specific or demonstrative bequest, but this has been construed as demonstrative, i.e., if the account is insufficient, the bequest is to be paid from other assets of the estate.[2]

Why do we bother to classify the different forms of testamentary gifts? Significant legal consequences flow from these classifications. Problems of ademption, satisfaction, abatement of various kinds, entitlement to income earned during administration of the estate, are resolved by reference to these classifications.

The classification of bequests and devises applies to the testamentary trust as well as to outright bequests and devises. The trust may be a specific bequest or devise in trust: "I bequeath my 5,000 shares of IBM common stock to Bank, in trust ..." It may be a general bequest in trust: "I bequeath $200,000 to Bank, in

2. In re Cline's Estate, 67 Cal.App.2d 800, 155 P.2d 390 (1945); Lavender v. Cooper, 248 Ga. 685, 285 S.E.2d 528 (1982); Maxim v. Maxim, 129 Me. 349, 152 A. 268 (1930); Leaver v. McBride, 506 S.W.2d 141 (Tenn.1974).

trust ..." It may be a residuary bequest and devise in trust: "I bequeath and devise all the rest and residue of my estate, real and personal, to Bank, in trust ..."

It should be noted that in the case of the living gift, in trust or outright, there is only one classification because by definition it is a transfer of specific property. There is no such thing as a general or residuary living gift.

SECTION 2. INTEGRATION AND INCORPORATION BY REFERENCE

If the will is on one page, there is obviously no problem of integration of the pages of the will. If the will consists of five pages, and all five pages are present at the time of execution, those five pages constitute the will of the testator. All pages intended as the will must be present at the time and place of execution if they are to constitute the will.[3] Those pages present at the time and place of execution and intended by the testator to be the will constitute the will.

Problems of proof of the pages of the will can arise at the testator's death. If the testator and the witnesses initialled each page for identification purposes, there is not likely to be any difficulty of proof. Frequently this is not done. If the pages are found fastened together at the testator's death, it will be rebuttably presumed that the will was executed in this condition and that the fastened pages were intended by the testator as his will. If the pages are not fastened at testator's death but they are connected by language and logic, they will be rebuttably presumed to have been present at execution and intended by the testator as his will.[5] Of course, there may be supportive testimony from the witnesses or the lawyer who presided at execution, or negative evidence from the witnesses or others present at the execution.

The doctrine of incorporation by reference has to do with a writing which has testamentary effectiveness although it is not executed in compliance with testamentary formalities and is not part of the testator's will in the physical sense. A testator wants to make a certain disposition but for some reason does not want it in his will. If the provision is in a separate writing which is in

---

3. See Matter of Will of Carter, 565 A.2d 933 (Del.1989); Palmer v. Owen, 229 Ill. 115, 82 N.E. 275 (1907); Cole v. Webb, 220 Ky. 817, 295 S.W. 1035 (1927); Appeal of Sleeper, 129 Me. 194, 151 A. 150 (1930); In re Estate of Beale, 15 Wis.2d 546, 113 N.W.2d 380 (1962).

4. See Estate of Moore, 143 Cal. App.2d 64, 300 P.2d 110 (1956); Appeal of Sleeper, 129 Me. 194, 151 A. 150 (1930); In re Will of Roberts, 251 N.C. 708, 112 S.E.2d 505 (1960); Estate of Woodruff, 379 P.2d 692 (Okl.1963).

5. Matter of Will of Sessoms, 254 N.C. 369, 119 S.E.2d 193 (1961); In re Estate of Van Gilder, 421 Pa. 520, 220 A.2d 21 (1966).

existence at the time the will is executed, and is described in the will with reasonable certainty and as being in existence, and the will evidences the intention to incorporate it, the writing will be given testamentary effect.[6]

Let us assume testator executes a valid will containing, among other provisions, the following clause: "I direct my executor to distribute $50,000 among such persons and in such amounts as I have designated in a paper signed and dated this day by me prior to the execution of this will." Shortly before the execution of the will testator typed out on a piece of paper a list of five persons by name with dollar amounts opposite their names totalling $50,000, wrote the date, and signed his name. The paper was not present at the execution of the will. The paper is found with the will at his death several years later. All requirements of the doctrine are met: the will evidences the intention to incorporate, the writing is identified with specificity, the writing was in existence at the time the will was executed, and it was referred to as being in existence. This paper will be deemed to be incorporated by reference, be binding upon the executor, and have testamentary effectiveness although it is not part of the attested will of the testator in the physical sense and was not executed in accordance with testamentary formalities. The incorporated document is not usually probated with the formal will. For all functional purposes, however, it is a part of the testator's will. In effect, the doctrine constitutes an exception to the rule that all pieces of paper constituting the will must be present at execution.

It should be emphasized that the writing not only must be in existence when the will is executed but must be described in the will with reasonable certainty and as being in existence. Suppose the will provides as follows: "I direct my executor to distribute $50,000 among such persons and in such amounts as appear in a paper to be found with my will." This language is ambiguous with respect to whether the writing is or is not in existence at the time of execution, and does not describe the paper with specificity. Consequently the incorporation is likely to be ineffective, even assuming that the writing in fact was in existence at the time of execution.[7]

6. Wagner v. Clauson, 399 Ill. 403, 78 N.E.2d 203 (1948); Lawless v. Lawless, 187 Va. 511, 47 S.E.2d 431 (1948); Baarslag v. Hawkins, 12 Wash.App. 756, 531 P.2d 1283 (1975); In re Estate of Erbach, 41 Wis.2d 335, 164 N.W.2d 238 (1969).

7. Bryan's Appeal, 77 Conn. 240, 58 A. 748 (1904); Estate of Sweet, 519 A.2d 1260 (Me.1987); Kellom v. Beverstock, 100 N.H. 329, 126 A.2d 127 (1956); Lawless v. Lawless, 187 Va. 511, 47 S.E.2d 431 (1948). Some courts have not applied the incorporation by reference criteria strictly: Simon v. Grayson, 15 Cal.2d 531, 102 P.2d 1081 (1940); Smith v. Weitzel, 47 Tenn.App. 375, 338 S.W.2d 628 (1960).

The requirement that the writing be in existence when the will is executed is essential if the testamentary formalities are to have any significance. If the informal writing could come into existence after the execution of the will and be validly incorporated, the testator could arrange to dispose of his estate by an informal paper to be attached to his will which could be changed from time to time, the last being the effective instrument. This would open the door to disposition at death without any formalities except the initial instrument which allowed for disposition by subsequent informal writings. The requirement that the informal writing be in existence at the time of the will execution creates certain risks but it limits informal disposition. The requirement that the will refer to the writing as in existence is merely an aspect of the requirement that the writing be identified with certainty.

The Uniform Probate Code provision is as follows:

Section 2–510. [Incorporation by Reference.]

Any writing in existence when a will is executed may be incorporated by reference if the language of the will manifests this intent and describes the writing sufficiently to permit its identification.

A number of states have legislation in this form.[8] It should be noted that there is no requirement that the will refer to the incorporated document as being in existence.

Although the writing is not a part of the will in a physical sense, it is effective as a testamentary provision, is binding on the executor, and makes legatees or devisees of those designated. It should be a part of the file in the probate court as much as the will is, and consequently a matter of public record. Why would a lawyer use the doctrine instead of putting those terms in the will itself? Secrecy must be the testator's motive. There probably is not going to be any secrecy after the testator's death, but the testator may not want anyone else, including his lawyer or his lawyer's secretary, to know about it during his lifetime.

It should be noted parenthetically that in jurisdictions in which holographic wills are recognized, the writing which is in the handwriting of the testator and signed by him may be valid as a holographic will or codicil. Incorporation by reference need be considered only if the writing is not a valid holographic instrument.

Pre–1990 Uniform Probate Code § 2–513 is a novel provision which permits certain property to be disposed of by a writing that comes into existence after the execution of the will and that does not comply with testamentary formalities or the requirements for a

8. E.g., Ariz.Rev.Stat.Ann. § 14–2510; Minn.Stat.Ann. § 524.2–510; N.M.Stat.Ann. § 45–2–510; Wash.Rev. Code Ann. § 11.12.255.

holographic will. Jewelry, gold, and works of art of great value could be disposed of under this section, which reads as follows:

> Section 2–513. [Separate Writing Identifying Bequest of Tangible Property.]
>
> Whether or not the provisions relating to holographic wills apply, a will may refer to a written statement or list to dispose of items of tangible personal property not otherwise specifically disposed of by the will, other than money, evidences of indebtedness, documents of title, and securities, and property used in trade or business. To be admissible under this section as evidence of the intended disposition, the writing must either be in the handwriting of the testator or be signed by him and must describe the items and the devisees with reasonable certainty. The writing may be referred to as one to be in existence at the time of the testator's death; it may be prepared before or after the execution of the will; it may be altered by the testator after its preparation; and it may be a writing which has no significance apart from its effect upon the dispositions made by the will.

A number of states have legislation in this form.[9] This legislation bypasses the doctrine of incorporation by reference and acts of independent significance, to say nothing of execution formalities, with respect to certain forms of property. 1990 Code § 2–513 changes this provision by requiring that the writing be signed by the testator; if the writing is in the handwriting of the testator but unsigned it is not effective.

SECTION 3. ACTS OF INDEPENDENT SIGNIFICANCE

The identity of a legatee or devisee or of property to be bequeathed or devised is often determined by acts of the testator or another or both after the will is executed. If these acts have a purpose other than a testamentary purpose, i.e., other than to determine who is to be a legatee or what property is to be disposed of, the provisions of the will based on those acts are valid. If the act has only testamentary significance, the provision of the will based on the act is invalid because the legatee or property would be determined by means other than the execution of an instrument complying with the requisite formalities.

Testator's will contains the following clause: "I bequeath $1,000 to each person who is employed in my retail store at my death." The legatees can be determined by subsequent acts of

---

9. E.g., Fla.Stat.Ann. § 732.515; N.J.Stat.Ann. § 3B:3–11.

employment within the testator's discretion, but those acts obviously have significance independent of their testamentary significance, and consequently the bequests are valid.[10]

Testator's will contains the following clause: "I devise the residence I own at my death to my son John." The identity of the land obviously has significance other than its testamentary significance, and consequently the devise is valid.

Testator bequeaths "$10,000 to such person whose name appears on a sheet of paper attached to my will at my death." The paper is not in existence at the execution of the will. It does not comply with the requirements for incorporation by reference. Does the paper have significance other than testamentary significance? It clearly does not, and consequently this provision is invalid.

There are standard types of testamentary gifts which technically involve the doctrine of acts of independent significance but are never considered in that light. Testator bequeaths and devises "all the rest and residue of my estate to my descendants who survive me, per stirpes." The identity of the takers is dependent upon acts of independent significance, but this obviously valid gift is never thought of in those terms. Indeed, most class gifts involve this doctrine, strictly speaking, but are never analyzed in those terms, and their validity is taken for granted. Testator bequeaths "all my household furnishings to my daughter Sue." This probably means household furnishings owned at death, and involves this doctrine, but its validity is taken for granted without considering this doctrine. A bequest of the "balance at my death in my savings account at Home Savings Bank," is assumed to be valid without analysis, although the amount of the bequest is clearly dependent upon deposits and withdrawals after the execution of the will.[11]

There have been cases in which the testator bequeathed the contents of a bank safe deposit box, or the contents of a certain receptacle in the home. The contents may be valuable, such as stocks, bonds or jewelry, and the gift may be changed by simply removing or adding to the contents. Nevertheless these gifts have usually been upheld.[12] The courts have not examined whether in the particular instance alterations were made for testamentary purposes. If changes may be made for nontestamentary purposes,

10. Boyle v. Howe, 126 Fla. 662, 171 So. 667 (1935); Koch v. Wix, 108 Ind. App. 20, 25 N.E.2d 277 (1940); Shoup v. American Trust Co., 245 N.C. 682, 97 S.E.2d 111 (1957).

11. Matter of Estate of Roberts, 182 Cal.App.2d 6, 5 Cal.Rptr. 720 (1960); Odom v. Odom, 238 Ga. 733, 235 S.E.2d 29 (1977); Lavin v. Banks, 496 Ill. 605,

94 N.E.2d 876 (1950); In re Oliverio's Will, 99 Misc.2d 9, 415 N.Y.S.2d 335 (1979).

12. Gaff v. Cornwallis, 219 Mass. 226, 106 N.E. 860 (1914); In re Estate of Evans, 165 Ohio St. 27, 133 N.E.2d 128 (1956); Silverthorn v. Jennings, 620 S.W.2d 894 (Tex.Civ.App.1981).

that seems to suffice. The doctrine of acts of independent signifi-cance rarely is applied to invalidate a testamentary gift.

Uniform Probate Code § 2–512 recognizes this doctrine and that section has been legislated in a number of states.[13]

SECTION 4. POUR–OVER WILLS

Let us assume that a settlor has created a living trust, reserv-ing the power to revoke or amend at any time and from time to time. The trust was created primarily to avoid estate administra-tion with respect to the trust property. The dispositive provisions are income to the settlor for life, and upon his death, income to his wife for life, remainder to his children.

The settlor has retained substantial assets which he intends to dispose of under his will. He wants to dispose of these assets at death in the same way as his trust assets. He also wishes to have these retained assets administered with the living trust assets as one trust. He executes a will in which he bequeaths and devises all of his property to the trustee under his previously created living trust, to be administered and disposed of as part of such trust. This is described as a pour-over will; the testamentary assets pass through estate administration and are poured over into an existing living trust.

The settlor could have created a separate trust under his will with identical terms to those of the living trust, instead of using the pour-over technique. There are, however, administrative econo-mies in having one trust rather than two. If two trusts are created, in many states the living trust is subject to the jurisdiction of the court of general jurisdiction, and the testamentary trust is subject to a court of limited jurisdiction over probate and related matters. As a consequence, judicial accounting proceedings may have to be conducted separately. In some jurisdictions the living trust is not subject to as close judicial supervision as the testamen-tary trust; for example, the testamentary trustee frequently is required by statute to submit an account to the probate court periodically, such as every year or every two or three years, where-as the inter vivos trustee often has no statutory obligation to submit periodic accounts. These are some of the reasons why the settlor may prefer to have the testamentary assets added to the living trust to be administered as one living trust.

Note that we have described the pouring-over of estate assets into a living trust which is revocable and amendable. The trust terms could be changed after the will was executed. If this occurs

---

13. E.g., Ariz.Rev.Stat.Ann. § 14–2512; Idaho Code § 15–2–512; Me.Rev. Stat.Ann. tit. 18–A, § 2–512; Utah Code Ann. § 75–2–512.

it means that estate property would pass in accordance with a writing which effectively came into existence after the execution of the will. The trust in its original form and the amendment to it are not likely to be executed in accordance with testamentary formalities. The amended terms would not be valid as applied to estate assets under the doctrine of incorporation by reference. If the trust had been irrevocable and unamendable at the execution of the will, incorporation by reference would sustain the application of the trust terms to the estate assets.

In the past there has been judicial authority that the pouring-over into the revocable and amendable trust was an invalid will provision if the trust was amended after the execution of the will, because of failure to comply with the doctrine of incorporation by reference. There was also authority that the pouring-over was valid but the estate assets would have to be disposed of in accordance with the terms of the trust as they existed at the time of the execution of the will, and any change in the trust terms would be ineffective as to probate assets. Then there were cases which upheld the pour-over to be disposed of in accordance with amendments to the trust after the execution of the will on the ground that the living trust as amended was an act of independent significance because it disposed of the original trust assets as well as the poured-over estate assets.

There was also the additional question of whether the estate assets would be held by the trustee of the existing living trust, or would be held by the same trustee under a different trust, i.e., a testamentary trust, containing the same terms as the living trust. If incorporation by reference theory is used to validate the pour-over, then it seems logical that the living trust terms become part of the will and the estate assets are held in a testamentary trust. The intention, however, was clearly to have the estate assets held in the living trust. If acts of independent significance theory is used, there is no problem in having the estate assets held in the living trust.[14]

All these problems brought on uniform legislation validating the pour-over of estate assets into a living trust, whether or not the living trust was revocable and amendable, and whether or not the living trust was in fact amended after the execution of the will. The legislation provides that what the testator wants to do can be done, and common law doctrine is irrelevant. The 1960 Uniform Testamentary Additions to Trusts Act, which became Section 2–511 of the pre–1990 Uniform Probate Code, is as follows:

14. For a discussion of the common law of pour-over wills, see 1 Scott, Law of Trusts § 54.3 (4th ed., Fratcher, 1987).

A devise or bequest, the validity of which is determinable by the law of this state, may be made by a will to the trustee of a trust established or to be established by the testator or by the testator and some other person or by some other person (including a funded or unfunded life insurance trust, although the trustor has reserved any or all rights of ownership of the insurance contracts) if the trust is identified in the testator's will and its terms are set forth in a written instrument (other than a will) executed before or concurrently with the execution of the testator's will or in the valid last will of a person who has predeceased the testator (regardless of the existence, size, or character of the corpus of the trust). The devise is not invalid because the trust is amendable or revocable, or because the trust was amended after the execution of the will or after the death of the testator. Unless the testator's will provides otherwise, the property so devised (1) is not deemed to be held under a testamentary trust of the testator but becomes a part of the trust to which it is given and (2) shall be administered and disposed of in accordance with the provisions of the instrument or will setting forth the terms of the trust, including any amendments thereto made before the death of the testator (regardless of whether made before or after the execution of the testator's will), and, if the testator's will so provides, including any amendments to the trust made after the death of the testator. A revocation or termination of the trust before the death of the testator causes the devise to lapse.

This legislation, or something similar, has been enacted in almost all states.

1990 Code § 2–511 has modified the section to make it clear that the trust need not be funded during the testator's life, and may be funded by the testator's bequest or devise. It also modifies the section by permitting the trust instrument to be executed after the execution of the testator's will. The 1960 Uniform Testamentary Additions to Trusts Act was revised in 1991 to conform to the 1990 Code § 2–511.

SECTION 5. REPUBLICATION BY CODICIL

Republication by codicil has two aspects. One has to do with the situation of a revoked will, which is still physically in existence, that is revived by a validly executed codicil to it. Testator has validly executed Will # 1. Testator validly executes Will # 2 which revokes Will # 1. Will # 1 is not destroyed. Testator then revokes Will # 2 by physical act. In the jurisdiction this revocation of the revoking will cannot revive Will # 1; testator has no will at this point. Next, testator validly executes an instrument which states that it is a codicil to Will # 1. Will # 1 comes back to life by the execution of the codicil, under the doctrine of republication by codicil. Many states have statutes which state this principle.[15] It should be emphasized that Will # 1 is still physically in existence when the codicil is executed; if it has been destroyed the doctrine does not apply. Also, if Will # 1 had been revoked by operation of law, in whole or in part, rather than by subsequent instrument, and was physically still in existence, the codicil similarly brings Will # 1 back to life.[16]

There is a situation that looks like republication by codicil but is different. Testator thinks she has executed a will but she hasn't because the formalities were not complied with. Testator is not aware of the invalidity, and validly executes what she thinks is a codicil to that instrument. The second instrument states that it is a codicil to the first instrument. This subsequent instrument, executed with the testamentary formalities, incorporates the first instrument by reference, thereby making a will out of the first instrument and the second instrument combined. This is not republication by codicil because there was no initial publication and there is no codicil, but courts often refer to it in that way.[17]

The other, and more significant, aspect of republication by codicil has to do with the standard situation of a valid will which is later amended by a codicil. It is said that the will is republished by the codicil, which in this context means that the will is, for certain purposes, read as if it had been executed at the time the codicil was executed. Testator executes a will devising to Jones "all the land I now own in Orange County." After the execution of the will testator acquires additional land in Orange County. Next, testator executes a codicil in which he changes his designation of the executor. Testator dies owning the additional land. The will is probably going to be read as if it had been executed at the time of

15. Price v. Marshall, 255 Ala. 447, 52 So.2d 149 (1951); Estate of Lane, 492 So.2d 395 (Fla.Dist.Ct.App.1986); Farmers' Bank & Trust Co. v. Harding, 209 Ky. 3, 272 S.W. 3 (1925); Crosby v. Alton Ochsner Medical Foundation, 276 So.2d 661 (Miss.1973); In re Estate of Eberhardt, 1 Wis.2d 439, 85 N.W.2d 483 (1957); Ark.Stat.Ann. § 60–408; D.C.Code Ann. § 18–109; Fla.Stat.Ann. § 732.511; Ky.Rev.Stat.Ann. § 394.100; N.J.Stat.Ann. § 3B:3–15.

16. In re Riddel's Estate, 104 Cal. App.2d 162, 230 P.2d 863 (1951); In re Coffield's Will, 216 N.C. 285, 4 S.E.2d 870 (1939); Florey v. Meeker, 194 Or. 257, 240 P.2d 1177 (1952); White v. Conference Claimants Endowment Commission, 81 Idaho 17, 336 P.2d 674 (1959).

17. Abel v. Bittner, 470 N.W.2d 348 (Iowa 1991); Hurley v. Blankinship, 313 Ky. 49, 229 S.W.2d 963 (1950); In re Kaiser's Estate, 150 Neb. 295, 34

the codicil, and the additional land is included in the devise.[18]

Suppose testator executes a will which purports to incorporate a writing by reference but the writing is not in existence at the time of the execution of the will. Subsequently it comes into existence. Next, testator executes a codicil in which he changes the designation of the executor. The will speaks as of the time of the codicil at which time the writing is in existence, and consequently the writing may be incorporated by reference.[19]

The will is not considered to speak as of the time of the codicil if the result would appear to be contrary to the testator's intention. Testator executes a will containing a $10,000 bequest to Sister. Several years later testator makes a gift of $10,000 to Sister, and this gift is intended to be and is effective as a satisfaction of the legacy; this renders the legacy a nullity as explained in the section below on the doctrine of satisfaction. Next, testator executes a codicil in which she changes certain administrative terms of the will. If the will speaks as of the time of the codicil there is no satisfaction because the gift would have been made before the will was executed, and a gift made before the will cannot possibly be treated as a satisfaction of a legacy contained in the will. In this situation, however, it has been held that the testator intended the satisfaction to be effective, and the will is not deemed to speak as of the time of the codicil for this purpose.[20] In sum, the will speaks as of the time of the codicil unless that would be inconsistent with what the court views to be the intent of the testator.

SECTION 6. MISDESCRIPTION AND AMBIGUITY

Previously we have discussed the testator's mistake as it relates to the admissibility of the will to probate. Here we are assuming that the will is admitted to probate, and we are concerned with the construction of descriptions of persons or property which are mistaken or ambiguous.

Testator devises to his son "my property located at 123 Vine Street in Smithville." Testator's property in Smithville was not located there, but rather at 231 Vine Street. The court will take extrinsic evidence to establish the mistake and correct it.[21]

N.W.2d 366 (1948); Johnson v. Johnson, 279 P.2d 928 (Okl.1954).

18. See Evans, Testamentary Republication, 40 Harv.L.Rev. 71 (1926).

19. Simon v. Grayson, 15 Cal.2d 531, 102 P.2d 1081 (1940).

20. Colley v. Britton, 210 Md. 237, 123 A.2d 296 (1956); Lansdale v. Dearing, 351 Mo. 356, 173 S.W.2d 25 (1943);

In re Lutz' Estate, 201 Misc. 539, 107 N.Y.S.2d 388 (1951).

21. Spencer v. Gutierrez, 99 N.M. 712, 663 P.2d 371 (App.1983); In re Will of Goldstein, 46 A.D.2d 449, 363 N.Y.S.2d 147 (1975); aff'd 38 N.Y.2d 876, 382 N.Y.S.2d 743, 346 N.E.2d 544 (1976); Fenzel v. Floyd, 289 S.C. 495, 347 S.E.2d 105 (App.1986); Matter of

Testator bequeaths "$5,000 to my friend, Wilbur Smith." Testator has no friend by that name, but does have a friend named Willis Smith. The court will admit extrinsic evidence to establish the mistake and correct it.[22] Probate courts have no problem rectifying such mistaken descriptions.

Suppose testator bequeaths "$5,000 to my friend, Wilbur Smith." Testator had a friend, Wilbur Smith, and he also had a friend named Willis Smith. Will the probate court admit evidence to establish that testator intended the legatee to be Willis Smith rather than Wilbur Smith? This is likely to be resolved by the "plain meaning" rule: If language accurately describes property of the testator, or an individual who is a likely legatee or devisee of the testator, the court will not admit evidence that something or someone else was intended. Wilbur Smith is the legatee. This is the prevailing position.[23]

Suppose testator bequeaths "$10,000 to my niece, Mary." Testator had two nieces by that name. This is ambiguity in the language of the will, not a misdescription. The ambiguity is described as latent, because it is not apparent on the face of the will. Extrinsic evidence is admissible to establish the ambiguity and to resolve the ambiguity.[24] This ambiguity may be resolved by evidence that the testator was close to one niece and saw her regularly, and saw the other infrequently.

Suppose testator bequeaths "$10,000 to my nephew Rob, of New York City." Testator had a nephew Rob who lived in Boston, and a nephew Roy who lived in New York City. This gift combines elements of misdescription and latent ambiguity. Evidence is admissible to determine which nephew was intended to be the legatee.[25]

Estate of Cohorn, 622 S.W.2d 486 (Tex. App.1981).

22. Shulman v. Connecticut Bank and Trust Co., 5 Conn.App. 561, 501 A.2d 759 (1985); Breckheimer v. Kraft, 133 Ill.App.2d 410, 273 N.E.2d 468 (1971); Hollenbeck v. Gray, 185 N.W.2d 767 (Iowa 1971); In re Estate of Gibb, 14 Wis.2d 490, 111 N.W.2d 413 (1961).

23. Gustafson v. Svenson, 373 Mass. 273, 366 N.E.2d 761 (1977); Ladd v. Estate of Kellenberger, 314 N.C. 477, 334 S.E.2d 751 (1985); In re Estate of Kelly, 473 Pa. 48, 373 A.2d 744 (1977); Greater Providence Chapter v. John E. Fogarty Foundation, 488 A.2d 1228 (R.I. 1985); Vadman v. American Cancer Society, 26 Wash.App. 697, 615 P.2d 500

(1980). See Connecticut Junior Republic v. Sharon Hospital, 188 Conn. 1, 448 A.2d 190 (1982).

24. Matter of Estate of Hayden, 23 Ill.App.3d 242, 318 N.E.2d 668 (1974); Bell v. Forti, 85 Md.App. 345, 584 A.2d 77 (1991); Clymer v. Mayo, 393 Mass. 754, 473 N.E.2d 1084 (1985); Matter of Estate of Kremlick, 417 Mich. 237, 331 N.W.2d 228 (1983); Baliles v. Miller, 231 Va. 48, 340 S.E.2d 805 (1986).

25. Matter of Estate of Cleaver, 126 Cal.App.3d 341, 178 Cal.Rptr. 729 (1981); Phipps v. Barbera, 23 Mass.App. 1, 498 N.E.2d 411 (1986); Bond v. Riley, 317 Mo. 594, 296 S.W. 401 (1927); Siegley v. Simpson, 73 Wash. 69, 131 P. 479 (1913).

plain ambiguities (handwritten)

Finally, there is the question of the patent ambiguity, one that is apparent on the face of the will, as distinguished from the latent ambiguity. As examples, a will may devise certain land to Son in fee in one clause of the will, and in another clause devise the same land to Son for life with a power of sale; or a will may bequeath "all my personal property" to Daughter in one clause of the will, and in the residuary clause of the will "bequeath and devise all the rest and residue of my personal and real property" to Son. Some courts insist upon resolving the patent ambiguity by constructional rules or by inference of intention without benefit of extrinsic evidence as to intention.[26] Why this should be is a mystery. The trend of authority appears to be that extrinsic evidence is admissible to resolve a patent ambiguity as it is to resolve a latent ambiguity.[27]

SECTION 7. LAPSE

Let us assume that testator bequeaths $1000 to A. If A was alive at the time the will was executed but predeceased the testator, the bequest to A is said to lapse.[28] This means that the bequest to A is invalid, and the property passes as if there were no bequest to A in the will. The $1000 passes to the residuary legatees in the will, assuming there is a residuary clause, and if not, it passes to the intestate takers. The conceptual explanation for the principle of lapse is that the will is effective as of the date of the testator's death, and the gift cannot be made to one who is not alive to receive it. Statutes have been enacted in most jurisdictions, however, which provide for substitutional gifts under certain circumstances in the event of lapse, as discussed later in this section.

The question of lapse may arise in connection with the apparent simultaneous death of the testator and a legatee in an accident. Under the 1940 Uniform Simultaneous Death Act, which was enacted in almost all states, if there is no sufficient evidence that the testator and the legatee or devisee have died otherwise than simultaneously, the legatee or devisee is treated as having predeceased the testator, unless the will provides otherwise. Pre–1990 Uniform Probate Code § 2–601 and 1990 Code § 2–702 go beyond

26. Kirk v. Lee, 402 S.W.2d 838 (Ky. 1965); Helmer v. Voss, 646 S.W.2d 738 (Mo.1983); Breckner v. Prestwood, 600 S.W.2d 52 (Mo.App.1980); In re Estate of Corrigan, 218 Neb. 723, 358 N.W.2d 501 (1984).

27. In re Estate of Russell, 69 Cal.2d 200, 70 Cal.Rptr. 561, 444 P.2d 353 (1968); Estate of Redenius, 455 N.W.2d 295 (Iowa App.1990); Matter of Estate of Kremlick, 417 Mich. 237, 331 N.W.2d

228 (1983); Matter of Estate of Arend, 373 N.W.2d 338 (Minn.App.1985); Matter of Estate of Bergau, 103 Wash.2d 431, 693 P.2d 703 (1985).

28. The death of the legatee prior to that of the testator is the most common form of lapse. There are, however, other forms including renunciation of the legacy and dissolution of a corporate legatee prior to testator's death.

simultaneous death to provide that a legatee or devisee who does not survive the testator for 120 hours is treated as if he predeceased the testator, unless the will provides otherwise. This provision has been legislated in a minority of states. In 1991 the 1940 Uniform Simultaneous Death Act was revised to require that a legatee or devisee survive the testator by 120 hours.

The lapsed bequest or devise is to be distinguished from the void bequest or devise. Lapse occurs when an event subsequent to the execution of the will renders the gift ineffective; a void gift is one which would be invalid if the testator died immediately upon the execution of the will. A bequest or devise lapses when the legatee was alive at the time the will was executed but predeceased the testator. If the legatee was dead at the time the testator executed the will, the gift is said to be void.[29] The consequences of the void gift and the lapsed gift are the same, except in some states with respect to the application of the lapse statutes discussed below. The incidence of a bequest or devise to one who is dead at the time of the execution of the will is, of course, quite rare, whereas the incidence of the lapsed bequest or devise is not unusual due to the lengthy gap that frequently exists between the execution of the will and the testator's death.

Let us assume that after several specific and general bequests the testator bequeaths and devises all the rest and residue of her property to A. A predeceases the testator. The residuary gift lapses, and the property that otherwise would have gone to A passes to the testator's intestate takers. The lapse is of the entire residuary estate and intestacy is all that remains.

Suppose the testator, after several specific and general bequests, bequeaths and devises all the rest and residue of her property one-half to A and one-half to B. A predeceases the testator but B survives the testator. Assume that A's gift is not covered by the anti-lapse statute discussed later in this section. Does the gift to A lapse and pass to the intestate takers, or does it pass to the other residuary legatee? Some courts have taken the rather mechanical view that after the residue there is only intestacy, and that is the fate of the lapsed fractional residuary gift.[30] Other courts have taken what seems to be a more sensible view,

---

29. Equitable Trust Co. v. Smith, 26 Md.App. 204, 337 A.2d 205 (1975); Padgett v. Black, 229 S.C. 142, 92 S.E.2d 153 (1956). Bequests and devises may, of course, be void for other reasons, e.g., violation of the rule against perpetuities, or on a condition that is deemed contrary to public policy.

30. Moffett v. Howard, 392 So.2d 509 (Miss.1981); Dean v. Moore, 380 P.2d 934 (Okl.1962); In re Estate of O'Hara, 549 S.W.2d 233 (Tex.Civ.App. 1977). Expression of intent by testator will, of course, result in distributing share of predeceasing residuary legatee among surviving residuary legatees. Bahan v. Citizens and Southern National Bank, 267 S.C. 303, 227 S.E.2d 671 (1976); In re Estate of Kugler, 52 Wis.2d 532, 190 N.W.2d 883 (1971).

and one which is certainly consonant with the presumption against intestacy, that the gift passes to B, the other residuary legatee.[31] Pre–1990 Uniform Probate Code § 2–606 and 1990 Code § 2–604 provide that the lapsed residuary gift passes to the other residuary legatees rather than by intestacy, as do the statutes in many states.[32]

Suppose testator bequeaths $100,000 in trust to pay the income to A for life, remainder to B. A survives the testator and B predeceases the testator. The remainder interest lapses, and upon the termination of A's life estate the principal of the trust passes to the residuary legatees. Of course, if A predeceases the testator and B survives the testator, B is entitled to the principal upon the testator's death.

Most jurisdictions have statutes which provide for substitutional gifts in the event of lapse in certain circumstances. These anti-lapse statutes vary considerably. The principal differences are the definitions of the predeceasing legatees and devisees to whom the statute applies. Pre–1990 Uniform Probate Code § 2–605 is limited to the predeceasing legatee or devisee (or one who does not survive the testator for 120 hours) who is a grandparent or a descendant of a grandparent of the testator; under the corresponding 1990 Code § 2–603, step-children of the testator qualify, as well as grandchildren and descendants of grandchildren. The statutes of some states are limited to the predeceasing legatee or devisee who is a descendant of the testator,[33] or a descendant or a sibling of the testator.[34] Some statutes apply to all predeceasing legatees or devisees.[35] Most of the statutes designate the descendants of the predeceasing legatee who survive the testator as the substitutional takers.[36]

Under these statutes, if testator bequeaths $100,000 to his son A, and A predeceases the testator leaving two children who survive the testator, the $100,000 does not pass into the residue but instead passes to the two children of A. If, however, A had no children or grandchildren who survived the testator, the money would pass to the residuary legatees. It should be stressed that the statutes

---

31. In re Estate of Jackson, 106 Ariz. 82, 471 P.2d 278 (1970); In re Leavy's Estate, 122 N.H. 184, 442 A.2d 588 (1982); In re Slack's Trust, 126 Vt. 37, 220 A.2d 472 (1966).

32. E.g., Md.Est. & Trusts Code Ann. § 4–404; Mass.Gen.Laws Ann. c. 191, §§ 1A, 22; N.C.Gen.Stat. § 31–42; Pa.Stat.Ann. tit. 20, § 2514.

33. E.g., Ill.Ann.Stat. ch. 110½, § 4–11; Miss.Code Ann. § 91–5–7; Tex.Probate Code Ann. § 68.

34. E.g., Conn.Gen.Stat.Ann. § 45–276a; N.Y.Est.Powers & Trusts Law § 3–3.3; Pa.Stat.Ann. tit. 20, § 2514.

35. E.g., R.I.Gen.Laws § 33–6–19; Tenn.Code Ann. § 32–3–105; Va.Code § 64.1–64; W.Va.Code § 41–3–3.

36. E.g., D.C.Code Ann. § 18–308; Ga.Code Ann. § 113–812; Ky.Rev.Stat. Ann. § 394.400; N.H.Rev.Stat.Ann. § 551.12.

provide for substitutional legatees; the lapsed gift does not pass through the estate of the predeceased legatee. Many lapse statutes, including pre–1990 Uniform Probate Code § 2–605 and 1990 Code § 2–603, apply to the void bequest (legatee dead at execution of will) as well as the lapsed bequest.[37]

It should be emphasized that the doctrine of lapse, and the lapse statutes, apply only to the situation of the legatee or devisee who predeceases the testator. If testator devises Blackacre to A for life, remainder to B in fee, and B survives the testator but predeceases A, there is no issue of lapse. There may possibly be a question of whether B must survive A in order to take the remainder, but this is not a lapse question and the lapse statute has no applicability.

The doctrine of lapse, and the application of lapse statutes, are subject to the control of the testator. The testator could bequeath "$10,000 to A, or if he predeceases me, to A's residuary legatees and devisees who survive me, or if there are none, to A's intestate takers". Here testator has circumvented the doctrine of lapse by providing an alternative gift to those who succeed to A's property. A testator can always provide for alternative gifts in the event a legatee predeceases him, such as "$10,000 to A, or if he predeceases me, to B, or if she predeceases me, to C".

Testator may bequeath "$10,000 to A if he survives me," without providing for an alternative legatee. If A predeceases the testator, it has been held that the lapse statute is not applicable because the testator has anticipated that A may predecease him and has provided that there is to be no gift in that event.[38] The application of a lapse statute is subject to the expression of a contrary intent by the testator.[39] The theory of lapse statutes is that the provision for substitutional takers reflects the presumed intent of the testator had he thought of the possibility that the legatee might predecease him; consequently, any indication that the testator did not wish the lapse statute to operate will be controlling.

There is also contrary authority that words requiring survivorship of the testator do not negate the application of the lapse

37. E.g., Del.Code Ann. tit. 12, § 2313; Ind.Code Ann. § 29–1–6–1; N.J.Stat.Ann. § 3B:3–35; Ohio Rev. Code Ann. § 2107.52; S.D.Comp.Laws Ann. § 29–6–8; Wyo.Stat. § 2–6–106.

38. In re Estate of Kerr, 433 F.2d 479 (D.C.Cir.1970); Estate of Stroble, 6 Kan.App.2d 955, 636 P.2d 236 (1981); In re Estate of Evans, 193 Neb. 437, 227 N.W.2d 603 (1975); In re Robinson's

Will, 37 Misc.2d 546, 236 N.Y.S.2d 293 (1963); Shalkhauser v. Beach, 14 Ohio Misc. 1, 233 N.E.2d 527 (1968).

39. Uniform Probate Code § 2–603; Iowa Code Ann. § 633.273; Or.Rev.Stat. § 112.395; Tenn.Code Ann. § 32–3–105; Vt.Stat.Ann. tit. 14, § 558; Wis.Stat. Ann. § 853.27.

statute.[40] This makes it necessary to expressly negate the application of the lapse statute if that is the intention. 1990 Code § 2–603(b)(3) supports this position. It provides that words of survivorship such as "if he survives me," or to "my surviving children," are not, in the absence of additional evidence, a sufficient indication of an intent to negate the application of the lapse statute.

If the bequest is "$10,000 to A if he survives me, or if he does not survive me, to B", both A and B predecease the testator and have descendants, and both A and B are within the lapse statute, there is a lapse of the bequest to B and the gift passes to B's substitutional takers because there has been no expression of an intention that the lapse statute is not to be applied to his gift. 1990 Code §§ 2–603(b)(4) and (c), however, provide for a different result in this situation. The alternative bequest to B does not replace the bequest to A unless B personally is entitled to take under the will. The fact that B has descendants available to take under the lapse statute does not cut off the interest of A's descendants under the lapse statute. Bear in mind that under 1990 Code § 2–603 the language of survivorship imposed upon A's gift does not negate the application of the lapse statute to his bequest.

The testator can protect against intestacy resulting from lapse in the residue by providing in the residuary clause that his property is to go "to A and B in equal parts, or if either A or B predeceases me, then her share to the survivor, or if both A and B predecease me, then to C if she survives me, or if not, to Charity Hospital". The last legatee is bound to be there.

SECTION 8.   ADEMPTION

If the testator executes a will containing a specific bequest or devise, and the subject of the specific gift is not in the estate of the testator at his death, the specific gift is said to be adeemed and is ineffective. The property in question may have been sold or given away by the testator, or taken by eminent domain, or destroyed or lost. The rule is usually applied mechanically; the gift was of specific property and if it is not in the estate for disposition, it fails.[41] In some circumstances it might be reasonable to infer that the testator would have wanted the proceeds of the sale of the property, or the insurance payable because of its loss or destruc-

---

40. Estate of Bulger, 224 Ill.App.3d 456, 166 Ill.Dec. 715, 586 N.E.2d 673 (1991); Gale v. Keyes, 45 Ohio App. 61, 186 N.E. 755 (1933); Estate of Kehler, 488 Pa. 165, 411 A.2d 748 (1980).

41. In re Estate of Reposa, 121 N.H. 114, 427 A.2d 19 (1981); In re Wright's Will, 7 N.Y.2d 365, 197 N.Y.S.2d 711, 165 N.E.2d 561 (1960); McGee v. McGee, 122 R.I. 837, 413 A.2d 72 (1980); Taylor v. Goddard, 265 S.C. 327, 218 S.E.2d 246 (1975); Shriner's Hospital For Crippled Children v. Stahl, 610 S.W.2d 147 (Tex.1980).

tion, substituted for the specific property, but the prevailing position does not examine intent. Some jurisdictions, however, have adopted a contrary view that the testator's manifested intention not to adeem is controlling, particularly where the proceeds of sale of the specifically devised or bequeathed property or the insurance money paid on account of its loss or destruction can be traced.[42] It should be noted that ademption is sometimes referred to as "ademption by extinction."

The rather rigid nature and sometimes harsh consequences of the prevailing position have been mitigated somewhat by certain constructional devices. If a testator bequeaths "my household furnishings," or "my jewelry," or "my stocks," without specifying whether she meant the property she owned at execution or at her death, the court may employ a date of death construction to avoid the harsh consequences of ademption.[43] If the date of execution construction is employed, items sold or given away are adeemed and their replacements are not bequeathed; if the date of death construction is used, the replacements are included in the bequest to the extent they are owned at death.

Another mitigating technique is to construe a bequest as general rather than specific if it is plausible to do so. Testator bequeaths "200 shares of IBM stock." Testator owned 200 shares of IBM stock when she executed the will, but the stock was not described as "my 200 shares ...," but merely as "200 shares ..." Testator sells her 200 shares of IBM stock and does not own any IBM stock at her death. A court may construe the bequest as general, thereby preserving the bequest.[44] Obviously ademption has nothing to do with general bequests or residuary bequests.

Another means of mitigating the harshness of ademption is to construe a change in the property as one of form only. Testator bequeaths "the balance in my deposit account at First National Bank at my death." Testator closed out that account a year before her death and transferred the funds to a deposit account with City Bank, which she owned at death. The court is likely to hold that there is no ademption because this is merely a change in the form of the gift, the identity of the bank being incidental to the sub-

---

42. Estate of Austin, 113 Cal.App.3d 167, 169 Cal.Rptr. 648 (1980); Sorensen v. First National Bank of Chicago, 59 Ill.App.3d 150, 17 Ill.Dec. 125, 376 N.E.2d 18 (1978); Matter of Estate of Wolfe, 208 N.W.2d 923 (Iowa 1973); White v. White, 105 N.J.Super. 184, 251 A.2d 470 (1969).

43. See cases and statutes cited supra note 1.

44. In re Jones' Estate, 60 Cal. App.2d 795, 141 P.2d 764 (1943); Feder v. Weissman, 81 Nev. 668, 409 P.2d 251 (1965); In re McFerren's Estate, 365 Pa. 490, 76 A.2d 759 (1950); In re Blomdahl's Will, 216 Wis. 590, 257 N.W. 152 (1934).

stance of the gift which is a specific legacy of a bank account.[45] In a similar vein, assume a specific gift of "my 100 shares of ABC Corp. stock." Later ABC Corp. is merged into XYZ Corp., and the testator receives 100 shares of XYZ Corp. stock in place of the 100 shares of ABC Corp. stock she owned prior to the merger. Testator dies owning the 100 shares of XYZ Corp. stock. This is likely to be considered merely a change in form and the bequest is not adeemed.[46]

The prevailing mechanical approach to ademption has also been modified in the situation of the sale of specifically bequeathed or devised property by a guardian, or conservator, of the property of the testator. The testator's will contains a specific bequest or devise, and the guardian properly sells the subject property to provide funds for the support of the testator. To the extent the funds are expended by the guardian for the support of the testator, there is an ademption. However, any remaining funds held by the guardian at the testator's death are payable to the specific legatee or devisee.[47]

Pre–1990 Uniform Probate Code §§ 2–607 and 2–608 protect the specific legatee or devisee from ademption in various situations including changes in the form of securities, condemnation awards, insurance proceeds, and guardian sales, as follows:

Section 2–607. [Change in Securities; Accessions; Nonademption.]

(a) If the testator intended a specific devise of certain securities rather than the equivalent value thereof, the specific devisee is entitled only to:

(1) as much of the devised securities as is a part of the estate at time of the testator's death;

(2) any additional or other securities of the same entity owned by the testator by reason of action initiated by the entity excluding any acquired by exercise of purchase options;

45. Willis v. Barrow, 218 Ala. 549, 119 So. 678 (1929); Matter of Estate of Hall, 60 N.J.Super. 597, 160 A.2d 49 (1960); Matter of Estate of Biss, 232 Or. 26, 374 P.2d 382 (1962).

46. Curtis v. Curtis, 23 Del.Ch. 27, 2 A.2d 88 (1938); In re Estate of Watkins, 284 So.2d 679 (Fla.1973); Goode v. Reynolds, 208 Ky. 441, 271 S.W. 600 (1925); Wyckoff v. Young Women's Christian Association, 37 N.J.Super. 274, 117 A.2d 162 (1955); In re Oliver-io's Will, 99 Misc.2d 9, 415 N.Y.S.2d 335 (1979).

47. In re Estate of Mason, 62 Cal.2d 213, 42 Cal.Rptr. 13, 397 P.2d 1005 (1965); Our Lady of Lourdes v. Vanator, 91 Idaho 407, 422 P.2d 74 (1967); Stake v. Cole, 257 Iowa 594, 133 N.W.2d 714 (1965); Matter of Estate of Graham, 216 Kan. 770, 533 P.2d 1318 (1975); Walsh v. Gillespie, 338 Mass. 278, 154 N.E.2d 906 (1959).

(3) securities of another entity owned by the testator as a result of a merger, consolidation, reorganization or other similar action initiated by the entity; and

(4) any additional securities of the entity owned by the testator as a result of a plan of reinvestment if it is a regulated investment company.

(b) Distributions prior to death with respect to a specifically devised security not provided for in subsection (a) are not part of the specific devise.

Section 2–608. [Nonademption of Specific Devises in Certain Cases; Unpaid Proceeds of Sale, Condemnation or Insurance; Sale by Conservator.]

(a) A specific devisee has the right to the remaining specifically devised property and:

(1) any balance of the purchase price (together with any security interest) owing from a purchaser to the testator at death by reason of sale of the property;

(2) any amount of a condemnation award for the taking of the property unpaid at death;

(3) any proceeds unpaid at death on fire or casualty insurance on the property; and

(4) property owned by testator at his death as a result of foreclosure, or obtained in lieu of foreclosure, of the security for a specifically devised obligation.

(b) If specifically devised property is sold by a conservator, or if a condemnation award or insurance proceeds are paid to a conservator as a result of condemnation, fire, or casualty, the specific devisee has the right to a general pecuniary devise equal to the net sale price, the condemnation award, or the insurance proceeds. This subsection does not apply if after the sale, condemnation or casualty, it is adjudicated that the disability of the testator has ceased and the testator survives the adjudication by one year. The right of the specific devisee under this subsection is reduced by any right he has under subsection (a).

These provisions of the Code have been legislated in a number of states.[48]

1990 Code § 2–606 changes the law of ademption in two major respects. First, it provides that a specific legatee or devisee is

---

48. E.g., Cal.Prob.Code §§ 6171, 6172, 6173; Fla.Stat.Ann. §§ 732.605, 732.606; Minn.Stat.Ann. §§ 524.2–607, 524.2–608; N.J.Stat.Ann. §§ 3B:3–42, 3B:3–43, 3B:3–44; Wyo.Stat. §§ 2–6–108, 2–6–109.

entitled to real property or tangible personal property owned by the testator at death which the testator acquired as a replacement for specifically devised or bequeathed real property or tangible personal property.   Second, if replacement has not occurred, a specific legatee or devisee is entitled to the value of any specifically bequeathed personal property (tangible and intangible) or specifically devised real property to the extent that such property is not in the testator's estate at death, unless it appears that ademption was intended by the testator.   This latter provision creates, in effect, a presumption against ademption.

SECTION 9.   SATISFACTION

A testator executes a will which contains a general bequest of $20,000 to Sister.   Several years later testator makes a living gift to Sister of $20,000 and states at the time that the gift is intended to be in satisfaction of the bequest to her in the will.   If testator dies with the will, the bequest is considered to have been satisfied and is ineffective.[49]   The doctrine of satisfaction has the effect of revocation of a clause in the will on the basis of an expression of an intention to do so which at common law may be oral.   It should be emphasized that satisfaction consists of two elements, the living gift and the contemporaneous intention that it be in satisfaction of the bequest.   A bequest may be partially satisfied; in our example a $10,000 gift accompanied by the intention to satisfy the bequest by that amount would reduce the bequest to $10,000.[50]   Satisfaction can occur only if the will is in existence when the gift is made; there can be no intention to satisfy if the gift is made first and the will follows.   It should be noted that satisfaction is sometimes referred to as "ademption by satisfaction."

The doctrine of satisfaction is restricted at common law to certain testamentary gifts.   It applies at common law only to general and residuary bequests (personalty).   It has generally been held that devises (real property) are not subject to satisfaction.[51]   It has usually been considered that a specific bequest cannot be satisfied.[52]   If the testator makes a living gift to the specific legatee

---

49.   Trustees of Baker University v. Trustees of the Endowment Association, 222 Kan. 245, 564 P.2d 472 (1977); Colley v. Britton, 210 Md. 237, 123 A.2d 296 (1956); Matter of Will of Williams, 71 N.M. 39, 376 P.2d 3 (1962); Matter of Estate of Spadoni, 71 Wash.2d 820, 430 P.2d 965 (1967).

50.   Rowe v. Newman, 290 Ala. 289, 276 So.2d 412 (1972); Matter of Will of Williams, 71 N.M. 39, 376 P.2d 3 (1962); In re Hall's Will, 120 N.Y.S.2d 188 (Sur.

1953), aff'd 284 App.Div. 1013, 135 N.Y.S.2d 295 (1954).

51.   Kemp v. Kemp, 92 Ind.App. 268, 154 N.E. 505 (1926); In re Brown's Estate, 139 Iowa 219, 117 N.W. 260 (1908); Graham v. Karr, 331 Mo. 1157, 55 S.W.2d 995 (1932); Maestas v. Martinez, 107 N.M. 91, 752 P.2d 1107 (App.1988).

52.   Roquet v. Eldridge, 118 Ind. 147, 20 N.E. 733 (1889); Heileman v. Dakan, 211 Iowa 344, 233 N.W. 542 (1930).

of the subject of the specific bequest, the specific bequest is, of course, adeemed. If the testator makes a living gift of other property with the intention of satisfying the specific bequest, it seems that satisfaction should occur, but there is little judicial authority for this result.

At common law there is authority for the proposition that a substantial living gift to a child of the testator who is a legatee is rebuttably presumed to be in satisfaction, in whole or in part, of the legacy if those who benefit under the will from the satisfaction are other children of the testator.[53] Suppose testator's will disposes of his entire estate to his children equally, and testator has three children. Testator makes a living gift of $50,000 to one child, without expressing any intention of satisfaction. Testator later dies with a net estate of $100,000. The legacy to the child who received the living gift has been presumptively satisfied, and the $100,000 would be divided equally between the other two children. The presumption is rebuttable by evidence that no satisfaction was intended. The obvious purpose of the presumption is to avoid disparate treatment of children.

Pre–1990 Uniform Probate Code § 2–612, which has been legislated in a number of states,[54] changes the law by requiring that the intention to satisfy be in writing, and permitting devises to be satisfied:

> Section 2–612. [Ademption by Satisfaction.]
>
> Property which a testator gave in his lifetime to a person is treated as a satisfaction of a devise to that person in whole or in part, only if the will provides for deduction of the lifetime gift, or the testator declares in a contemporaneous writing that the gift is to be deducted from the devise or is in satisfaction of the devise, or the devisee acknowledges in writing that the gift is in satisfaction. For purpose of partial satisfaction, property given during lifetime is valued as of the time the devisee came into possession or enjoyment of the property or as of the time of death of the testator, whichever occurs first.

It should be noted that the word "devise" is defined in the Code to include the testamentary gift of personal property as well as real property. Pre–1990 Uniform Probate Code § 2–612 does not provide explicitly for the application of satisfaction to the

---

53. Heileman v. Dakan, 211 Iowa 344, 233 N.W. 542 (1930); Colley v. Britton, 210 Md. 237, 123 A.2d 296 (1956); In re Hall's Will, 120 N.Y.S.2d 188 (Sur.1953), aff'd 284 App.Div. 1013, 135 N.Y.S.2d 295 (1954); Hayes v. Welling, 38 R.I. 553, 96 A. 843 (1916).

54. E.g., Fla.Stat.Ann. § 732.609; Minn.Stat.Ann. § 524.2–612; Mo.Ann. Stat. § 474.425; N.J.Stat.Ann. § 3B:3–46.

specific gift, but the language of the section is broad enough to include it, and the Comment in the Code to this section implies that result.

It should be noted that if the intention to satisfy must be evidenced by a writing to that effect, as in the Code, there can be no presumption of satisfaction arising merely from the fact that a substantial gift has been made to a child.

1990 Code § 2–609 dealing with satisfaction changes the pre-1990 Code section on the subject by permitting the testator to satisfy a bequest or devise to A by making a living gift to B which is intended to satisfy the bequest or devise to A. The 1990 Code provision also makes it explicit that if a legatee or devisee predeceases the testator, any living gift to her in full or partial satisfaction of her bequest or devise satisfies in the same fashion any substituted bequest or devise pursuant to the antilapse statute. The Comment to the section also states explicitly that specific bequests and devises are subject to satisfaction. In addition, the Comment states that living gifts in satisfaction may take the form of will substitutes such as the beneficiary of a life insurance policy or remainderman of a revocable trust.

SECTION 10. EXONERATION OF LIENS

When a will contains a specific devise, and at the testator's death there is a mortgage or other lien on the devised land, the question arises whether the devisee takes the land subject to and burdened by the lien or is entitled to the land free of the lien by having the debt paid from the general assets of the estate. The common law rule is that if the testator was personally liable on the debt, it is rebuttably presumed that the testator intended that the debt be paid from general estate assets, thereby enabling the devisee to have the land free of the lien.[55] If, however, the testator was not personally liable on the debt, as occurs when a purchaser acquires title to land which is subject to a mortgage but the purchaser does not personally assume the mortgage debt, the presumption that the specifically devised property is to be exonerated of the lien by payment from other estate assets does not apply.[56] The presumption of exoneration of the lien has been applied to

55. In re Estate of Dolley, 265 Cal. App.2d 63, 71 Cal.Rptr. 56 (1968); Eaton v. MacDonald, 154 Me. 227, 145 A.2d 369 (1958); In re Lienhart's Estate, 146 Neb. 821, 21 N.W.2d 749 (1946); Bethel v. Magness, 296 P.2d 792 (Okl.1956); In re Nawrocki's Estate, 200 Or. 660, 268 P.2d 363 (1954).

56. In re Estate of Brown, 240 Cal. App.2d 818, 50 Cal.Rptr. 78 (1966); Kent v. McCaslin, 238 Miss. 129, 117 So.2d 804 (1960); In re Taylor's Estate, 30 N.J.Super. 65, 103 A.2d 268 (1954).

liens on specifically bequeathed personalty as well as specific devises.[57]

The will may, of course, expressly provide that the debt is to be paid out of the specifically devised or bequeathed property. The executor is, however, ultimately responsible to pay the personal debts of the testator. If the specific devisee does not pay the lien debt, the executor may force the sale of the property and pay the debt from the proceeds.

There are circumstances which may rebut by implication the presumption of exoneration. If the lien was on the property when the will was executed and it is a long-term debt, it is inferable that the testator intended that the devise was burdened with the lien. If the lien debt is large, and the payment out of residuary assets would distort the apparent dispositive plan, it is inferable that the testator intended that the devise was burdened with the debt.[58]

In many states the presumption has been reversed by statute, and the specific devisee or legatee of property subject to a lien takes the property burdened by the lien, unless the will indicates otherwise.[59] Uniform Probate Code § 2–609, which is to this effect, is as follows:

Section 2–609. [Non-Exoneration.]

A specific devise passes subject to any mortgage interest existing at the date of death, without right of exoneration, regardless of a general directive in the will to pay debts.

Pre–1990 Uniform Probate Code § 2–603 makes it clear that § 2–609 is subject to a contrary expression of intention in the will. The 1990 Code does the same.

It is standard practice to include a directive in the will that the executor is to pay the testator's debts. Such language is not usually construed as a direction that the specific devisee is to take the property free of the lien.[60] Such language is routine and is not indicative of the testator's intent with respect to the payment of

---

57. Ashkenazy v. Ashkenazy's Estate, 140 So.2d 331 (Fla.App.1962); Lange v. Lange, 127 N.J.Eq. 315, 12 A.2d 840 (1940).

58. In re Tunison's Estate, 75 F.Supp. 573 (D.D.C.1948); Ashkenazy v. Ashkenazy's Estate, 140 So.2d 331 (Fla. App.1962); Taylor's Executor v. Broadway Methodist Church, 269 Ky. 108, 106 S.W.2d 69 (1937); Kellam's Executors v. Jacob, 152 Va. 725, 148 S.E. 835 (1929).

59. E.g., Ariz.Rev.Stat.Ann. § 14–2609; Hawaii Rev.Stat. § 560:2–609; N.M.Stat.Ann. § 45–2–609; N.C.Gen.

Stat. § 28A–15.3; N.D.Cent.Code § 30.1–09–09.

60. Fidelity Union Trust Co. v. Laise, 142 N.J.Eq. 366, 60 A.2d 250 (1948); In re Ide's Will, 120 N.Y.S.2d 650 (Sur.1953); In re McNulta's Estate, 168 Wash. 397, 12 P.2d 389 (1932); In re Estate of Budd, 11 Wis.2d 248, 105 N.W.2d 358 (1960). There is contrary authority: In re Estate of Miller, 127 F.Supp. 23 (D.D.C.1955); Blansfield v. Bang, 20 Conn.Sup. 269, 131 A.2d 841 (1956).

lien indebtedness on specifically bequeathed or devised property. It should also be noted that such language in the will is surplusage because the executor is obligated by law to pay creditors' claims. Pre–1990 Uniform Probate Code § 2–609 and 1990 Code § 2–607 explicitly provide that such language has no bearing on the issue of exoneration.

SECTION 11.　ABATEMENT AND ALLOCATION OF DEATH TAXES

Suppose the testator's will contains a specific devise of Blackacre to Son, a general bequest of $100,000 to Daughter, and a residuary gift to Grandchildren. Blackacre has a value of $100,000, and the assets in the residue have a value of $300,000. Testator had debts of $50,000, and the expenses of administration, including but not limited to executor's and lawyer's fees, are $50,000. The gross estate is $500,000; the net estate (disregarding death taxes) is $400,000. From whose share are the debts and administration expenses paid?

In most states the debts and expenses are paid first from intestate property if there is partial intestacy, and if that is not sufficient, then from residuary property, and if that is not sufficient, then from general bequests and devises, and if that is not sufficient, then from specific bequests and devises.[61] All bequests and devises in the same category abate ratably. Uniform Probate Code § 3–902 provides for abatement in this way.

There is another position adopted in a few states which follows the pattern described in the preceding paragraph, except that within each category, such as residuary property, for example, the personalty is to be used first, and if that is insufficient, the realty is to be used.[62] There is still another view in effect in a few states that personalty in the estate is used first to pay debts and administration expenses, and only after that source is exhausted is land used.[63]

It should be noted that the order of abatement can be controlled by the testator in his will. That is to say, the testator could direct that certain categories of bequests or devises be used first to pay debts and expenses although it is inconsistent with the order otherwise applicable. The statutes of a number of states provide

61. E.g., Colo.Rev.Stat. § 15–12–902; Md.Est. & Trusts Code Ann. § 9–103; N.J.Stat.Ann. § 3B:22–3; N.C.Gen.Stat. § 28A–15–5; Wis.Stat.Ann. § 863.11.

62. Del.Code Ann. tit. 12, § 2317; Hawaii Rev.Stat. § 560:3–902; Kan. Stat.Ann. § 59–1405.

63. Mass.Gen.Laws Ann. ch. 202, § 1; Miss.Code Ann. § 91–7–91; W.Va. Code § 44–8–7.

that if the statutory order of abatement distorts the testator's dispositive plan, the court can make modifications in the order of abatement.

The issue of abatement also arises when a surviving spouse elects to take his statutory forced share of his spouse's estate. The forced share is discussed in Chapter 8, Section 2. It suffices for present purposes to state that in most states the spouse who has been disinherited by the will of his deceased spouse may claim a share of the estate, such as what he would receive on intestacy or a lesser amount. Uniform Probate Code § 2–207 and the statutes in many states provide that the burden of this claim is distributed pro rata among all the legatees or devisees,[64] but in a few states it is payable out of the residue, and if that is insufficient, out of general gifts, and if that is insufficient, out of specific gifts.[65]

The issue of abatement also arises when the pretermitted (omitted) child claims his share of his parent's estate. The pretermitted child's claim is discussed in Chapter 8, Section 6. It suffices for present purposes to state that in most states the child who is born after the execution of his parent's will and is not provided for and not referred to in the will can, in certain circumstances, claim his intestate share of the estate. In some states the claim is paid first out of the residue, and if that is inadequate, out of general gifts, and if that is inadequate, out of specific gifts.[66] Uniform Probate Code § 2–302 so provides. In other states the burden of the claim is distributed pro rata among all the legatees and devisees.[67]

Another form of abatement is the allocation of the burden of death taxes. Some states have inheritance taxes, which are theoretically imposed on the privilege of receiving property from the decedent. The inheritance tax is determined by the relationship of the legatee or devisee to the decedent, which rate may be 3% for gifts to children, and 10% for gifts to siblings, and 15% for gifts to nonrelatives, for the same size of gift. The federal death tax is an estate tax, as are the death taxes of some states. The estate tax is imposed theoretically upon the privilege of transfer by the decedent. The estate tax is on the estate as a whole and the rate of the tax is determined by the size of the estate. By statute most states apportion death taxes among those gifts which are subject to tax,

---

64. E.g., Ala.Code § 43–8–75; Me. Rev.Stat.Ann. tit. 18–A, § 2–207; Neb. Rev.Stat. § 30–2319; Or.Rev.Stat. § 114.165; Utah Code Ann. § 75–2–207.

65. E.g., Ark.Stat.Ann. § 28–53–107; Iowa Code Ann. § 633.436.

66. E.g., Ariz.Rev.Stat.Ann. § 14–2302; Colo.Rev.Stat. § 15–11–302;

Minn.Stat.Ann. § 524.2–302; Mont. Code Ann. § 72–2–602; Utah Code Ann. § 75–2–302.

67. E.g., Cal.Prob.Code § 6573; Ill. Ann.Stat. ch. 110½, § 4–10; Mass.Gen. Laws Ann. ch. 191, § 25; N.J.Stat.Ann. § 3B:5–16; Wash.Rev.Code Ann. § 11.-12.090.

making allowances for gifts which qualify for marital or charitable deductions or exemptions, and variations in inheritance tax rates and other equitable considerations; Uniform Probate Code § 3–916 and the Uniform Estate Tax Apportionment Act, which are the same, so provide.[68]

The Internal Revenue Code §§ 2206 and 2207 provide that the federal estate tax attributable to life insurance or property subject to a general power of appointment is payable out of those assets. These federal statutory provisions would control, of course, over conflicting state law.

The testator may provide in the will that death taxes are to be paid from a specified category, such as the residue, which direction prevails over any provision for allocation otherwise applicable.

SECTION 12. MISCELLANEOUS CONSTRUCTIONAL QUESTIONS

Questions have arisen as to whether a gift to "children" includes adopted children or nonmarital children. The traditional common law view has been that the adopted child is included in the gift to "children" where the adoptive parent is the testator or donor;[69] if, however, the gift is by one other than the adoptive parent, the adopted child is not included[70] unless the adoption existed and was known to the testator or donor at the time the will was executed or the gift made, or there is other evidence of intention to include the adopted child.[71] The law, however, has changed on this question. Pre–1990 Uniform Probate Code § 2–611 provides that the adopted child is included in a class gift in a will if the adopted child is included in intestate succession, which she invariably is. The statutes of some states simply provide that the adopted child is a child for the purposes of all dispositive instruments.[72] There are also a number of recent cases which

68. E.g., Cal.Prob.Code § 20110; N.M.Stat.Ann. § 45–3–916; Utah Code Ann. § 75–3–916.

69. Parker v. Mullen, 158 Conn. 1, 255 A.2d 851 (1969); Stewart v. Lafferty, 12 Ill.2d 224, 145 N.E.2d 640 (1957); Sewall v. Roberts, 115 Mass. 262 (1874); In re Chemical Bank, 90 Misc.2d 727, 395 N.Y.S.2d 917 (1977). See Simes & Smith, Law of Future Interests § 724 (2d ed. 1956).

70. Morgan v. Keefe, 135 Conn. 254, 63 A.2d 148 (1948); Stewart v. Lafferty, 12 Ill.2d 224, 145 N.E.2d 640 (1957); Central Trust Co. v. Bovey, 25 Ohio St.2d 187, 267 N.E.2d 427 (1971).

71. In re Estate of Clancy, 159 Cal. App.2d 216, 323 P.2d 763 (1958); Whittle v. Speir, 235 Ga. 14, 218 S.E.2d 775 (1975); Mesecher v. Leir, 241 Iowa 818, 43 N.W.2d 149 (1950); Bullock v. Bullock, 251 N.C. 559, 111 S.E.2d 837 (1960); Estes v. Ruff, 267 S.C. 396, 228 S.E.2d 671 (1976); In re Estate of Breese, 7 Wis.2d 422, 96 N.W.2d 712 (1959).

72. E.g., Conn.Gen.Stat.Ann. 45–64a; Ill.Ann.Stat. ch. 110½ § 2–4; N.J.Stat.Ann. § 9:3–30; N.Y.Est.Powers & Trusts Law § 2–1.3; N.C.Gen.Stat. § 48–23; Pa.Stat.Ann. tit. 20, § 2514(7).

presume that the adopted child is included in the class gift.[73]

There has been a traditional common law presumption that the nonmarital child is not included in a gift to "children." [74] This presumption has been overcome in some cases by evidence that inclusion was intended.[75] In recent years the law has become more inclined to include the nonmarital child in the gift to "children." Pre–1990 Uniform Probate Code § 2–611 provides that in a will the nonmarital child is included among the "children" of a person if he is an intestate taker of that person, and in the case of the father, the nonmarital child has been openly treated as a child by the father. The nonmarital child is an intestate taker of the mother, and in some circumstances of the father. There have also been recent decisions which do away with the presumption against inclusion of the nonmarital child in the class designation.[76]

A stepchild is not included within the term "children" in a dispositive instrument unless there is evidence of intention to include her.[77]

The constructional rules concerning the inclusion or exclusion of adopted children, nonmarital children and stepchildren with respect to the class designation of "children" are also generally applicable with respect to class designations of "descendants," "issue," "grandchildren," "nieces and nephews," etc.

1990 Uniform Probate Code § 2–705 provides that the adopted child and the nonmarital child are generally included in dispositions to classes such as "children," "descendants," "nieces and nephews," etc., in wills, living trusts, and will substitutes. (Pre–1990 Code § 2–611 dealing with this constructional issue was concerned only with wills.) There are two qualifications to this 1990 Code provision. One is that if the testator, settlor or donor is not the natural parent of the child, such child is not considered to

---

73. McCaleb v. Brown, 344 So.2d 485 (Ala.1977); Estate of McCallen, 53 Cal.App.3d 142, 125 Cal.Rptr. 645 (1975); Elliott v. Hiddleson, 303 N.W.2d 140 (Iowa 1981); In re Trusts of Harrington, 311 Minn. 403, 250 N.W.2d 163 (1977); Estate of Sykes, 477 Pa. 254, 383 A.2d 920 (1978); Wheeling Dollar Savings & Trust Co. v. Hanes, 160 W.Va. 711, 237 S.E.2d 499 (1977).

74. Simes & Smith, Law of Future Interests § 724 (2d ed. 1956).

75. Meyer v. Rogers, 173 Kan. 124, 244 P.2d 1169 (1952); Old Colony Trust Co. v. Attorney General, 326 Mass. 532, 95 N.E.2d 649 (1950); Fiduciary Trust Co. v. Michou, 73 R.I. 190, 54 A.2d 421 (1947); In re Kaufer's Will, 203 Wis. 299, 234 N.W. 504 (1931).

76. Walton v. Lindsey, 349 So.2d 41 (Ala.1977); Powers v. Wilkinson, 399 Mass. 650, 506 N.E.2d 842 (1987); Will of Hoffman, 53 A.D.2d 55, 385 N.Y.S.2d 49 (1976); Estate of Dulles, 494 Pa. 180, 431 A.2d 208 (1981); In re Trust of Parsons, 56 Wis.2d 613, 203 N.W.2d 40 (1973). Restatement (Second) of Property, Donative Transfers § 25.2 provides that "children" includes nonmarital children.

77. Davis v. Mercantile Trust Co., 206 Md. 278, 111 A.2d 602 (1955); In re Estate of Goetzinger, 12 Misc.2d 197, 176 N.Y.S.2d 899 (1958). See Annot., 28 A.L.R.3d 1307 (1969).

be the child of his natural parent unless the child lived while a minor as a regular member of the household of that natural parent or of that natural parent's parent, brother, sister, spouse, or surviving spouse. Assume that T's will left his entire estate in trust to pay the income to Son for life, principal at Son's death to Son's descendants. Son and Sue had a child; Son and Sue never married and never lived together. Sue raised the child; Son never lived with the child. The child does not have an interest in the trust.

The other qualification to the generality of 1990 Code § 2–705 is as follows: If the testator, settlor or donor is not the adoptive parent of the child, the adopted child is not considered to be the child of the adoptive parent unless the adopted child lived while a minor, either before or after the adoption, as a regular member of the household of the adoptive parent. Assume that T's will left his entire estate in trust to pay the income to Daughter for life, principal at Daughter's death to Daughter's descendants. Daughter adopts a person aged 30, who was never a member of Daughter's household as a minor. That person does not have an interest in the trust. Case law has been mixed on facts of this nature.[78]

1990 Code § 2–705 also provides that dispositions in wills, living trusts and will substitutes that do not differentiate relationships by blood from those by affinity, such as "uncles," "aunts," "nieces," or "nephews," are construed to exclude relatives by affinity. The common law is unclear on this point. 1990 Code § 2–705 also provides that terms of relationship that do not differentiate relationships by the half-blood from those by the whole blood, such as "brothers," "sisters," "nieces," or "nephews," are construed to include both types of relationships. This is the likely result at common law as well.

1990 Code § 2–708 states that a disposition in a will, trust or will substitute to "descendants" or "issue" of a person passes to the members of that group who would take from such person in intestacy and in the shares they would take in intestacy. Assume that T devised his land to his "issue." T was survived by two sons, each of whom had three children who survived T. The two sons take the land equally. If one son was dead at T's death, the children of such son would each take one-sixth, and the living son would take one-half. This is consistent with the prevailing common law position. This and the other constructional rules of the

---

78. Adult adoptee included in class gift: Chichester v. Wilmington Trust Co., 377 A.2d 11 (Del.1977); Estate of Fortney, 5 Kan.App.2d 14, 611 P.2d 599 (1980); Evans v. McCoy, 291 Md. 562, 436 A.2d 436 (1981); Solomon v. Central Trust Co., 63 Ohio St.3d 35, 584 N.E.2d 1185 (1992). Adult adoptee not included in class gift: Cross v. Cross, 177 Ill.App.3d 588, 126 Ill.Dec. 801, 532 N.E.2d 486 (1988); Minary v. Citizens Fidelity Bank, 419 S.W.2d 340 (Ky. 1967).

1990 Code are subject, of course, to a finding of a different intention of the testator, settlor or donor.

1990 Code § 2–707 reforms the law of future interests by providing that the beneficiary of a future interest under a trust must survive to the time of distribution in order to take. Assume T's will left her entire estate in trust to pay the income to A for life, and upon A's death, to pay over the principal to B. A and B survived T; B predeceased A. The gift to B does not lapse because B survived T. The historical and contemporary conclusion is that there is no implied condition that B must survive A in order to take; B's remainder was indefeasibly vested, and at B's death the remainder is held by his estate. When A dies the property passes to those who are entitled to B's estate. The 1990 Code changes this result by making all future interests under trusts contingent upon survivorship by the beneficiary to the time of distribution. If the beneficiary predeceases the time of distribution, the 1990 Code provides for a substitute gift to the descendants (by representation) of the predeceased beneficiary who survive the time of distribution. If there are no such descendants, the interest fails. The implied condition of survivorship and the substitute gift are subject to a finding of a contrary intention of the testator or settlor.

It is made clear in the 1990 Code that the implied condition of survivorship to the time of distribution applies only to future interests under a trust, and does not apply to legal future interests in land. It is also made clear that there is no substitute gift in the event the holder of the legal future interest in land predeceases the time for distribution. Where legal interests in land are concerned, the common law conclusion is undisturbed. In the transfer of land to A for life, remainder to B, the future interest passes to B's estate if B predeceases A. The reason given for the difference in treatment has to do with the transferability of land titles. If the remainder is contingent upon survivorship and there is a substitute gift to descendants of the remainderman, it would be difficult to sell the fee during A's life because of the proliferation of interests. In the case of property held in trust, the trustee almost invariably has the power to sell the fee.

Chapter 7

WILL SUBSTITUTES

In 1989 and 1990 changes were made in certain sections of the Uniform Probate Code dealing with will substitutes. In this chapter there are references to the pre-1989 Uniform Probate Code, to the pre–1990 Uniform Probate Code, to the 1989 Uniform Probate Code, and to the 1990 Uniform Probate Code, to identify the provisions of the Code before and after the changes. There are also references to the Uniform Probate Code in instances in which no substantial change has been made by the 1989 and 1990 revisions. The reader is referred to the introduction to Chapter 2 for further information on the development of the Uniform Probate Code.

SECTION 1. INTRODUCTION

In the brief summary of wealth transmission in Chapter 1, it was pointed out that the transmission of wealth at death is a bifurcated process. Those assets owned by the decedent in his name solely, or as tenant in common with another, pass through formal estate administration, and are disposed of by the terms of the will or in accordance with the intestacy statute. A great deal of wealth, however, avoids formal estate administration by means of several conceptual devices frequently referred to collectively as will substitutes, and passes to individuals designated by the property owner in a relatively informal fashion. The principal will substitutes are joint tenancy property, joint and payable-on-death bank accounts, life insurance, and living trusts, all of which are discussed in this chapter.

The formalism and court oversight of traditional estate administration, including the probate of the will, the appointment of the personal representative to manage the estate, and the submission of accounts to the court, presumably serve the ends of assuring that the intended beneficiaries of the wealth are properly identified and receive what they are entitled to, that the creditors are paid, and that the government receives its death taxes. Why, then, does the law permit the alternative informal method of wealth transmission, which does not involve probate or the appointment of a personal representative or the submission of accounts, but simply allows property to pass directly by informal designation of the recipient? The answer is that no one planned it this way; it simply evolved. There is no evidence that transmission without administration is tainted by any more fraud than transmission by formal administration. It should be noted that will substitutes are usually subject to death taxation. The forced share of the surviving spouse, however, may not apply to the will substitute, and creditors of the decedent may not be able to reach the will substitute.

It should be pointed out that there are certain living transfers which to the untutored eye appear to be testamentary in nature but are not. If a person has the power to possess and transfer certain property up to the time of his death, his disposition of that property at his death is testamentary in nature. In such case he can dispose only by will or by one of the recognized will substitutes. A person may, however, during his lifetime make an irrevocable transfer of an interest in property which does not become possessory in the transferee until the death of the transferor. Such a transfer is not testamentary in nature. An example is as follows: Owner irrevocably transfers corporate stock to Bank, as trustee, to pay the income to Owner for his life, and upon his death, to pay the principal of the trust outright to Owner's descendants then living. Note that the trust is irrevocable. Owner made a living transfer of the descendants' future interest. The transfer of the future interest is made when the trust is created but the future interest does not become a possessory, or present, interest until Owner's death. Owner gave up all control of the principal when he created the trust. If the trust had been revocable, but Owner had not revoked during his life, Owner would have retained the power to possess and dispose until his death because he could have taken the property back at any time and have done with it as he wished. The provisions of the revocable trust which dispose of the property after Owner's death are testamentary in nature. The revocable trust is a valid will substitute.

The first category of will substitute to be considered is the joint tenancy of which the salient characteristic is the right of survivorship which avoids estate administration.

SECTION 2.   JOINT TENANCY AND
TENANCY BY THE ENTIRETY

Joint tenancy, tenancy by the entirety, and tenancy in common are the three principal common law forms of concurrent ownership and they are still with us. There is also community property, a form of concurrent ownership that was not part of the common law but rather derived from the civil law of the European continent, which exists in nine states. We deal with that topic in Chapter 8, Section 7. Business partners also hold property in a form of concurrent ownership which is beyond the scope of this book. Joint tenancy, tenancy in common and tenancy by the entirety share certain characteristics but differ markedly in several respects. Our focus here is on joint tenancy and tenancy by the entirety because of their survivorship characteristic. There is no survivorship aspect to the tenancy in common. We discuss first the joint tenancy.

In most states two or more persons may own personalty or realty as joint tenants. As a practical matter, almost invariably only two people own property as joint tenants, usually husband and wife or two close family members. Each joint tenant has an equal undivided interest in the whole of the property. If it is land, each grain of earth is owned by the joint tenants concurrently, and if it is a certificate for 100 shares of corporate stock, each share represented by the certificate is owned by the joint tenants concurrently. A joint tenant cannot claim any part of the property as his exclusively to do with as he pleases. As a practical matter, if it is land to be farmed or lived on, the use or occupancy is shared, or some agreement exists as to the use or occupancy by one of the joint tenants or the property is rented to others. If it is stocks or bonds, the dividend and interest checks are payable to all the joint tenants and the checks cannot be negotiated without the endorsement of all.

Since almost all joint tenancies are held by only two people, usually husband and wife or two close family, the remainder of this discussion assumes a two-person joint tenancy to simplify the discussion. The salient characteristic of the joint tenancy is the right of survivorship. Upon the death of a joint tenant his interest disappears and becomes the property of the surviving joint tenant. This occurs by operation of law; it inheres in the nature of the joint tenancy. There is no need for an instrument of transfer. If there are two joint tenants to begin with, the survivor becomes absolute owner of the property in fee. The interest which moves from the deceased former joint tenant to the survivor does not pass through formal estate administration, thereby avoiding delay in transmission and expense of administration. This characteristic makes the joint tenancy attractive.

It should be noted that the original Uniform Simultaneous Death Act (promulgated in 1940), which has been enacted in almost all states, provides that if it cannot be established which joint tenant survived, one-half of the property passes to the estate of each joint tenant. The 1991 Uniform Simultaneous Death Act, and 1990 Uniform Probate Code § 2–702, provide that if it cannot be established that one joint tenant survived the other by 120 hours, one-half of the property passes to the estate of each joint tenant.

While the joint tenants are living, either of them can transfer his interest as joint tenant to another. This transfer, however, brings about a transformation of the title in the property from a joint tenancy to a tenancy in common. The transferee and the other erstwhile joint tenant are now tenants in common. This transformation through transfer by one joint tenant is called severance of the joint tenancy. It is a function of the violation of the requisite "four unities" of the joint tenancy, which feudal hangover need not concern us here.[1] The tenancy in common is a form of concurrent ownership which has in many respects the same characteristics as the joint tenancy but the salient difference is that the tenancy in common does not have the survivorship aspect. When one tenant in common dies, his undivided interest passes to his estate. Another difference between the joint tenancy and the tenancy in common is that joint tenants must own equal undivided interests, whereas tenants in common may own unequal undivided interests. One tenant in common may own a one-third interest and the other tenant a two-thirds interest; this unequal division is impermissible in the joint tenancy. Severance of a joint tenancy occasionally happens with land, but virtually never occurs with respect to stocks or bonds because there is no market for an undivided interest in stocks and bonds. It should also be noted that the creditors of a joint tenant can levy upon his interest, the purchaser at the execution sale becoming a tenant in common with the other tenant.

Each joint tenant has the right to partition the property. What this means is that each is entitled to terminate the joint tenancy and the concurrent ownership and take his share in the form of an individually owned portion. If land is involved the joint tenant can obtain a judicial decree granting him individual ownership in fee of a specified portion of the land which represents 50% of the total value. If stocks or bonds are involved, each joint tenant is entitled to a judgment awarding him one-half the shares or the bonds in the form of individual ownership. If the property does not lend itself to partition in kind, as is sometimes the case with land, the court will order the sale of the whole and the division of the proceeds. The joint tenants can, of course, partition voluntarily without judicial action, but one joint tenant cannot partition unilaterally by self-help.

When a joint tenant dies, as we have said, his interest moves to the survivor without an instrument of transfer or estate administration. That interest which passes is not subject to the claims of the deceased joint tenant's creditors. During that joint tenant's life his interest could be reached by his creditors, but at his death his interest disappears, so there is nothing for the creditors to reach. Under the traditional forced share statute for the surviving spouse the interest that passes at the joint tenant's death is not

---

1. See 2 American Law of Property § 6.1 (Casner ed. 1952).

subject to the forced share rights of his spouse, but under the Uniform Probate Code § 2–201 it may be subject to the forced share; the forced share is discussed in Chapter 8, section 2. The interest that passes at the joint tenant's death may be subject to death taxation, depending on circumstances.

The joint tenancy can be created in most jurisdictions, but a few states have statutes which prohibit its creation except for fiduciaries. In general, a transfer to individuals as concurrent owners creates a tenancy in common unless it is clearly expressed that a joint tenancy is intended, except that executors and trustees are presumed to hold as joint tenants.

It should be emphasized that the joint tenancy interest that passes on the death of the first to die is in the nature of a testamentary transfer. The joint tenant retains full control over his interest until the time of his death. He can transfer it by sale or gift, and he can partition, in each instance depriving the other joint tenant of his survivorship right in that interest. If there is no transfer or partition prior to death, the interest passes to the surviving tenant by the nature of the joint tenancy. The movement of the interest to the surviving tenant is, in effect, a testamentary transfer by the deceased tenant.

The survivorship aspect of the joint tenancy has been applied in modern times to the joint bank account, which is discussed in the next section. The joint bank account, however, is not a true joint tenancy; this has caused problems with respect to the survivorship aspect and brought about legislation to validate it.

It is reiterated that the tenancy in common is not treated here as a separate topic because it is not a form of will substitute. The interest of a tenant in common passes through estate administration.

The tenancy by the entirety is a form of concurrent ownership which is limited to husband and wife. Like the joint tenancy, it has the survivorship characteristic. It is recognized in less than half the states. In some states it is applicable only to real property.[2]

In the tenancy by the entirety each spouse has an equal undivided interest in the whole of the property. If it is land, each grain of earth is owned concurrently, and if it is a certificate for 100 shares of corporate stock, each share represented by the certificate is owned concurrently. A tenant by the entirety cannot claim any part of the property as his or hers exclusively to do with as he or she pleases. Upon the death of the first to die the interest of the decedent disappears and becomes the property of the survivor.

2. See Cunningham, Stoebuck and Whitman, Law of Property 203, 208 (2d ed. 1993).

This occurs by operation of law; it inheres in the nature of the tenancy by the entirety. There is no need for any instrument of transfer. The interest of the deceased tenant does not pass through estate administration.

In most jurisdictions the husband or the wife cannot separately transfer his or her interest to a third party, nor may a creditor of one of them reach his or her interest in the property. Acting together, however, husband and wife can convey the title to the property or mortgage it, and if both are liable on a debt the creditor can reach the property. In a few states the husband or the wife may separately transfer his or her interest, and a creditor of one of them can reach his or her interest. In such states the transferee stands in the shoes of the transferring tenant and becomes, in effect, a tenant by the entirety with the other tenant. The transfer does not transform the tenancy by the entirety into a tenancy in common. In such states the survivorship characteristic remains unimpaired by the transfer; upon the death of the first spouse to die, the surviving spouse, or his or her transferee, becomes the owner of the whole.

Neither tenant can compel partition of the tenancy by the entirety property. Acting together, however, they can partition if they choose.

It should be apparent from the above discussion that once a tenancy by the entirety is established, neither tenant can unilaterally change its characteristics. There is no right of partition, and the right of survivorship is indestructible. Of course, the parties can join to do whatever they like with the property. In all jurisdictions the creditors at the death of the first spouse to die cannot reach the interest that passes to the survivor.

It should be noted that although the tenancy by the entirety is often loosely referred to as a will substitute, the transfer by operation of law of the decedent tenant's interest to the surviving tenant is not testamentary in nature. The tenant by the entirety does not have full control of his or her interest up to the time of his or her death as the joint tenant does. The tenant by the entirety does not have the right to partition, and he or she does not have the power to deny the other tenant his or her survivorship right. The survivorship right is indestructible. The tenant has the right to use but he or she does not control disposition. He or she is locked into survivorship when the property is received as a tenancy by the entirety. The determination of who takes at the death of the tenant has been placed beyond his or her control by action taken during his or her lifetime, i.e., the creation of the tenancy by the entirety.

SECTION 3. JOINT BANK ACCOUNTS AND PAYABLE–ON–DEATH PROVISIONS

The joint bank account in which two parties have the right to draw on the account usually provides that the survivor is entitled to the balance of the account on the death of the first to die. It resembles a joint tenancy, and it is obviously patterned after it, but it is not a joint tenancy. The fact that it is not a joint tenancy has created problems with respect to the validity of the survivorship provision.

Why is it not a joint tenancy? Let us assume A and B make deposits into their joint account, and they intend that each is to use the account for his needs and that the survivor should have the balance at the death of the first to die. The principal reason why this is not a joint tenancy in a chose in action (a claim against the bank) is that one depositor may properly draw out more than one-half the account. In a joint tenancy the interests must be equal.

Since it is not a joint tenancy, the survivorship aspect is legally questionable. Let us assume that A and B own the joint account, and that A has contributed 90% of the account. A then dies intestate; C is A's sole heir. If B is entitled to the balance in the account, on what theory is this rationalized? The joint account agreement which provides for the survivor to receive the account balance was not signed in accordance with the formalities for a will, so B's rights cannot be rationalized on that basis. As we said, it is not a joint tenancy. It is the contention of C, A's heir, that the survivorship provision of the agreement with the bank is ineffective to dispose of A's property at his death, so that portion of the balance which represents A's contribution, i.e., 90%, passes through A's intestate estate.

Some courts have come up with rationales to uphold the transfer to B at A's death. One is that A, B, and the bank contracted that B was to receive the balance in the account at A's death; the transfer to B was not an invalid testamentary disposition for failure to comply with requirements for a will, but rather a contractual payment triggered by A's death.[3] This is the same reasoning used by courts to uphold life insurance payments to beneficiaries; the payment by the life insurance company is not an invalid testamentary disposition for failure to comply with the requirements for a will, but rather a contractual payment triggered by the death of the insured.

3. Matter of Estate of Smith, 199 Kan. 89, 427 P.2d 443 (1967); Perry v. Leveroni, 252 Mass. 390, 147 N.E. 826 (1925); Eger v. Eger, 39 Ohio App.2d 14, 314 N.E.2d 394 (1974); Barbour v. First Citizens National Bank, 77 S.D. 106, 86 N.W.2d 526 (1957).

Another rationale that has been used is that the transfer to B at A's death is the product of an inter vivos gift. By entering into the joint bank account arrangement, A made a living gift to B of access to A's deposits while both lived, and A's contribution to the balance in the account at the time of A's death if B survives A.[4]

There have been cases in which A and B have entered into a joint bank account agreement with a survivorship provision, A is the sole contributor to the account, and the only reason for the account is to enable B to make withdrawals from the account to pay A's bills or for A's benefit in other respects. There is no intention that the balance is to pass to B on A's death. This form of account with its survivorship provision happened to have been chosen for their purpose, instead of a pure agency account which would have been precisely responsive to their needs. In these circumstances courts have denied B the balance at A's death.[5] There was no intention to make a gift to B, and there was no intention to contract for survivorship in accordance with the language contained in the bank's form.

There is now legislation in a large majority of states which validates the property interest of the surviving depositor, unless there is clear and convincing evidence that the depositors did not intend to create such a survivorship right,[6] and pre–1989 Uniform Probate Code § 6–104 so provides. 1989 Code § 6–212 also validates the property interest of the surviving depositor.

The validity of the survivorship interest as against the legatees or heirs of the deceased joint account party is one thing, but the rights of the creditors of the deceased party if his estate assets are insufficient is another. Pre–1989 Uniform Probate Code § 6–107 and the statutes of a number of states give those creditors access to the account, through the decedent's personal representative, to the extent of the decedent's net contribution if estate assets are insufficient.[7] 1989 Code § 6–215 is to the same effect, but § 6–211 creates a rebuttable presumption that in a husband and wife account the contributions are equal.

There is a further problem with respect to the joint bank account which is tangential to our concern here, and that has to do

4. Murgic v. Granite City Trust & Savings Bank, 31 Ill.2d 587, 202 N.E.2d 470 (1964); McLeod v. Hennepin County Savings Bank, 145 Minn. 299, 176 N.W. 987 (1920); Burns v. Nolette, 83 N.H. 489, 144 A. 848 (1929); Slepkew v. Robinson, 113 R.I. 550, 324 A.2d 321 (1974).

5. Matter of Estate of Schroeder, 74 Ill.App.3d 690, 30 Ill.Dec. 781, 393 N.E.2d 1128 (1979); Matter of Estate of Johnson, 27 Or.App. 461, 556 P.2d 969 (1976); Matter of Estate of Boots, 73 Wis.2d 207, 243 N.W.2d 225 (1976).

6. E.g., Conn.Gen.Stat.Ann. § 36–3; N.Y. Banking Law § 675; Or.Rev.Stat. § 708.616; Utah Code Ann. § 75–6–104; Va.Code § 6.1–125.5.

7. E.g., Ariz.Rev.Stat.Ann. § 14–6107; Colo.Rev.Stat. § 15–15–107; Minn.Stat.Ann. § 528.08; Neb.Rev.Stat. § 30–2707; Tex.Prob.Code Ann. § 442.

with the rights of the parties to the account while both are alive. The bank is usually protected by statute in honoring any withdrawal,[8] but the property rights of the depositors and the rights of their creditors are another issue. Pre–1989 Uniform Probate Code § 6–103 and the statutes of a number of states provide that their ownership is determined by their net contributions.[9] 1989 Code § 6–211 is to the same effect except that it creates a rebuttable presumption that in a husband and wife account the contributions are equal.

Whether or not the decedent's share of the account is subject to the surviving spouse's forced share depends on the statute or case law of the jurisdiction, as discussed in Chapter 8, Section 2. The decedent's share may be subject to federal estate taxation.

There is another type of bank account which may serve as a will substitute, the payable-on-death account. Here A opens an account in her name, with a provision that any balance at her death is payable to B if B survives A. While A lives, only A can withdraw; B has only a survivorship interest. A can close the account at anytime. This type of account with its survivorship provision is not patterned after the joint tenancy; it is a straightforward circumvention of the will and intestacy statutes. It is obviously testamentary in nature. In the absence of statute this survivorship provision is ineffective. Pre–1989 Uniform Probate Code § 6–104, 1989 Code § 6–212 and statutes in about half the states validate this type of survivorship provision.[10] At the decedent depositor's death, pre–1989 Uniform Probate Code § 6–107, 1989 Code § 6–215, and the statutes of many states provide that the decedent's creditors can reach the account, through the decedent's personal representative, if her estate has insufficient assets to pay her debts.[11] Whether or not the account is subject to the forced share of the depositor's surviving spouse is discussed in Chapter 8, Section 2. The account is subject to the federal estate tax.

The Uniform TOD Security Registration Act, promulgated in 1989, was incorporated into the Uniform Probate Code in that year (§§ 6–301 through 6–311). TOD stands for "transfer on death." These provisions of the Code validate a "transfer on death" provision in the registration of a security. It is the equivalent of a "payable-on-death" provision for a bank account. The security is

---

8. E.g., Del.Code Ann. tit. 5, § 923; Iowa Code Ann. § 524.806; Md.Fin.Inst. Code Ann. § 5–303; Mo.Ann.Stat. § 362.470; N.M.Stat.Ann. § 45–6–112; N.C.Gen.Stat. § 41–2.1.

9. E.g., Alaska Stat. § 13.31.015; Hawaii Rev.Stat. § 560:6–103; Idaho Code § 15–6–103; Me.Rev.Stat.Ann. tit. 18–A, § 6–103.

10. E.g., Ga.Code Ann. § 7–1–813; Ind.Code Ann. § 32–4–1.5–4; N.J.Stat. Ann. § 17:16I–5; N.M.Stat.Ann. § 45–6–104; N.D.Cent.Code § 30.1–31–04.

11. E.g., Colo.Rev.Stat. § 15–15–107; Hawaii Rev.Stat. § 560:6–107; Minn. Stat.Ann. § 528.08; Tex.Prob.Code Ann. § 442; Va.Code § 6.1–125.8.

registered in the name of the owner, Jones, and the registration provides that title passes to Smith at Jones' death. The designated death beneficiary must survive the owner. The "transfer on death" registration has no effect on Jones' title until her death. Jones can cancel or change the death beneficiary designation at any time. If Jones transfers the security during her life, the title passes free of the death beneficiary designation. "Security" is defined very broadly to include "a share, participation, or other interest in property, in a business, or in an obligation of an enterprise or other issuer, and includes ... a security account." The provisions of the 1989 Code do not deal with the rights of creditors of an insolvent decedent who owned securities so registered; 1989 Code § 6–309 states that the rights of creditors are to be determined under other laws of the state.

Pursuant to federal regulations, federal government bonds may be issued in the names of "A or B," which permits A or B to redeem or to receive payment upon presentation at maturity and gives the survivor full ownership. Regulations also provide for the issuance of federal government bonds in the names of "A, payable on death to B," which gives A full control while A lives, and if not redeemed or paid during A's life, gives B full ownership at A's death.[12] Clearly the latter form is testamentary in nature, since A has full dispositive power over the bond until her death. The former type is testamentary in nature also because either party can redeem at any time or receive payment at maturity or thereafter, and if she does not, full ownership passes to the other at her death. The "A or B" form is likely to be used in the situation in which A purchases and physically retains the bond, intending that B is to have it at A's death or possibly before. The "A or B" form is very different from joint tenancy because either is entitled to the proceeds as her own at any time. The federal regulations authorizing these forms of ownership and succession are deemed to preempt state law and are valid.[13]

Frequently parties enter into contracts with "payable-on-death" provisions, other than the bank accounts, securities and government bonds described above. Life insurance proceeds payable to a beneficiary upon the death of an insured is the most significant example, and the insurance beneficiary designation is clearly valid; life insurance is described in the next section.

Business partners sometimes contract that upon the death of one of them his interest shall pass to the other partner or partners,

12. 31 C.F.R. §§ 315.7, 315.37, 315.38, 315.70.

13. Yiatchos v. Yiatchos, 376 U.S. 306, 84 S.Ct. 742, 11 L.Ed.2d 724 (1964); Free v. Bland, 369 U.S. 663, 82 S.Ct. 1089, 8 L.Ed.2d 180 (1962); McKee v. Hassebroek, 337 F.2d 310 (10th Cir. 1964); Marcum v. Marcum, 377 S.W.2d 62 (Ky.1964).

or possibly to some third person. Promissory notes sometimes provide that upon the death of the payee the remaining amount due is cancelled or is payable to a designated party. Installment land contracts occasionally provide that if the purchase price has not been paid in full at the time of the seller's death, the remaining payments are to be made to a designated person. If such a provision for payment at death cannot be changed unilaterally by the person making the transfer, it seems that such provision is not testamentary in nature and should be upheld. Such a provision is testamentary in nature, however, if it is subject to change unilaterally by the person making the transfer, and accordingly it appears to be vulnerable. The case law on the validity of such contractual provisions is mixed, results are frequently unpredictable, and the reasoning of many of the cases leaves much to be desired.[14] Pre–1989 Uniform Probate Code § 6–201, which has been legislated in a number of states,[15] is a very broad validating provision as follows:

> Section 6–201. [Provisions for Payment or Transfer at Death.]
>
> (a) Any of the following provisions in an insurance policy, contract of employment, bond, mortgage, promissory note, deposit agreement, pension plan, trust agreement, conveyance or any other written instrument effective as a contract, gift, conveyance, or trust is deemed to be nontestamentary, and this Code does not invalidate the instrument or any provision:
>
>> (1) that money or other benefits theretofore due to, controlled or owned by a decedent shall be paid after his death to a person designated by the decedent in either the instrument or a separate writing, including a will, executed at the same time as the instrument or subsequently;
>>
>> (2) that any money due or to become due under the instrument shall cease to be payable in event of the death of the promisee or the promissor before payment or demand; or
>>
>> (3) that any property which is the subject of the instrument shall pass to a person designated by the

---

14. See Wilhoit v. People's Life Insurance Co., 218 F.2d 887 (7th Cir. 1955); Williams v. Williams, 438 So.2d 735 (Ala.1983); Valenzuela v. Anchonda, 22 Ariz.App. 332, 527 P.2d 109 (1974); Matter of Estate of Hillowitz, 22 N.Y.2d 107, 291 N.Y.S.2d 325, 238 N.E.2d 723 (1968); McCarthy v. Pieret, 281 N.Y. 407, 24 N.E.2d 102 (1939); In re Lewis' Estate, 2 Wash.2d 458, 98 P.2d 654 (1940); Juneau v. Dethgens, 200 Wis. 360, 228 N.W. 496 (1930).

15. E.g., Ariz.Rev.Stat.Ann. § 14–6201; Colo.Rev.Stat. § 15–15–201; Me. Rev.Stat.Ann. tit. 18–A, § 6–201; Mo. Ann.Stat. § 456.231; Wash.Rev.Code Ann. § 11.02.090.

decedent in either the instrument or a separate writing, including a will, executed at the same time as the
instrument or subsequently.

(b) Nothing in this section limits the rights of creditors
under other laws of this state.

The Comment to the above section is of interest, but it may
overstate the vulnerability of such provisions under existing case
law. The Comment reads, in part, as follows:

> This section authorizes a variety of contractual ar-
> rangements which have in the past been treated as testa-
> mentary. For example most courts treat as testamentary
> a provision in a promissory note that if the payee dies
> before payment is made the note shall be paid to another
> named person, or a provision in a land contract that if the
> seller dies before payment is completed the balance shall
> be cancelled and the property shall belong to the vendee.
> These provisions often occur in family arrangements. The
> result of holding the provisions testamentary is usually to
> invalidate them because not executed in accordance with
> the statute of wills. On the other hand the same courts
> have for years upheld beneficiary designations in life insur-
> ance contracts. Similar kinds of problems are arising in
> regard to beneficiary designations in pension funds and
> under annuity contracts. The analogy of the power of
> appointment provides some historical base for solving some
> of these problems aside from a validating statute. Howev-
> er, there appear to be no policy reasons for continuing to
> treat these varied arrangements as testamentary. The
> revocable living trust and the multiple-party bank ac-
> counts, as well as the experience with United States gov-
> ernment bonds payable on death to named beneficiaries,
> have demonstrated that the evils envisioned if the statute
> of wills is not rigidly enforced simply do not materialize.
> The fact that these provisions often are part of a business
> transaction and in any event are evidenced by a writing
> eliminate the danger of "fraud."

1989 Code § 6–101 is substantially the same as the pre–1989
Code provision; it does make explicit that it covers securities of all
kinds and employee benefit plans.

SECTION 4. LIFE INSURANCE

A life insurance policy is a contract in which the insurance
company ("insurer') promises to pay a certain amount ("proceeds")
to a designated person ("beneficiary") at the death of a named

person ("insured"), in consideration of payments ("premiums") made usually by the person who owns the rights under the policy ("owner"). The owner of the policy and the insured are usually the same person, because normally an individual takes out a policy on his own life. He may subsequently assign his rights in the policy, however, in which case the owner and the insured are different parties. Since the owner and the insured are usually the same person, we shall assume that is the case in our discussion.

There is a large variety of life insurance contracts that may be purchased, descriptions of which are beyond the scope of this book. There are, however, several basic categories that require mention. First, there is "term" insurance. This form of life insurance is for a specific term, such as five years. It is often written for successive five-year terms which are guaranteed to be renewable by the insured at his option until age 65 or 70, at increasing premiums for each successive term for the same amount of coverage. In the term policy the insured purchases life insurance only; that is to say, the policy does not build up any cash surrender value. When the insured opts out of the contract by ceasing to pay the premiums, or the policy expires when the insured reaches age 65 or 70, there is no residual value in the contract. If the insured dies when the policy is in effect, the insurance company pays the full amount of the policy to the beneficiary; when the policy comes to an end and the insured is alive, the insurer owes nothing. Term insurance is the least expensive form of life insurance.

There is a variety of insurance policies in which the insured purchases not only life insurance but also cash value in the policy. Probably the most common is the policy that is called "ordinary life," or "straight life," or "whole life." Here the insured pays a constant premium for the rest of his life for insurance of, let us say, $100,000, and at the same time he is building cash value. If the insured wishes to terminate the policy after a certain number of years, he is entitled to its cash value which equals at least a major portion of the premiums paid. The insured may keep the $100,000 policy in effect and borrow from the insurance company up to the amount of the cash value. If an insured should die with the $100,000 policy in effect, having a $25,000 cash value, the total amount payable by the insurance company is $100,000, less any amount borrowed against the cash value. Because of the asset value characteristic, the premiums in an ordinary life policy are considerably greater than the premiums for a term policy in the same face amount. The ordinary life policy is a form of saving as well as life insurance.

Another form of policy with cash value is the "endowment" policy. Here the cash value of the policy becomes equal to the face amount of the policy at a designated age well within the life expectancy of the insured, such as 60. If the policy is for $100,000, the cash value at age 60 is $100,000, and the insured is then entitled to his $100,000. Because of the accelerated build up of cash value, the premium for this type of policy is greater than for ordinary life. Actually the ordinary life policy has an "endowment" characteristic because at an age far beyond the life expectancy of the insured, such as 95, the cash value will equal the face amount of the policy.

The contract of life insurance invariably provides that the insured may change his beneficiary at any time. If it is a policy with cash value, the insured may at any time terminate the contract and take out the cash value. The insured retains full control during life and disposes of the property at death by means of the informal beneficiary designation. The disposition at death is testamentary in nature, but the validity of the beneficiary designation has been established for many years on contract theory and is now often confirmed by statute. The insured and the insurance company contract to pay a certain sum at the insured's death to a person designated by the insured.

If a designated beneficiary predeceases the insured, the beneficiary designation fails. Lapse statutes providing for substituted takers in the event certain legatees predecease a testator do not apply to predeceasing insurance beneficiaries. It is common practice to provide for alternative beneficiaries in the event of the death of a prior life insurance beneficiary. If there is no beneficiary to take, the proceeds pass to the insured's estate.

By statute in most states the proceeds of life insurance policies are exempt from the claims of the insured's creditors either entirely or up to a certain amount. Under some statutes the exemption applies only if the proceeds are payable to certain specified family members. Some statutes also exempt the cash value of a policy from claims of the insured's creditors during his life. Life insurance payable to a specific beneficiary (other than the insured's estate) is usually not subject to the surviving spouse's forced share. Life insurance in most instances is subject to federal estate taxation.

The fact that life insurance is often exempt from the claims of the insured's creditors should not be confused with the practice of using an insurance policy as collateral for a loan to the insured. The insured borrows from Bank and assigns his policy to Bank as security for the loan. Bank becomes the beneficiary of the policy and is secured in that respect, and also holds cash value as security if it is that type of policy. If the debt is paid when due, the policy is, of course, reassigned to the insured.

Usually the proceeds of the life insurance policy are payable in a lump sum on the death of the insured. However, policies invariably offer optional modes of payment which may be selected by the insured, or if he does not choose to do so, the beneficiary may do so. One optional mode may be the payment of the proceeds in installments over a fixed period; these payments will, of course, total more than the face amount of the policy because an interest element is added in the deferred mode of payment. Another settlement option is a lifetime annuity, i.e., periodic payments in a fixed amount for the life of the beneficiary. The beneficiary has, in effect, purchased an annuity contract with the proceeds of the policy. The annuity option may provide for guaranteed payments for a specified number of years to protect against the economic loss to the beneficiary that would result from extraordinarily premature death following the purchase of the contract. The beneficiary who selects an optional settlement may also designate a beneficiary of his own to receive whatever payments remain to be made if he dies before all the payments are made. This informal beneficiary designation is probably valid without compliance with the will formalities.

It should be mentioned that frequently employee pension plans provide for a death benefit if the employee dies before he retires or in some circumstances after he retires. The employee designates the beneficiary and usually is entitled to change the designation as he wishes. The beneficiary designation is probably valid without compliance with the will formalities.

Life insurance policies are sometimes the corpus of living trusts. This is discussed in Section 7 of this chapter.

SECTION 5. THE REVOCABLE TRUST

Settlor transfers to T, in trust, to pay the income to A for life, and upon A's death, to pay the principal to B; the settlor retains the power to revoke the trust at any time during his lifetime. The trust instrument is not executed with the formalities required for a will. The settlor dies without having revoked. A is alive at the settlor's death. Is the trust effective after the settlor's death, or are the trust terms viewed as an invalid testamentary disposition? The trust is effective prior to and after the settlor's death because it is viewed as an effective inter vivos transaction, despite the retention of the power of revocation. A living trust is irrevocable unless it is expressly provided that it is revocable. A testamentary trust, of course, is necessarily irrevocable.

It appears that the retention of the power of revocation is tantamount to ownership of the trust property, and therefore when the revocable trust settlor dies without having exercised his power, he was effectively the owner of the trust property to the moment of his death. But the law views the power of revocation differently. The conveyance in trust is a good inter vivos transfer, albeit subject to recall. This may be legal conceptualism divorced from reality, but that is how it is. It should be noted that the settlor may reserve the power to revoke the living trust at his death by his will as well as during his lifetime.

Suppose in the revocable trust example the life interest is in the settlor rather than in A. Does this make the revocable trust testamentary? The answer is no. The trust is still a valid inter vivos transfer. To digress for a moment, it should be emphasized that if the settlor transfers to T, in trust, to pay the income to the settlor for life, and to transfer the principal at settlor's death to B, and the trust is irrevocable, the trust is clearly not testamentary in nature. The settlor has retained a life interest, but he has during his life disposed of the remainder without reserving any power to change the disposition. The irrevocable living trust is not testamentary in nature because there is no retention of control of disposition until death, although there is retention of benefit until death.

If a settlor of a living trust reserves a power of revocation, is such power subject to the claims of his creditors? In the absence of statute, the answer usually is no.[16] The power of revocation is not "property" of the settlor. Once again, we encounter conceptualism divorced from economic reality. Many states, however, have statutes which subject the power of revocation to the claims of the settlor's creditors.[17] It should be noted that if the settlor retains a beneficial interest in the trust, that interest is subject to the claims of his creditors. If the power of revocation is subject to the claims of the settlor's creditors by statute, there is the further issue as to whether the creditors can reach the trust assets after his death, as well as during his life, if he never revokes. This will, of course, depend on the language of the statute and how it is construed.[18] It

16. Hill v. Cornwall & Bros., 95 Ky. 512, 26 S.W. 540 (1894); Guthrie v. Canty, 315 Mass. 726, 53 N.E.2d 1009 (1944). However, Restatement (Second) of Property, Donative Transfers § 13.3 (1984) subjects the power of revocation to the claims of settlor's creditors.

17. E.g., Minn.Stat.Ann. § 502.76; N.Y.Est. Powers & Trusts Law § 10–10.6; Ohio Rev.Code Ann. § 1335.01; S.D.Comp.Laws Ann. § 43–11–17.

18. See Granwell v. Granwell, 20 N.Y.2d 91, 281 N.Y.S.2d 783, 228 N.E.2d

779 (1967); Schofield v. Cleveland Trust Co., 135 Ohio St. 328, 21 N.E.2d 119 (1939). In State Street Bank & Trust Co. v. Reiser, 7 Mass.App.Ct. 633, 389 N.E.2d 768 (1979), without a statute the court held that the settlor's creditors could reach the trust assets after his death. See also ITT Commercial Finance Corp. v. Stockdale, 25 Mass.App. Ct. 986, 521 N.E.2d 417 (1988). Restatement (Second) of Property, Donative Transfers § 34.3 (1992) permits creditors of settlor of revocable trust to reach trust assets at settlor's death.

also appears that if the settlor is placed in bankruptcy, his power of revocation is included in the bankruptcy estate.[19]

The revocable trust may be subject to the surviving spouse's forced share. It is subject to federal estate taxation.

SECTION 6. THE BANK ACCOUNT TRUST

Suppose Jones declares himself trustee of 1,000 shares of his General Motors common stock, to accumulate the income for his life, and upon his death, to pay the principal and accumulated income to his son, Bob, if he survives Jones. In the trust instrument Jones reserves the power to revoke the trust in whole or in part at any time and from time to time. The trust instrument also provides that Jones can contribute additional assets to the trust at any time and from time to time.[20] There would be no question in most jurisdictions that this trust is valid.[21]

Let us change the facts somewhat. Jones places $50,000 in an account with a bank. The bank form which Jones signs when he opens the account states that he is trustee for his son Bob, who may withdraw whatever is left in the account at Jones' death. It is provided that Bob must survive Jones in order to be entitled to withdraw. If Bob predeceases Jones, the trust terminates because the entire legal and equitable interests are in Jones.[22] The agreement with the bank also allows Jones to withdraw, at any time and from time to time, all or any part of the balance in the account, and to make additional deposits to the account at any time and from time to time. The trust property is the claim against the bank in the amount of the balance from time to time.

Does the bank account trust differ in any substantial respect from the trust of General Motors shares? It appears not. In each case Jones has made a declaration of trust to accumulate the income and to pay the accumulated income and principal to his son at his death, reserving the power of revocation and providing for future contributions to the trust. If it is concluded that what

19. 11 U.S.C.A. § 541 (Bankruptcy Code of 1978).

20. It is common to provide for additions of trust property. Does each addition technically constitute a new trust on the same terms? Clearly the intention is that the original trust property and all additions are one trust, and that is the legal result. See 2A Scott, Law of Trust § 179.2 (4th ed., Fratcher, 1987).

21. Jones, as trustee, would be considered to hold the legal fee, as discussed in Section 8 of Chapter 5. If Jones held only a legal life estate for his own life as trustee, Bob's future interest would be a legal future interest, and would be testamentary and probably invalid because of Jones' reserved power to revoke it up to the time of his death.

22. Jones would hold the legal fee in trust, and there would be no equitable interest other than his own as equitable reversioner.

purports to be a trust of the savings account is not a trust, then upon Jones' death the bank balance passes to Jones' estate.[23]

Some courts have held that a trust is not created in the savings account situation.[24] The reason for this is that it has been questionable to them that Jones intends to create a trust when he signs the bank form, although the bank form says that he is a trustee. Jones gives up no control of the money and may not consider that he is making any kind of property transfer to his son or that he is making himself a fiduciary when he opens the account. Jones may look upon it merely as a type of will which leaves his bank balance to his son, without complying with the statutory formalities for a will. It is the rather casual manner in which the transaction is accomplished that casts doubt upon Jones' intention to create a living trust.

The modern tendency, however, is for the courts to hold that a revocable trust is created in this situation.[25] In addition pre–1989 Uniform Probate Code § 6–104, 1989 Code § 6–212 and the statutes of many states, now validate bank account trusts.[26] The bank account trust is functionally the same as the payable-on-death bank account.

Pre–1989 Uniform Probate Code § 6–107, 1989 Code § 6–215, and the statutes of a number of states subject bank account trust assets to the claims of the decedent-settlor's creditors if his estate assets are insufficient.[27] The trust assets may be subject to the surviving spouse's forced share. The trust assets are subject to federal estate taxation.

SECTION 7. THE LIFE INSURANCE TRUST

If the owner of a life insurance policy wishes to have the proceeds of the policy at his death held in trust, he can designate his estate as beneficiary and provide for a trust in his will. He may

23. In the absence of a living trust, the "remainder" in Bob is an invalid attempt to dispose of property at death without a will because of Jones' retention of the power to retake the property to the time of his death. A statute which validates payable-on-death bank accounts should, of course, permit Bob to take in any event.

24. Stamford Savings Bank v. Everett, 132 Conn. 92, 42 A.2d 662 (1945); Estate of Hoffman, 175 Ohio St. 363, 195 N.E.2d 106 (1963); Fleck v. Baldwin, 141 Tex. 340, 172 S.W.2d 975 (1943). See Underwood v. Bank of Huntsville, 494 So.2d 619 (Ala.1986).

25. Estate of Petralia, 32 Ill.2d 134, 204 N.E.2d 1 (1965); Blue Valley Federal Savings v. Burrus, 617 S.W.2d 111 (Mo.App.1981); Byrd v. Lanahan, 105 Nev. 707, 783 P.2d 426 (1989); Estate of Stokes, 747 P.2d 300 (Okl.1987); Estate of McFetridge, 472 Pa. 546, 372 A.2d 823 (1977); Estate of Adams, 155 Vt. 517, 587 A.2d 958 (1990).

26. E.g., Cal.Prob.Code § 5302; Ga. Code Ann. § 7–1–813; Hawaii Rev.Stat. § 560:6–104; Ind.Code Ann. § 32–4–1.5–4; N.J.Stat.Ann. § 17:16I–5.

27. E.g., Ind.Code Ann. § 32–4–1.5–7; Minn.Stat.Ann. § 528.08; Neb.Rev. Stat. § 30–2707; Tex.Prob.Code Ann. § 442; Va.Code § 6.1–125.8.

prefer, however, to have the insurance proceeds held in trust without passing through estate administration. This can be accomplished by creating an inter vivos life insurance trust.

There are several types of inter vivos life insurance trusts. Let us examine first the "thinnest" form of life insurance trust. The settlor enters into a trust agreement with Bank, as trustee, which provides that Bank is to be designated as beneficiary under three life insurance policies of the settlor in which the settlor's life is insured in amounts totalling $200,000. The trust agreement provides that Bank is to receive the proceeds at the settlor's death and hold the proceeds in trust to pay the income to the settlor's son for his life and upon the son's death, to pay the principal to the son's children who survive the son. The settlor retains title to and possession of the policies, and reserves the power of revocation. It is understood that the settlor has the responsibility for paying the insurance premiums. The trustee has nothing to do while the settlor is alive.

In order for there to be a living trust, there must be a transfer of property to the trustee. What does the Bank hold in trust during the settlor's life? The beneficiary of a life insurance policy has a contract right; that is to say, under the contract with the insurance company the beneficiary has the right to the proceeds upon the death of the insured. It is this contract right which is deemed to be the trust property.[28] The beneficiary of a life insurance policy usually can be changed at any time by the owner of the policy, but until this is done the beneficiary has a contract right, however tenuous it may be. In the case of this life insurance trust, the settlor would revoke the trust and change the beneficiary simultaneously if he changed his mind about having a trust.

The insurance trust we have just described is referred to as a revocable, unfunded life insurance trust. The term "unfunded" refers to the fact that the trustee has not been given the funds to pay the premiums under the policy. It should be noted that in this type of trust it is likely that the settlor will give the Bank possession of the policies at the creation of the trust, but it is not necessary that this be done.

Now let us examine the most "substantial" life insurance trust. The settlor and Bank enter into a trust agreement in which the settlor irrevocably transfers to Bank, in trust, possession of and

---

28. Rosen v. Rosen, 167 So.2d 70 (Fla.App.1964); Gurnett v. Mutual Life Insurance Co., 356 Ill. 612, 191 N.E. 250 (1934); Connecticut General Life Insurance Co. v. First National Bank, 262 N.W.2d 403 (Minn.1977); Gordon v. Portland Trust Bank, 201 Or. 648, 271 P.2d 653 (1954); Brault v. Bigham, 493 S.W.2d 576 (Tex.Civ.App.1973). A number of states have statutes which validate this form of trust, e.g., Fla.Stat. Ann. § 733.808; Mo.Ann.Stat. § 456.-030; N.C.Gen.Stat. § 36A–100; Tenn. Code Ann. § 35–50–103; Wash.Rev.Code § 48.18.450.

title to three life insurance policies insuring the settlor's life in the total amount of $200,000. Bank is, of course, made beneficiary of the policies as well. The settlor also transfers to Bank, in trust, cash or other assets sufficient to pay all remaining premiums on the policies. Bank is to receive the life insurance proceeds at the settlor's death as trustee and is to pay the income therefrom to the settlor's son for his life, and to pay the principal to the son's children who survive the son. In this living trust the trust property consists originally of the life insurance contracts and the assets for paying the premiums. The trust property subsequently takes the form of the $200,000 insurance proceeds. During the settlor's life the trustee holds the policies, invests the funds held to pay the premiums, and pays the premiums when due. This type of insurance trust is called an irrevocable, funded life insurance trust. The term "funded" refers to the fact that the settlor has furnished the Bank with the funds to pay the premiums on the policies.

The life insurance trust may take somewhat different forms from the ones we have described. For instance, the settlor may transfer title to the policies irrevocably but not transfer to the trustee the funds for paying the premiums. Or the settlor may transfer title to the policies and the funds for the premiums but reserve the power of revocation.

There is another technique which may be available for placing life insurance proceeds in trust. Suppose Jones owns an insurance policy on his life and designates as the beneficiary of the policy, "the trustee under my will admitted to probate." Jones dies leaving a valid will in which his entire estate is left to Bank in trust. Do the insurance proceeds pass to the executor of Jones' estate to be administered with the other probate assets and to be ultimately distributed to the testamentary trustee if the probate estate is solvent? Or do the insurance proceeds bypass probate administration and go directly to the trustee under the will? The intention is to bypass probate administration and have the insurance proceeds paid directly to the testamentary trustee as insurance beneficiary. It has not been clear under case law that probate administration of the insurance proceeds could be avoided by this means.[29] A number of states have enacted statutes, however, which provide that such a beneficiary designation avoids probate

---

29. See Pavy v. Peoples Bank & Trust Co., 135 Ind.App. 647, 195 N.E.2d 862 (1964); Frost v. Frost, 202 Mass. 100, 88 N.E. 446 (1909); Prudential Insurance Co. v. Bloomfield Trust Co., 104 N.J.Eq. 372, 145 A. 735 (1929); Bellinger v. Bellinger, 180 Misc. 948, 46 N.Y.S.2d 263 (1943). The following cases tend to support the technique: United States v. First National Bank & Trust Co., 133 F.2d 886 (8th Cir.1943); Boston Safe Deposit & Trust Co. v. Commissioner, 100 F.2d 266 (1st Cir. 1938); Prudential Insurance Co. v. Gatewood, 317 S.W.2d 382 (Mo.1958).

and passes the insurance proceeds directly to the trustee under the will.[30]

SECTION 8. SURVIVORSHIP; LAPSE; REVOCATION BY DIVORCE; DISCLAIMER

(a) Survivorship

1990 Uniform Probate Code § 2–702 provides that an individual who is required to survive the death of another person, or any other event, under the terms of the Code or the terms of any instrument such as a deed, will, trust, insurance policy, or payable-on-death designation, must survive the person or event by 120 hours, and if he does not, he is deemed to have predeceased the person or event. In the case of a joint tenancy, tenancy by the entirety, and joint and survivorship bank account, if the survivor does not survive for 120 hours, one-half the property passes to the estate of each party. This survivorship requirement is subject to the terms of the instrument which explicitly deals with the matter in a different way. This provision also specifically excludes from its coverage securities which have a TOD (transfer on death) beneficiary designation. Pre–1990 Code § 2–601 contained a 120–hour survivorship provision for legatees and devisees under wills; the 1990 Code provision extends this to other forms of disposition.

(b) Lapse

1990 Uniform Probate Code § 2–706 contains antilapse provisions for death beneficiary designations under life insurance policies, annuity policies, payable-on-death accounts, securities with TOD (transfer on death) registration, pension plans, and other employee benefit plans, which are substantially the same as those applicable to legatees and devisees under a will as set forth in 1990 Code § 2–603. If a death beneficiary fails to survive the decedent (or is deemed to have failed to survive), and is a grandparent, a descendant of a grandparent, or a stepchild of the decedent, and the death beneficiary is survived by descendants who survive the decedent, such descendants of the death beneficiary take by representation what the death beneficiary would have taken had he survived the decedent.

At common law and by statute death beneficiaries under most will substitutes are required to survive the decedent in order to take; if the death beneficiary predeceases the decedent, the beneficiary designation fails and the property passes to the estate of the decedent unless there is an alternative designation of a beneficiary who survives the decedent. The 1990 Code provision reforms the

---

30. E.g., Ohio Rev.Code § 2107.64; tit. 20, § 6108; W.Va.Code § 44–5–11; N.C.Gen.Stat. § 36A–100; Pa.Stat.Ann. Wis.Stat.Ann. § 701.09.

law significantly by providing for a substitute gift in the event the death beneficiary predeceases the decedent if the beneficiary has the requisite relationship to the decedent.

The antilapse provision for will substitutes does not apply if it appears that it would be contrary to the intention of the person who created the will substitute. The prevailing position in wills law is that a devise or bequest to "Jones, if he survives me," is a sufficient expression of intention that the antilapse statute is not to apply. 1990 Code § 2–603 dealing with antilapse for wills provides that such language is not a sufficient indication of an intention to negate the antilapse statutory provision; 1990 Code § 2–706 has the same provision with respect to death beneficiaries under will substitutes.

Suppose the death beneficiary designation is to "A, if he survives me, or if not, to B." A and B are children of the decedent, and both predecease the decedent leaving children who survive the decedent. 1990 Code § 2–706 provides expressly that in this situation A's children take the substitute gift rather than B's children; if B had survived the decedent, however, B would take.

(c) Revocation By Divorce

1990 Code § 2–804 provides that by operation of law a divorce revokes any provision in a will, living trust, or will substitute made by the divorced person for the benefit of her former spouse, unless the express terms of the instrument provide otherwise. In addition, the divorce revokes any provision in a will, living trust or will substitute made by the divorced person for the benefit of a relative of the former spouse. "Relative" is defined to include an individual who is related to the divorced person's former spouse by blood, adoption or affinity, and who after the divorce is not related to the divorced person by blood, adoption or affinity. In most states divorce has no effect upon beneficiary designations under will substitutes.

1990 Code § 2–804 also provides that a divorce transforms a joint tenancy between husband and wife, and a tenancy by the entirety, into a tenancy in common. In most states today divorce has no effect upon a joint tenancy.

(d) Disclaimer

1990 Code § 2–801 is the Uniform Disclaimer of Property Interests Act which covers disclaimers (renunciations) of testamentary and intestate interests and disclaimers of interests under nontestamentary instruments (will substitutes). Disclaimer of testamentary and intestate interests is discussed in Chapter 2, Section

7. There are complex provisions for the timing and manner of making the disclaimer of interests under nontestamentary instruments. If the disclaimer is made, the interest passes as if the disclaimant predeceased the effective date of the instrument, and if the antilapse statute applies, the disclaimed interest passes to the disclaimant's descendants.

Chapter 8

LIMITATIONS UPON DISPOSITIVE POWER

In 1990 changes were made in certain sections of the Uniform Probate Code dealing with limitations upon the dispositive power. In this chapter there are references to the pre–1990 Uniform Probate Code (or pre–1990 Code) and to the 1990 Uniform Probate Code (or 1990 Code). There are also references to the Uniform Probate Code in instances in which no substantial change has been made by the 1990 revision. The reader is referred to the introduction to Chapter 2 for further information on the development of the Uniform Probate Code.

Ownership of property may be defined as the protection by the state of use and transferability. This use and transferability, however, is not absolute. Nuisance, environmental and zoning laws restrict the use of land in the interest of certain societal objectives. The law restricts donative transferability of personal and real property in the interest of several societal objectives. That is the subject of this chapter. One objective is the protection of the immediate family of the decedent. Another objective is the protection of beneficiaries from the imposition by the decedent of conditions to their taking which are considered contrary to public policy. Another is the limitation upon the period of time that a donor or testator can exercise control over who shall own his property. First we deal with the protection of family.

SECTION 1. DOWER

In the common law property system the wife was protected from disinheritance by dower. Dower is a property interest which attaches by operation of law to all real property owned in fee or fee tail by the husband during the marriage. While the husband is alive, dower provides the wife no possessory interest in or other benefit from the land to which it attaches. If the wife predeceases the husband, dower becomes a nullity. If, however, the husband dies survived by the wife, she is entitled to a possessory life estate in one-third of the land to which dower attached. The court determines what form this possessory dower is to take; the widow is assigned a specific portion of the land if practicable, or if the land does not lend itself to division, she may be given one-third of the income from the land.

The wife's dower interest is not subject to the claims of the husband's creditors during his life or at his death. Once dower attaches there is nothing the husband can do without the wife's consent to get rid of it. Any transferee of the husband's interest, by voluntary sale or gift or by execution sale pursuant to a judgment against the husband, takes subject to dower.

The wife can voluntarily join with her husband in a deed for the purpose of releasing her dower interest in the conveyed land to the transferee. While the husband is living the wife cannot otherwise transfer her dower interest to third parties. After dower becomes possessory following the husband's death, the widow can transfer her interest as she wishes. It should be noted that the law permits the wife to release generally her right to dower by agreement with her husband if certain conditions are met, as discussed in Section 5 of this chapter. Divorce terminates the dower interest. It should be emphasized that dower does not apply to personal property.

A majority of states have abolished dower, as do pre-1990 Uniform Probate Code § 2–113 and 1990 Code § 2–112. Of those that have retained it, some have modified it in certain respects. For example, some states have limited dower to land owned by the husband at death [1]; this enables the husband to transfer good title to his land during his life without any participation by his wife. Modern statutes typically provide that shortly after the husband's death the wife must manifest an election to claim the benefit of her dower. If the wife elects dower, she waives any provision in her favor under the deceased husband's will or any share in his intestate estate.

The states that have retained dower usually give the husband the same interest in the lands owned by the wife during the marriage. Historically the husband had much broader rights in the lands of his wife under the doctrines of the estate by the marital right and curtesy. These gave the husband the possessory and beneficial interest in all the wife's lands during the marriage, and, if a child of the marriage was born alive, a continuing possessory interest for the husband's life after the wife's death. This was essentially a sexist perquisite of marriage, and served a very different function from dower. The estate by the marital right and curtesy no longer exist; if the husband has something called curtesy today in a particular jurisdiction, it is the same as dower or substantially so. It should also be noted that historically the wife's personal property became the property of the husband upon marriage; this also is no part of modern law.[2]

1. Mass.Gen.Laws Ann. ch. 189, § 1; Vt.Stat.Ann. tit. 14, § 461.

2. For an extended discussion of dower and curtesy, see 1 American Law

Dower was not a part of the law of the states which adopted the European community property system. As discussed in Section 7 of this chapter, the community property system deals with spousal property rights very differently from the common law property system.

As wealth came to be held predominantly in forms other than land, such as corporate stocks, bonds and bank accounts, dower ceased to be adequate protection against disinheritance. During the past century most states in the common law property tradition, as distinguished from the community property tradition, have enacted forced share statutes to better protect the surviving spouse from disinheritance.

SECTION 2. SURVIVING SPOUSE'S FORCED SHARE

Because of the inadequacy of dower as protection against disinheritance, most states, other than the community property states, during the past century have enacted forced share statutes, often called elective share statutes, which apply to both personal and real property. The essence of the forced share statutes is to provide the surviving spouse, husband or wife, the right to elect to take a specified fraction of the decedent spouse's estate, both personalty and realty, in the face of dispositive provisions in the will which are unfavorable to the surviving spouse. The spouse gets a fee interest in the property received pursuant to the forced share, unlike dower which provides only a life estate. Unlike dower, the forced share statute does not give a spouse any property interest in the other spouse's personal or real property during the marriage. Each spouse has complete ownership of his or her property during the marriage; the forced share comes into effect only at death. The decedent spouse's creditors come ahead of the surviving spouse's forced share; if the decedent spouse is insolvent at his death, the forced share usually avails the surviving spouse nothing. In this respect, the forced share is less protective than dower. But on balance the forced share is far more protective than dower because of its applicability to personalty as well as realty, and the fee interest that it provides.

The right to elect the forced share is personal to the spouse and cannot be assigned. After the other spouse has died and the election has been made, the property interests that result can be assigned. Husband and wife may contract to waive their forced share rights, as discussed in Section 5 of this chapter.

The traditional forced share statute applies only to the decedent spouse's probate estate, that is to say, those assets which pass

of Property §§ 5.1–.76 (Casner ed.1952).   Stoebuck and Whitman, Law of Property
For a brief discussion, see Cunningham,   69–77 (2d ed. 1993).

through estate administration and are disposed of by will.[3] These are assets owned by the decedent solely in his name or as tenant in common with another. The amount of the forced share varies; in some states it is one-third of the net estate if the decedent is survived by a descendant, or one-half if he is not.[4] It never exceeds the intestate share; it would make no sense to provide for a fraction which exceeded that which would pass to the spouse if there were no disinheriting will.

The traditional statute has no applicability to non-probate assets, that is, will substitutes such as joint tenancies, joint bank accounts, life insurance payable to beneficiaries, and revocable trusts. This makes it possible to avoid the forced share by placing one's assets in certain forms of will substitutes, such as a revocable living trust. Some courts have subjected certain will substitutes, such as revocable trusts, to the forced share despite the language of the statutes which limit the applicability of the forced share to estate assets. Judicial reactions to efforts to circumvent the forced share is discussed in the next section.

Some states now have statutes which subject revocable trusts and other will substitutes to the forced share.[5] It is obvious that any forced share statute which does not include commonly used will substitutes is inadequate, but many of them do not.

The pre–1990 Uniform Probate Code §§ 2–201 and 2–202 have introduced a very comprehensive and in some respects complex forced share statute which has been legislated in some states.[6] It provides that the surviving spouse can elect to take one-third of the decedent spouse's "augmented estate." The augmented estate includes, first of all, assets owned by the decedent at death which pass through estate administration. Second, it includes a variety of donative transfers to or for the benefit of others than the surviving spouse, made by the decedent while married to the surviving spouse, including will substitutes such as revocable trusts, joint tenancies, and joint bank accounts, as well as irrevocable trusts with life income retained by the decedent, and outright living gifts made within two years of death to the extent the gifts exceed a specified amount per donee in any one of the two years. Third, it includes living gifts of property by the decedent to the surviving spouse to the extent the surviving spouse owns such property at the

3. E.g., Fla.Stat.Ann. § 732.206; Mass.Gen.Laws Ann. ch. 191, § 15; Ohio Rev.Code Ann. § 2107.39; Va.Code § 64.1–16.

4. E.g., Md.Est. and Trusts Code Ann. § 3–203; Mo.Ann.Stat. § 474.160; N.H.Rev.Stat.Ann. § 560:10.

5. E.g., Del.Code Ann. tit. 12, § 902; N.J.Stat.Ann. § 3B:8–3; N.Y.Est. Powers and Trusts Law § 5–1.1; Pa.Stat. Ann. tit. 20, § 2203.

6. E.g., Colo.Rev.Stat. § 15–11–202; Me.Rev.Stat.Ann. tit. 18–A, § 2–202; Mont.Code Ann. § 72–2–705; Utah Code Ann. § 75–2–202.

decedent spouse's death, and will substitutes for the benefit of the surviving spouse.

This is a complex statute which must be read carefully for full understanding; the above is merely a synopsis. The essence is that the surviving spouse can reach not only estate assets but other living transfers and will substitutes made by the decedent spouse during marriage in favor of others, but credited against the surviving spouse's share are donative transfers by the decedent to the surviving spouse if owned or received at the death of the decedent spouse. As an example, if probate property left to others and will substitutes left to others total $500,000, and life insurance left to the surviving spouse totals $250,000, the surviving spouse has received her one-third of the augmented estate and there is no reason for her to elect to take her one-third share of the augmented estate because she already has one-third. If the life insurance which the surviving spouse received amounted to $100,000, she would then elect to take her one-third share which would cause $100,000 of the estate property and will substitutes for the benefit of others to be distributed to her.

As we have emphasized, the traditional forced share statute is only concerned with the estate assets. This means that whatever the surviving spouse may have received in the form of will substitutes is irrelevant and disregarded, just as whatever passes to others than the surviving spouse in the form of will substitutes is irrelevant and disregarded.

There is one remarkable aspect of the pre–1990 Code's augmented estate. There is a sentence in the subsection concerned with will substitutes in favor of others than the spouse which reads as follows: "Nothing herein shall cause to be included in the augmented estate any life insurance, accident insurance, joint annuity, or pension payable to a person other than the surviving spouse ..." But in the subsection concerned with gifts and will substitutes made by the decedent to or for the surviving spouse, such transfers are included in the augmented estate. Why this difference? The Comment to the section explains as follows: "... life insurance is not included in the first category of transfers to other persons, because it is not ordinarily purchased as a way of depleting the probate estate and avoiding the elective share of the spouse; but life insurance proceeds payable to the surviving spouse are included in the second category, because it seems unfair to allow a surviving spouse to disturb the decedent's plan if the spouse has received ample provision from life insurance." Is this explanation plausible? Why would a uniform act permit life insurance or annuity or pension benefits to be used to avoid the surviving spouse's forced share? The author leaves this to the reader's imagination.

Some states which have legislated the forced share have also retained dower. If the surviving spouse is dissatisfied with the provision for her in the decedent's will, she must make an election between dower and the forced share. Almost invariably the forced share will be more valuable, because it applies to personalty as well as realty, and provides a fee interest. Dower has the advantage if the decedent's estate is insolvent.

Why are we concerned about the disinheritance of the spouse? Why do we have a forced share? Certainly one reason is to provide support to the surviving spouse. The forced share is not limited, however, to the surviving spouse who is in need; it is available to the survivor who has substantial property of her own, or who is capable of earning an adequate living. The forced share also deals inadequately with the need for support because the fraction does not vary with the size of the estate; one-third of a $1,000,000 estate would provide adequate support for a surviving spouse without means, but one-third of a $200,000 estate would not.

Another reason for the forced share is to compensate the survivor for her indirect contribution to the accumulation of wealth by the decedent. The traditional family consists of a husband-father who earns money and a wife-mother who keeps house and cares for the children. The homemaker's efforts free the husband to work and thereby contribute to the wealth accumulated in the husband's name. The forced share, however, is not limited to the earnings accumulated during the marriage. It is also available to the working husband who survives the homemaking wife whose estate consists of inherited wealth from her parents. The forced share is also available to the surviving spouse of the second marriage late in life during which there was no homemaking or wealth accumulation.

The forced share is a rather crude means of achieving the objectives of support and compensation for contribution in circumstances in which such considerations obtain. If such considerations do not obtain, the forced share may be justified as the sharing which inheres in the marriage relationship regardless of financial need or compensation. It is interesting to note that Great Britain places discretion in the court to change the dispositive terms of the decedent spouse's will or the intestate division, as the case may be, if necessary to provide adequately for the surviving spouse; this is the only protection afforded the surviving spouse from disinheritance. In this country we have generally chosen not to vest such discretionary power in our probate courts for the purpose of support.

It should be noted that some states, in addition to their forced share statutes, have statutes which are protective of the surviving spouse but serve a somewhat different function. These statutes provide, in essence, that if a single person has a will, later marries, then dies survived by his spouse and leaves his premarital will which makes no provision for the spouse and gives no indication that the omission of the spouse was intentional, the spouse is entitled to the share of the estate she would take if the decedent spouse had died intestate.[7] Pre–1990 Uniform Probate Code § 2–301 is to this effect.

The purpose of this type of statute is to protect against the inadvertent failure to provide for the surviving spouse in the premarital will rather than willful disinheritance. If the will antedates the marriage and makes no provision for the spouse, it may be that the testator forgot to change his will to adjust to his new circumstance. What does this statute do that the forced share statute does not do? This statute gives the surviving spouse her intestate share which may be the entire estate. Under the forced share statutes the spouse typically receives no more than one-half, and frequently receives less than her intestate share. It should be emphasized that under this type of statute, as under the forced share statute, the will is valid but distribution under it is reduced by the portion payable to the spouse.

1990 Code § 2–301 changes the definition of the share that the surviving spouse takes in the circumstance of the premarital will, as follows: The share she would receive in intestacy if the decedent spouse had died intestate as to that portion of his estate other than that which is left to a child of the decedent spouse who was born before the decedent spouse married the surviving spouse and who is not a child of the surviving spouse, or which is left to a descendant of such child, or which passes to a descendant of such child under the anti-lapse statute. This revision has the effect of protecting testamentary gifts to children of prior marriages (or relationships) under a premarital will from the claim of the surviving spouse. It should be reiterated that this statute is distinct from the forced share of the surviving spouse.

We have previously mentioned that in some states a testator's marriage entirely revokes his previously executed will by operation of law, unless the will anticipates the subsequent marriage.[8] If a jurisdiction has such a statute, obviously there is no need for a statute protecting the spouse against inadvertent omission.

It is reiterated that the forced share statute protects the surviving spouse regardless of when the will was executed and

---

7. E.g., Ariz.Rev.Stat.Ann. § 14–2301; Colo.Rev.Stat. § 15–11–301; Minn.Stat.Ann. § 524.2–301; N.J.Stat. Ann. § 3B:5–15; N.M.Stat.Ann. § 45–2–301.

8. See Chapter 4, Section 4.

regardless of the expression of an intention to disinherit in the will. Indeed its purpose is to prevent intentional disinheritance.

SECTION 3. AVOIDANCE OF FORCED SHARE

In many states the forced share statute applies only to estate assets; wealth which bypasses estate administration, such as life insurance, joint bank accounts, joint tenancies, and revocable trusts, is not subject to the surviving spouse's claim. This provides an opportunity for the spouse intent upon disinheriting his or her partner. Some courts, however, have subjected certain will substitutes, usually revocable trusts or bank account trusts, to the forced share in certain circumstances, despite the language of the statute. Such judicial action is the subject of this section.

Before we discuss those lines of authority, however, it should be reiterated that there is a reverse twist to the limitation of the forced share to estate assets. Suppose a husband dies with life insurance in the amount of $300,000 payable to his wife, and net probate assets in the amount of $300,000 which he leaves to his children in his will. The wife keeps the $300,000 of life insurance and elects her forced share in estate assets which entitles her to one-third, or $100,000. The fact that she received one-half the husband's economic estate in the form of life insurance is irrelevant. If in the jurisdiction all will substitutes were included in the determination of the forced share, the wife would be entitled to only $200,000, and since she took $300,000 of life insurance she would obviously not make the election. So it is possible that the forced share statute limited to estate assets can work in the surviving spouse's favor.

Let us return to the use of the will substitute to disinherit the surviving spouse. Husband and Wife have been previously married and have children by their previous marriages. Husband and Wife married in their sixties. Husband has substantial wealth, and transfers most of it to Bank, as trustee, to pay the income to Husband for his life, and upon his death, to pay the principal outright to Husband's children. The trust is expressly made revocable, and Husband has expressly retained the power to direct the Bank with respect to investments. The trust is clearly valid as a living transfer. Husband dies without having revoked the trust. Ten percent of his assets was not transferred in trust, and was disposed of by his will to Wife.

Some courts have, of course, taken the position that the statute in the jurisdiction applies only to estate assets, and Wife has no claim to the trust assets.[9] There are cases, however, in which

9. Cherniack v. Home National Bank   (1964); Leazenby v. Clinton County
& Trust Co., 151 Conn. 367, 198 A.2d 58   Bank and Trust Co., 171 Ind.App. 243,

courts have, in essence, disregarded the language of the statute and subjected revocable trusts to the forced share, but the reasoning of the cases varies. Some courts have adopted the so-called "illusory" rationale: If the decedent's living transfer enables him to keep the benefit and control of the transferred property despite the transfer, the transfer is illusory and is subject to the forced share.[10] The illusory rationale has its logical difficulties because there is no question that the transfer is otherwise valid from a property standpoint. The term "illusory" is inept. The courts which adopt this position are making a policy judgment that the statute should not be subject to circumvention by these means, but the rationale is inadequate.

A few courts in circumstances such as this have adopted a more convincing rationale which has been called the "equitable" standard: If it appears unjust to deprive the surviving spouse of access to the revocable trust, it will be subjected to the forced share. The factors to be considered are whether the decedent spouse intended the living transfer as a disinheriting device, the amount which the surviving spouse received from the decedent under the will and from other will substitutes, and other property owned by the surviving spouse.[11]

A few courts have held and a couple of statutes provide that if a living transfer is made for the purpose of disinheriting the spouse, it will be subjected to the forced share.[12] Retention of benefit and control is not central under this view. An absolute transfer without retention of any strings may be subjected to the forced share. This view has sometimes been referred to as the "intent" or "fraud" view.

There is yet another view adopted recently by a couple of courts and the Restatement (Second) of Property, Donative Transfers § 34.1, to the effect that a revocable trust is subject to the forced share because of the underlying policy of the forced share

355 N.E.2d 861 (1976); Matter of Halpern, 303 N.Y. 33, 100 N.E.2d 120 (1951); Smyth v. Cleveland Trust Co., 172 Ohio St. 489, 179 N.E.2d 60 (1961).

10. Montgomery v. Michaels, 54 Ill.2d 532, 301 N.E.2d 465 (1973); Ackers v. First National Bank of Topeka, 192 Kan. 319, 387 P.2d 840 (1963); Staples v. King, 433 A.2d 407 (Me.1981); Newman v. Dore, 275 N.Y. 371, 9 N.E.2d 966 (1937); Thomas v. Bank of Oklahoma, 684 P.2d 553 (Okl.1984); Johnson v. Farmers and Merchants Bank 180 W.Va. 702, 379 S.E.2d 752 (1989).

11. Windsor v. Leonard, 475 F.2d 932 (D.C.Cir.1973); Whittington v. Whittington, 205 Md. 1, 106 A.2d 72 (1954); Davis v. KB & T Co., 172 W.Va. 546, 309 S.E.2d 45 (1983).

12. Harris v. Rock, 799 S.W.2d 10 (Ky.1990); Hanke v. Hanke, 123 N.H. 175, 459 A.2d 246 (1983); Patch v. Squires, 105 Vt. 405, 165 A. 919 (1933); Mo.Ann.Stat. § 474.150; Tenn.Code Ann. § 31-1-105.

statute. In this straightforward view, intention to disinherit, "illusoriness," and other "equitable considerations" are not relevant.[13]

The piecemeal judicial treatment of attempted avoidance of the forced share by will substitutes or other living gifts is inadequate because of its unpredictability. Also, it does not deal with the situation discussed above in which the surviving spouse is left out of the will but receives a very ample share under a will substitute such as life insurance.

It should be noted that the courts which have chosen to subject non-estate assets to the forced share have done so where the decedent died intestate.[14] It would make no sense to include will substitutes where there was a disinheriting will and not do so if there was intestacy. Once the forced share statute is disregarded to reach non-estate assets, it is a small step to disregard the statute again to apply it to the intestate situation.

The pre–1990 Uniform Probate Code deals with the forced share intelligently. The surviving spouse can elect to take one-third of the augmented estate, whether the decedent spouse dies with a will or intestate. The augmented estate includes (1) estate assets, (2) will substitutes left to others than the spouse and certain outright gifts within two years of death to others than the spouse, and (3) living gifts to the spouse which are still held at the decedent's death, and will substitutes left to the spouse. If the surviving spouse receives one-third or more of the total by will substitute or otherwise, the surviving spouse obviously has no claim. Under the pre–1990 Code the will substitute left to someone other than the spouse and included in the augmented estate is valid in accordance with its terms except to the extent that a portion of it is given to the spouse pursuant to her election. All interests included in the augmented estate abate pro rata to satisfy the spouse's elective share.

It should be noted again that the pre–1990 Uniform Probate Code leaves an opportunity for disinheriting the surviving spouse. The augmented estate does not include "... life insurance, accident insurance, joint annuity, or pension payable to a person other than the surviving spouse." Such assets are included in the augmented estate if they are payable to the surviving spouse. This is a most obvious and unjustified gap in an otherwise comprehensive and sound system of spousal protection.

13. Sullivan v. Burkin, 390 Mass. 864, 460 N.E.2d 572 (1984); Moore v. Jones, 44 N.C.App. 578, 261 S.E.2d 289 (1980).

14. Montgomery v. Michaels, 54 Ill.2d 532, 301 N.E.2d 465 (1973); Ackers v. First National Bank of Topeka, 192 Kan. 319, 387 P.2d 840 (1963); Staples v. King, 433 A.2d 407 (Me.1981).

SECTION 4. 1990 UNIFORM PROBATE CODE ELECTIVE SHARE

1990 Uniform Probate Code §§ 2–201 through 2–207 radically revise the surviving spouse's forced share. It is a complex system, but its outline can be presented briefly.

It is necessary first to describe the assets which are to be considered in the determination of the surviving spouse's forced share. Those assets are called the "augmented estate." The augmented estate, in general terms, includes the following: (1) the net probate estate of the decedent spouse (assets subject to estate administration); (2) property designed to pass to any person other than the surviving spouse but which was subject to a power exercisable by the decedent spouse in favor of himself immediately before his death; (3) decedent spouse's fractional share of property owned by decedent spouse and any person other than the surviving spouse, with right of survivorship, immediately before decedent spouse's death; (4) proceeds of insurance on the life of the decedent spouse payable to any person other than the surviving spouse, if the decedent spouse owned the policy or had the power to change the beneficiary immediately before the decedent spouse's death; (5) any donative transfer by the decedent spouse to any person other than the surviving spouse made during the marriage to the surviving spouse, to the extent the decedent spouse retained at his death the enjoyment or possession of, or the right to income from, the property, or to the extent the property at the decedent spouse's death was subject to a power exercisable by the decedent spouse in favor of himself or his estate; (6) certain donative transfers to any person other than the surviving spouse made during the marriage to the surviving spouse and within two years of the decedent spouse's death; (7) property to which the surviving spouse succeeds by reason of the decedent spouse's death other than by testate or intestate succession, i.e., by means of will substitutes including life insurance and retirement benefits; (8) the net value of property owned by the surviving spouse at the decedent spouse's death.

It should be emphasized that the augmented estate includes under (8) above all property owned by the surviving spouse at the time of the decedent spouse's death, however acquired. Under the pre–1990 Code counterpart provision, only property owned by the surviving spouse at the decedent spouse's death which had been acquired from the decedent spouse by living gift or by will substitute was included in the augmented estate.

The 1990 Code provides for an elective share of a percentage of the augmented estate which varies in accordance with the duration of the marriage. If the duration of the marriage has been 15 years or more at the decedent's death, the elective share is 50%. If the duration of the marriage was one year or more but less than two years, the elective share is 3%. The percentage moves up in 3% annual increments to 30% for the marriage of 10 years or more but less than 11 years. Thereafter it moves up in annual increments of 4% to 50% for marriages of 15 years or more.

The elective share is first satisfied from the decedent's probate property (property subject to estate administration) passing to the surviving spouse, decedent's will substitutes passing to the surviving spouse, and property owned by the surviving spouse at the decedent's death. If these assets do not satisfy the elective share, the other components of the augmented estate must contribute.

In determining the amount of the surviving spouse's owned property which is to be applied to satisfy the elective share, a percentage of that property equal to twice the applicable elective share percentage is used. If the duration of the marriage is 15 years or more, then all the owned property is applied, i.e., twice the 50%. If the duration of the marriage was 10 years, 30% is the elective share percentage, and 60% of the surviving spouse's owned property is applied to the elective share. The reasoning behind this is set forth in the third paragraph following this one.

The novel features of the 1990 Code elective share are the variable percentages and the inclusion of the surviving spouse's owned property in the augmented estate. These innovations are efforts to approximate, in a very rough way, the results of the community property system which adopts the marital sharing principle with respect to property acquired during marriage (other than by gift or inheritance). Such property is deemed to be owned equally by husband and wife; one-half is owned and disposed of by the decedent spouse and one-half is owned by the surviving spouse, regardless of how the property is nominally titled. The community property system treats marriage as a partnership with respect to property acquired during marriage (other than by gift or inheritance). Property owned prior to marriage is not community property. The community property states do not have the forced share. Community property is described briefly in Section 7 of this chapter.

It is emphasized that the 1990 Code is a very rough approximation of the community property concept as applied at the time of the death of the decedent spouse. There is no effort to distinguish property acquired during marriage as a result of earnings, from property acquired during marriage by gift or inheritance, or from property acquired prior to marriage. The 1990 Code assumes that the shorter the marriage, the less the husband's and wife's property consists of community property, and therefore the lower the elective share percentage. A marriage of three years would produce very little community property. A marriage of ten years would probably produce a good deal of community property; 60% of the total property of the two is deemed to be community, and one-half of that belongs to each. After 15 years of marriage all the husband's and wife's property is treated as if it were community property for purposes of the elective share. After 15 years the surviving spouse is entitled to one-half of the total of the decedent's property and the survivor's property. Of course, if the survivor already owns more than one-half, she does not have to give anything up to the decedent's estate; all that is involved here is the forced share of the survivor. It is reiterated that the community property system is simply the "notion" which underlies the 1990 Code forced share. The 1990 Code does not adopt the system in any sense.

Let us return to the amount of the surviving spouse's property which is applied to satisfy her elective share. The elective share is intended to reflect the surviving spouse's share of what is deemed to be community (or marital) property. If the marriage has had a duration of 15 years or more, the elective share is 50% of the property of both because all their property is deemed to be community (or marital) property. This means that in satisfying the elective share from the property of the surviving spouse, all of the surviving spouse's property is deemed to be marital property and credited to her elective share. If the marriage has had a duration of 10 years, the elective share is 30% because 60% of their property is deemed to be marital property. This means that in satisfying the elective share from the property of the surviving spouse, 60% of the surviving spouse's property is deemed to be marital property and credited to her elective share.

The 1990 Code elective share can produce harsh results. Assume a decedent spouse with net assets of $500,000. He leaves his entire estate to his children in his will. He is also survived by a widow to whom he was married late in life for five years and who has no assets. The elective share is 15%; she is entitled to $75,000. Is that the way it should be? This raises the question of the meaning and responsibility of marriage, whatever its duration.

Assume a decedent spouse with net assets of $200,000, who leaves his entire estate to his children in his will. He is survived by a widow to whom he was married for 30 years who has assets of $200,000. The elective share is 50%; she is entitled to nothing. Is that the way it should be?

The 1990 Code elective share may work satisfactorily when both spouses have substantial means, but it can work harsh results where the property held is modest. Also, the elective share and intestacy involve different considerations, but nevertheless the gross discrepancy between them should be noted.

It should be pointed out that the 1990 Code has a "safety valve" which assures the surviving spouse not less than $50,000 from the augmented estate if the total of what she owns, receives from the decedent, and is entitled to under the elective share percentage formula amounts to less than $50,000.

SECTION 5. PREMARITAL CONTRACTS BARRING SPOUSAL RIGHTS

Prior to marriage the prospective husband and wife may enter into a contract wherein each, or one of them, releases or limits his or her dower, forced share and intestate rights in the estate of the other in the event he or she survives. The law of the premarital contract of this nature has developed largely by judicial decision. In recent years, however, a number of states have legislated on the subject as a result of the pre–1990 Uniform Probate Code which has a section dealing with it. The opinions of the courts in this area are frequently less than models of precise deductive logic. A distillation of the cases does, however, produce certain principles which are purportedly determinative of the validity of such contracts in the absence of statute.

The courts have viewed the premarital estate contract very differently from the conventional arm's length trading transaction. The premarital estate contract provides for a release of rights of the surviving spouse without compensation therefor, or in exchange for a designated amount paid at or about the time of the marriage or to be paid from the estate, or for a fraction of the estate which is less than what the survivor would be entitled to pursuant to his or her rights at law. The prevailing judicial view is that if the premarital settlement of the rights of the surviving spouse in the estate of the decedent spouse is not substantively fair under the circumstances existing at the time the contract is executed, the contract is not enforceable, unless at the time of the contract the surviving spouse was adequately informed of the property of the decedent spouse and its value, either by express disclosure by the decedent spouse or from other sources, was aware of the rights she was giving up, and was not unduly pressured to execute the contract.[15] In other words, if the provision is not reasonable as of the time of the

---

15. Watson v. Watson, 5 Ill.2d 526, 126 N.E.2d 220 (1955); Hartz v. Hartz, 248 Md. 47, 234 A.2d 865 (1967); Hook v. Hook, 69 Ohio St.2d 234, 431 N.E.2d 667 (1982); Kosik v. George, 253 Or. 15, 452 P.2d 560 (1969); Batleman v. Rubin, 199 Va. 156, 98 S.E.2d 519 (1957); Estate of Crawford, 107 Wash.2d 493, 730 P.2d 675 (1986).

This section 5, and the discussion on page 153 above, previously appeared in Haskell, The Premarital Estate Contract And Social Policy, 57 N.C.L.Rev. 415, 423 (1979).

contract, then it must appear that the deprived spouse knew what she was doing when she signed the contract and did it voluntarily. Enforceability is determined in accordance with the alternative criteria of substantive fairness or fairness in the making of the contract. It is usually held that if the spouse challenging the contract establishes that the contract was substantively unfair, a presumption arises that she was uninformed or unduly pressured, which places the burden of proof on those issues upon the party upholding the contract.[16]

It should be noted that there is authority that the requirement of substantive fairness may be satisfied although the surviving spouse has waived her interest completely and has received nothing in exchange; this would be so if the surviving spouse had independent means or the capacity to earn an adequate living.[17] If the surviving spouse does not have property or a vocation which would assure her an adequate income, substantive fairness will usually require a provision which is not disproportionate to her rights at law on the basis of the property of the decedent spouse at the time of the contract. It should be emphasized that the question of substantive fairness is to be resolved as of the time of the contract, not as of the time of the decedent spouse's death; that is to say, if the provision for the surviving spouse was fair in relation to the decedent spouse's assets at the time of the contract but unfair in relation to the decedent spouse's assets at his death, the criterion of substantive fairness would be satisfied.[18] It is reiterated that the provision for the surviving spouse may be either a transfer of assets at or about the time of the marriage or a promise to provide a specified amount from or a fraction of the estate in the will of the decedent spouse.

The alternative criteria of substantive fairness and fairness in the making of the contract are the consequence of the relationship of trust and confidence between individuals about to be married which may cause one of them to relax his or her guard. Obviously the one with property or the potential therefor who is proposing the waiver of rights, in whole or in part, is on his or her guard, but the one who is giving something up may not be on guard. It is inequitable to allow one of the parties in these circumstances to take advantage of the other's trust by obtaining a partial or total

16. Faver v. Faver, 266 Ark. 262, 583 S.W.2d 44 (1979); Fleming v. Fleming, 85 Ill.App.3d 532, 40 Ill.Dec. 676, 406 N.E.2d 879 (1980); Hook v. Hook, 69 Ohio St.2d 234, 431 N.E.2d 667 (1982); Kosik v. George, 253 Or. 15, 452 P.2d 560 (1969).

17. Hartz v. Hartz, 248 Md. 47, 234 A.2d 865 (1967); In re Estate of Davis, 20 N.Y.2d 70, 281 N.Y.S.2d 767, 228 N.E.2d 768 (1967).

18. Hosmer v. Hosmer, 611 S.W.2d 32 (Mo.App.1980); Rocker v. Rocker, 13 Ohio Misc. 199, 232 N.E.2d 445 (1967); In re Estate of Vallish, 431 Pa. 88, 244 A.2d 745 (1968).

release which is unfair to the trusting party, unless the releasing party has been fully informed and not subject to undue pressure. In the litigation that has occurred, often the initiator of the contract is the business-wise prospective husband and the waiving party is the financially and legally unsophisticated prospective wife who survives and challenges the validity of the contract. Unquestionably such bargaining imbalance reflecting the traditional economic dependence of the female has influenced the courts to require an openness in the making of the contract which is not required between parties bargaining at arm's length.

Pre–1990 Uniform Probate Code § 2–204, which has been legislated in a number of states,[19] deals with this subject and reads in part as follows:

Section 2–204. [Waiver of Right to Elect and of Other Rights.]

The right of election of a surviving spouse and the rights of the surviving spouse to homestead allowance, exempt property and family allowance, or any of them, may be waived, wholly or partially, before or after marriage, by a written contract, agreement or waiver signed by the party waiving after fair disclosure ...

The pre–1990 Uniform Probate Code provision requires that there be fair disclosure in all cases and makes no reference to substantive fairness. This means presumably that a premarital contract which is substantively fair but concerning which there was no disclosure of the decedent spouse's assets is invalid. The prevailing common law view, of course, is that such a contract would be enforceable. The pre–1990 Uniform Probate Code provision appears to follow generally, but not in detail, a line of common law authority to the effect that premarital estate contracts are valid if there has been disclosure of the decedent spouse's assets, but if the provision for the surviving spouse is disproportionate to the decedent spouse's assets at the time of the contract, a presumption arises that there has not been adequate disclosure, thereby placing the burden of proof with respect to disclosure upon the party upholding the contract. Substantive fairness is never determinative of validity; disclosure alone determines validity.[20]

Occasionally the estate contract is entered into during marriage. It appears from the reported litigation that this is uncommon relative to the premarital settlement. The courts have gener-

---

19. E.g., Alaska Stat. § 13.11.085; Del.Code Ann. tit. 12, § 905; N.J.Stat. Ann. § 3B:8–10; N.D.Cent.Code § 30.1–05–04; Utah Code Ann. § 75–2–204; Wyo.Stat. § 2–5–102.

20. Rankin v. Schiereck, 166 Iowa 19, 147 N.W. 180 (1914); Potter's Ex'r v. Potter, 234 Ky. 769, 29 S.W.2d 15 (1930).

ally employed the same considerations with respect to validity as in the premarital contract,[21] as does the pre–1990 Code provision.

1990 Code § 2–204 radically changes the law on this subject. It sets forth two circumstances in which the waiver by the surviving spouse of statutory rights in the estate of the decedent spouse would be unenforceable. First, it is unenforceable if its execution by the surviving spouse was not done "voluntarily." Second, the waiver is unenforceable if it was unconscionable when executed, provided that the surviving spouse did not have adequate knowledge of the decedent spouse's financial circumstances, and did not expressly and voluntarily waive in writing any right to disclosure of the decedent spouse's financial circumstances. It follows that an unconscionable waiver of the forced share is enforceable if the surviving spouse does not have knowledge of the decedent spouse's financial circumstances and waives her right to such information, as long as the surviving spouse acted "voluntarily." It should be noted that under this section the waiver of statutory rights in the estate of the decedent spouse which is merely "unfair" rather than "unconscionable" is enforceable regardless of the question of disclosure. What 1990 Code § 2–204 permits is the enforceability of an unconscionable marital agreement by the use of the formal device of a waiver of disclosure. This, of course, makes for certainty of enforcement of the marital agreement at the price of decency.

It should be noted that the unconscionable waiver of the forced share is valid if the surviving spouse is informed of the decedent spouse's financial circumstances. Note also that the 1990 Code provision applies to waivers made before or during marriage.

The 1990 Code provision is taken from the Uniform Premarital Agreement Act, adopted in about fifteen states, which deals with all aspects of the marital relationship, including property consequences on divorce as well as at death, and support during marriage.

SECTION 6. PRETERMITTED CHILD

A testator is entitled to disinherit his children if he wishes in all states except Louisiana which has a form of forced heirship for certain children derived from its French property tradition.[22] Most states, however, have enacted statutes which protect children who are not provided for in the will unless it appears that the failure to

---

21. Rockwell v. Rockwell, 24 Mich. App. 593, 180 N.W.2d 498 (1970); Estate of Murphy, 661 S.W.2d 657 (Mo. App.1983); In re Estate of Kester, 486 Pa. 349, 405 A.2d 1244 (1979); In re Estate of Beat, 25 Wis.2d 315, 130 N.W.2d 739 (1964).

22. Forced heirship is limited to children under 23, and disabled children of any age. La.Civ.Code Ann. arts. 1493 et seq.

make provision for them was intentional. The apparent purpose of these statutes is to protect the child who has been omitted by the testator through oversight. If the statute applies, the child is usually entitled to what she would have received if the parent-testator had died intestate. A small number of statutes protect omitted grandchildren of the testator by children who have predeceased the testator.[23] To simplify the discussion of the subject we shall discuss these statutes in terms only of children of the testator.

The statutes differ in various respects of which several are central. Most statutes apply only to children born or adopted after the execution of the will,[24] but a small number of statutes apply to all children whether alive at the execution of the will or born thereafter.[25] A small number of statutes bar the child's claim only if an intention to disinherit appears on the face of the will.[26] Many states bar the child's claim not only in that circumstance but also if the child received a living gift or will substitute from the testator which was intended to be in lieu of a testamentary gift, or if the testator had a child at the time of execution of the will and left substantially all of his estate to the other parent of the omitted child.[27]

Pre–1990 Uniform Probate Code § 2–302, which has been legislated in a number of states, includes these circumstances, and reads in part as follows:

Section 2–302   [Pretermitted Children.]

(a) If a testator fails to provide in his will for any of his children born or adopted after the execution of his will, the omitted child receives a share in the estate equal in value to that which he would have received if the testator had died intestate unless:

  (1) it appears from the will that the omission was intentional;

  (2) when the will was executed the testator had one or more children and devised substantially all his estate to the other parent of the omitted child; or

  (3) the testator provided for the child by transfer outside the will and the intent that the transfer be in

23. E.g., Md.Est. & Trusts Code Ann. § 3–301; Mass.Gen.Laws Ann. ch. 191, § 20; R.I.Gen.Laws § 33–6–23.

24. E.g., Fla.Stat.Ann. § 732.302; Ill.Ann.Stat. ch. 110½, § 4–10; Iowa Code Ann. § 633.267; Neb.Rev.Stat. § 30–2321; N.J.Stat.Ann. § 3B:5–16; Tenn.Code Ann. § 32–3–103.

25. E.g., Ark.Stat.Ann. § 28–39–407.

26. E.g., N.C.Gen.Stat. § 31–5.5; Ill. Ann.Stat. ch. 110½, § 4–10; Or.Rev. Stat. § 112.405; Pa.Stat.Ann. tit. 20, § 2507.

27. E.g., Ariz.Rev.Stat.Ann. § 14–2302; Hawaii Rev.Stat. § 560:2–302; Ky.Rev.Stat.Ann. § 394.382; Mo.Ann. Stat. § 474.240; Wis.Stat.Ann. § 853.-25.

lieu of a testamentary provision is shown by statements of the testator or from the amount of the
transfer or other evidence.

The pre-1990 Code provision that the child cannot take under
the statute if the testator leaves his estate to the child's other
parent, provided there was a child living at the time of the execution of the will, is very sensible because it is natural for a testator
to leave his entire estate to his spouse, but under many pretermitted child statutes the failure to mention children in the will in this
circumstance may make the statute applicable. If, however, the
testator leaves all to the spouse, and in addition provides that in
the event the spouse predeceases him he leaves all to his issue who
survive him, there should be no problem with the pretermitted
child statute in any jurisdiction.

The purpose of the statutes is presumably to correct for the
testator's failure to provide for a child through oversight. A child
born after the execution of the will may be overlooked. It is highly
unlikely that the omission of a child alive at the time of the
execution of the will would be the result of oversight. If the
statute applies to children living at the making of the will, and
intention to disinherit is limited to the four corners of the will, it
appears that the statute may well be applied to situations in which
the child was not overlooked.

The pretermitted child statute can produce erratic results.
Assume a testator with a wife and one child. He executes a will
leaving $40,000 to the one child and the residue of his estate to his
wife. He subsequently has another child but dies without changing
his will, survived by his wife and the two children. There is no
evidence of any intention to disinherit the second child. His net
estate is $240,000. If the intestate share for children is two-thirds,
the afterborn child gets $80,000 and the legatee child gets $40,000.
Assume the same facts except that the will provides for a trust of
the entire estate to pay the income to the wife for her life,
remainder outright to the child who was living at the making of the
will. The afterborn child gets $80,000 now, and the other child
may wait many years for the rest of the estate property.

1990 Code § 2–302 leaves certain provisions unchanged and
substantially changes others. Only children born or adopted after
the execution of the will are protected. The omitted child is denied
a share of the estate if it appears from the will that the omission
was intentional, or the testator provided for the child by transfer
outside the will and such transfer was intended to be in lieu of a
testamentary provision. The 1990 Code also denies the omitted
child a share if there was no child living when the will was
executed, the will leaves all or substantially all of the estate to the

other parent of the child, and that parent survives the testator. In addition, the omitted child is not entitled to any share of the estate if a child or children were living when the will was executed, and nothing was left in the will to him or them.

1990 Code § 2–302 gives the omitted child his intestate share if there was no child living when the will was executed, unless the will leaves all or substantially all of the estate to the other parent of the child and that parent survives the testator. If a child or children were living when the will was executed, and the will makes a gift or gifts to them, the omitted child is entitled to a pro-rata share of the gift or gifts to such child or children; that is to say, the gift or gifts to the child or children living at the execution of the will are reduced ratably to provide for the share of the omitted child.

There is a related point of law that needs mentioning. Suppose a testator leaves his entire estate to several people, and includes in his will the following statement: "I have deliberately left nothing to my son Robert in this will, and I hereby direct that if for any reason any part of my estate shall pass by intestacy, my son Robert is to receive no part of my intestate estate." At testator's death a portion of his estate passes by intestacy because of a lapse in the residue. Son Robert is an heir and takes his intestate share.[28] A testator cannot disinherit an intestate taker by fiat. The only way a testator can disinherit an heir is to dispose of his estate to others. The law disposes of the estate in the absence of a testamentary disposition. 1990 Uniform Probate Code § 2–101(b) changes the law in this respect by providing that a testator may in his will exclude a person from taking any property which may pass to him as a result of intestacy, in which circumstance such property passes as if the person had disclaimed his intestate interest.

SECTION 7.　COMMUNITY PROPERTY

In most states husband and wife own property in the same way as an unmarried person. If husband receives a pay check, the money belongs to him absolutely; he may have an obligation of support, but the ownership is his exclusively. If husband and wife become divorced, for equitable reasons the court may award some of the husband's property to the wife, or vice-versa, and upon death the surviving spouse may be entitled to claim a share of the decedent spouse's estate, but these considerations do not bear

28. In re Estate of Barnes, 63 Cal.2d 580, 47 Cal.Rptr. 480, 407 P.2d 656 (1965); Estate of Cancik, 121 Ill.App.3d 113, 76 Ill.Dec. 659, 459 N.E.2d 296 (1984); Estate of Stroble, 6 Kan.App.2d 955, 636 P.2d 236 (1981); In re Estate of Stewart, 113 N.H. 179, 304 A.2d 361 (1973).

directly upon the basically individualistic nature of ownership in the common law property system. The only qualification to individual ownership between married people in common law property states is dower, which is of limited significance today because of the forced share.

Individual ownership of property in the marital relationship derives from the English property tradition. Nine states, Washington, Idaho, California, Nevada, Arizona, New Mexico, Texas, Louisiana and Wisconsin have a different system of ownership for married people which derives from the Spanish and French property traditions. This system provides that the earnings of each spouse during the marriage are community property, which means that they are owned in equal undivided shares by husband and wife. Any property acquired with such earnings is also community property. Income derived from community property is, of course, community property.

All other property owned by husband or wife is called separate property, which means that it is owned individually as property is owned in the large majority of states which do not have the community property system. Property owned by a spouse prior to marriage is separate property, and property acquired by gift or inheritance during marriage is separate property. Some of the community property states treat income from separate property during the marriage as separate property, and others treat such income as community property.

At the death of a husband or wife domiciled in a community property state, the decedent has dispositive power by will over all his separate property and one-half the community property. The other half of the community property belonged to the surviving spouse and becomes his or hers absolutely on the death of the decedent spouse. This is all the protection against disinheritance the surviving spouse has in the community property system. There is no forced share or dower. If the spouses have not labelled their separate and community property systematically, there may be problems of determining what is community and what is separate. Upon the death of a spouse domiciled in a community property state, if the origins of property are not clear, such property is rebuttably presumed to be community.

If the spouse dies intestate, his or her separate property and his or her share of the community property pass in accordance with the intestacy statute which usually has different provisions for community and separate property.

In most community property states husband and wife are free to transform by agreement community property into separate property and vice-versa.

It should also be noted that community property cannot be held in joint tenancy. Community property is analogous to the common law tenancy in common which does not have a survivorship characteristic. Joint tenancy is a common law property concept, not a community property concept. If husband and wife own as joint tenants in a community property state, the property is separate property. None of the community property states recognizes tenancy by the entirety.

It should be emphasized that the community property law in each of the nine states has its distinctive statutory and judicially determined characteristics. The states have a common conceptual base, but there are many differences in detail. This discussion is a grossly simplified statement of the principles of the system.

The rationale of the community property system is that the product of the common endeavor of marriage should belong equally to the marital partners. In the traditional family the husband works for pay and the wife cares for the home and the children. The money should be shared as all else is. Protection against disinheritance is not the purpose of the system, although in many situations it may be a by-product. However, it may occur that the married couple consumes their earnings, and their accumulated capital is from inheritance from their parents; in such circumstance community property provides no protection against the potential of disinheritance. In the case of a second marriage late in life in which both spouses are retired or work for a few years and then retire, there is little, if any, community property. It is reiterated that there is no forced share or dower for the surviving spouse.

If a couple moves from a common law property state into a community property state, the property they bring with them retains its individually-owned nature, i.e., it is separate property. Of course, earnings of the couple thereafter are community property. At the time of death in the community property state, all the separate property of the decedent spouse is his to dispose of as he sees fit. Two of the community property states, however, have legislated that in the case of the death of a spouse where the couple has migrated from a noncommunity property state, property of that spouse acquired during marriage while in the noncommunity property state will be treated as community property if such property would have been community property had it been acquired during marriage in that state. However, any such property of the surviving spouse is treated as his or hers absolutely. This category of property of the deceased spouse is referred to as quasi-community property. This is a form of protection against disinheritance in the case of the couple that migrates to the community property state from a noncommunity property state and has accumulated little community property in the community property state.

If a couple migrates from a community property state to a common law property state, the community property acquired while in the former state retains that characteristic and at the death of a spouse he or she can dispose of only one-half of such property. Of course, all property acquired while domiciled in the common law property state is owned individually.

It is beyond the purpose of this book, but there is the issue of management of community property during the marriage. When the husband receives his pay check and deposits it, does withdrawal require the consent of both husband and wife? In general, each acting alone can exercise managerial power over community property. One exception to this is that real estate transactions usually require that both join. Another exception is that a substantial living gift of community property by one spouse to a third party may be set aside by the nonconsenting spouse. It should also be noted that there are problems concerning the rights of creditors of one or the other spouse with respect to community property.[29]

SECTION 8. EXEMPT PROPERTY, FAMILY ALLOWANCE, HOMESTEAD ALLOWANCE

By statute certain property of the decedent is distributed to the surviving spouse or children and is not subject to the terms of the will of the decedent or the intestacy statute. In addition, these statutory dispositions are exempt from the claims of the decedent's creditors. Usually these dispositions are in addition to the provisions for the spouse or children in the will or by intestacy.

Most states have statutes which give to the surviving spouse, or if there is none, to the children, certain personal effects of the decedent up to a certain value.[30] These statutes vary greatly. Pre-1990 Uniform Probate Code § 2–402, which has been legislated in some states, is as follows:

Section 2–402. [Exempt property.]

In addition to the homestead allowance, the surviving spouse of a decedent who was domiciled in this state is entitled from the estate to value not exceeding $3,500 in excess of any security interests therein in household furni-

29. Texts on community Property: de Funiak and Vaughn, Principles of Community Property (2d ed.1971); Mennell, Community Property In A Nutshell (1982).

30. E.g., Ala.Code § 43–8–111; Hawaii Rev.Stat. § 560:2–402; Idaho Code § 15–2–402; R.I.Gen.Laws § 33–10–1; Tenn.Code Ann. § 30–2–101; Va.Code § 64.1–151.2.

ture, automobiles, furnishings, appliances and personal effects. If there is no surviving spouse, children of the decedent are entitled jointly to the same value. If encumbered chattels are selected and if the value in excess of security interests, plus that of other exempt property, is less than $3,500, or if there is not $3,500 worth of exempt property in the estate, the spouse or children are entitled to other assets of the estate, if any, to the extent necessary to make up the $3,500 value. Rights to exempt property and assets needed to make up a deficiency of exempt property have priority over all claims against the estate, except that the right to any assets to make up a deficiency of exempt property shall abate as necessary to permit prior payment of homestead allowance and family allowance. These rights are in addition to any benefit or share passing to the surviving spouse or children by the will of the decedent unless otherwise provided, by intestate succession, or by way of elective share.

1990 Code § 2–403 is substantially the same as the pre–1990 provision, except that the exempt property amount is increased to $10,000.

Most states have statutes which authorize payments from the estate to the surviving spouse and minor children for support during the administration of the estate.[31]   These statutes vary greatly. Pre–1990 Uniform Probate Code § 2–403, which has been legislated in some states, reads as follows:

Section 2–403. [Family Allowance.]

In addition to the right to homestead allowance and exempt property, if the decedent was domiciled in this state, the surviving spouse and minor children whom the decedent was obligated to support and children who were in fact being supported by him are entitled to a reasonable allowance in money out of the estate for their maintenance during the period of administration, which allowance may not continue for longer than one year if the estate is inadequate to discharge allowed claims. The allowance may be paid as a lump sum or in periodic installments. It is payable to the surviving spouse, if living, for the use of the surviving spouse and minor and dependent children; otherwise to the children, or persons having their care and custody; but in case any minor child or dependent child is not living with the surviving spouse, the allowance may be

31. Ariz.Rev.Stat.Ann. § 14–2403; § 114.015; Wash.Rev.Code Ann. § 11.-
Conn.Gen.Stat.Ann. § 45–250; Okla. 52.040.
Stat.Ann.tit. 58, § 314; Or.Rev.Stat.

made partially to the child or his guardian or other person having his care and custody, and partially to the spouse, as their needs may appear. The family allowance is exempt from and has priority over all claims but not over the homestead allowance.

The family allowance is not chargeable against any benefit or share passing to the surviving spouse or children by the will of the decedent unless otherwise provided, by intestate succession, or by way of elective share. The death of any person entitled to family allowance terminates his right to allowances not yet paid.

1990 Code § 2–404 is substantially the same as the pre–1990 provision.

Finally there is the homestead allowance which exists in many states. The original purpose of this type of statute was to give the family home to the spouse in fee, or to the spouse for life and to the children during minority, free of the decedent's creditors' claims. However, in many states a dollar limit has been placed upon the allowance which is usually far below current land values, such as $5,000 or $12,000. It is only that value which is covered by the statute. This means that the homestead allowance is essentially a legislated disposition of a specific dollar amount not subject to creditors' claims. Some states, however, give the property interest without any dollar limit of value. The statutes vary all over the lot.[32] Pre–1990 Uniform Probate Code § 2–401, which has been legislated in some states, is as follows:

Section 2–401. [Homestead Allowance.]

A surviving spouse of a decedent who was domiciled in this state is entitled to a homestead allowance of [$5,000]. If there is no surviving spouse, each minor child and each dependent child of the decedent is entitled to a homestead allowance amounting to [$5,000] divided by the number of minor and dependent children of the decedent. The homestead allowance is exempt from and has priority over all claims against the estate. Homestead allowance is in addition to any share passing to the surviving spouse or minor or dependent child by the will of the decedent unless otherwise provided, by intestate succession or by way of elective share.

1990 Code § 2–402 is the same as the pre–1990 Code provision, except that the homestead allowance has been increased to $15,000.

32. See Ark. Const. Art. 9, §§ 4, 5, 6; Ky.Rev.Stat.Ann. §§ 427.060, 427.070; Me.Rev.Stat.Ann. tit. 18–A, § 2–401; Mass.Gen.Laws Ann. ch. 188, §§ 1, 4; N.H.Rev.Stat.Ann. §§ 480:1, 480:3–a; Okla.Stat.Ann. tit. 58, § 311; Utah Code Ann. § 75–2–401.

SECTION 9.   RULE AGAINST PERPETUITIES

Suppose the owner of Blackacre conveyed it to his son for life, remainder to his grandsons for their lives, remainder to his great-grandsons for their lives, remainder to his great-great-grandsons for their lives, and upon the death of the surviving great-great-grandson, remainder to his great-great-great-grandsons in fee. This type of transfer has been viewed as socially undesirable because it effectively removes the land from commerce and development for many years. This is because there is no market for a life estate, or a series of them; people interested in using and developing land want the fee interest. In this situation the fee can be conveyed only by the joinder of the son, all the grandsons, all the great-grandsons, all the great-great-grandsons, and all the great-great-great-grandsons, but unfortunately they are not all around to join in the deed. A court may appoint a guardian for those who are not around or who are not of age, and approve the sale of the fee, but this is a cumbersome procedure. The creation of successive future interests extending far into the future not only may have undesirable commercial effects, but also it seems to make little sense to permit a person to determine who is to enjoy the property far into the future.

The common law limited the duration of the "dead hand" control of wealth by the rule against perpetuities.[33] In its feudal origins it applied only to land because future interests were not created in personal property at that time. In the past century or two, equitable future interests in trusts of personal property, stocks and bonds, have become common, and the rule against perpetuities has been made applicable to such interests as well as to legal and equitable interests in land. Theoretically, the rule is also applicable to legal future interests in personalty, but these are virtually unheard of.

Suppose a modern property owner creates a trust of stocks and bonds, to pay the income to his children for their lives, and then to pay the income to his grandchildren for their lives, and then to pay the income to his great-grandchildren for their lives, and then to pay the income to his great-great-grandchildren for their lives, and upon the death of the last survivor of the great-great-grandchildren, to pay the principal to the great-great-great-grandchildren in fee. Does this result in taking the trust property out of commerce? The trustee holds only legal title to the assets and not equitable

---

33. For a detailed treatment of the historical development and the operation of the rule against perpetuities, see Simes and Smith, Law of Future Interests §§ 1201–1292 (2d ed.1956). For a briefer description of the operation of the rule and a discussion of modern reforms, see Bergin and Haskell, Preface To Estates In Land And Future Interests Ch. 8 (2d ed. 1984).

title, but invariably the trustee also has the power to sell the legal
and equitable fee, that is to say, the totality of the property
interests. After the trustee sells, the proceeds are held in trust,
and they are invested in other assets which are held in trust. In
the modern trust, nothing is taken out of commerce. The trust is a
changing fund. It is true, however, that trust investment policy is
such that trusts have the effect of channeling a substantial quantity
of capital funds into conservative investments. Although the economic consequences of the trust we have described are probably not
very significant, it does seem highly questionable to allow a property owner to control the enjoyment of and the investment policy
with respect to a substantial quantum of wealth for such a long
period of time.

The common law rule against perpetuities, which remains the
law in many jurisdictions, often with statutory modifications, is as
follows: No interest is good unless it must vest, if at all, not later
than 21 years after some life in being at the creation of the interest.
The interest referred to is, of course, a future interest. The vesting
referred to is vesting in interest, not vesting in possession. A
future interest may vest in interest long before it vests in possession. Despite the brevity of the rule, it has spawned one of the
most abstruse bodies of law in Anglo-American jurisprudence.
This is not the place to explain its operation. An example or two of
what the rule permits and what it prohibits will suffice for our
purposes.

Testator leaves a will in which he creates a trust to pay the
income to his wife for life, and then to pay the income to his
children for their lives, and upon the death of the last child to die,
to pay the principal to his grandchildren. Testator is survived by
his wife and three children. All the interests in the trust are
within the rule and therefore valid.

Suppose, however, that the dispositive terms of that testamentary trust had been as follows: Income to wife for life, and then
income to his children for their lives, and then income to his
grandchildren for their lives, and upon the death of the last
surviving grandchild, the principal to his great-grandchildren. The
remainder to the great-grandchildren violates the common law rule
and is invalid; upon the death of the last grandchild to die, the
trustee holds on resulting trust for the estate of the testator.

The common law approach is mechanically to chop off the
future interest which violates the rule, and let the rest of the
disposition remain. More than half the states have enacted statutes which authorize the court to modify the invalid provision in
accordance with the apparent intent of the settlor to make it
conform to the rule. This is known as the "cy pres" or "reforma-

tion" reform. Another legislative reform, adopted by more than half the states, is to judge whether or not there is a violation of the rule by waiting to see what the actual sequence of events is, in place of the common law approach which is to make the determination of whether or not there is a violation prospectively as of the time of the creation of the future interests. This is known as the "wait and see" reform.[34]

It should be emphasized that the rule against perpetuities has to do with the time period within which a future interest must vest in interest. The rule is not concerned with the duration of trusts as such. A trust may last beyond the period of rule, provided all the interests thereunder vest within the period of the rule. The life income interests of the grandchildren in the example in the immediately preceding paragraph vest within the rule and are valid, but the trust which remains for their lives may last longer than the period of the rule. Several states, however, have statutes which limit the duration of trusts.[35] It has also been maintained that if the trust lasts beyond the period of the rule, it should be subject to termination by the beneficiaries after the expiration of the period.[36] That is to say, at the expiration of the period of the rule, the beneficiaries should be able to compel the trustee to distribute the assets to them, thereby terminating the trust, regardless of the provisions of the trust.[37]

In most jurisdictions there is a rule which limits accumulations of income under a private trust to the period of the rule against perpetuities.[38] Charitable trusts are allowed to accumulate income without regard to the period of perpetuities, but the court will limit the period of accumulation if the provision therefor in the trust instrument is unreasonably long.[39] However, the Internal Revenue

34. These reforms are reflected in Uniform Statutory Rule Against Perpetuities, 8A U.L.A. 1992 Supp. 342, and Restatement (Second) of Property, Donative Transfers §§ 1.4, 1.5 (1983). The Uniform Statutory Rule establishes a 90–year period for the purpose of the wait-and-see reform.

35. E.g., Nev.Rev.Stat. § 166.140; Okla.Stat.Ann. tit. 60, § 172.

36. Restatement (Second) of Property, Donative Transfers § 2.1 (1983); 1 Scott, Law of Trusts § 62.10 (4th ed., Fratcher, 1987); Simes, Handbook of the Law of Future Interests § 145 (2d ed.1966).

37. Chapter 11 deals with the right of beneficiaries to terminate the trust.

38. Gertman v. Burdick, 75 U.S.App. D.C. 48, 123 F.2d 924 (1941), cert. denied 315 U.S. 824, 62 S.Ct. 917, 86 L.Ed.

1220 (1942); Gaess v. Gaess, 132 Conn. 96, 42 A.2d 796 (1945); In re Foster's Estate, 190 Kan. 498, 376 P.2d 784 (1962); Rentz v. Polk, 267 S.C. 359, 228 S.E.2d 106 (1976); Cal.Civ.Code § 724; Ill.Ann.Stat. ch. 30, § 153; Ind.Code Ann. § 32–1–4–2; N.Y.Est. Powers & Trusts Law § 9–2.1.

39. Waterbury Trust Co. v. Porter, 131 Conn. 206, 38 A.2d 598 (1944); Frazier v. Merchants National Bank, 296 Mass. 298, 5 N.E.2d 550 (1936); Trusts of Holdeen, 486 Pa. 1, 403 A.2d 978 (1979); Allaun v. First & Merchants National Bank, 190 Va. 104, 56 S.E.2d 83 (1949). See Restatement (Second) of Property, Donative Transfers § 2.2(2) (1983).

Code precludes accumulations of income by certain tax-exempt charitable trusts. It should be noted that the rule against perpetuities does not apply to charitable trusts, and that the law does not limit the duration of charitable trusts.[40]

SECTION 10.   CONDITIONAL GIFTS TO DISCOURAGE MARRIAGE, ENCOURAGE DIVORCE, OR INFLUENCE RELIGIOUS AFFILIATION

Testator creates a trust in his will which provides for the payment of income to his Brother for his life, principal on Brother's death to Cousin, but if Brother should marry, then the trust is to terminate and the principal is to be immediately payable to Cousin. Testator and Brother were both bachelors. Brother had a job which paid well. The trust terms appear to discourage marriage. Unless there is credible evidence that Testator had a reason for cutting short Brother's income other than to discourage marriage, the provision cutting short Brother's interest upon his marriage is invalid as contrary to public policy.[41] The condition subsequent is stricken, leaving a life estate in Brother, remainder in Cousin. Marriage is considered to be socially desirable, and the law will not countenance the use of one's wealth in this manner to influence another to avoid it.

Suppose Testator created a trust in his will to pay the income to Niece for her life, principal at her death to Son, but if Niece should marry, then the trust is to terminate and the principal is to be immediately payable to Son. Niece was 25 at Testator's death, unmarried, had no special vocational skills, worked only occasionally, and had been supported financially by Testator. Testator created the trust to assure that Niece was supported while she was single, and he did not consider it necessary or appropriate to continue this support after her marriage. The purpose of the trust was not to discourage marriage, although it possibly could have such an effect. The condition subsequent is therefore valid.[42]

Suppose we change the facts of the preceding example by substituting Testator's Widow for Niece. Testator had been the breadwinner and had accumulated substantial wealth; Widow did

---

40. See Chapter 12, Section 5.

41. Knost v. Knost, 229 Mo. 170, 129 S.W. 665 (1910); In re Seaman's Will, 218 N.Y. 77, 112 N.E. 576 (1916); Gard v. Mason, 169 N.C. 507, 86 S.E. 302 (1915); Goffe v. Goffe, 37 R.I. 542, 94 A. 2 (1915); Cal.Civ.Code § 710; Ga.Code Ann. § 19-3-6; N.D.Cent.Code § 47-2-25; S.D.Comp.Laws Ann. § 43-3-4. See Restatement (Second) of Property, Donative Transfers § 6.1 (1983).

42. Lewis v. Searles, 452 S.W.2d 153 (Mo.1970); Estate of Stone, 155 N.Y.S.2d 898 (Sur.1956), aff'd 3 A.D.2d 1009, 165 N.Y.S.2d 695 (1957); Winters v. Miller, 23 Ohio Misc. 73, 261 N.E.2d 205 (1970); Harbin v. Judd, 47 Tenn. App. 604, 340 S.W.2d 935 (1960). See Restatement (Second) of Property, Donative Transfers § 6.1 (1983).

not work and had no property of her own. Testator's purpose was to assure Widow an income while she was single, and he did not consider it necessary or advisable to provide the income after she remarried. On facts such as these, it has been held that the condition subsequent is valid.[43]

Suppose in the preceding example the Widow had considerable wealth of her own, and the Testator's purpose was to discourage her remarriage from a spirit of possessiveness. There is some authority that the condition of remarriage is valid without regard to any purpose of support in the case of the surviving spouse of the testator.[44]

Suppose a settlor created a trust to pay the income to Son for life, principal at his death to Son's issue, but if Son should marry someone who is not a practicing Roman Catholic, then the trust is to terminate and the principal is to be immediately payable to Daughter. Son is single at the time of the creation of the trust. This condition subsequent discourages marriage to non-Catholics, but it permits Son to choose a wife from a large group without incurring any penalty. This condition subsequent is held to be valid as a reasonable "restraint" on marriage.[45] The courts are not opposed to marriage restraints if they are limited in nature. The word "restraint" is sometimes used in this marriage context; there is, of course, no restraint in the literal sense, but money is used to discourage or encourage specific conduct.

A condition which terminates a beneficial interest in a trust upon marriage to someone who is not of the white race would probably be valid, provided it did not fail for indefiniteness. The courts have allowed settlors to be arbitrary in their marriage conditions as long as the beneficiary has an ample opportunity for marriage without losing his interest. It is arguable that judicial enforcement of religious and racial conditions in trusts and wills is violative of the equal protection clause of the Fourteenth Amendment, by analogy to the case of Shelley v. Kraemer,[46] but there does

43. Wilbur v. Campbell, 280 Ala. 268, 192 So.2d 721 (1966); Knight v. Mahoney, 152 Mass. 523, 25 N.E. 971 (1890); Latorraca v. Latorraca, 132 N.J.Eq. 40, 26 A.2d 522 (1942).

44. Matter of 1942 Gerald H. Lewis Trust, 652 P.2d 1106 (Colo.App.1982); N.D.Cent.Code § 47-2-25; S.D.Comp. Laws Ann. § 43-3-4. See Restatement (Second) of Property, Donative Transfers § 6.3 (1983). Ind.Code Ann. § 29-1-6-3 invalidates such a condition as to the spouse.

45. Gordon v. Gordon, 332 Mass. 197, 124 N.E.2d 228 (1955); Shapira v.

Union National Bank, 39 Ohio Misc. 28, 315 N.E.2d 825 (1974); United States National Bank v. Snodgrass, 202 Or. 530, 275 P.2d 860 (1954); Estate of Keffalas, 426 Pa. 432, 233 A.2d 248 (1967); In re Paulson's Will, 127 Wis. 612, 107 N.W. 484 (1906). See Restatement (Second) of Property, Donative Transfers § 6.2 (1983).

46. 334 U.S. 1, 68 S.Ct. 836, 92 L.Ed. 1161 (1948), holding that judicial enforcement of racially restrictive real estate covenants constituted state action violative of the equal protection clause of the Fourteenth Amendment.

not appear to be any authority for this.[47]

A condition that a beneficiary not marry a particular person has been upheld as a reasonable restraint.[48] Also, a condition that a beneficiary not marry without the consent of a particular person has been upheld.[49] It is likely, however, that a court would require that the withholding of consent be reasonable.

Trust conditions whose purpose is to encourage divorce have been held to be invalid as contrary to public policy. Testator creates a trust in his will to pay the income to Son for life when Son ceases to be married to his present wife. Son had a job that paid well, and his wife did not work and had no property of her own to speak of. In the absence of credible evidence that Testator had a reason for deferring the Son's interest other than to encourage divorce, the condition precedent to Son's interest is invalid as contrary to public policy.[50] The prevailing view is that the Son becomes entitled to the trust income presently as if the condition precedent did not exist.[51]

The settlor can control the effect of the invalidity of the condition upon the beneficial interest by anticipating that result in the trust instrument. For instance, the trust instrument may provide that if the condition precedent is invalid, the interest shall fail also, or that the interest shall vest immediately as if the condition precedent did not exist. We have seen that if a condition subsequent is invalid, it is stricken and the interest which it would have terminated continues in effect. The trust instrument, however, may provide that if a condition subsequent is invalid, the interest which the invalid condition subsequent would terminate fails also.

Suppose a settlor creates a trust to pay the income to his Daughter at such time as she is unmarried. Daughter is married at the time the trust is created and has two children. She has no

---

47. See Gordon v. Gordon, 332 Mass. 197, 124 N.E.2d 228 (1955); Shapira v. Union National Bank, 39 Ohio Misc. 28, 315 N.E.2d 825 (1974); United States National Bank v. Snodgrass, 202 Or. 530, 275 P.2d 860 (1954).

48. Taylor v. Rapp, 217 Ga. 654, 124 S.E.2d 271 (1962); Turner v. Evans, 134 Md. 238, 106 A. 617 (1919); In re Seaman's Will, 218 N.Y. 77, 112 N.E. 576 (1916).

49. Pacholder v. Rosenheim, 129 Md. 455, 99 A. 672 (1916). See Matter of Liberman, 279 N.Y. 458, 18 N.E.2d 658 (1939).

50. In re Estate of Gerbing, 61 Ill.2d 503, 337 N.E.2d 29 (1975); Fineman v.

Central National Bank, 175 N.E.2d 837, 18 O.O.2d 33 (Ohio App.1961); Matter of Collura, 98 Misc.2d 1104, 415 N.Y.S.2d 380 (1979); Estate of Keffalas, 426 Pa. 432, 233 A.2d 248 (1967); Graves v. First National Bank, 138 N.W.2d 584 (N.D.1965). See Restatement (Second) of Property, Donative Transfers § 7.1 (1983).

51. In re Estate of Gerbing, 61 Ill.2d 503, 337 N.E.2d 29 (1975); Fleishman v. Bregel, 174 Md. 87, 197 A. 593 (1938); Matter of Liberman, 279 N.Y. 458, 18 N.E.2d 658 (1939); Fineman v. Central National Bank, 175 N.E.2d 837, 18 O.O.2d 33 (Ohio App.1961); Graves v. First National Bank, 138 N.W.2d 584 (N.D.1965).

special vocational skills, and presumably would have difficulty supporting herself and the children. This condition precedent may be valid because the settlor's purpose apparently was to provide support rather than to encourage divorce.[52]

We have seen that a condition in a trust which penalizes a beneficiary for marrying someone of a particular faith is not considered to be against public policy. There also is authority that a condition that a person remain a member of a particular faith, or become a member of a particular faith, is valid. Trust terms which provide for the payment of income to Son as long as he remains a practicing Mormon, or to pay income to Daughter if she converts to Roman Catholicism, are probably valid.[53]

It is clear that the law sometimes upholds conditions which reflect the arbitrary, unreasonable or bigoted attitudes of the settlor. The question may well be asked why the law should permit a person to influence the conduct of others in this fashion with respect to such important and sensitive aspects of life as marriage and religion, for years after his death. The property owner while he is alive may, of course, bestow gifts upon those who comply with his wishes, and withhold them from those who do not. Why can't he do the same after his death? Ownership denotes the right of disposition, including the right to dispose whimsically, arbitrarily and unreasonably. The law does, however, place certain limitations upon the right of disposition, such as the surviving spouse's forced share, the rule against perpetuities, as well as the invalidity of the conditions discussed in this section. The right of disposition is not absolute. The issue is whether the law should add a few more prohibitions. The analogy to arbitrary lifetime giving has at least one flaw: While the property owner is alive, he may be importuned to change his views, but after his death the unfair condition in the trust instrument is written in cement.

The discussion in the preceding paragraph raises the question of the validity of conditions which are applicable only at the time of the testator's death. Suppose Jones has a daughter who is married to someone whom Jones did not want her to marry and Jones fervently wishes that she would divorce him. Jones can certainly decline to make living gifts to her as long as she is married to the man although he is making living gifts to other children of his.

---

52. Hamilton v. Ferrall, 92 Cal. App.2d 277, 206 P.2d 663 (1949); Alexander v. Hicks, 488 S.W.2d 336 (Ky. 1972); Hood v. St. Louis Union Trust Co., 334 Mo. 404, 66 S.W.2d 837 (1933); In re Hauck's Estate, 239 Wis. 421, 1 N.W.2d 773 (1942).

53. Delaware Trust Co. v. Fitzmaurice, 27 Del.Ch. 101, 31 A.2d 383 (1943), modified sub nom. Crumlish v. Delaware Trust Co., 27 Del.Ch. 374, 38 A.2d 463 (1944); United States National Bank v. Snodgrass, 202 Or. 530, 275 P.2d 860 (1954); In re Estate of Laning, 462 Pa. 157, 339 A.2d 520 (1975). See Restatement (Second) of Property, Donative Transfers § 8.1 (1983).

Suppose Jones' will provides that his daughter is to receive $100,-000 if she is no longer married to the man at Jones' death. This condition is functionally equivalent to his withholding money from her during her marriage while he was alive, and is valid.[54] He is not creating a condition which has continuing effect after his death. If the daughter was married to the man at Jones' death, and if Jones created a trust in his will of $100,000 to be paid to his daughter when she became divorced, the condition would be invalid.

54. Succession of Ruxton, 226 La. 1088, 78 So.2d 183 (1955). See Restatement (Second) of Property, Donative Transfers § 6.1, comment c, illustration 5 (1983).

Chapter 9

ADMINISTRATION OF THE DECEDENT'S ESTATE

SECTION 1. INTRODUCTION

As we have described in various contexts before, the economic estate of a decedent falls into the two categories of estate assets and will substitutes. Estate assets consist of the property owned solely by the decedent or owned by the decedent as tenant in common with another. Will substitutes consist of such things as life insurance, joint tenancies, joint and payable-on-death bank accounts, and revocable trusts. Estate assets pass under the will or by intestacy and are subject to estate administration; will substitutes pass in accordance with their terms rather than under the will or by intestacy, and are not subject to estate administration. This chapter deals with the administration of estate assets. Will substitutes pass free of the regulation to which estate assets are subject. There is no rhyme or reason for this difference in treatment; as we have said before, the dichotomization of the economic estate evolved without design.

Estate administration includes the judicial establishment of the validity of the decedent's will if there is one, the judicial appointment of a personal representative who administers the estate, and the procedures for the management of the estate. The law dealing with these matters is primarily statutory, and the statutes vary widely from state to state. Frequently the statutes are not as explicit as they could be, leaving gaps that are filled sometimes by judicial decisions and sometimes by custom. In significant measure estate administration is idiosyncratic to the specific state. Because of the multiple variations, we shall attempt to describe the administrative process by means of the Uniform Probate Code. The estate administration provisions of the Code have not been materially amended since the Code's promulgation in 1969. The administrative provisions of the Code have been adopted by a minority of states, but the provisions are detailed, explicit, and thoroughly considered. The Code provisions also touch upon the principal steps in estate administration provided in the statutes of most states. We shall make reference to parallel non-Code statutory provisions of various states throughout the discussion. This gener-

181

alized background should enable the reader to identify and understand the detailed statutory provisions of the particular jurisdiction with which she is concerned.

Chapter 13 deals with principles of fiduciary administration beyond the procedures of decedent estate administration covered in this chapter. In that chapter we deal with problems of delegation of authority by a fiduciary, conflicts of interest, investments, and the determination of principal and income, among other things. These issues apply to personal representatives as well as trustees. The personal representative has the short-term function of winding up the decedent's financial affairs; the trustee is a long-term manager of investments. Both are fiduciaries and their responsibilities as such are common. The different nature of their roles, however, means that certain areas of responsibility are more significant for the trustee than for the personal representative. This is certainly the case with respect to investments and the determination of principal and income. We shall deal in Chapter 13 with the problems of fiduciary responsibility common to the personal representative and the trustee after we have completed the substantive law of wills and trusts.

There is a matter of nomenclature that should be dealt with at the outset. "Personal representative" is the generic term for the person appointed by the court to administer the estate of the decedent. More specific titles, however, are commonly used. The person named in the will of a decedent and appointed by the court to administer the estate is called an executor. If the decedent has no will, the person appointed by the court to administer the estate is called an administrator.

If there is no will and the administrator does not complete his administration, the person appointed to succeed him is called an administrator of goods not administered, usually abbreviated to administrator d.b.n. (for the Latin de bonis non). If the decedent leaves a will but does not designate an executor, or if someone is designated but is not appointed by the court, the person appointed is called an administrator with the will annexed, usually abbreviated to administrator c.t.a. (for the Latin cum testamento annexo). If an executor does not complete his administration, or an administrator with the will annexed does not complete his administration, the person appointed to succeed him is called an administrator with the will annexed of goods not administered, usually abbreviated to administrator c.t.a.d.b.n.

Sometimes it is necessary to appoint a person to begin administration before a permanent executor or administrator is appointed. This temporary personal representative is usually called a special administrator.

The Uniform Probate Code uses the generic "personal representative" to describe an executor or administrator of various kinds, or sometimes "successor personal representative" in the appropriate circumstances, and "special administrator" to describe the temporary personal representative.

Before we begin our discussion of the mechanics of probate and administration we shall discuss why we have administration and the circumstances in which that frequently cumbersome and expensive process can be avoided.

SECTION 2. FUNCTION OF AND NECESSITY FOR ADMINISTRATION

When a person dies it is necessary to identify and collect what he owned, pay his debts and taxes, and determine who are entitled to what is left over. If there is a will, the judicial establishment of it, usually referred to as the probate of the will, determines who are entitled to the decedent's property after the payment of claims. If there is no will, the court usually identifies the intestate takers. The personal representative appointed by the court has the responsibility for identifying and collecting the assets of the decedent, paying the claims, and distributing the remainder of the property to those entitled to it. In a majority of states the personal representative takes title to the decedent's personal property, whereas title to real property usually passes directly to the heirs or devisees. However, real property may be sold by the personal representative to pay debts and administration expenses, and, in general, is within the fiduciary responsibility of the personal representative despite the location of the title. Uniform Probate Code §§ 3–101, 3–709, and 3–711 provide that title to personalty and realty is in the heirs, legatees and devisees, subject to the fiduciary management and power of sale of the personal representative. In a majority of states the personal representative is subject to judicial supervision and regulatory procedures in varying degrees and forms. The controls result in expense to the estate, and their value has been the subject of considerable controversy. It should be noted here that the thrust of the Uniform Probate Code is to minimize judicial oversight of the administration of estates.

The administration process is logical and orderly. The personal representative is the successor to the decedent for the purpose of winding up his financial affairs. The debtors of the decedent, such as a bank in which the decedent held a balance, pay the personal representative what is owed. Corporations whose stock was owned by the decedent transfer the stock into the name of the personal representative. If the personal representative needs to sell property, the purchaser receives good title from the personal representative. Creditors of the decedent submit their claims to the personal representative who pays them from the decedent's property. When all claims, administration expenses and death taxes are paid, the personal representative turns over the remainder to the takers under the will or to the intestate takers, thereby resolving the decedent's financial affairs. It is an orderly process of claims payment and title transfer in which debtors and creditors of the decedent, those dealing with property of the decedent, and those who are the ultimate beneficiaries of the decedent, are protected.

The administration process does, however, usually involve the hiring of a lawyer, personal representative's fees, and other procedural costs, as well as delay in the distribution of the property to the beneficiaries, and if they can be avoided, so much the better. Suppose the decedent died intestate survived by her husband and two adult children, leaving $10,000 in cash and $30,000 in municipal bonds in bearer form, all of which are in husband's safe deposit box in a bank. Bearer bonds are titled in the name of "bearer" and title to them passes to good faith purchasers by delivery in the same manner as title to cash passes. Under the intestacy law the husband takes one-third and the children take two-thirds. The decedent had debts of $2,000 under two credit card accounts. Husband deposits the cash in his bank account, and sells the bearer bonds, depositing the proceeds in that account. Husband pays the credit card debts, and files the state death tax return and pays the small tax due. Husband gives two-thirds of what remains to the children. There is no administration, no expense, no delay in distribution. This was possible because there is no need to establish by documentation the transfer of title from decedent to personal representative to beneficiaries with respect to assets in the form of cash or bearer bonds. Has the family done anything wrong? Absolutely not. Everything has been done that should have been done; no one has any basis for complaint.

Suppose that, in addition to the cash and the bearer bonds, the decedent had an account with First Bank in her sole name with a balance of $20,000 at her death. Husband requests First Bank to release the funds to him, or if it prefers, to him and the children in their intestate shares. If First Bank were to accede to the request, what risk is it taking? First, suppose an undisclosed third child turned up a year later. If the family does not give him his share, that child could petition for the appointment of a personal representative who would collect the assets of the estate. If the personal representative could not obtain the estate assets from the husband and the other children, he could recover the balance that had been in the account with First Bank. First Bank would have to pay again. First Bank had no legal protection by virtue of its unauthorized payment to husband and children. First Bank will get back its overpayment if husband and the two children are ultimately forthcoming on their obligation to restore estate property to the personal representative, but that remains to be seen.

Suppose, instead of a third child, another creditor turns up with a $10,000 claim. If the family does not pay the claim, the creditor could petition for the appointment of a personal representative who would collect the assets of the estate. If the personal representative could not obtain the estate assets from the husband and the children, he could recover the balance that had been in the account with First Bank. First Bank's payment provided it no legal protection. In sum, if First Bank pays to anyone other than the personal representative it may have to pay again if it turns out that there is an unpaid creditor, or tax collector, or beneficiary.

It should be apparent that the undisclosed third child and the creditor could not require First Bank to pay them directly without formal administration because that would be another unauthorized and unprotected payment. There may be still further creditors or children who would be disadvantaged by such payment.

If, on the other hand, First Bank knows the family and decides to cooperate by releasing the funds to the family, it has done nothing illegal. First Bank does not have to insist upon payment only to a personal representative. It can take whatever risk is involved if it chooses to do so. If all creditors and the tax collector are paid by the family, and the heirs are as represented to First Bank, everybody is taken care of and all is well.

Let us assume that instead of a bank account the decedent owned 100 shares of IBM common stock. The stock certificate is in the name of the decedent and, of course, the dividend checks are made payable to the decedent. The stock cannot be sold and the dividend checks cannot be cleared until the stock is transferred on the books of the corporation from the decedent to the personal representative and a new certificate issued in the name of the personal representative to replace the old one. The husband can present the same story to IBM that he presented to the bank, but IBM is not going to accede to the request. If it did, of course, it would be subject to the same risks discussed in connection with the bank. If another heir or creditor showed up who could not receive satisfaction from the family, a personal representative would probably be appointed who would be entitled to receive a new certificate from IBM. IBM will not transfer the stock on its books and issue a new certificate to anyone other than the personal representative or possibly the heirs on the direction of the personal representative.

Suppose instead of a bank account or stock the decedent owned a parcel of land. The family does not have to have the concurrence of a third party such as the bank or the corporation for the transfer of title to the property. Unless there is administration, however, the title to the land is probably unmarketable, i.e., no one will buy it. The last deed was to the decedent. This deed is in the land records. Title to the land passes from the decedent to her devisee under the will if there is one, or in intestacy to her heirs. Without administration the link in the record chain of title is missing. Not only is the identity of the devisee or heirs uncertain, but unpaid creditors of the decedent could compel the appointment of a personal representative at a later time to reach the land to pay the creditors.

In sum, if the estate includes stocks, bonds (other than bearer bonds), bank accounts or land, there is going to be administration in all likelihood. It should be noted that most states have statutes providing for the avoidance of administration for very small estates; this is discussed in Section 11 of this chapter.

Administration may be avoided when there is agreement as to who are beneficially entitled to the estate and the validity of claims, and the estate consists of property which legally or as a practical matter can be transferred without judicial establishment of title. Title to such assets as cash and bearer bonds pass to bona fide purchasers without proof of title. As a practical matter, chattels of limited value, such as household furnishings, can be sold without proof of title although the bona fide purchaser of chattels receives no better title than his transferor had. The purchaser of valuable chattels such as jewelry may insist upon proof of title because he receives no better title than his transferor has, and this makes administration necessary.

Administration may be avoided if the economic estate of the decedent consists wholly of will substitutes. Will substitutes by definition bypass administration. Life insurance payable to a beneficiary other than the estate of the insured passes directly to the beneficiary; joint tenancy property passes to the surviving joint tenant by operation of law; the revocable living trust continues in accordance with its dispositive terms after the death of the decedent; the joint bank account usually passes to the survivor. Large sums can pass by means of will substitutes. Sometimes will substitutes are subject, in whole or in part, to the claims of the decedent's creditors. Will substitutes are usually subject to death taxation, and there can be a problem of responsibility for the payment of the tax. It is possible that the tax authorities could force administration for that reason, but usually it is not necessary because someone interested in the estate assumes the responsibility for the filing of the return and the payment of the tax.

One anomalous line of authority concerning the avoidance of administration should be described. Suppose a decedent leaves a valid will disposing of his property among his immediate family who are also his intestate takers. They are all in agreement with respect to who is to receive what property. All creditors have been paid. The estate consists of cash, a bank account, and stock in a family corporation. The bank is willing to release the funds to the family, and the family corporation is willing to issue new certificates to the family. There is no need for administration and the family intends for there to be none. The will designates First Bank as executor. First Bank petitions the court for admission of the will to probate and appointment as executor. The family objects. In circumstances such as this there is limited authority that the will must be admitted and the executor appointed.[1] The basic reason offered for probate in these circumstances is that the law dictates that the intent and purposes of the decedent must be honored. In other words, the legatees and heirs are not the only parties whose interests are involved. The decedent's interest in having the will admitted and his property administered by his designated executor must also be considered. Another justification that has been offered is that if the family has agreed on a distribution which differs from the terms of the will, it is possible that creditors of those who receive less than they would under the will may be disadvantaged. This latter reasoning supports a petition for administration by a disadvantaged creditor, but not by an officious executor. It should be emphasized that most courts would not authorize probate and administration in these circumstances.

Most states have statutes which require that one in possession of a will deliver it to the probate court.[2] The statutes do not require, however, that the will be probated.

Sometimes a will contest by disappointed heirs is avoided by a compromise agreement among those who obtain an advantage under the will and disappointed heirs. It is assumed that there is going to be administration; the agreement has to do with the beneficial interests in the estate. The legal ramifications of these agreements are discussed in Section 12 of this chapter.

SECTION 3. PROBATE OF WILL; APPOINTMENT OF PERSONAL REPRESENTATIVE

The probate of a will is the judicial determination that the instrument is the will of the decedent. This means that the

1. Tator v. Valden, 124 Conn. 96, 198 A. 169 (1938); In re Estate of Harper, 202 Kan. 150, 446 P.2d 738 (1968); In re Nelson's Estate, 242 Pa. 167, 88 A. 974 (1913); In re Vasgaard's Estate, 62 S.D. 421, 253 N.W. 453 (1934). See Annot., 29 A.L.R.3d 8, 39 (1970), for abundant authority to the contrary.

2. E.g., Del.Code Ann. tit. 12, § 1301; Ill.Ann.Stat. ch. 110½, § 6–1; Nev.Rev.Stat. § 136.050; Okla.Stat. Ann. tit. 58, § 21.

testator intended it to be his will, that it has not been revoked, that it was executed in compliance with the statutory formalities, that the testator had the requisite mental capacity, that the testator was not subject to undue influence, that fraud was not practiced on the testator with respect to the inducement to the execution of the will or the inclusion of its provisions, and that none of the clauses was inserted by mistake. Noncompliance with the formalities of execution, lack of testamentary capacity, undue influence, fraud, and mistake are the principal bases for contesting the validity of a will.

Probate is not concerned with the construction or the interpretation of the provisions of the will; matters of this nature may be litigated after probate of the will during administration. Probate is not concerned with the substantive validity of the terms of the will; as examples, questions involving violations of the rule against perpetuities, or the invalidity of a condition to a bequest as violative of public policy such as one requiring divorce, are matters to be litigated during administration.

The state in which the decedent was domiciled at her death has jurisdiction over the decedent by virtue of that fact. The administration in that state is referred to as the principal or domiciliary administration. The law of the domiciliary state governs the disposition of all personal property of the decedent whether located in the state or elsewhere, and all real property located in the state.[3] The disposition of real property located in another state is governed by the law of that state.[4] If there is land outside the state of domicile there will in all likelihood be ancillary administration in the state in which the land is located. If there is personal property having a situs in a state other than the domiciliary state, it is possible, but unlikely, that there will be ancillary administration for the benefit of local creditors in that state, but the law of the domiciliary state controls its disposition to the extent the property is not used to satisfy local creditors. Ancillary administration is discussed in Section 8 of this chapter.

The will is probated in the state in which the decedent was domiciled at death. If the decedent has no property, real or personal, located in another state, that is the only place it will be probated. If there is a need for ancillary administration, the will is probated also in the ancillary state, and in that event it is almost invariably, although not necessarily, probated first in the domiciliary state. Venue for probate within the domiciliary state is the county in which the testator was domiciled at death.

3. Restatement (Second) of Conflict of Laws §§ 260–266, 236–243 (1971); Scoles and Hay, Conflict of Laws §§ 20.6–20.14 (2d ed. 1992).

4. Restatement (Second) of Conflict of Laws §§ 236–243 (1971); Scoles and Hay, Conflict of Laws §§ 20.6–20.8 (2d ed. 1992).

There were two probate procedures in England historically, probate in "common form," and probate in "solemn form." Probate in common form was an ex parte proceeding in which the will was admitted to probate on petition of an interested party without notice to the heirs or anyone else. Those with standing to contest the probate of the will could do so by bringing an action at a later time. Probate in solemn form was an inter partes action brought by an interested party in which other interested parties such as heirs were joined and given notice. Anyone who chose to contest the validity of the will was required to do so in that proceeding. The judgment in that proceeding was final as to that will, subject, of course, to appeal.

Many states have an ex parte probate procedure similar in nature to the old common form. An interested party can contest the probate by bringing an action within a period of time specified by statute, such as six months or three years.[5] The action to contest the validity of the will is an inter partes proceeding in which all interested parties must be joined and given notice. Those states which have the ex parte probate procedure may provide for the inter partes procedure in the first instance in which interested parties such as heirs are joined and given notice and are bound by the judgment as to that will, subject to appeal. The proponent of the will would have the option of the use of the ex parte or the inter partes procedure. If no trouble is anticipated, as is the case in the vast majority of situations, the ex parte proceeding is used; if there is the potential for a contest, the inter partes procedure may be chosen by the proponent.

Some states have only the inter partes procedure for probate of the will, in which interested parties such as heirs are joined and given notice, and the judgment in the action is final as to that will, subject to appeal.[6]

The Uniform Probate Code (herein "U.P.C.") provides both an ex parte proceeding and an inter partes proceeding. The ex parte proceeding is called "informal probate," the inter partes proceeding is called "formal testacy." The proponent of the will may elect either procedure. A person who wishes to contest the ex parte informal probate of a will does so by means of the inter partes formal testacy procedure. We first consider informal probate.

---

5. E.g., Ga.Code Ann. § 53–3–12; Ky.Rev.Stat.Ann. § 394.240; Miss.Code Ann. § 91–7–23; N.C.Gen.Stat. § 31–32.

6. E.g., N.Y.Sur.Ct.Proc.Act §§ 1403 et seq.; Okla.Stat.Ann. tit. 58, §§ 25 et seq.; S.D.Comp.Laws Ann. §§ 30–6–7 et seq.

U.P.C. § 3–302 is as follows:

Section 3–302. [Informal Probate; Duty of Registrar; Effect of Informal Probate.]

Upon receipt of an application requesting informal probate of a will, the Registrar, upon making the findings required by Section 3–303 shall issue a written statement of informal probate if at least 120 hours have elapsed since the decedent's death. Informal probate is conclusive as to all persons until superseded by an order in a formal testacy proceeding. No defect in the application or procedure relating thereto which leads to informal probate of a will renders the probate void.

The Comment to U.P.C. § 3–302 reads in part as follows:

... This "umbrella" section and the sections it refers to describe an alternative procedure called "informal probate." It is a statement of probate by the Registrar. A succeeding section describes cases in which informal probate is to be denied. "Informal probate" is subjected to safeguards which seem appropriate to a transaction which has the effect of making a will operative and which may be the only official reaction concerning its validity. "Informal probate," it is hoped, will serve to keep the simple will which generates no controversy from becoming involved in truly judicial proceedings. The procedure is very much like "probate in common form" as it is known in England and some states.

U.P.C. § 3–303(c), concerning informal probate, is as follows:

(c) A will which appears to have the required signatures and which contains an attestation clause showing that requirements of execution under Section 2–502, 2–503, or 2–506 have been met shall be probated without further proof. In other cases, the Registrar may assume execution if the will appears to have been properly executed, or he may accept a sworn statement or affidavit of any person having knowledge of the circumstances of execution, whether or not the person was a witness to the will.

U.P.C. § 3–306 provides that no prior notice concerning informal probate needs to be given to anyone other than an appointed personal representative and an interested person who has filed with the court a demand for notice of any order or filing pertaining to the estate. In any event, there is no provision for a hearing before informal probate is granted. If a personal representative is appointed, as will normally be the case, he has the duty to inform legatees of the probate.

U.P.C. § 3–305 is as follows:

Section 3–305. [Informal Probate; Registrar Not Satisfied.]

If the Registrar is not satisfied that a will is entitled to be probated in informal proceedings because of failure to meet the requirements of Sections 3–303 and 3–304 or any other reason, he may decline the application. A declination of informal probate is not an adjudication and does not preclude formal probate proceedings.

The Uniform Probate Code provides both an ex parte procedure for the appointment of a personal representative, called "informal appointment proceeding," and an inter partes procedure for the appointment of a personal representative, called "formal appointment proceeding." The applicant may choose the form of proceeding she wishes. Anyone who wishes to challenge the appointment made in an informal proceeding must do so by means of a formal inter partes proceeding.

Traditional American procedure contemplates the probate of the will or determination of intestacy and the appointment of the personal representative. The Uniform Probate Code makes it clear that those are separate matters. Under the Uniform Probate Code there is a procedure for the probate of the will or a determination of intestacy without any appointment of a personal representative. In other words, the Code provides for the judicial determination of who are beneficially interested in the estate without requiring that there be any judicially sanctioned administration. As a practical matter there is usually going to be administration, and the probate of the will and the appointment of a personal representative are likely to take place at the same time. We proceed now to consider the informal appointment proceeding.

U.P.C. § 3–307 reads in part as follows:

Section 3–307. [Informal Appointment Proceedings; Delay in Order; Duty of Registrar; Effect of Appointment.]

(a) Upon receipt of an application for informal appointment of a personal representative other than a special administrator as provided in Section 3–614, if at least 120 hours have elapsed since the decedent's death, the Registrar, after making the findings required by Section 3–308, shall appoint the applicant subject to qualification and acceptance; ....

(b) The status of personal representative and the powers and duties pertaining to the office are fully established by informal appointment.

U.P.C. §§ 3–308 and 3–311 provide that there may be no informal appointment of a personal representative if there is a will unless the will has been formally or informally probated; if the will has not been probated, a special (interim) administrator may be appointed.

U.P.C. § 3–203 sets forth the priorities for appointment of the personal representative, combining intestacy with the existence of a will, and reads in part as follows:

Section 3–203. [Priority Among Persons Seeking Appointment as Personal Representative.]

(a) Whether the proceedings are formal or informal, persons who are not disqualified have priority for appointment in the following order:

(1) the person with priority as determined by a probated will including a person nominated by a power conferred in a will;

(2) the surviving spouse of the decedent who is a devisee of the decedent;

(3) other devisees of the decedent;

(4) the surviving spouse of the decedent;

(5) other heirs of the decedent;

(6) 45 days after the death of the decedent, any creditor.

U.P.C. § 3–310 provides for prior notice of informal appointment only to an interested person who has filed with the court a demand for notice of any order or filing pertaining to the estate, and to anyone having a prior or equal right to appointment. There is no provision for a hearing prior to the informal appointment.

U.P.C. § 3–309 reads as follows:

Section 3–309. [Informal Appointment Proceedings; Registrar Not Satisfied.]

If the Registrar is not satisfied that a requested informal appointment of a personal representative should be made because of failure to meet the requirements of Sections 3–307 and 3–308, or for any other reason, he may decline the application. A declination of informal appointment is not an adjudication and does not preclude appointment in formal proceedings.

The Uniform Probate Code thus provides informal procedures for the probate of a will and for the appointment of the personal representative. There may be probate of the will without the appointment of a personal representative. There is no informal procedure to determine that the decedent died intestate or to determine the heirs.

U.P.C. § 3–401 and following sections, provide for formal, inter partes proceedings to probate a will, to set aside an informal probate of a will, and to determine intestacy and heirship. U.P.C. § 3–401 reads in part as follows:

Section 3–401. [Formal Testacy Proceedings; Nature; When Commenced.]

A formal testacy proceeding is litigation to determine whether a decedent left a valid will. A formal testacy proceeding may be commenced by an interested person filing a petition as described in Section 3–402(a) in which he requests that the Court, after notice and hearing, enter an order probating a will, or a petition to set aside an informal probate of a will or to prevent informal probate of a will which is the subject of a pending application, or a petition in accordance with Section 3–402(b) for an order that the decedent died intestate.

A petition may seek formal probate of a will without regard to whether the same or a conflicting will has been informally probated. A formal testacy proceeding may, but need not, involve a request for appointment of a personal representative.

During the pendency of a formal testacy proceeding, the Registrar shall not act upon any application for informal probate of any will of the decedent or any application for informal appointment of a personal representative of the decedent.

U.P.C. § 3–403 sets forth the notice of hearing requirements:

Section 3–403. [Formal Testacy Proceedings; Notice of Hearing on Petition.]

(a) Upon commencement of a formal testacy proceeding, the Court shall fix a time and place of hearing. Notice shall be given in the manner prescribed by Section 1–401 by the petitioner to the persons herein enumerated and to any additional person who has filed a demand for notice under Section 3–204 of this Code.

Notice shall be given to the following persons: the surviving spouse, children, and other heirs of the decedent, the devisees and executors named in any will that is being, or has been, probated, or offered for informal or formal probate in the [county,] or that is known by the petitioner to have been probated, or offered for informal or formal probate elsewhere, and any personal representative of the decedent whose appointment has not been terminated.

Notice may be given to other persons. In addition, the petitioner shall give notice by publication to all unknown persons and to all known persons whose addresses are unknown who have any interest in the matters being litigated.

U.P.C. § 3–405 provides for the requirements of proof in uncontested formal probate proceedings:

Section 3–405. [Formal Testacy Proceedings; Uncontested Cases; Hearings and Proof.]

If a petition in a testacy proceeding is unopposed, the Court may order probate or intestacy on the strength of the pleadings if satisfied that the conditions of Section 3–409 have been met, or conduct a hearing in open court and require proof of the matters necessary to support the order sought. If evidence concerning execution of the will is necessary, the affidavit or testimony of one of any attesting witnesses to the instrument is sufficient. If the affidavit or testimony of an attesting witness is not available, execution of the will may be proved by other evidence or affidavit.

U.P.C. § 3–409, referred to in § 3–405, reads in part as follows:

Section 3–409. [Formal Testacy Proceedings; Order; Foreign Will.]

After the time required for any notice has expired, upon proof of notice, and after any hearing that may be necessary, if the Court finds that the testator is dead, venue is proper and that the proceeding was commenced within the limitation prescribed by Section 3–108, it shall determine the decedent's domicile at death, his heirs and his state of testacy. Any will found to be valid and unrevoked shall be formally probated....

U.P.C. § 3–406 provides for proof of execution in contested cases:

Section 3–406. [Formal Testacy Proceedings; Contested Cases; Testimony of Attesting Witnesses.]

(a) If evidence concerning execution of an attested will which is not self-proved is necessary in contested cases, the testimony of at least one of the attesting witnesses, if within the state, competent and able to testify, is required. Due execution of an attested or unattested will may be proved by other evidence.

(b) If the will is self-proved, compliance with signature requirements for execution is conclusively presumed and other requirements of execution are presumed subject to rebuttal without the testimony of any witness upon filing the will and the acknowledgment and affidavits annexed or attached thereto, unless there is proof of fraud or forgery affecting the acknowledgment or affidavit.

The Comment to § 3–406 reads in part as follows:

The "conclusive presumption" described here would foreclose questions like whether the witnesses signed in the presence of the testator. It would not preclude proof of undue influence, lack of testamentary capacity, revocation or any relevant proof that the testator was unaware of the contents of the document.

U.P.C. § 3–407 provides for the burdens of proof in contested cases:

Section 3–407. [Formal Testacy Proceedings; Burdens in Contested Cases.]

In contested cases, petitioners who seek to establish intestacy have the burden of establishing prima facie proof of death, venue, and heirship. Proponents of a will have the burden of establishing prima facie proof of due execution in all cases, and, if they are also petitioners, prima facie proof of death and venue. Contestants of a will have the burden of establishing lack of testamentary intent or capacity, undue influence, fraud, duress, mistake or revocation. Parties have the ultimate burden of persuasion as to matters with respect to which they have the initial burden of proof. If a will is opposed by the petition for probate of a later will revoking the former, it shall be determined first whether the later will is entitled to probate, and if a will is opposed by a petition for a declaration of intestacy, it shall be determined first whether the will is entitled to probate.

U.P.C. § 3–412, providing for the effect of the judicial determination in formal testacy proceedings, reads in part as follows:

Section 3–412. [Formal Testacy Proceedings; Effect of Order; Vacation.]

Subject to appeal and subject to vacation as provided herein and in Section 3–413, a formal testacy order under Sections 3–409 to 3–411, including an order that the decedent left no valid will and determining heirs, is final as to all persons with respect to all issues concerning the decedent's estate that the court considered or might have considered incident to its rendition relevant to the question of whether the decedent left a valid will, and to the determination of heirs, except that:

(1) the court shall entertain a petition for modification or vacation of its order and probate of another will of the decedent if it is shown that the proponents of the later-offered will were unaware of its existence at the time of the earlier proceeding or were unaware of the earlier proceeding and were given no notice thereof, except by publication.

(2) If intestacy of all or part of the estate has been ordered, the determination of heirs of the decedent may be reconsidered if it is shown that one or more persons were omitted from the determination and it is also shown that the persons were unaware of their relationship to the decedent, were unaware of his death or were given no notice of any proceeding concerning his estate, except by publication.

The question of what the legal consequences are when a later will is presented after an earlier will has been probated or there has been an earlier determination of intestacy, and the estate has been administered, is discussed in Section 9 of this chapter.

In states that do not have the Uniform Probate Code, the proof required for probate of the will in uncontested situations varies. We are referring now both to the ex parte proceeding and to an uncontested inter partes proceeding. Frequently the witnesses are required to appear before the court if they are alive and available. Sometimes affidavits of the witnesses will suffice. If the witnesses are deceased or unavailable, proof of their signatures and the testator's signature may be required. Other proof may also be called for.[7] It should be noted that many states that have not adopted the Uniform Probate Code have enacted the "self-proved" will provisions of § 2–504 of the Code, described in Section 1 of Chapter 3. In such case, there is no need for witnesses to appear or for any other evidence of compliance with the formalities of execution in the ex parte or uncontested inter partes situation. If it is concluded that the will has been properly executed with respect to the formalities, it is generally recognized that there is a presumption that the testator had testamentary capacity.[8]

7. E.g., Ill.Ann.Stat. ch. 110½, § 6–6; Mo.Ann.Stat. § 473.053; Nev.Rev.Stat. § 136.170; N.C.Gen.Stat. § 31–18.1; Wash.Rev.Code Ann. § 11.20.040.

8. Estate of Lacy, 431 P.2d 366 (Okl. 1967); Estate of Gentry, 32 Or.App. 45,

573 P.2d 322 (1978); Estate of Kuzma, 487 Pa. 91, 408 A.2d 1369 (1979); Hellams v. Ross, 268 S.C. 284, 233 S.E.2d 98 (1977).

U.P.C. § 3–414 describes the formal proceeding for the appointment of a personal representative pursuant to the priorities under U.P.C. § 3–203. Prior notice must be given to heirs and devisees if there is a will. There is no explicit provision for a hearing, but it would appear to be implicit in any formal proceeding. It appears that if there is a will it must be informally or formally probated at the time of or before the appointment of the personal representative.

So there may be formal proceedings for the probate of the will, setting aside an informal probate of a will, or for determination of intestacy. There may be a formal proceeding for the appointment of a personal representative. Clearly there may be a formal probate or intestacy determination without the appointment of a personal representative. The Code allows for the judicial determination of who are beneficially interested in the estate without requiring that there be any judicially sanctioned administration.

The fact that the probate of the will is in formal proceedings does not preclude the appointment of the personal representative in informal proceedings, and the reverse is also permissible. Determination of intestacy can only be made in formal proceedings, but despite such proceedings the appointment of the personal representative may be by informal proceedings.

U.P.C. § 3–601 provides that the personal representative shall qualify by filing with the appointing court any required bond and a statement of acceptance of the duties of the office. Sections 3–603, 604 and 605 set forth the rules for requiring or not requiring the personal representative to furnish a bond, that is, a surety to guarantee the proper performance of his duties. The provisions are detailed, but their essence is that the court has broad discretion in the matter, including the discretion to dispense with the bond even where the will provides that a bond is to be furnished. In most states that do not have the U.P.C. the bond is required unless the will provides that it is not necessary or all the beneficiaries waive it.

U.P.C. § 3–108 provides, in general, that any informal or formal probate proceeding or proceeding for the appointment of a personal representative must be commenced within three years after the decedent's death, except that a proceeding to contest an informally probated will may be commenced within twelve months after such informal probate or three years after the decedent's death, whichever is later.

U.P.C. § 3–101 provides that title to the decedent's property passes to devisees or heirs at the decedent's death, subject to administration. If there is no probate proceeding or proceeding for the appointment of a personal representative within three years after the decedent's death, title is clear in the heirs (intestate takers) of the decedent.[9] Under U.P.C. § 3–803, if there has been no administration the claims of unsecured creditors are also barred after one year following the decedent's death. Under U.P.C. § 3–108 it is possible to have a proceeding to determine the identity of heirs after the expiration of three years following the decedent's death should this be necessary.

SECTION 4.   DUTIES AND POWERS OF PERSONAL REPRESENTATIVE

U.P.C. § 3–704 reads as follows:

Section 3–704.   [Personal Representative to Proceed Without Court Order; Exception.]

A personal representative shall proceed expeditiously with the settlement and distribution of a decedent's estate and, except as otherwise specified or ordered in regard to a supervised personal representative, do so without adjudication, order, or direction of the Court, but he may invoke the jurisdiction of the Court, in proceedings authorized by this Code, to resolve questions concerning the estate or its administration.

Supervised administration referred to in U.P.C. § 3–704 is discussed in Section 7 of this chapter. It must be specifically applied for by an interested person or by the personal representative. Supervised administration includes formal proceedings for the probate of the will or determination of intestacy and for the appointment of the personal representative. Under supervised administration the personal representative may administer the estate in all respects without touching base with the court, except that he may not make distributions without permission of the court, and there must be a judicial proceeding for the settlement of his accounts. He may, however, be subject to direction by the court on its own motion or on the motion of an interested party. In the absence of supervised administration the personal representative may administer and distribute the estate without touching base with the court in any respect, but he may ask the court to resolve questions concerning the estate or its administration.

In most jurisdictions which have not adopted the Uniform Probate Code, the personal representative must report to and receive permission of the court with respect to various matters. In most states the personal representative must file an inventory of

---

9. In 1987 U.P.C. § 3–108 was amended to allow for a formal testacy proceeding more than three years after the decedent's death for the purpose of establishing a devise in specified limited circumstances.

estate assets with the court.[10] In some states the court appoints an appraiser to value the assets of the estate.[11] Many states require court permission for the sale of real estate [12] and sometimes personal property,[13] court approval for the payment of creditors' claims,[14] filing by the personal representative of periodic and final accounts with the court,[15] and court authorization of distribution of the estate.[16] In many states some of these provisions may be waived in the will, such as court authorization for the sale of property.[17] Some states that have not adopted the Uniform Probate Code provide in certain circumstances for the administration of the estate substantially free of court supervision; [18] this is referred to as "independent administration."

U.P.C. § 3–706 requires the personal representative to prepare an inventory as follows:

Section 3–706. [Duty of Personal Representative; Inventory and Appraisement.]

Within 3 months after his appointment, a personal representative, who is not a special administrator or a successor to another representative who has previously discharged this duty, shall prepare and file or mail an inventory of property owned by the decedent at the time of his death, listing it with reasonable detail, and indicating as to each listed item, its fair market value as of the date of the decedent's death, and the type and amount of any encumbrance that may exist with reference to any item.

The personal representative shall send a copy of the inventory to interested persons who request it. He may also file the original of the inventory with the court.

10. E.g., Ark.Stat.Ann. § 28–49–110; Iowa Code Ann. § 633.361; Ky.Rev.Stat. Ann. § 395.250; Ohio Rev.Code Ann. § 2115.02.

11. E.g., Miss.Code Ann. § 91–7–109; N.H.Rev.Stat.Ann. § 554:2; Okl. Stat.Ann. tit. 58, § 282.

12. E.g., Ga.Code Ann. § 53–8–23; Mass.Gen.Laws Ann. ch. 202, §§ 6, 7; R.I.Gen.Laws § 33–19–3; Tex.Prob. Code Ann. § 346.

13. E.g., Ark.Stat.Ann. § 28–51–103; Ill.Ann.Stat. ch. 110½, § 19–1; Mo.Ann. Stat. § 473.487.

14. E.g., Ark.Stat.Ann. § 28–50–105; Cal.Prob.Code § 711; Okl.Stat.Ann. tit. 58, § 337; Tex.Prob.Code Ann. § 312.

15. E.g., Md.Est. & Trusts Code Ann. § 7–305; Mass.Gen.Laws Ann. ch. 206, §§ 1, 22; Wash.Rev.Code Ann. §§ 11.76.010, .030; W.Va.Code § 44–4–2.

16. E.g., Conn.Gen.Stat.Ann. § 45–272; Ind.Code Ann. § 29–1–17–2; Wis. Stat.Ann. § 863.25; Wyo.Stat. § 2–7–813.

17. E.g., Fla.Stat.Ann. § 733.613; Ill.Ann.Stat. ch. 110½, §§ 19–1, 20–15; Ohio Rev.Code Ann. §§ 2113.39, 2127.-01; Tex.Prob.Code Ann. § 332.

18. E.g., Ill.Ann.Stat. ch. 110½, §§ 28–1 et seq.; Mo.Ann.Stat. §§ 473.-780 et seq.; S.D.Comp.Laws Ann. § 30–18A–1; Tex.Prob.Code Ann. §§ 145 et seq.; Wash.Rev.Code Ann. § 11.68.010.

Note that filing the inventory with the court is optional with the personal representative. In most states that do not have the Uniform Probate Code the inventory is required to be filed with the court. The Comment to this section states, "This and the following sections eliminate the practice now required by many probate statutes under which the judge is involved in the selection of appraisers."

U.P.C. § 3–707 reads as follows:

Section 3–707. [Employment of Appraisers.]

The personal representative may employ a qualified and disinterested appraiser to assist him in ascertaining the fair market value as of the date of the decedent's death of any asset the value of which may be subject to reasonable doubt. Different persons may be employed to appraise different kinds of assets included in the estate. The names and addresses of any appraiser shall be indicated on the inventory with the item or items he appraised.

U.P.C. § 3–709 reads in part as follows:

Section 3–709. [Duty of Personal Representative; Possession of Estate.]

Except as otherwise provided by a decedent's will, every personal representative has a right to, and shall take possession or control of, the decedent's property, except that any real property or tangible personal property may be left with or surrendered to the person presumptively entitled thereto unless or until, in the judgment of the personal representative, possession of the property by him will be necessary for purposes of administration.

U.P.C. § 3–715 gives the personal representative very broad powers to administer the estate. Several of the more significant provisions are as follows:

Section 3–715. [Transactions Authorized for Personal Representatives; Exceptions.]

Except as restricted or otherwise provided by the will or by an order in a formal proceeding and subject to the priorities stated in Section 3–902, a personal representative, acting reasonably for the benefit of the interested persons, may properly:

(1) retain assets owned by the decedent pending distribution or liquidation including those in which the repre-

sentative is personally interested or which are otherwise improper for trust investment;

* * *

(5) if funds are not needed to meet debts and expenses currently payable and are not immediately distributable, deposit or invest liquid assets of the estate, including moneys received from the sale of other assets, in federally insured interest-bearing accounts, readily marketable secured loan arrangements or other prudent investments which would be reasonable for use by trustees generally;

(6) acquire or dispose of an asset, including land in this or another state, for cash or on credit, at public or private sale; and manage, develop, improve, exchange, partition, change the character of, or abandon an estate asset;

* * *

(18) pay taxes, assessments, compensation of the personal representative, and other expenses incident to the administration of the estate;

* * *

(21) employ persons, including attorneys, auditors, investment advisors, or agents, even if they are associated with the personal representative, to advise or assist the personal representative in the performance of his administrative duties; act without independent investigation upon their recommendations; and instead of acting personally, employ one or more agents to perform any act of administration, whether or not discretionary;

* * *

(23) sell, mortgage, or lease any real or personal property of the estate or any interest therein for cash, credit, or for part cash and part credit, and with or without security for unpaid balances;

It should be noted that the introductory clause qualifies all the broad powers that follow by the requirement that the personal representative act reasonably in the interests of all interested parties, i.e., heirs, devisees, creditors. Subsection (1) permits the retention of assets owned by the decedent although they are not proper investments. It must, however, be reasonable to retain them; that is to say, if the investment carries very high risk it may not be proper to retain it. Such authorization to retain assets owned by the decedent is commonly found in legislation dealing with the powers of personal representatives.[19]

Subsection (5) adopts the "prudent person" standard for investments by the personal representative. This standard is the prevailing standard for trustees and is discussed in Chapter 13, Section 6. Many states that have not adopted the Uniform Probate Code have legislated that investment standard for personal representatives.[20] In the past many states restricted investments, by personal representatives to specified debt securities, and a few still do.[21] In such states the testator may provide in the will that the personal representative may invest in accordance with the prudent person standard.

Subsections (6) and (23) grant broad authority to buy property and dispose of estate property.

Subsection (21) authorizes broad delegation of authority and self-dealing. This is a controversial clause, and its ramifications are discussed in Chapter 13, Sections 1 and 2. These forms of delegation and self-dealing are in conflict with traditional fiduciary principles.

U.P.C. § 3–717 reads in part as follows:

Section 3–717. [Co-representatives; When Joint Action Required.]

If two or more persons are appointed co-representatives and unless the will provides otherwise, the concurrence of all is required on all acts connected with the administration and distribution of the estate. This restriction does not apply when any co-representative receives and receipts for property due the estate, when the concurrence of all cannot readily be obtained in the time reasonably available for emergency action necessary to preserve the estate, or when a co-representative has been delegated to act for the others.

The first sentence states the common law position. The provision in the last clause of the second sentence for express delegation by one personal representative to another is inconsistent with common law principles, as discussed in Chapter 13, Section 10.

19. E.g., Ga.Code Ann. § 53–8–2; Iowa Code Ann. § 633.348; N.J.Stat. Ann. § 3B:20–11; Ohio Rev.Code Ann. § 2109.38.

20. E.g., Iowa Code Ann. § 633.123; N.C.Gen.Stat. § 36A–2; S.C.Code Ann. § 62–3–715.

21. E.g., Ala.Code § 19–3–120; Ohio Rev.Code Ann. § 2109.37(B); Pa.Stat. Ann. tit. 20, § 3316.

U.P.C. § 3–718 reads as follows:

Section 3–718. [Powers of Surviving Personal Representative.]

Unless the terms of the will otherwise provide, every power exercisable by personal co-representatives may be exercised by the one or more remaining after the appointment of one or more is terminated, and if one of 2 or more nominated as co-executors is not appointed, those appointed may exercise all the powers incident to the office.

This provision generally reflects the common law.

U.P.C. § 3–719 reads as follows:

Section 3–719. [Compensation of Personal Representative.]

A personal representative is entitled to reasonable compensation for his services. If a will provides for compensation of the personal representative and there is no contract with the decedent regarding compensation, he may renounce the provision before qualifying and be entitled to reasonable compensation. A personal representative also may renounce his right to all or any part of the compensation. A written renunciation of fee may be filed with the Court.

Many states have statutory schedules for the compensation of personal representatives.[22] The Comment to § 3–719 states in part, "This section has no bearing on the question of whether a personal representative who also serves as attorney for the estate may receive compensation in both capacities ..." There is judicial authority that permits the personal representative to receive a fee as attorney for the estate as well.[23]

U.P.C. § 3–712 reads as follows:

Section 3–712. [Improper Exercise of Power; Breach of Fiduciary Duty.]

If the exercise of power concerning the estate is improper, the personal representative is liable to interested persons for damage or loss resulting from breach of his fiduciary duty to the same extent as a trustee of an express trust.

SECTION 5.   CREDITORS' CLAIMS

Virtually all states have had legislation which provides that the personal representative is to publish in a newspaper a notice to

22. E.g., Cal.Prob.Code § 10800; Md.Est. & Trusts Code Ann. § 7–601; Ohio Rev.Code Ann. § 2113.35; Tex. Prob.Code Ann. § 241.

23. See Chapter 13, note 31.

creditors of the decedent to present their claims within a specified number of months, and if they fail to do so, their claims will be barred. Such notice by publication barred claims regardless of whether the creditors were known or reasonably ascertainable by the personal representative. These statutes are usually referred to as nonclaim statutes. In effect, they are very short statutes of limitations triggered by publication of notice. Some statutes, however, have permitted tardy presentment of claims in specified justifiable circumstances.

In 1988 in the case of Tulsa Professional Collection Services, Inc. v. Pope,[24] the U.S. Supreme Court held the Oklahoma nonclaim statute of this nature unconstitutional as a violation of the Due Process Clause of the Fourteenth Amendment with respect to a creditor whose identity was known or reasonably ascertainable by the personal representative. With respect to such a creditor, the Due Process Clause requires that notice be given by mail or other means to ensure actual notice. The traditional nonclaim statute remains effective to bar the claims of creditors not known or reasonably ascertainable by the personal representative.

Former Uniform Probate Code §§ 3–801 and 3–803 constituted a nonclaim statute which barred claims that were not presented within four months of publication of notice. Because of the new constitutional requirement, in 1989 these sections were revised to provide that the personal representative may give notice by publication which bars claims not presented within four months, or give notice by mail or other delivery to creditors which bars claims not presented within 60 days of such actual notice, or give both forms of notice; in the last circumstance the claims of creditors receiving actual notice are barred four months after publication or 60 days after actual notice, whichever is later. It has become necessary for all states to amend their nonclaim statutes to comply with the constitutional requirements.

Most states also have statutes which bar claims of creditors of the decedent which are not presented within a certain number of years from the decedent's death, such as three years, regardless of any publication or notice from the personal representative. This form of statute is designed to cover the situation in which the personal representative has failed to publish the notice to creditors or to give actual notice, and the situation in which there has been no administration. The original Uniform Probate Code § 3–803 was such a statute which barred claims not presented within three years of the decedent's death. In 1989 that section was revised to reduce the period to one year after the decedent's death. The U.S. Supreme Court decision did not deal with this type of statute,

24. 485 U.S. 478, 108 S.Ct. 1340, 99 L.Ed.2d 565 (1988).

which is a so-called self-executing statute of limitations like a three-year statute of limitations for contract claims. The Court stated that the Due Process Clause does not require notice of the impending expiration of the period of such a statute. The statute before the Court was a short-term one involving direct state involvement through a court-appointed personal representative who triggers the running of the period by a form of notice by publication.

U.P.C. § 3–802 provides that the general statute of limitations applicable to a claim against the decedent while he was living is suspended for a period of four months following the death of the decedent, and then resumes after the expiration of that period. If the claim becomes barred by the special statutes relating to the death of the decedent described above, before the expiration of the period of the general statute of limitations applicable to the claim, the general statute becomes irrelevant. If, however, the general statute of limitations bars the claim after the decedent's death before the expiration of the period of the special statutes relating to the death of the decedent, the special statutes become irrelevant.

U.P.C. § 3–804 provides that the claim may be presented by filing with the personal representative or with the court, or commencing a suit against the personal representative within the statutory period.

U.P.C. § 3–806 provides for notice of disallowance of a claim by the personal representative to the creditor. It also provides that the creditor must act within 60 days of notice of disallowance or be barred, as follows:

> Every claim which is disallowed in whole or in part by the personal representative is barred so far as not allowed unless the claimant files a petition for allowance in the Court or commences a proceeding against the personal representative not later than 60 days after the mailing of the notice of disallowance or partial allowance if the notice warns the claimant of the impending bar. Failure of the personal representative to mail notice to a claimant of action on his claim for 60 days after the time for original presentation of the claim has expired has the effect of a notice of allowance.

In the event the estate is insolvent U.P.C. § 3–805 provides for priority of payment of claims as follows:

Section 3–805. [Classification of Claims.]

(a) If the applicable assets of the estate are insufficient to pay all claims in full, the personal representative shall make payment in the following order:

(1) costs and expenses of administration;

(2) reasonable funeral expenses;

(3) debts and taxes with preference under federal law;

(4) reasonable and necessary medical and hospital expenses of the last illness of the decedent, including compensation of persons attending him;

(5) debts and taxes with preference under other laws of this state;

(6) all other claims.

(b) No preference shall be given in the payment of any claim over any other claim of the same class, and a claim due and payable shall not be entitled to a preference over claims not due.

Problems of payment arise with respect to claims which come due in the future, such as a promissory note, and contingent claims such as a guaranty of payment of another's debt, and unliquidated claims such as tort claims and breach of contract claims. U.P.C. § 3–810 deals with this problem as follows:

Section 3–810. [Claims Not Due and Contingent or Unliquidated Claims.]

(a) If a claim which will become due at a future time or a contingent or unliquidated claim becomes due or certain before the distribution of the estate, and if the claim has been allowed or established by a proceeding, it is paid in the same manner as presently due and absolute claims of the same class.

(b) In other cases the personal representative or, on petition of the personal representative or the claimant in a special proceeding for the purpose, the Court may provide for payment as follows:

(1) if the claimant consents, he may be paid the present or agreed value of the claim, taking any uncertainty into account;

(2) arrangement for future payment, or possible payment, on the happening of the contingency or on liquidation may be made by creating a trust, giving a mortgage, obtaining a bond or security from a distributee, or otherwise.

Secured claims present special issues. The secured creditor is entitled to enforce his security interest without regard to the special provisions limiting enforcement of claims against an estate as discussed above.[25] To the extent, however, of the amount of the

25. E.g., D.C.Code Ann. § 20–903; Fla.Stat.Ann. § 733.702; Md.Est. & Trusts Code Ann. § 8–103; Mo.Ann. Stat. § 473.360.

claim in excess of the value of the security, the creditor is subject to the special provisions relating to claims against the estate. U.P.C. § 3–809 deals with the situation of the secured creditor as follows:

Section 3–809. [Secured Claims.]

Payment of a secured claim is upon the basis of the amount allowed if the creditor surrenders his security; otherwise payment is upon the basis of one of the following:

(1) if the creditor exhausts his security before receiving payment, [unless precluded by other law] upon the amount of the claim allowed less the fair value of the security; or

(2) if the creditor does not have the right to exhaust his security or has not done so, upon the amount of the claim allowed less the value of the security determined by converting it into money according to the terms of the agreement pursuant to which the security was delivered to the creditor, or by the creditor and personal representative by agreement, arbitration, compromise or litigation.

There may be claims against the estate which were not obligations of the decedent. Contract, tort, or other claims may be incurred during the process of administration. U.P.C. § 3–803(c) provides that such a claim based on a contract with the personal representative must be presented within four months after performance by the personal representative is due, and any other such claim must be presented within the later of four months after it arises or one year after the decedent's death.

The provisions of U.P.C. §§ 3–804 and 3–806 dealing with the methods of presentation and the consequences of disallowance are applicable to such claims arising after the decedent's death.

SECTION 6. CLOSING THE ESTATE

Many states require a personal representative to file a formal account of his administration with the court upon completion of administration. The personal representative may also be required to file interim periodic accounts with the court.[26] If the court is satisfied with the final account, it issues an order terminating the personal representative's appointment, and directing the distribution of the estate. The accounts may also be distributed to those beneficially interested in the estate. In the absence of a judicial

26. See statutes cited note 15 supra.

proceeding described in the next paragraph, the filing of the final account with the court and the judicial order terminating the personal representative's appointment and directing distribution do not affect the potential liability for mismanagement of the personal representative to those beneficially interested in the estate. After the submission of the final account to the beneficiaries, they may bring an action against the personal representative within the period of the applicable statute of limitations.

The personal representative may resolve any potential liability for his administration at the time he submits his final account by bringing an inter partes action to settle his account in which all those beneficially interested in the estate are joined as parties. Those beneficially interested must make their claims in this proceeding, and if they do not they are forever barred from doing so with respect to matters disclosed in the account.[27] Any claims of mismanagement are adjudicated in this proceeding. If no objections are made to the account, the judgment of the court approving the account is res judicata as to all matters that could have been raised; the court orders distribution to the proper parties and the personal representative is discharged of liability. This judicial proceeding is mandatory in some states. It should be emphasized that the judgment is effective as a bar to liability to the extent of the disclosure in the account. That is to say, if there is a failure to disclose information relevant to mismanagement, the judgment does not bar liability based on such undisclosed information. Sometimes the personal representative and all the beneficiaries avoid the judicial proceeding by an agreement in which the personal representative is released from liability.

The Uniform Probate Code does not require the personal representative to submit annual accounts or a final account to the court. The personal representative can administer and distribute without touching base with the court. However, U.P.C. § 3–1003 provides for an optional ex parte closing of the estate by means of a sworn statement filed with the court, as follows:

> Section 3–1003. [Closing Estates; By Sworn Statement of Personal Representative.]
>
> (a) Unless prohibited by order of the Court and except for estates being administered in supervised administration proceedings, a personal representative may close an estate by filing with the court no earlier than 6 months after the date of original appointment of a general personal representative for the estate, a verified statement stating that the personal representative or a previous personal representative, has:

---

27. See Chapter 13, Section 10, note 22.

(1) determined that the time limited for presentation of creditors' claims has expired;

(2) fully administered the estate of the decedent by making payment, settlement or other disposition of all claims that were presented, expenses of administration and estate, inheritance and other death taxes, except as specified in the statement, and that the assets of the estate have been distributed to the persons entitled. If any claims remain undischarged, the statement must state whether the personal representative has distributed the estate subject to possible liability with the agreement of the distributees or state in detail other arrangements that have been made to accommodate outstanding liabilities; and

(3) sent a copy of the statement to all distributees of the estate and to all creditors or other claimants of whom the personal representative is aware whose claims are neither paid nor barred and has furnished a full account in writing of the personal representative's administration to the distributees whose interests are affected thereby.

(b) If no proceedings involving the personal representative are pending in the Court one year after the closing statement is filed, the appointment of the personal representative terminates.

Note that the personal representatives must send a final account to all those beneficially interested in the estate. Note also that one year thereafter the appointment of the personal representative terminates. U.P.C. § 3–1003 does not address the question of the termination of the personal representative's potential liability.

U.P.C. § 3–1005 deals with the termination of liability of the personal representative six months after the filing of the closing statement, as follows:

Section 3–1005. [Limitations on Proceedings Against Personal Representative.]

Unless previously barred by adjudication and except as provided in the closing statement, the rights of successors and of creditors whose claims have not otherwise been barred against the personal representative for breach of fiduciary duty are barred unless a proceeding to assert the same is commenced within 6 months after the filing of the closing statement. The rights thus barred do not include rights to recover from a personal representative for fraud, misrepresentation, or inadequate disclosure related to the settlement of the decedent's estate.

U.P.C. §§ 3–1001 and 3–1002 provide the personal representative with the option of bringing an inter partes proceeding in which all interested parties are joined for the purpose of obtaining a court order settling the personal representative's account, discharging the personal representative from further liability, and directing the distribution of the estate to designated beneficiaries. This is the judicial accounting proceeding in which the beneficiaries must make their claims against the personal representative or be barred.

SECTION 7.   SUPERVISED ADMINISTRATION

We have mentioned that most states which have not enacted the Uniform Probate Code provide for general supervision by the court of the administration of the estate by the personal representative. The Uniform Probate Code, on the other hand, presumes that administration is not to be judicially supervised. The Code, however, does provide for judicially supervised administration, in the discretion of the court, if it is requested by an interested party. In supervised administration there must be formal, inter partes probate of the will or determination of intestacy and heirship, formal appointment of the personal representative, an inter partes judicial settlement of the account of the personal representative, and a judicial order of distribution of the estate; there may also be other forms of judicial intervention.

U.P.C. §§ 3–501, 3–502, and 3–504, are as follows:

Section 3–501.   [Supervised Administration; Nature of Proceeding.]

Supervised administration is a single in rem proceeding to secure complete administration and settlement of a decedent's estate under the continuing authority of the Court which extends until entry of an order approving distribution of the estate and discharging the personal representative or other order terminating the proceeding. A supervised personal representative is responsible to the Court, as well as to the interested parties, and is subject to directions concerning the estate made by the Court on its own motion or on the motion of any interested party. Except as otherwise provided in this Part, or as otherwise ordered by the Court, a supervised personal representative has the same duties and powers as a personal representative who is not supervised.

Section 3–502. [Supervised Administration; Petition; Order.]

A petition for supervised administration may be filed by any interested person or by a personal representative at any time or the prayer for supervised administration may be joined with a petition in a testacy or appointment proceeding. If the testacy of the decedent and the priority and qualification of any personal representative have not been adjudicated previously, the petition for supervised administration shall include the matters required of a petition in a formal testacy proceeding and the notice requirements and procedures applicable to a formal testacy proceeding apply. If not previously adjudicated, the Court shall adjudicate the testacy of the decedent and questions relating to the priority and qualifications of the personal representative in any case involving a request for supervised administration, even though the request for supervised administration may be denied. After notice to interested persons, the Court shall order supervised administration of a decedent's estate: (1) if the decedent's will directs supervised administration, it shall be ordered unless the Court finds that circumstances bearing on the need for supervised administration have changed since the execution of the will and that there is no necessity for supervised administration; (2) if the decedent's will directs unsupervised administration, supervised administration shall be ordered only upon a finding that it is necessary for protection of persons interested in the estate; or (3) in other cases if the Court finds that supervised administration is necessary under the circumstances.

Section 3–504. [Supervised Administration; Powers of Personal Representative.]

Unless restricted by the Court, a supervised personal representative has, without interim orders approving exercise of a power, all powers of personal representatives under this Code, but he shall not exercise his power to make any distribution of the estate without prior order of the Court. Any other restriction on the power of a personal representative which may be ordered by the Court must be endorsed on his letters of appointment and, unless so endorsed, is ineffective as to persons dealing in good faith with the personal representative.

SECTION 8. ANCILLARY ADMINISTRATION

We have previously mentioned that the state in which the decedent is domiciled at his death has jurisdiction for purposes of estate administration by virtue of the domicile. The law of the domiciliary jurisdiction governs the disposition of personalty situated in that state as well as personalty having its situs in other states at the time of death.[28] That is to say, the validity of the will, the construction of its terms, and intestate distribution, are governed by the law of the domiciliary jurisdiction with respect to personalty having a situs in a state other than the domiciliary state, under conflict of laws principles. However, the state of the situs of personalty may exercise jurisdiction to administer such personalty for the purpose of assisting local creditors. The situs of a chattel is the place where it is located at death. The prevailing modern view is that the situs of a stock certificate or bond is the place where the document is located at death. The situs of a debt (other than a bond or debenture) such as a bank account is the place where the debtor is subject to suit.[29]

Obviously the law of the domiciliary jurisdiction controls the disposition of real property located in that state. If the decedent owned land at his death situated outside the domiciliary state, the law of the state in which it is located governs the testate and intestate disposition of the land, and that state has jurisdiction over the administration of that land.[30]

Invariably the will is probated and the personal representative is appointed initially in the domiciliary state. This is called the principal or domiciliary administration. If land is situated in another state, in all likelihood there will be some form of ancillary administration in that state. In order to make the title to the land marketable, the will must be probated in that state or heirship must be judicially determined there. The probate of the will or the determination of heirship is the link in the record chain of title to the land. By statute the ancillary jurisdiction may give effect to the determination by the domiciliary court of the validity of the will, thereby avoiding an additional probate proceeding. An ancillary personal representative may be appointed to carry out the process of administration in order to remove the potential cloud of the decedent's creditors' rights in the land. If an ancillary representative is appointed it may be the party who is the domiciliary representative. In addition to its title function, ancillary administration serves the purpose of protecting local creditors by permitting them to deal with a local representative and to sue locally and reach local assets.

If there is only personal property having a situs outside the domiciliary state, ancillary administration may occur but it is

28. See supra note 3.

29. Scoles and Hay, Conflict of Laws §§ 22.7, 22.10, 22.11, 22.12 (2d ed.

1992); Restatement (Second) of Conflict of Laws §§ 318, 324, 326 (1971).

30. See supra note 4.

usually avoided. Ancillary administration is not necessary to establish title to personal property because there is no public record of title to personalty. Ancillary administration with respect to personalty exists to protect the interests of local creditors; it enables them to present their claims to a local personal representative, to sue in a local court if that becomes necessary, and to reach local assets of the estate. If only personalty is involved, the ancillary jurisdiction usually gives effect to the determination of the validity of the will by the domiciliary court. An ancillary personal representative is appointed who may be the domiciliary personal representative.

If ancillary administration has been established, those holding personalty must transfer it to the ancillary personal representative. If, however, there has been no ancillary administration established, those holding personalty may transfer it to the domiciliary personal representative. That is to say, the party holding personalty is not required to await the appointment of an ancillary personal representative or initiate ancillary administration in order to be protected. If only personal property is involved, there usually is no ancillary administration. If there is ancillary administration, upon its completion the ancillary representative usually transfers the personal property remaining after paying local creditors and the state tax collector to the domiciliary representative.[31]

U.P.C. § 4–201 provides for the payment or delivery of personal property situated in other than the domiciliary state to the domiciliary personal representative if there is no ancillary administration, as follows:

Section 4–201. [Payment of Debt and Delivery of Property to Domiciliary Foreign Personal Representative Without Local Administration.]

At any time after the expiration of sixty days from the death of a nonresident decedent, any person indebted to the estate of the nonresident decedent or having possession or control of personal property, or of an instrument evidencing a debt, obligation, stock or chose in action belonging to the estate of the nonresident decedent may pay the debt, deliver the personal property, or the instrument evidencing the debt, obligation, stock or chose in action, to the domiciliary foreign personal representative of the nonresident decedent upon being presented with proof of his appointment and an affidavit made by or on behalf of the representative stating:

---

31. Scoles and Hay, Conflict of Laws §§ 22.21, 22.24 (2d ed. 1992); Restatement (Second) of Conflict of Laws §§ 364–366 (1971).

(1) the date of death of the nonresident decedent,

(2) that no local administration, or application or petition therefor, is pending in this state,

(3) that the domiciliary foreign personal representative is entitled to payment or delivery.

If there has been no ancillary personal representative appointed, U.P.C. §§ 4–204, 4–205, and 4–206 set forth a procedure to permit the domiciliary representative to function in the ancillary jurisdiction, as follows:

Section 4–204.   [Proof of Authority-Bond.]

If no local administration or application or petition therefor is pending in this state, a domiciliary foreign personal representative may file with a Court in this State in a [county] in which property belonging to the decedent is located, authenticated copies of his appointment and of any official bond he has given.

Section 4–205.   [Powers.]

A domiciliary foreign personal representative who has complied with Section 4–204 may exercise as to assets in this state all powers of a local personal representative and may maintain actions and proceedings in this state subject to any conditions imposed upon nonresident parties generally.

Section 4–206.   [Power of Representatives in Transition.]

The power of a domiciliary foreign personal representative under Section 4–201 or 4–205 shall be exercised only if there is no administration or application therefor pending in this state. An application or petition for local administration of the estate terminates the power of the foreign personal representative to act under Section 4–205, but the local Court may allow the foreign personal representative to exercise limited powers to preserve the estate

. . .

Sometimes ancillary administration is required because the domiciliary representative is deemed not to have the power to sue in the ancillary jurisdiction on a claim owing to the estate by a debtor in the ancillary jurisdiction. U.P.C. § 4–205 permits the domiciliary representative to sue if there is no ancillary administration, as do the statutes in many states.[32]

---

32.   Scoles and Hay, Conflict of Laws
§ 22.14 (2d ed. 1992).

SECTION 9. WILL PRESENTED
AFTER ADMINISTRATION

Let us assume that a will is admitted to probate, an executor is appointed, and the estate is fully administered and distributed to the legatees and devisees. Two months thereafter a legatee under a later will whose terms are significantly different from the probated will and which revokes it, petitions the court for probate of the later will. Assuming the later will has been validly executed, is it entitled to probate? If it is, what is the status of the action taken in the previous administration?

The answer to the first question is that the later will is admissible to probate, regardless of whether the first will was admitted to probate in an ex parte proceeding or an inter partes proceeding. The decree of probate of the first will is a determination that the will was validly executed, but it does not preclude the judicial determination of the existence of a later valid will which revokes the earlier will.[33] If the estate had been administered and distributed as an intestate estate, the later-offered will would be admissible to probate.[34] These conclusions are qualified, however, by the fact that there are statutes in many states which place a time limit upon the petition for the probate of a will, such as three years from death.[35] If the petition for probate is not made within that time, the will cannot be probated.

The response to the second question—what is the status of the actions taken in the previous administration—is a bit more involved. Clearly all parties who dealt with the duly appointed personal representative are protected, such as creditors, debtors, corporations, purchasers, etc. Purchasers for value from heirs, legatees and devisees of estate property distributed to such beneficiaries are usually protected and receive good title.[36] In short, everyone who has relied on the previous judicial determination is usually protected. However, the heirs, legatees and devisees are only donees, and consequently they are obligated to return to the estate what they received or its value, for redistribution to those entitled under the later will.[37] It may well be, however, that the

33. Estate of Morris, 577 S.W.2d 748 (Tex.Civ.App.1979); In re Bentley's Will, 175 Va. 456, 9 S.E.2d 308 (1940); In re Winzenrith's Will, 133 W.Va. 267, 55 S.E.2d 897 (1949).

34. See Annot., 2 A.L.R.4th 1315 (1980).

35. E.g., Uniform Probate Code § 3-108 (3 years), legislated in a number of states; Ala.Code § 43–8–161 (5 years); Ky.Rev.Stat.Ann. §§ 413.160, 394.295 (10 years).

36. Eckland v. Jankowski, 407 Ill. 263, 95 N.E.2d 342 (1950); Matthews v.

Fuller, 209 Md. 42, 120 A.2d 356 (1956); Doughty v. Hammond, 207 Tenn. 545, 341 S.W.2d 713 (1960). Statutes sometimes protect the purchaser only if the later-offered will is not probated within a specified period of time after the death of the testator or the probate of the first will. Ohio Rev.Code Ann. § 2107.47; Va.Code §§ 64.1–95, 64.1–96.

37. Gross v. Slye, 360 So.2d 333 (Ala.1978); In re Mitchell's Estate, 115 Cal.App. 348, 1 P.2d 536 (1931); Miller v. McNamara, 135 Conn. 489, 66 A.2d 359 (1949). See In re Cecala's Estate, 104 Cal.App.2d 526, 232 P.2d 48 (1951);

heirs, legatees and devisees in certain circumstances would have a defense based on change of position in reliance on the judicial determination.

U.P.C. § 3–108 provides, subject to several exceptions, that no proceedings for the informal or formal probate of a will may be commenced later than three years after the death of the decedent. If a will has been admitted to probate in a formal testacy proceeding, U.P.C. § 3–412 places stricter time limits on the probate of a later-offered will, as well as other restrictions, as follows:

Section 3–412.   [Formal Testacy Proceedings; Effect of Order; Vacation.]

Subject to appeal and subject to vacation as provided herein and in Section 3–413, a formal testacy order under Sections 3–409 to 3–411, including an order that the decedent left no valid will and determining heirs, is final as to all persons with respect to all issues concerning the decedent's estate that the court considered or might have considered incident to its rendition relevant to the question of whether the decedent left a valid will, and to the determination of heirs, except that:

(1) the court shall entertain a petition for modification or vacation of its order and probate of another will of the decedent if it is shown that the proponents of the later-offered will were unaware of its existence at the time of the earlier proceeding or were unaware of the earlier proceeding and were given no notice thereof, except by publication.

(2) If intestacy of all or part of the estate has been ordered, the determination of heirs of the decedent may be reconsidered if it is shown that one or more persons were omitted from the determination and it is also shown that the persons were unaware of their relationship to the decedent, were unaware of his death or were given no notice of any proceeding concerning his estate, except by publication.

(3) A petition for vacation under either (1) or (2) above must be filed prior to the earlier of the following time limits:

(i) If a personal representative has been appointed for the estate, the time of entry of any order approving final distribution of the estate, or, if the estate is closed by statement, 6 months after the filing of the closing statement.

Maynard v. Hustead, 185 Okl. 20, 90 P.2d 30 (1939).

> (ii) Whether or not a personal representative has been appointed for the estate of the decedent, the time prescribed by Section 3-108 when it is no longer possible to initiate an original proceeding to probate a will of the decedent.
>
> (iii) 12 months after the entry of the order sought to be vacated.

U.P.C. § 3-714 provides that purchasers from the personal representative in the prior administration are protected, and U.P.C. § 3-910 protects purchasers of estate property from heirs, legatees and devisees who received it under the prior administration. Under U.P.C. § 3-909 the heirs, legatees and devisees must return what they received under the prior administration, but U.P.C. § 3-1006 bars such obligation to return after the later of three years from the decedent's death or one year from the time of distribution to them.

SECTION 10. LIABILITY OF PERSONAL REPRESENTATIVE TO THIRD PERSONS

In Chapter 13, Section 11, we discuss the common law personal liability of fiduciaries to third persons. In summary, the common law position is that the personal representative is personally liable on contracts entered into in his representative capacity unless he expressly negates personal liability in the contract. If the contract was within his powers as personal representative, i.e., was not a breach of his fiduciary duty, he is entitled to reimbursement from the estate. The personal representative is personally liable for torts committed in the course of his management of the estate. If the personal representative is not personally at fault in its commission, as would be the case if a servant he properly hired was negligent, he is entitled to reimbursement from the estate.

The Uniform Probate Code § 3-808 changes these outmoded rules as follows:

Section 3-808. [Individual Liability of Personal Representative.]

(a) Unless otherwise provided in the contract, a personal representative is not individually liable on a contract properly entered into in his fiduciary capacity in the course of administration of the estate unless he fails to reveal his representative capacity and identify the estate in the contract.

(b) A personal representative is individually liable for obligations arising from ownership or control of the estate or for torts committed in the course of administration of the estate only if he is personally at fault.

A number of states have enacted statutes of this nature which bring the law into line with the parties' expectations that the personal representative should be personally liable only if he acts beyond his authority or is negligent in performing his duties.[38]

SECTION 11. SMALL ESTATES

Most states have a statute which, in the case of very small estates, permits heirs or legatees of the decedent to acquire her personal property directly without formal administration.[39] These statutes are usually limited to estates not exceeding amounts such as $5,000 or $25,000, or the value of exempt property and administration expenses. The Uniform Probate Code has such a provision. U.P.C. §§ 3–1201 and 3–1202 are as follows:

Section 3–1201. [Collection of Personal Property by Affidavit.]

(a) Thirty days after the death of a decedent, any person indebted to the decedent or having possession of tangible personal property or an instrument evidencing a debt, obligation, stock or chose in action belonging to the decedent shall make payment of the indebtedness or deliver the tangible personal property or an instrument evidencing a debt, obligation, stock or chose in action to a person claiming to be the successor of the decedent upon being presented an affidavit made by or on behalf of the successor stating that:

(1) the value of the entire estate, wherever located, less liens and encumbrances, does not exceed $5,000;

(2) 30 days have elapsed since the death of decedent;

(3) no application or petition for the appointment of a personal representative is pending or has been granted in any jurisdiction; and

(4) the claiming successor is entitled to payment or delivery of the property.

(b) A transfer agent of any security shall change the registered ownership on the books of a corporation from

---

38. E.g., Md.Est. & Trusts Code Ann. § 8–109; Mass.Gen.Laws Ann. ch. 195, § 17; Minn.Stat.Ann. § 524.3–808; Mo.Ann.Stat. § 473.820; Vt.Stat.Ann. tit. 14, § 1208.

39. E.g., Ark.Stat.Ann. § 28–41–101; Ind.Code Ann. § 29–1–8–1; Mass.Gen. Laws Ann. ch. 195, § 16; Mo.Ann.Stat. § 473.090; Tex.Prob.Code Ann. § 137.

the decedent to the successor or successors upon the presentation of an affidavit as provided in subsection (a).

Section 3–1202. [Effect of Affidavit.]

The person paying, delivering, transferring, or issuing personal property or the evidence thereof pursuant to affidavit is discharged and released to the same extent as if he dealt with a personal representative of the decedent. He is not required to see to the application of the personal property or evidence thereof or to inquire into the truth of any statement in the affidavit. If any person to whom an affidavit is delivered refuses to pay, deliver, transfer, or issue any personal property or evidence thereof, it may be recovered or its payment, delivery, transfer, or issuance compelled upon proof of their right in a proceeding brought for the purpose by or on behalf of the persons entitled thereto. Any person to whom payment, delivery, transfer or issuance is made is answerable and accountable therefor to any personal representative of the estate or to any other person having a superior right.

The last sentence of U.P.C. § 3–1202 should be noted. If administration follows, or if those who receive under the statute are not entitled, recovery can be had from those who have received the property. Presumably in most instances these complications will not occur.

It should be emphasized that "estate" in this statute and other state statutes means the estate subject to administration, and does not include will substitutes.

Some states also have a statute which permits small estates to be administered summarily.[40] The Uniform Probate Code § 3–1203 which so provides, is as follows:

Section 3–1203. [Small Estates; Summary Administration Procedure.]

If it appears from the inventory and appraisal that the value of the entire estate, less liens and encumbrances, does not exceed homestead allowance, exempt property, family allowance, costs and expenses of administration, reasonable funeral expenses, and reasonable and necessary medical and hospital expenses of the last illness of the decedent, the personal representative, without giving notice to creditors, may immediately disburse and distribute

---

40. E.g., Md.Est. & Trusts Code Ann. § 5–601; Minn.Stat.Ann. § 524.3– 1203; Okla.Stat.Ann. tit. 58, § 241; Vt. Stat.Ann. tit. 14, § 1901.

the estate to the persons entitled thereto and file a closing statement as provided in Section 3–1204.

In summary administration the closing statement under U.P.C. § 3–1204 has the same effect as a closing statement in conventional administration.

SECTION 12. WILL CONTEST SETTLEMENT AGREEMENTS; ANTI–CONTEST CLAUSES IN WILLS; STANDING TO CONTEST

Sometimes an heir (intestate taker) or heirs who are left nothing in the will or less than they would receive in intestacy, contest the probate of the will, or threaten to do so, on grounds of noncompliance with the formalities of execution, lack of testamentary capacity, undue influence, or possibly other grounds. The contest is a form of litigation, and the settlement of litigation by compromise is generally encouraged. As a general proposition the settlement by compromise of the will contest is permissible, but the nature of the matter being settled causes there to be certain qualifications to this generality.

The parties to the conflict are those who take under the will and the heirs. Some or all of the heirs may also be legatees or devisees, but in order for there to be a conflict one or more of the heirs must receive less under the will than they would receive in intestacy. By its nature the settlement provides for a distribution which takes something from one or more of the will beneficiaries and gives it to one or more of the heirs. In order to be completely effective, all the legatees, devisees and heirs must join in the settlement; no taker under the will or heir can be bound unless he joins. It is, of course, possible that a settlement agreement in which one or more interested parties did not join would be functionally effective because such party or parties do not choose to take action that would upset the settlement, such as petitioning for probate or contesting probate as the case may be.

The settlement agreement can take several forms. The parties may agree to probate the will and to have the takers under the will distribute a part of what they take to an heir or heirs. Or the parties may agree not to probate the will, administer the estate as an intestate estate, and have the heirs distribute part of what they take to the takers under the unprobated will. The third form is to have the court order the personal representative to distribute the estate among takers under the unprobated will and the heirs in accordance with the agreement, but some probate courts have determined that such an order of distribution is not within their power. The last form is obviously the most desirable from the standpoint of the parties because they receive their agreed upon shares directly from the personal representative. Under the other forms there is always the possibility that a party will default in his contractual obligation to pay over what he is entitled to from the personal representative.[41]

A few courts have not been hospitable to the will contest settlement. Suppose the legatees and heirs agree not to probate the will and agree to administer the estate as an intestate estate. Despite this agreement the executor designated in the will petitions for probate of the will. The beneficially interested parties object to the probate because of their agreement. A few courts have admitted the will to probate on the ground that the intent of the decedent was entitled to judicial implementation.[42] The probate, of course, does not preclude the interested parties from agreeing to redistribute the assets after distribution by the personal representative in accordance with the will. Another reason that has been given for the probate of the will in the face of a settlement agreement not to probate is the protection of possible creditors of legatees or devisees; the agreement not to probate could be a means of keeping testamentary assets from the reach of such creditors. It is emphasized that most courts would not probate the will in this circumstance.

There is a special circumstance in which the settlement agreement has generally run into difficulty. The will leaves the entire estate to Bank, in trust, to pay the income to A for life, and principal to B at A's death. C is the sole heir. C threatens to contest the probate of the will. A, B and C enter into an agreement in which the will is not to be probated, A and B are each to receive one-fourth of the estate outright, and C is to receive one-half outright. Bank, as trustee, does not join in the agreement. Bank is also designated as executor in the will, and petitions for probate of the will; A, B and C object on the basis of their agreement. Most trusts are not subject to termination by agreement of all beneficiaries unless the trustee concurs in the termination, and here the trustee has not. If the settlement agreement is given effect, it amounts to a termination of the trust because it does not come into being. There is substantial authority in this situation that the will is to be probated despite the settlement agreement in order to give effect to the testator's intention as manifested by the trust.[43] The settlement agreement has been used as a means by A

---

41. For discussion and citation of authority on judicial approval of distribution in accordance with settlement agreement, see Annot., 29 A.L.R.3d 112–122 (1970).

42. See cases cited supra note 1.

43. Adams v. Link, 145 Conn. 634, 145 A.2d 753 (1958); In re Swanson's Estate, 239 Iowa 294, 31 N.W.2d 385 (1948); St. Louis Union Trust Company v. Conant, 499 S.W.2d 761 (Mo.1973); Cahill v. Armatys, 185 Neb. 539, 177 N.W.2d 277 (1970). Contra: Budin v.

and B to avoid the trust, because C does not care whether the other half is in trust or not.

Assume the same will as in the preceding paragraph, and C is the sole heir. Bank petitions for probate and C contests the will. Before judgment, C, A and B enter into a settlement that one-half the estate is to be paid to C outright, and the other half is to be disposed of in trust in accordance with the probated will. If this is a good faith settlement of litigation, the court will direct the executor and trustee to comply with it. But note that the will is probated and the trust remains as to the other half. C has no interest in how the other half is disposed of; A and B have not used the settlement as a means of avoiding the trust set up by the testator.

Courts have imposed other limitations upon the settlement agreement. There are some cases that have held that the settlement agreement is valid only if the heirs have reasonable grounds for contesting the will,[44] and others have held that the agreement is valid only if the contest is in good faith.[45] In other words, a court is not likely to recognize or uphold the settlement agreement simply because it has been entered into.

We have described the will contest as between the beneficiaries of a will and the heirs. The contest may also arise between takers under successive wills presented for probate. The takers under the prior will contest the probate of the later will. The heirs, of course, may also challenge the validity of both wills.

The Uniform Probate Code has very broad provisions favorable to the enforcement of settlement agreements. U.P.C. § 3–912 requires the personal representative to comply with agreements concerning the distribution of the estate made by interested parties, including a testamentary trustee and the beneficiaries of the trust, without a court order.

U.P.C. §§ 3–1101 and 3–1102 set forth a formal procedure for judicial approval of a settlement agreement made by all living holders of beneficial interests except those whose identity cannot be ascertained or whose whereabouts is unknown, and parents of minor children having beneficial interests in the settlement, which agreement may be binding upon unborn and unascertained beneficiaries without the appointment of a guardian ad litem, although

Levy, 343 Mass. 644, 180 N.E.2d 74 (1962).

44. Boyd v. Boyd, 417 So.2d 577 (Ala.1982); Warner v. Warner, 124 Conn. 625, 1 A.2d 911 (1938); Anderson v. Anderson, 380 Ill. 488, 44 N.E.2d 43 (1942); Murphy v. Henry, 311 Ky. 799,

225 S.W.2d 662 (1949); Holt v. Holt, 304 N.C. 137, 282 S.E.2d 784 (1981).

45. Blount v. Dillaway, 199 Mass. 330, 85 N.E. 477 (1908); Stanley v. Sumrall, 167 Miss. 714, 147 So. 786 (1933); Rutledge v. Hoffman, 81 Ohio App. 85, 75 N.E.2d 608 (1947).

the court may make such an appointment if it deems it appropriate. The standards for judicial approval are that the agreement is made in good faith and is just and reasonable. The judicial approval, of course, requires the personal representative and any testamentary trustee to comply with the agreement.

A word should be said about "no contest" clauses in wills. Sometimes a will contains a provision that if any beneficiary contests the will, she forfeits the gift to her in the will. A beneficiary may contest if she is an heir and takes more as an heir, or if she is a beneficiary under an earlier will which gives her more than the later will which contains the clause. If the beneficiary contests the will and succeeds, she is in good shape; if she contests and loses, she loses all if the no-contest clause is enforced.

Obviously there is a policy against the admission of wills to probate which are improperly executed, or are the product of undue influence or the lack of capacity, which weighs against the enforceability of such a clause. The argument for the validity of the clause is that the testator should be allowed to discourage a law suit in which his personality and character and the character of others may be smeared, and family conflict may be aggravated. Many states have adopted the sensible rule, by statute or judicial decision, that the clause is unenforceable if there is probable cause for the contest.[46] That is to say, if there is probable cause for the contest and the contest fails, the contesting legatee retains her legacy. This is the position of Uniform Probate Code § 3–905, and Restatement (Second) of Property, Donative Transfers § 9.1. Some states, however, have adopted the position that the clause is enforceable in all circumstances.[47] It should be emphasized that proceedings to construe a will, or to challenge a provision as violative of the rule against perpetuities, are not considered to be a "contest" of the validity of the will, nor is the petition to probate a later will a "contest" of the earlier will.[48]

A word about standing to contest a will. In order to have standing one must have a direct pecuniary interest in the denial of probate,[49] or one must be a fiduciary for someone who has such a

46. In re Cocklin's Estate, 236 Iowa 98, 17 N.W.2d 129 (1945); Haynes v. First National State Bank, 87 N.J. 163, 432 A.2d 890 (1981); Estate of Seymour, 93 N.M. 328, 600 P.2d 274 (1979); Ryan v. Wachovia Bank & Trust Co., 235 N.C. 585, 70 S.E.2d 853 (1952).

47. Estate of Friedman, 100 Cal. App.3d 810, 161 Cal.Rptr. 311 (1979); Commerce Trust Co. v. Weed, 318 S.W.2d 289 (Mo.1958); Elder v. Elder, 84 R.I. 13, 120 A.2d 815 (1956); Dainton v. Watson, 658 P.2d 79 (Wyo.1983).

48. Ivancovich v. Meier, 122 Ariz. 346, 595 P.2d 24 (1979); In re Kline's Estate, 138 Cal.App. 514, 32 P.2d 677 (1934); Estate of Bergland, 180 Cal. 629, 182 P. 277 (1919); Reed v. Reed, 569 S.W.2d 645 (Tex.Civ.App.1978); N.Y.Est.Powers & Trusts Law § 3–3.5.

49. Hooper v. Huey, 293 Ala. 63, 300 So.2d 100 (1974); Estate of Powers, 91 Cal.App.3d 715, 154 Cal.Rptr. 366 (1979); In re Estate of Pearson, 319 N.W.2d 248 (Iowa 1982); Zinn v. Imperial Council, 253 Md. 183, 252 A.2d 76

direct pecuniary interest.[50]   Obviously an heir who receives less
under the will than he would receive in intestacy has standing.   A
beneficiary under an earlier will has standing to contest the probate
of a later will which revokes the prior will if he is disadvantaged by
the later will.   A trustee designated under an earlier will can
contest a later will if his beneficiaries are disadvantaged by the
later revoking will.   It seems that an executor under an earlier will
should have standing to contest a later will as the representative of
the beneficiaries' interests, but the law is mixed on this point.[51]

A creditor of the decedent cannot contest a will because his
position is unaffected by its probate.   A creditor of the decedent can
petition for probate as a part of the process of bringing about
administration so that he can get paid, but he has no economic
interest in the validity or invalidity of the will.   Unsecured creditors of heirs or beneficiaries under earlier wills present a different
question.   They have an interest in whether their debtor receives
property, but it has consistently been held that it is not a sufficiently substantial interest to allow standing to contest probate.[52]   However, if the creditor is a judgment, attachment or lien creditor who
would by virtue of that status obtain a lien on property received by
the debtor heir or beneficiary, such creditor has standing to contest
probate,[53] but there is also authority to the contrary.[54]

(1969);   In re Will of Calhoun, 47
N.C.App. 472, 267 S.E.2d 385 (1980),
cert. denied 301 N.C. 90, 273 S.E.2d 311
(1980).

50.   In re Estate of Getty, 85 Cal.
App.3d 755, 149 Cal.Rptr. 656 (1978);
Ashby v. Haddock, 140 So.2d 631 (Fla.
App.1962), rev'd on other grounds 149
So.2d 552 (Fla.1962); Johnston v. Willis,
147 Md. 237, 127 A. 862 (1925); Reed v.
Home National Bank of Brockton, 297
Mass. 222, 8 N.E.2d 601 (1937); In re
Estate of Maricich, 140 Mont. 319, 371
P.2d 354 (1962).

51.   Standing: Estate of Costa, 191
Cal.App.2d 515, 12 Cal.Rptr. 920 (1961);
Freasman v. Smith, 379 Ill. 79, 39
N.E.2d 367 (1942); Marshall's Executor
v. Pogue, 226 Ky. 767, 11 S.W.2d 918
(1928); In re Murphy's Estate, 153
Minn. 60, 189 N.W. 413 (1922).   No
standing: Johnston v. Willis, 147 Md.
237, 127 A. 862 (1925); Reed v. Home
National Bank of Brockton, 297 Mass.

222, 8 N.E.2d 601 (1937); Hermann v.
Crossen, 81 Ohio L.Abs. 322, 160 N.E.2d
404 (Ohio App.1959); In re O'Brien's
Estate, 13 Wash.2d 581, 126 P.2d 47
(1942).

52.   Lockard v. Stephenson, 120 Ala.
641, 24 So. 996 (1899); San Diego Trust
& Savings Bank v. Heustis, 121 Cal.App.
675, 10 P.2d 158 (1932); Keeler v.
Lauer, 73 Kan. 388, 85 P. 541 (1906); In
re Shepard's Estate, 170 Pa. 323, 32 A.
1040 (1895).

53.   In re Harootenian's Estate, 38
Cal.2d 242, 238 P.2d 992 (1951); In re
Duffy's Estate, 228 Iowa 426, 292 N.W.
165 (1940); Marcus v. Pearce Woolen
Mills, 353 Mass. 483, 233 N.E.2d 29
(1968); In re Van Doren's Estate, 119
N.J.Eq. 80, 180 A. 841 (1935).

54.   Lockard v. Stephenson, 120 Ala.
641, 24 So. 996 (1899); Lee v. Keech,
151 Md. 34, 133 A. 835 (1926).

Chapter 10

SPENDTHRIFT, DISCRETIONARY, SUPPORT AND PROTECTIVE TRUSTS

SECTION 1. ALIENABILITY

Unless the trust instrument or a statute in the jurisdiction otherwise provides, equitable interests under a trust are alienable (transferable) inter vivos and by will. Let us assume that Bank is trustee to pay the income to Mary for her life, and upon her death to pay over the trust assets to John in fee. Mary can transfer her life interest to Jane, gratuitously or for consideration, thereby making Jane the owner of the equitable interest for the life of Mary. John during his life can transfer his remainder to Bill, gratuitously or for consideration, thereby making Bill the owner of the equitable remainder in fee. If John's remainder had been a contingent remainder, as it would have been if the trust instrument had provided that John would take only if he survived Mary, it would also be transferable inter vivos.[1] Assuming John's taking was not contingent upon his surviving Mary, and John predeceased Mary, John could bequeath or devise his equitable remainder interest to Bill in his will.

An assignment of an equitable interest under a trust of personalty can be made orally,[2] unless there is a statute which requires that such an assignment be made or evidenced by a writing of the assignor, as there is in some states.[3] In most states there are statutes which require that inter vivos transfers of equitable interests under a trust of land be made or evidenced by a writing of the

---

1. Johnson v. Swann, 211 Md. 207, 126 A.2d 603 (1956); All Persons v. Buie, 386 So.2d 1109 (Miss.1980); McNeal v. Bonnel, 412 S.W.2d 167 (Mo. 1967); Martin v. Martin, 54 Ohio St.2d 101, 374 N.E.2d 1384 (1978). Historically legal contingent future interests in land were not assignable, and vestiges of that rule remain today in a few states. See Simes and Smith, Law of Future Interests §§ 1857–1859 (2d ed. 1956).

In this book we frequently use the example of a trust for A for life, remainder to B in fee. It should be understood that usually there is no implied condition that B must survive A in order to take. B's remainder is vested; B's estate takes if B predeceases A.

2. 2A Scott, Law of Trusts § 138 (4th ed., Fratcher, 1987). See Gwin v. Gwin, 240 Mo.App. 782, 219 S.W.2d 282 (1949).

3. E.g., Ind.Code Ann. § 32-2-1-3; Minn.Stat.Ann. § 513.03; Nev.Rev.Stat. § 111.235; S.D.Comp.Laws Ann. §§ 43–35-2, 55-1-14.

assignor.[4] A minor or a person otherwise incompetent cannot assign his beneficial interest under a trust, any more than he can transfer legal interests in property.

Unless the trust instrument or a statute in the jurisdiction provides otherwise, the interest of a beneficiary under a trust is subject to the claims of his creditors.[5] If the beneficiary has a life income interest, the court may order the sale of the interest. This may be harsh on the debtor-beneficiary because of the uncertain duration of the life interest and the consequent speculative nature of its value. For that reason the court may order the trustee to pay the income to the judgment creditor until the debt is satisfied, rather than order the sale of the interest.[6] If the debtor-beneficiary has a future interest, the court may not order the sale of the interest because of the speculative nature of its value, but rather impose a lien upon the interest which will enable the judgment creditor to have his claim satisfied from the property in the event the future interest becomes possessory.[7]

The trust is frequently employed by the settlor to assure the financial security of members of his family over an extended period of time. Obviously the settlor does not want the beneficiaries to sell their interests or to have their interests subjected to the claims of their creditors, because this would defeat the purpose of providing security to the beneficiaries. It is therefore common for the trust instrument to include clauses which purport to restrain directly such voluntary and involuntary alienation, or which qualify the interests of the beneficiaries in such a manner as to effectively preclude alienation of the interests. Spendthrift trusts, discretionary trusts, support trusts, and protective trusts are of this nature.

Before these several types of trusts are discussed, it would be helpful to summarize briefly the law concerning direct, or express, restraints on alienation with respect to legal interests. If an owner of legal title to land transfers title and wishes to prevent or discourage the transferee from transferring his title or creditors of the transferee from reaching it, he may attempt to effect this result by including an appropriate clause in the deed to restrain alienation. Such clauses fall into three basic categories: the disabling restraint, the forfeiture restraint, and the promissory restraint.

---

4. E.g., Colo.Rev.Stat. § 38–10–106; Fla.Stat.Ann. § 689.06; Idaho Code § 9–503; Pa.Stat.Ann. tit. 33, § 2.

5. Chandler v. Hale, 173 Conn. 276, 377 A.2d 318 (1977); Henderson v. Collins, 245 Ga. 776, 267 S.E.2d 202 (1980); Miller v. Maryland Cas. Co., 207 Ark. 312, 180 S.W.2d 581 (1944); New England Merchants Nat. Bank v. Hoss, 356 Mass. 331, 249 N.E.2d 635 (1969).

6. Showalter v. G.H. Nunnelley Co., 201 Ky. 595, 257 S.W. 1027 (1924); Dillon v. Spilo, 250 App.Div. 543, 294 N.Y.S. 876 (1937), aff'd 275 N.Y. 275, 9 N.E.2d 864 (1937).

7. Equitable Life Assur. Society v. Patzowsky, 131 N.J.Eq. 49, 23 A.2d 561 (1942); Mid-America Corp. v. Geismar, 380 P.2d 85 (Okl.1963); Meyer v. Reif, 217 Wis. 11, 258 N.W. 391 (1935).

The disabling restraint purports to deprive the transferee of the power to alienate; that is to say, any attempt to alienate voluntarily or any attempt by a creditor to reach the property is ineffective, a nullity. The forfeiture restraint provides that if the transferee attempts to convey, or a creditor attempts to levy or attach, the interest of the transferee terminates and title returns to the transferor or passes to a third party. The promissory restraint provides that the transferee promises that he will not alienate, and any attempt to do so is enjoinable.

The disabling restraint upon the alienation of legal interests in land has usually been held to be invalid, and this has been the result whether the interest so restrained is a fee, a life estate, or an estate for years. The forfeiture restraint and the promissory restraint, when imposed upon a fee interest, have generally been held to be invalid also, except that such restraints have sometimes been held to be valid where they are limited in duration or where they restrict alienation only to a limited group of people. However, the forfeiture restraint and the promissory restraint have been held to be valid when imposed upon a legal life estate or an estate for years.[8] It should be emphasized that where the restraint upon alienation is invalid, the transfer of the property which included the restraint is otherwise effective; the restraint clause is stricken and the transferee is free to alienate as he pleases.[9]

SECTION 2. SPENDTHRIFT TRUSTS

It is common for the settlor to include a clause which imposes a disabling restraint upon the alienation of beneficial interests under a trust. Such restraints purport to render ineffective any attempt to alienate, voluntarily or involuntarily. As indicated above, such restraints are usually held to be invalid when imposed upon legal interests. The law is different, however, with respect to equitable interests in a trust. The disabling restraint upon the equitable right to receive income for life or years has generally been held to be valid in this country.[10] The disabling restraint upon the equita-

---

8. For discussion of the law of direct, or express, restraints on alienation, see Simes and Smith, Law of Future Interests §§ 1136–1167 (2d ed. 1956). See also Restatement (Second) of Property, Donative Transfers, Chapter 4 (1983).

9. The law concerning direct restraints on alienation of legal interests has developed primarily with respect to land, but the same principles presumably apply to direct restraints on legal interests in personalty. Certain direct restraints on alienation of stock in close-ly-held corporations have been upheld as reasonable. See 2 O'Neal, Close Corporations §§ 7.05 et seq. (2d ed. 1971); Simes and Smith, Law of Future Interests § 1166 (2d ed. 1956).

10. American Security & Trust Co. v. Utley, 127 U.S.App.D.C. 235, 382 F.2d 451 (1967); Watterson v. Edgerly, 40 Md.App. 230, 388 A.2d 934 (1978); Estate of Edgar, 425 Mich. 364, 389 N.W.2d 696 (1986); Lundgren v. Hoglund, 219 Mont. 295, 711 P.2d 809

ble right to receive principal in remainder is also valid in most jurisdictions.[11] If a disabling restraint is included in a trust instrument in a jurisdiction in which it is invalid, the equitable interest remains in effect free of the restraint.

If the restraint is valid, the creditor is unable to reach the interest of the beneficiary prior to distribution to the beneficiary, but the creditor can reach the assets after payment to the beneficiary. The spendthrift trust, in effect, exempts property in the hands of the trustee, but does not exempt the same property in the hands of the beneficiary.[12] It would be, of course, much simpler for the creditor to reach the property before it leaves the hands of the trustee than to do so after the money is in the hands of the beneficiary who is disinclined to pay his debts. The spendthrift trust puts the creditor at a distinct disadvantage.

If a settlor makes himself a beneficiary of the trust, any attempt to impose a disabling restraint upon his beneficial interest is invalid,[13] although disabling restraints upon other beneficial interests in the trust are valid. Accordingly, if the settlor transfers to T, in trust, to pay the income to the settlor and A, equally, for their lives, and upon their respective deaths to pay one-half the principal to their issue, and the trust instrument prohibits alienation of beneficial interests, the settlor's income interest is alienable and the other interests are not.

Conceivably a settlor may attempt to prohibit involuntary alienation of a beneficiary's interest but permit voluntary alienation. It would seem improper to prevent creditors from reaching that which the beneficiary could transfer, and accordingly the restraint upon involuntary alienation in such circumstances should

---

(1985); Erickson v. Bank of California, 97 Wash.2d 246, 643 P.2d 670 (1982).

11. Brent v. State of Maryland Central Collection Unit, 311 Md. 626, 537 A.2d 227 (1988); Bank of New England v. Strandlund, 402 Mass. 707, 529 N.E.2d 394 (1988); Lamberton v. Lamberton, 229 Minn. 29, 38 N.W.2d 72 (1949); First Nat. Bank of Omaha v. First Cadco Corp., 189 Neb. 734, 205 N.W.2d 115 (1973); In re Estate of Vought, 25 N.Y.2d 163, 303 N.Y.S.2d 61, 250 N.E.2d 343 (1969). It appears that some courts have recognized the spendthrift restraint on income interests but not on principal interests. See 2A Scott, Law of Trusts § 153 (4th ed., Fratcher, 1987).

Some states have statutes which recognize the validity of spendthrift trusts as to income and principal interests: E.g., Del.Code Ann. tit. 12, § 3536; Ind. Code Ann. § 30–4–3–2; Ky.Rev.Stat. Ann. § 381.180; R.I.Gen.Laws § 18–9.1–1; Wis.Stat.Ann. § 701.06.

There are states which do not recognize the validity of the spendthrift trust in any respect: E.g., Athorne v. Athorne, 100 N.H. 413, 128 A.2d 910 (1957).

12. See notes 23 and 24 below, and accompanying text.

13. Matter of Witlin, 640 F.2d 661 (5th Cir.1981); Deposit Guaranty Nat. Bank v. Walter E. Heller & Co., 204 So.2d 856 (Miss.1967); Morton v. Morton, 394 Pa. 402, 147 A.2d 150 (1959); Farmers State Bank v. Janish, 410 N.W.2d 188 (S.D.1987).

be invalid.[14] On the other hand, if the trust prohibited voluntary alienation but permitted involuntary alienation, the restraint upon voluntary alienation should be valid. It is very rare for a trust to restrain one form of alienation and not the other; almost invariably spendthrift trust provisions restrain alienation of all kinds.

In some jurisdictions there are statutes which impose certain disabling restraints upon beneficial interests under a trust as a matter of law. There are statutes which provide that certain beneficial interests cannot be voluntarily alienated; [15] some statutes provide that so much of a beneficial income interest as is necessary for the education and support of the beneficiary is exempt from creditors' claims; [16] other statutes provide that income up to a certain dollar amount is exempt from creditors' claims.[17]

In some states in which spendthrift provisions are valid, certain types of creditors of the beneficiary have been allowed to reach the trust assets in the hands of the trustee despite the spendthrift aspect, sometimes by judicial decision, sometimes by statute. Children and the spouse of the beneficiary have been allowed to reach the trust assets to satisfy claims for support or alimony, on the ground that the settlor did not intend the spendthrift provisions to apply to such claims, or on the ground that it would be contrary to public policy to exempt trust assets from such claims, or by statute.[18] There is authority that those who have furnished necessaries to the beneficiary can reach trust assets.[19] The government has been permitted to reach the trust assets for unpaid taxes of the beneficiary.[20] There is authority that those who have conferred a

14. See 2A Scott, Law of Trusts § 152.3 (4th ed., Fratcher, 1987). See Bank of New England v. Strandlund, 402 Mass. 707, 529 N.E.2d 394 (1988) for a contrary view.

15. E.g., Mich.Stat.Ann. § 26.69.

16. E.g., Ala.Code § 19–3–1; Cal. Civ.Code § 859; Mich.Stat.Ann. § 26.-63; N.Y.Est.Powers & Trusts Law § 7–3.4; Okla.Stat.Ann. tit. 60, § 140.

17. E.g., Okla.Stat.Ann. tit. 60, § 175.25.

18. Howard v. Spragins, 350 So.2d 318 (Ala.1977); Council v. Owens, 28 Ark.App. 49, 770 S.W.2d 193 (1989); In re Marriage of Parscal, 148 Cal.App.3d 1098, 196 Cal.Rptr. 462 (1983); Bacardi v. White, 463 So.2d 218 (Fla.1985); Zouck v. Zouck, 204 Md. 285, 104 A.2d 573 (1954); Shelley v. Shelley, 223 Or. 328, 354 P.2d 282 (1960); Ky.Rev.Stat.

Ann. § 381.180; Okla.Stat.Ann. tit. 60, § 175.25; Pa.Stat.Ann. tit. 20, § 6112; Wis.Stat.Ann. § 701.06.

19. American Security & Trust Co. v. Utley, 127 U.S.App.D.C. 235, 382 F.2d 451 (1967); Matter of Estate of Dodge, 281 N.W.2d 447 (Iowa 1979); Lang v. Commonwealth, Dept. of Public Welfare 515 Pa. 428, 528 A.2d 1335 (1987); Erickson v. Bank of California, 97 Wash.2d 246, 643 P.2d 670 (1982); Ky.Rev.Stat. Ann. § 381.180; La.Rev.Stat.Ann. § 9:2005; Okla.Stat.Ann. tit. 60, § 175.-25.

20. First Northwestern Trust Co. v. Internal Revenue Service, 622 F.2d 387 (8th Cir.1980); Leuschner v. First Western Bank & Trust Co., 261 F.2d 705 (9th Cir.1958); Ky.Rev.Stat. § 381.180. See Restatement (Second) of Trusts § 157 (1959).

benefit upon the beneficiary's interest, such as an attorney for the beneficiary in connection with litigation concerning his interest, can reach the trust assets,[21] but there is also authority to the contrary.[22] Arguably tort claimants against the beneficiary should be allowed to reach the trust assets because they have no opportunity to check out the beneficiary's financial status in advance.

There is some authority for the proposition that when an interest under a spendthrift trust becomes due and payable to the beneficiary, the beneficiary can then validly assign the amount due and his creditors can reach the amount due in the hands of the trustee.[23] That is to say, an assignment or attachment of that which becomes due in the future is wholly ineffective, but if after a distribution under the trust becomes due, the beneficiary makes an assignment of, or the creditor attaches the amount due, the assignment and the attachment are valid. There is, however, contrary authority that the assignment and attachment under these limited circumstances are also ineffective, and that under no circumstances can the trust assets in the hands of the trustee be assigned or attached.[24]

It is important to distinguish between an assignment and a revocable direction or authorization to pay. An assignment of a beneficial interest under a trust or a portion of such an interest is a transfer of a property interest. A direction to the trustee to pay the next installment of income to X, which direction to the trustee may be revoked at any time prior to the payment, is not a transfer of a property interest. In the case of the assignment, the beneficiary loses control; in the case of the direction, the beneficiary can change his mind and revoke the direction up to the time the distribution is made. The revocable direction is not prohibited by the spendthrift provision in the trust; that is to say, the trustee is not in violation of the terms of the trust if he honors the direction

21. In re Williams, 187 N.Y. 286, 79 N.E. 1019 (1907). See Restatement (Second) of Trusts § 157 (1959).

22. McKeown v. Pridmore, 310 Ill. App. 634, 35 N.E.2d 376 (1941); Pond v. Harrison, 96 Kan. 542, 152 P. 655 (1915).

23. Brent v State of Maryland Central Collection Unit, 311 Md. 626, 537 A.2d 227 (1988); Boston Safe Deposit & Trust Co. v. Paris, 15 Mass.App.Ct. 686, 447 N.E.2d 1268 (1983); First National Bank of Omaha v. First Cadco Corp., 189 Neb. 734, 205 N.W.2d 115 (1973); Trust Co. of New Jersey v. Gardner, 133 N.J.Eq. 436, 32 A.2d 572 (1943); In re Gould's Will, 39 Misc.2d 942, 242

N.Y.S.2d 153 (1963); Milner v. Outcalt, 36 Wash.2d 720, 219 P.2d 982 (1950).

24. Connecticut Bank & Trust Co. v. Hurlbutt, 157 Conn. 315, 254 A.2d 460 (1968); Matter of Trust Created Under Agreement With McLaughlin, 361 N.W.2d 43 (Minn.1985); Williams v. Frisbee, 419 S.W.2d 99 (Mo.1967); Clark v. Clark, 411 Pa. 251, 191 A.2d 417 (1963); First Bank & Trust v. Goss, 533 S.W.2d 93 (Tex.Civ.App.1976). In 2A Scott, Law of Trusts §§ 152.5 and 153 (4th ed., Fratcher, 1987), it is indicated that creditors can attach past due principal but cannot attach past due income, but it is not clear that the cases bear this out or why it should be so.

as long as it is not revoked prior to the time distribution is made.[25]

It is surprising that the spendthrift trust has been so widely accepted in this country since it is primarily a creditor avoidance technique. The creditor of the spendthrift trust beneficiary with substantial income is prevented from reaching the income at its source, and instead must go to the trouble of locating the assets of the debtor in his hands. The social utility of the spendthrift trust is questionable. It seems that it can be justified only as an aspect of the settlor's ownership; that is to say, the property owner is entitled to dispose of his property on such terms as he wishes. This explanation begs the question, however, because limits are placed on the disposition of property where a social interest takes precedence over the dispositive aspects of ownership, e.g., the rule against perpetuities, surviving spouse's forced share, and, indeed, the rule against restraints on the alienation of legal interests. It has also been maintained that the creditor of the spendthrift trust beneficiary has only himself to blame if he has not checked on the exempt nature of his debtor's income. This last contention has several holes in it. For one, it is not economic for most creditors to check out in detail the debtor's financial situation. Also, the living trust of personalty is not a matter of record. The living trust of real property and the testamentary trust are of record, but heaven only knows in what jurisdiction that record may be. It is not easy for the creditor to discover the spendthrift nature of the debtor's income.

SECTION 3. DISCRETIONARY TRUSTS

It is not uncommon for a settlor to create a trust in which the trustee is given discretion concerning the disposition of the trust assets. Settlor transfers to T, in trust, to pay to A during his life so much of the income and so much of the principal, from time to time, as T shall determine in his absolute discretion, and upon A's death to pay over the remaining principal and accumulated income, if any, to B. There is no standard set forth in the trust instrument within which the discretion is to be exercised. That which is given to A is taken from B. T is a trustee and must exercise his discretion in accordance with his fiduciary responsibility, which requires that he act impartially and from proper motives. The trustee must make deliberative decisions, and his actions must not be arbitrary, capricious or biased. In making a distribution T is necessarily subject to fiduciary standards which always control the conduct of a trustee, but assuming his compliance with these standards, T's discretion is otherwise unfettered.

25. Clark v. Clark, 123 Kan. 646, 256 P. 1012 (1927); Matter of Will of Link, 119 Misc.2d 181, 462 N.Y.S.2d 582 (1983); In re Heyl's Estate, 156 Pa.Super. 277, 40 A.2d 149 (1944), aff'd 352 Pa. 407, 43 A.2d 130 (1945).

It follows that T is in breach of trust if he distributes to A because he detests B, or if he refuses to distribute to A because he detests A or is especially fond of B.[26]   T violates his fiduciary duty if he distributes to A because A is married to T's daughter.   Of course, T is permitted to distribute to A even though A is married to T's daughter, or to distribute to A even though he likes A and dislikes B, or to refuse to distribute to A even though he dislikes A, as long as T has not been motivated by these improper considerations.   The burden is upon the beneficiary to prove the improper motive, which may be very difficult to establish.   If, however, it can be established that T has these biases which could affect his decisions, a court may order the trustee's removal to avoid the possibility of improperly motivated decisions.

Let us suppose that A is destitute and living on welfare due to factors beyond his control such as physical or mental incapacity, that B is quite comfortable, and T refuses to make any distribution to A.   Is it possible that T's decision not to distribute is within the scope of his permissible discretion?   Even if it cannot be established that T is biased against A or in favor of B, there appears to be no justification for the withholding of funds from A.   A trustee who has discretion to pay out funds or not must make deliberative decisions, and it appears that T has not done so here because if he had he would necessarily decide to make a distribution.

The discretionary trust has the effect of making the trust assets unavailable to the beneficiary's creditors as long as the trustee chooses not to distribute to the beneficiary.   The creditor of the discretionary trust beneficiary has no better claim upon the trust assets than the beneficiary has.   If the unsatisfied judgment creditor levies upon the beneficiary's interest in the trust, he receives nothing as long as the trustee elects not to make a distribution.   In the event, however, that the trustee decides to make a distribution, the creditor will receive that distribution on account of the judgment debt.[27]   The net result is that the assets are insulated from the claims of creditors at the price of termination of distributions to the beneficiary.   This is very different from the spendthrift trust situation where the beneficiary can receive the distribution in the face of creditors' claims.   The discretionary trust keeps the assets out of the hands of creditors

26. See Connor v. Hart, 157 Conn. 265, 253 A.2d 9 (1968); Mesler v. Holly, 318 So.2d 530 (Fla.Dist.Ct.App.1975); In re Koretzky's Estate, 8 N.J. 506, 86 A.2d 238 (1951); Matter of Bruches, 67 A.D.2d 456, 415 N.Y.S.2d 664 (1979); In re Buchar's Estate, 225 Pa. 427, 74 A. 237 (1909).

27. Canfield v. Security-First Nat. Bank, 13 Cal.2d 1, 87 P.2d 830 (1939); Landmark First National Bank v. Haves, 467 So.2d 839 (Fla.Dist.Ct.App. 1985); Sand v. Beach, 270 N.Y. 281, 200 N.E. 821 (1936); First Nat. Bank of Enid v. Clark, 402 P.2d 248 (Okl.1965). But see Shelley v. Shelley, 223 Or. 328, 354 P.2d 282 (1960).

only if the trustee exercises his discretion to refrain from making distributions to the beneficiary. It should be kept in mind that a trust may contain both discretionary and spendthrift terms, in which case the distributions to the beneficiary are exempt from the claims of creditors.

It should be noted that in our example the trust is not discretionary with respect to the interest of the remainderman, B. B is absolutely entitled to receive his distribution at A's death, but, of course, his interest has virtually no value while A lives because there may be nothing to distribute. If, however, the trust provided that T could distribute so much of the income (but not principal) to A as T should determine in his discretion, and at A's death, all accumulated income, if any, and principal were to be paid to B, the value of the remainder interest of B would be substantial. In both examples, the rule with respect to creditors' rights to reach discretionary trust assets does not apply to B's interests. When the term discretionary trust is used, it describes only specific interests under the trust; there must always be a nondiscretionary interest entitled to the trust assets in the event the assets are not fully disposed of pursuant to the discretionary power.

The settlor of a discretionary trust may be a beneficiary of such trust. The settlor cannot, however, insulate the trust assets from his creditors by this means. His creditors can reach the trust assets to the extent of the trustee's power to make distributions to the settlor.[28] That is to say, in a trust providing that Trustee may distribute so much of the income and so much of the principal to Settlor as Trustee shall in his discretion determine, and at Settlor's death the remaining principal and accumulated income, if any, is to be paid to Jones, Settlor's creditors can at any time during Settlor's life reach all the principal and income because Trustee was empowered to distribute all of it at any time to Settlor. This means, in effect, that Settlor's creditors have rights to reach the trust assets which are greater than Settlor's right to demand distribution. It should be noted that after Settlor's death his creditors cannot levy upon the trust assets because Settlor ceases to have any beneficial interest.

SECTION 4. SUPPORT TRUSTS

It is common for the settlor to create a trust which provides for the distribution of income or principal, or both, only for the support of a beneficiary. Settlor transfers to T, in trust, to pay so much of

28. Ware v. Gulda, 331 Mass. 68, 117 N.E.2d 137 (1954); State Street Bank & Trust Co. v. Reiser, 7 Mass.App.Ct. 633, 389 N.E.2d 768 (1979); Vanderbilt Credit Corp. v. Chase Manhattan Bank, 100 A.D.2d 544, 473 N.Y.S.2d 242 (1984).

the income to A as is necessary for A's support, and upon A's death, to pay the undistributed income, if any, and the principal to B. Unlike the discretionary trust and the trust in which the beneficiary is absolutely entitled to income, the trustee in making his distributive decisions is limited by a standard.

The first issue that is presented by this type of trust is the definition of support. Support does not mean subsistence; that is to say, T is not limited in his distributions to that which is necessary to keep A's body and soul together. Support is a relative standard whose meaning varies in accordance with the social and economic classification of the beneficiary.[29] The support of Jones who is a blue collar laborer is very different from the support of Smith who is a member of the social and economic establishment in the community. To provide support is to provide funds to enable the beneficiary to live in the manner to which he is accustomed. The expenses of a condominium in Florida for vacationing would not be included within support for Jones, but they may be for Smith. It is obvious that support is a very flexible concept.

Another issue in the determination of what the trustee is to distribute is whether the trustee must take into consideration the support trust beneficiary's income, other than what he receives from the trust, in making his decision concerning the beneficiary's needs. If it is proper to consider the beneficiary's other income, then the beneficiary is not entitled to any distribution from the trust if he is earning a living which is in keeping with his accustomed standard of living. If, on the other hand, it is not proper to consider other income, and the beneficiary is earning a living which is in keeping with his accustomed standard, then he is entitled to receive distributions from the trust which in fact enable him to live substantially beyond his accustomed standard. Clearly the trust instrument can, and should, state whether or not other income is to be considered, but if the trust instrument is silent, the prevailing judicial construction is that other income is not to be considered;[30] there is, however, authority to the contrary.[31]

Why should this be the prevailing construction? A reason that has been offered is that if other income is to be considered, then

29. McElrath v. Citizens & Southern Nat. Bank, 229 Ga. 20, 189 S.E.2d 49 (1972); Kuykendall v. Proctor, 270 N.C. 510, 155 S.E.2d 293 (1967); Epp Estate, 17 Pa.D. & C.2d 278 (Orph.1959); Emmert v. Old National Bank of Martinsburg, 162 W.Va. 48, 246 S.E.2d 236 (1978). See Martin v. Simmons First Nat. Bank, 250 Ark. 774, 467 S.W.2d 165 (1971).

30. Estate of Wells v. Sanford, 281 Ark. 242, 663 S.W.2d 174 (1984); Ho-

lyoke Nat. Bank v. Wilson, 350 Mass. 223, 214 N.E.2d 42 (1966); Matter of Clark, 280 N.Y. 155, 19 N.E.2d 1001 (1939); Kuykendall v. Proctor, 270 N.C. 510, 155 S.E.2d 293 (1967); Estate of Tashjian, 375 Pa.Super. 221, 544 A.2d 67 (1988).

31. Dunklee v. Kettering, 123 Colo. 43, 225 P.2d 853 (1950); Board of Visitors v. Safe Deposit & Trust Co. of Baltimore, 186 Md. 89, 46 A.2d 280 (1946).

there is an inducement for the beneficiary not to work since whatever he produces is, in effect, deducted from his trust distribution. This makes some sense, but there is also the strange consequence that if the beneficiary earns a good living, the support trust becomes a luxury trust. It also should be noted that the support trust beneficiary may have substantial income from another trust, or from stocks and bonds which he owns; it appears that this income is also to be ignored under this construction. The argument about inducing sloth is less convincing where such "unearned" income is involved.

In the definition of support there is also the issue of whether the beneficiary's support, as that term is used in the trust instrument, includes his obligation to support others. It has been held that the beneficiary's support includes his legal obligations to support his wife and minor children.[32] In other words, the beneficiary's support includes what is necessary for his support and for the support of his wife and minor children. This, of course, is a matter of judicial construction of the settlor's intention, and the trust instrument can and should deal specifically with this issue.

It should be mentioned that support trusts frequently provide for the application of the trust assets to the payment of the beneficiary's expenses for support, as well as for payment directly to the beneficiary, as the trustee deems advisable. Also, it is common to allow for the distribution of principal, as well as income, for support, since it is impossible to project the beneficiary's needs and the trust income over the long term.

It has been generally held that support trusts are spendthrift even in the absence of any language in the trust instrument prohibiting alienation.[33] The reasoning is that the settlor intended that the trust be used for a specific purpose, the beneficiary's support, and that to permit voluntary alienation or creditors to reach the beneficiary's interest would be contrary to that purpose. Only the beneficial interest which is limited to support is spendthrift; in the case of a trust to pay income to A as needed for his support, and upon A's death to pay principal and any undistributed income to B, A's interest is spendthrift but B's interest is not. The support trust instrument may, of course, contain explicit spendthrift provisions.

32. Bridgeport-City Trust Co. v. Beach, 119 Conn. 131, 174 A. 308 (1934); In re Estate of Rockwell, 26 Misc.2d 709, 205 N.Y.S.2d 928 (Sur.Ct. 1960); Seattle First Nat. Bank v. Crosby, 42 Wash.2d 234, 254 P.2d 732 (1953). But see Martin v. Martin, 54 Ohio St.2d 101, 374 N.E.2d 1384 (19788).

33. In re McLoughlin, 507 F.2d 177 (5th Cir.1975); Reilly v. State, 119 Conn. 508, 177 A. 528 (1935); Lang v. Commonwealth, Dept. of Public Welfare, 515 Pa. 428, 528 A.2d 1335 (1987).

There is authority that a support trust is spendthrift even in a jurisdiction in which spendthrift trusts otherwise are invalid.[34] The reason the ordinary spendthrift trust is invalid is that it is considered to be contrary to public policy for a person to be entitled to property which his creditors cannot reach. In the case of the support trust, however, the beneficiary is not absolutely entitled to property, but rather is entitled to property only for a specific purpose, and it does not seem to be as offensive to place such property beyond the reach of creditors.

Presumably the types of creditors which are excepted from the application of the express restraints of the conventional spendthrift trust are also excepted from the implied restraints of the support trust.[35] Thus, creditors such as those who have furnished the necessities of life, and family dependents, can reach the interest of the support beneficiary in the trust. This makes good sense because payment to such creditors would constitute the application of the beneficiary's interest to the support of the beneficiary. Arguably all creditors whose advances contribute to the support of the beneficiary in accordance with the beneficiary's accustomed standard should be permitted to reach the beneficiary's interest.

If Settlor transfers to Trustee, to pay the income to Settlor as needed for his support, and upon Settlor's death, to pay the undistributed income, if any, and principal to X, the support trust for Settlor is perfectly valid, but Settlor's interest is not spendthrift.[36] Settlor's creditors can reach his interest in the trust despite the implied spendthrift provision, just as a settlor's interest in an express, non-support spendthrift trust is subject to the claims of his creditors. It is contrary to public policy to allow a property owner to place his property beyond his creditors' reach by means of the trust device. The settlor's creditors can reach the trust assets only to the extent of the settlor's interest; the settlor is not entitled to the income absolutely, but rather is entitled only to such income as is required for his support.

The trustee has considerable discretion in the support trust because of the imprecise nature of the support standard. It is common practice, however, to include discretionary language in connection with the support standard. Settlor transfers to T, in trust, to pay such income to A as T shall, in his discretion, deem necessary for A's support, and upon A's death, to pay the principal and any undistributed income to B. This may be referred to as a

34. See Athorne v. Athorne, 100 N.H. 413, 128 A.2d 910 (1957).

35. Restatement (Second) of Trusts § 157 (1959).

36. Restatement (Second) of Trusts § 156 (1959). See cases cited supra note 13.

discretionary support trust. T is limited in his distributions to A's support needs, but T is explicitly given the power to determine what A's support needs are. Certainly it is intended that T shall have greater latitude in his decisions than would be the case in the absence of the discretionary language. T is, of course, required to exercise his judgment in accordance with fiduciary standards which are generally applicable. The significance of these standards as applied to the exercise of trustee discretion was described above in the discussion of discretionary trusts. It seems that in a discretionary support trust such as this the trustee may, in his determination of support, consider the beneficiary's other income or not as he deems fit.[37]

In recent years there has been considerable litigation on the question of whether the state can compel reimbursement from a trust for the cost of state institutional care for a beneficiary of the trust which has been established by the beneficiary's parent or other person. It is clear that if the beneficiary is absolutely entitled to income from the trust, and there is no spendthrift provision, the state as creditor can reach the beneficiary's interest in the hands of the trustee. The matter is not as obvious if it is a spendthrift trust, a support trust, a discretionary trust, or a discretionary support trust. If the trust is spendthrift, there is the exception to the spendthrift constraint that a creditor who has furnished necessaries to the beneficiary can reach his interest. Certainly institutional care is a "necessary." If the trust is for support without language of discretion, which is unusual, certainly the institutional care qualifies as support and must be paid by the trustee, provided the beneficiary does not have other sources of support. If the trust is purely discretionary without any language of a standard, it may be very difficult for the state to establish that the trustee has violated its duty by refusing to make payments to the state for services which the beneficiary is entitled to. The trustee of a purely discretionary trust may decline to make distribution as long as the decision is deliberative and not arbitrary, capricious or biased; reasons for withholding distribution may include the need to provide for other expenses of the institutionalized beneficiary, or to protect against the day when he ceases to be institutionalized, or to provide for the remaindermen under the trust. If the trust is a discretionary support trust, it may be that the trustee has a duty to pay the state as a creditor which is furnishing essential support; that is to say, it would be arbitrary for the trustee to decline to reimburse the state for such services. On the other hand, it may be a reasonable exercise of discretion to retain all trust income and principal for the purpose of providing

---

37. See Martin v. Martin, 54 Ohio St.2d 101, 374 N.E.2d 1384 (1978); Es- tate of Tashjian, 375 Pa.Super. 221, 544 A.2d 67 (1988).

for other needs of the institutionalized beneficiary, or to protect against the day when he ceases to be institutionalized. In the absence of a statute to the contrary, it seems to be legally permissible to include language in a discretionary support trust to the effect that trust assets are not to be used to reimburse the state for the expenses of care of the beneficiary unless the state services would be reduced or terminated because of such nonreimbursement.

Entitlement to certain medical and disability benefits from the state often are based upon need. There is the question of whether a beneficial interest in a trust is an asset whose value is to be attributed to the applicant for the services. Does the beneficiary of a discretionary or discretionary support trust have such access to the assets in the trust that the assets are to be deemed to be his property? This presents legal problems similar to those relating to the reimbursement of the state for institutional care.[38]

SECTION 5. PROTECTIVE TRUSTS

At the beginning of this chapter we discussed the several forms of restraints upon alienation, i.e., the disabling restraint, the forfeiture restraint, and the promissory restraint. The spendthrift trust involves the disabling restraint. Sometimes, however, a forfeiture restraint is employed to protect against creditors and voluntary alienation, and in such case the trust is frequently referred to as a protective trust.

Settlor transfers to Trustee to pay the income to A for life, but if A should assign his interest or if A's creditors should attempt to levy upon or attach his interest, then the Trustee shall pay such income to A as Trustee shall in his absolute discretion determine; upon the death of A, the principal and any undistributed income is to be paid to B. In this trust, the power of voluntary alienation and the rights of creditors with respect to A's interest have not been denied as such, but rather any attempt by A to alienate or any attempt by creditors to reach A's interest produces a transformation of A's interest from an absolute right to income to an interest in which Trustee decides in his discretion whether or not A is to receive income. A's power of alienation, voluntary and involuntary, has been restrained by means of the imposition of a forfeiture of his absolute income interest. The consequence is that if the alienation is attempted, A may not receive any further income, and

---

38. For discussion of the issues in this and the preceding paragraph, see Frolik, Discretionary Trusts for a Disabled Beneficiary: A Solution or a Trap for the Unwary? 46 Pitt.L.Rev. 335 (1985); Mooney, Discretionary Trusts: An Estate Plan to Supplement Public Assistance for Disabled Persons, 25 Ariz. L.Rev. 939 (1983); Silber, The Effect of a Trust on the Eligibility or Liability of the Trust Beneficiary for Public Assistance, 26 Real Prop., Prob. & Trust J. 133 (1992).

his creditors may not obtain satisfaction of their claims. If Trustee exercises his discretion by withholding distributions, A gets nothing and his creditors get nothing; if Trustee decides to distribute, A's creditors get the distribution. If the creditors' claims are paid from other assets, Trustee can start paying income directly to A again. Under the spendthrift trust, the income continues to flow to A despite the creditors' claims, and his creditors get nothing; under the protective trust, A's income is interrupted when the creditors close in. Instead of transforming the absolute income trust into a discretionary income trust for A, the protective trust may provide that the trust is transformed into a discretionary income trust for the spouse and children of A, as well as for A. In this case the income may continue to flow.

Obviously the spendthrift trust offers more to the beneficiary than the protective trust does. There are, however, jurisdictions in which the spendthrift trust is invalid; it appears that in such jurisdictions the protective trust is likely to be valid.[39] The protective trust is frequently employed in such jurisdictions. It goes without saying that the protective trust is valid wherever the spendthrift trust is valid. The protective trust is less offensive to one's sense of justice since the beneficiary cannot have his income while his creditors remain unpaid. The protective trust also has the virtue of disciplining the irresponsible beneficiary, since his income is going to be cut off, at least temporarily, if he gets into financial difficulty.

The protective trust may contain a forfeiture clause which terminates A's interest in the trust completely in the event of an attempted voluntary or involuntary alienation, rather than transforming it into a discretionary interest. This has the effect of making it absolutely certain that A's creditors do not receive any of the trust assets, but it also can produce the harsh consequence that A may be deprived of any future benefits if he becomes financially embarrassed.[40]

Suppose Settlor transfers to Trustee to pay the income to Settlor for life, but if Settlor should assign his interest or if Settlor's creditors should attempt to levy upon or attach his interest, then Trustee shall pay such income to Settlor as Trustee shall

---

39. Duncan v. Elkins, 94 N.H. 13, 45 A.2d 297 (1946). See N.C.Gen.Stat. § 36A–115. In a given jurisdiction, the forfeiture restraint may be valid as to an income interest, but invalid as to a principal interest, as is the case with the spendthrift restraint in some jurisdictions.

40. It may be that the creditors who are excepted from the spendthrift restraint, such as children and spouse for support and alimony, should also be excepted from the protective restraint. See United States v. Riggs National Bank, 636 F.Supp. 172 (D.D.C.1986).

in his absolute discretion determine; upon Settlor's death, the principal and any undistributed income is to be paid to X. Settlor has made himself a protective trust beneficiary. If Settlor's creditors attach his interest, his interest becomes discretionary in accordance with the terms of the trust, but, as we have seen in our discussion of the discretionary trust, Settlor's creditors can reach whatever income Trustee could pay to Settlor. If the trust terms provided that Settlor lost his beneficial interest absolutely upon levy or attachment, then the issue is presented as to whether Settlor can insulate his assets from his creditors in this fashion. It seems that Settlor should not be permitted to do so; Settlor's right to income should remain absolute as far as Settlor's creditors are concerned.

The settlor of the private trust usually has as his purpose the financial security of members of his family or close friends for their lives, and frequently for the lives of two or more persons or classes successively. If he simply gives life interests and remainder interests without controls of any kind, the beneficiaries may sell their interests or run into debt and lose their interests to creditors. A life beneficiary who is absolutely entitled to income may have a substantial earned income and have no need for the trust income; the income might be put to better use if it were accumulated for future distribution to that beneficiary should he come on hard times, or distributed to others. Spendthrift, discretionary, support, and protective trusts are employed to deal with these situations. They are devices which enable the settlor to achieve his objectives with greater precision.

Chapter 11

TRUST TERMINATION AND DEVIATION

SECTION 1. TERMINATION BY AGREEMENT
OF BENEFICIARIES AND TRUSTEE

We have seen that when a settlor transfers property irrevocably in trust without retaining any reversionary or other beneficial interest, he has completely relinquished all control over and interest in the transferred property.[1] This would be the case if Settlor transferred irrevocably to Trustee to pay the income to A for life, and at A's death to pay the principal to B in fee. This is to be distinguished from other similar transfers. Suppose that the foregoing is modified to provide that the principal is payable to B if B survives A; Settlor has retained a future interest, specifically an equitable reversion, which becomes possessory upon A's death in the event B predeceases A. Suppose that in the original example Settlor expressly reserved a power of revocation in the trust instrument; this power may not be an equitable future interest in the technical sense, but it is the next thing to absolute ownership because Settlor can cause absolute ownership to return to himself at any time.

If Settlor transfers in trust irrevocably and without retaining any reversionary interest or creating any other beneficial interest in himself, are the beneficiaries free to deal with the trust property as they see fit regardless of the provisions of the trust? The answer is that it all depends.

Assume that Settlor irrevocably transfers stocks and bonds having a value of $100,000 to Bank, in trust, to pay the income to A for life, and upon A's death, to pay the principal to B in fee. A is dissatisfied with receiving the income of about $6,000 annually, and would prefer to have the trust terminated and a portion of the principal, equal to the value of his life income interest determined actuarially, distributed outright to him. B is not interested, however, and wishes to have the trust remain in existence in accordance with its terms. Bank does not wish to comply with A's request. Settlor opposes A's request. What are the rights and duties of the parties?

1. Chapter 5, Section 7, note 31.

First of all, Settlor no longer has any interest in the property and has no standing to enforce the trust provisions. The creation of the trust was a transfer of property with the title divided into legal and equitable interests. Settlor did not contract with the trustee or the beneficiaries with respect to the manner in which the trust property was to be administered or enjoyed. It is possible for a settlor to transfer title in trust and purport to contract with the trustee or the beneficiaries concerning administration and enjoyment, but it is not implied in the creation of a trust and the trust instrument did not provide for it in our example. It is not clear, however, that such contractual provisions would be enforceable.[2] It should be noted that trust instruments rarely provide for the retention of contractual rights by the settlor.

B has an equitable remainder. He is entitled to the principal of the trust outright whenever A dies. A may die tomorrow, or precisely at the time of his actuarial expectancy, or many years after his actuarial expectancy. B cannot be required to settle currently for a portion of the principal equal to the value of his remainder determined actuarially. The earlier A dies, the better off B is financially, and B's property interest entitles him to this opportunity. So A cannot deprive B of the full benefit of his property interest, regardless of how fair his offer is. And Bank, as trustee, cannot accede to A's request because it would constitute a violation of its fiduciary obligation to B.

Suppose, however, that B was willing to go along with A's suggestion for terminating the trust and dividing up the principal, and Bank was also agreeable to it. Is there anything illegal about their accomplishing this result? As we have pointed out, Settlor is now a stranger to the trust assets, without any property interest or contractual rights. The only interested parties are Bank, A and B. They own the totality of the property interests. If they all agree, there is nobody to complain about the alteration of the trust. To say that Bank commits a breach of its fiduciary duty by acting in violation of the trust terms is meaningless if the only parties who have standing to complain request Bank to do so. There can be no breach of a legal obligation to someone who consents. So in these circumstances the trust may be terminated.[3] We defer discussion

2. It is arguable that the inclusion of contractual provisions would avail the Settlor nothing because he has no interest to be protected and never can show damages.

It is worth repeating that when Settlor creates a trust for A for life, remainder to B, there is no implied condition that B must survive A to take; if B predeceases A, B's estate takes on A's death. There can be no return of the property to the Settlor.

3. Croslow v. Croslow, 38 Ill.App.3d 373, 347 N.E.2d 800 (1976); Hagerty v. Clement, 195 La. 230, 196 So. 330 (1940); Partridge v. Clary, 228 Mass. 290, 117 N.E. 332 (1917); Matter of Boright, 377 N.W.2d 9 (Minn.1985).

of the situation in which A and B agree to terminate the trust but
the trustee refuses to comply.

Suppose Settlor had transferred irrevocably to Bank, in trust,
to pay the income to A for life, and upon A's death, to pay the
principal to A's children. A is 45, and the father of two children,
both of whom are over 21. A and his children wish to terminate
the trust and divide up the principal, and Bank is agreeable to it.
Is this the same as the preceding example? Clearly not, because
not all the beneficiaries have consented.[4] There are contingent
interests in unborn children of A. The Bank would be in breach of
trust if it made distribution of the principal; it would violate its
fiduciary obligation to the unborn beneficiaries. If Settlor got wind
of the plan, and it appeared that it might be consummated, he
would have no standing personally to challenge the action, but he
could bring the matter to the attention of the court, in which case
the court would proceed to appoint a guardian for the unborn to
protect their interests, or the court might enjoin the breach on its
own motion. It should be noted that if A were older, and it could
be established that he was incapable of having children, and the
term "children" in the trust instrument did not include adopted
children, then the Bank, A and the two children of A may be able
legally to terminate the trust.[5]

Assume Settlor transfers irrevocably to Bank, in trust, to pay
the income to A for life, and upon A's death to pay the principal to
B in fee if B survives A. A and B wish to terminate the trust and
divide the principal, and Bank is agreeable. Settlor, however, has
retained an equitable reversion because he is entitled to the trust
property if B predeceases A. Consequently, Bank cannot accede to
any termination without Settlor's consent.

Suppose Settlor transfers to Bank, in trust, to pay the income
to A for life, and to pay the principal to B on A's death, and Settlor
retains the power to revoke the trust at any time. Are Bank, A and
B legally entitled to terminate the trust without Settlor's consent
prior to revocation by Settlor? The answer clearly is negative,
although Settlor was not a trust beneficiary in the conventional
sense. The Settlor did not retain an equitable reversion, as is the
case where B must survive A in order to be entitled to the principal.

4. Sawyer v. Sawyer, 261 Iowa 112,
152 N.W.2d 605 (1967); Madden v. Mer-
cantile-Safe Deposit and Trust Co., 262
Md. 406, 278 A.2d 55 (1971); Ajax Elec-
trothermic Corp. v. First Nat. Bank of
Princeton, 7 N.J. 82, 80 A.2d 559 (1951);
Schmucker v. Walker, 226 Va. 582, 311
S.E.2d 108 (1984).

5. The equivocation here has to do
with the common law conclusive presumption of fertility. There is limited
modern authority, however, which allows proof of the inability of a person to
have children. For a discussion of this
issue, see Bergin and Haskell, Preface
To Estates In Land and Future Interests
143, 221 (2d ed. 1984).

The revocable transfer in trust creates the same equitable property interests as the irrevocable transfer of the same nature, but it is clear that all the legal and equitable interests are subject to termination by the Settlor. The power of revocation appears to be something like the power of termination (sometimes called right of entry) which is the future interest occasionally retained by the grantor of legal interests in land, but it is not characterized as that in trust law.[6] It also is the functional equivalent of the general power of appointment, but traditionally it has not been placed in that conceptual category in trust law.[7] It is in a conceptual category of its own as a power to vest title in the settlor of a trust, and the nature of the power is such that the Bank would clearly be liable to Settlor if it distributed principal to A and B without Settlor's consent and Settlor subsequently exercised his power of revocation.

There is an aspect of this subject which may be referred to as the partial termination question. Settlor irrevocably transfers to Bank, in trust, to pay one half the income to A and one half the income to B, and upon the death of the first to die, to pay one half the principal to First Baptist Church and to continue to pay the income from the remaining principal to the survivor, and upon the death of the survivor, to pay the remaining principal to First Baptist Church. A and First Baptist Church would like to divide up the principal, but B does not wish to do so. Since B does not consent, A and First Baptist Church propose to Bank that it distribute one half the principal to them and continue to pay the income from the remaining principal to B; their contention is that this would not constitute any violation of Bank's fiduciary duty to B because his interest would be unaffected.

Can Bank comply without violating its fiduciary duty to B? It has been held that the Bank cannot comply, because B's interest would be affected; while A and B are both alive, B is entitled to one half the income from the entire principal, rather than the entire income from one half the principal.[8] The investment opportunities for the larger principal are greater than for the smaller principal; this may make a difference with respect to the nature and quality of the investments and the diversification of investments. There is, however, authority that partial termination is permissible in these

---

6. They differ in the respect that under the power of revocation the property returns to the settlor's possession at his option at any time, whereas under the power of termination the property returns at the option of the grantor following the breach of a condition.

7. Restatement (Second) of Property, Donative Transfers § 11.1 (1983) defines the power of appointment to include the power of revocation.

8. Dunn v. Dobson, 198 Mass. 142, 84 N.E. 327 (1908); Shaller v. Mississip-

circumstances.[9]

SECTION 2.   TERMINATION: THE "MATERIAL PURPOSE" TRUST

To this point we have discussed the situation in which all the beneficiaries agree to terminate the trust and the trustee is willing to comply, and the situation in which less than all those beneficially interested in the trust wish to terminate. Let us now examine the situation in which all the beneficiaries wish to terminate, but the trustee does not wish to comply.

Settlor irrevocably transfers to Bank, in trust, to pay the income to A for life, and upon A's death to pay the principal to B. A and B wish to terminate and have agreed upon the division of the principal. Bank, however, refuses to terminate the trust. Settlor has told Bank that he definitely is opposed to termination, and although Settlor no longer has any interest in the assets held in trust, Bank feels honor-bound to comply with Settlor's wishes. Of course, Settlor may be dead, or it may have been a testamentary trust, and yet Bank very likely would be disinclined to go along with the request for termination; the professional trustee who cooperates with beneficiaries who want to make off with the principal prematurely may find that prospective settlors will go elsewhere with their trust business. The property owner who goes to the trouble of creating a trust presumably anticipates that the trustee will administer it in accordance with its terms.

In this situation, can A and B compel the trustee to terminate the trust? Surprisingly the answer may be yes. The result depends upon whether or not there appears to be a material purpose for the Settlor's creation of the trust, other than that of mere successive enjoyment, which is as yet unfulfilled. That is to say, if there remains such an unfulfilled material purpose, the trustee cannot be required to comply with the request for termination although all the beneficiaries join in the request; if, however, there is no such unfulfilled material purpose, the trustee is required to comply with the request provided all the beneficiaries join in the request. The salient issue, therefore, is what constitutes a material purpose other than mere successive enjoyment, and what constitutes mere successive enjoyment.

One example of a trust with an unfulfilled material purpose is as follows: Settlor irrevocably transfers to Bank, in trust, to pay the income to A until he reaches age 35, and upon A's reaching age

pi Valley Trust Co., 319 Mo. 128, 3 S.W.2d 726 (1928).

9. Whittingham v. California Trust Co., 214 Cal. 128, 4 P.2d 142 (1931);

Ames v. Hall, 313 Mass. 33, 46 N.E.2d 403 (1943); Matter of Boright, 377 N.W.2d 9 (Minn.1985).

35, to pay the principal to A, or if A dies under 35, to pay the principal at A's death to A's estate. A, who is the sole beneficiary, is 30, and requests Bank to distribute the principal to him now and terminate the trust. Bank refuses to do so and is justified in taking this position because there remains an unfulfilled material purpose.[10] Settlor established this trust to provide only the income to A until he had attained sufficient maturity to handle the principal; Settlor clearly did not want A to get control of the principal when, in Settlor's view, he could not properly manage it.

Suppose, in the preceding example, Settlor advised Bank that now he thought that A could manage the principal, and that he had no objection to the distribution of it to A, or Settlor joined with A in asking for termination. Would Bank be entitled to withhold the distribution? The answer is no, because there is no longer any unfulfilled material purpose.[11] The carrying out of the Settlor's wishes is the justification for the rule which prevents the beneficiary from forcing termination, and if the Settlor has changed his mind, the trustee cannot use the Settlor's original purpose to justify its retention of the principal. Of course, if this had been a testamentary trust, or if the Settlor had died without having indicated any change of attitude concerning when the beneficiary might be capable of managing the principal, the material purpose would remain unfulfilled and Bank would be entitled to refuse to comply with the beneficiary's request.

Let us suppose, however, that Bank is willing to comply with A's request for distribution of the principal at age 30, despite the fact that Settlor considers A to be unqualified to manage the principal and protests vigorously. Can Bank distribute without liability? Settlor has no cause of action. A owns the entire beneficial interest. There is no one to complain; no one is damaged. If there is a material purpose which is unfulfilled, and all the beneficiaries request termination, the trustee need not comply, but the trustee is not liable if he does comply.

Suppose Testator leaves his estate to Bank, in trust, to pay so much of the income to A as is necessary for A's support, and upon A's death, to pay any undistributed income and the principal to B. A and B request distribution of all the trust assets to them, but Bank does not comply. Can A and B compel termination? No,

---

10. Lafferty v. Sheets, 175 Kan. 741, 267 P.2d 962 (1954); Claflin v. Claflin, 149 Mass. 19, 20 N.E. 454 (1889); Cannistra Estate, 384 Pa. 605, 121 A.2d 157 (1956); Rhode Island Hospital Trust Co. v. Smith, 97 R.I. 480, 198 A.2d 664 (1964).

11. Botzum v. Havana Nat. Bank, 367 Ill. 539, 12 N.E.2d 203 (1937); St.

Louis Union Trust Co. v. Conant, 499 S.W.2d 761 (Mo.1973); Dunnett v. First Nat. Bank & Trust Co. of Tulsa, 184 Okl. 82, 85 P.2d 281 (1938); In re Bowers' Trust Estate, 346 Pa. 85, 29 A.2d 519 (1943); Fowler v. Lanpher, 193 Wash. 308, 75 P.2d 132 (1938).

because there remains an unfulfilled material purpose.[12] Testator wanted to assure sufficient funds for the support of A for A's entire life; the premature termination of the trust might defeat this purpose.

The support trust is to be distinguished from the trust which provides for the payment of income to A, and upon A's death, the payment of the principal to B. Can A and B compel termination? Is there an unfulfilled material purpose other than successive enjoyment? On its face, the only purpose of the trust appears to be to provide that A shall have the benefit of the property for his life, and B thereafter, i.e., successive enjoyment. The settlor wanted to assure the preservation of the trust assets in order that both A and B might derive benefit from them successively. Consequently the trustee can be compelled to terminate. The result is that A and B get something different from what the settlor had in mind, but the courts have not considered the settlor's purpose to be sufficiently "material" to prevent the beneficial owners from forcing a change in the terms.[13]

Suppose, however, that in the immediately preceding example the trust instrument provided expressly, or it was reasonably inferable, that the settlor desired that A be assured an adequate income for his lifetime, and that any premature termination of the trust and division of the principal between A and B would be contrary to the settlor's purpose in the creation of the trust. In such a case, it is clear that the settlor's purpose involves more than mere successive enjoyment; the settlor also wanted to protect A and doubted that A would use principal prudently if it was made available to him. Consequently it appears that A and B do not have a cause of action to compel distribution of the principal.[14] It is clear that the settlor can give a trust a "material" purpose by including the appropriate language in the trust instrument.

The spendthrift trust is another example of a "material purpose" trust. Testator creates a trust to pay income to A, and to

12. Clemenson v. Rebsamen, 205 Ark. 123, 168 S.W.2d 195 (1943); Danahy v. Noonan, 176 Mass. 467, 57 N.E. 679 (1900); Heritage Bank-North v. Hunterdon Medical Center, 164 N.J.Super. 33, 395 A.2d 552 (1978); Estate of Brown, 148 Vt. 94, 528 A.2d 752 (1987).

13. Bennett v. Tower Grove Bank and Trust Co., 434 S.W.2d 560 (Mo. 1968); Ambrose v. First Nat. Bank of Nevada, 87 Nev. 114, 482 P.2d 828 (1971); In re Estate of Ransom, 89 N.J.Super. 224, 214 A.2d 521 (1965); Estate of Weeks, 485 Pa. 329, 402 A.2d

657 (1979); Clayton v. Behle, 565 P.2d 1132 (Utah 1977).

14. Adams v. Link, 145 Conn. 634, 145 A.2d 753 (1958); Hopp v. Rain, 249 Iowa 891, 88 N.W.2d 39 (1958); Frost National Bank v. Newton, 554 S.W.2d 149 (Tex.1977); Estate of Brown, 148 Vt. 94, 528 A.2d 752 (1987).

In this situation A might defeat the settlor's purpose by selling his life interest, since this is not a spendthrift trust. Because the settlor has not used all possible means to protect A, it does not follow that A and B should be permitted to compel termination.

pay principal to B on A's death, with a provision that the interest of A shall not be voluntarily or involuntarily alienable. Clearly the testator was thinking of more than successive enjoyment here; he had a protective purpose with respect to A. A and B cannot compel termination.[15] It should be noted, once again, that if the trustee should agree to terminate, he could do so with impunity.

The discretionary trust has also been held to be a "material purpose" trust. Testator creates a trust to pay so much of the income to A as trustee shall, in his absolute discretion, determine, and upon A's death, to pay the principal and any accumulated income to B. It appears that the testator had more than mere successive enjoyment in mind. The testator did not want A to have the income absolutely, but rather wanted the income to be available to A if the trustee thought it was necessary or advisable for A to receive the income. There is a protective aspect to a trust of this kind.[16]

Suppose the beneficiary of a "material purpose" trust assigns his interest to a stranger, with the consequence that the purpose which the settlor had in mind when the trust was created is now incapable of being accomplished. Settlor irrevocably transfers in trust to pay the income to A until he reaches age 35, and upon A's reaching age 35, to pay the principal to A, or if A dies under 35, to pay the principal at A's death to A's estate. At age 25, A assigns his entire interest in the trust to X, who is a total stranger to Settlor. X then requests the trustee to distribute the principal to him. The trustee declines, relying on the "material purpose" principle, which appears to have no relevance at this point because Settlor would have no interest in protecting X. It has been held, however, that X cannot compel termination.[17] The reasoning which supports this conclusion is that if X were permitted to compel termination, then A would be able to circumvent the rule against termination simply by getting together with X who would transfer to A what he received from the trustee. In cases of the spendthrift trust and the support trust, where alienation of the beneficial interest cannot be accomplished, this situation, of course, cannot arise.

The issue of termination has arisen in connection with the settlement of a will contest involving a will which contains a

15.　Mahan v. Mahan, 320 Md. 262, 577 A.2d 70 (1990); Hay v. Le Bus, 317 Mich. 698, 27 N.W.2d 309 (1947); Heritage Bank-North v. Hunterdon Medical Center, 164 N.J.Super. 33, 395 A.2d 552 (1978); In re Estate of Davis, 449 Pa. 505, 297 A.2d 451 (1972); Germann v. New York Life Ins. Co., 286 S.C. 34, 331, S.E.2d 385 (1985).

16.　Moxley v. Title Ins. & Trust Co., 27 Cal.2d 457, 165 P.2d 15 (1946); In re Roberts' Estate, 240 Iowa 160, 35 N.W.2d 756 (1949); Damon v. Damon, 312 Mass. 268, 44 N.E.2d 657 (1942).

17.　Stier v. Nashville Trust Co., 158 Fed. 601 (6th Cir.1908); Lewes Trust Co. v. Smith, 28 Del.Ch. 64, 37 A.2d 385 (1944).

"material purpose" trust. Let us assume that the will disposes of the entire estate in trust to pay the income to A, and principal on A's death to B; there is a clause which prohibits the voluntary or involuntary alienation of the beneficial interests. X is the testator's sole heir, and he receives nothing under the will. X contests the probate of the will on the ground, let us say, of testamentary incapacity. A, B and X enter into a settlement agreement, whereby the estate is to be distributed 50% outright to X and 25% outright to each of A and B. The settlement agreement is presented to the court for approval. Settlements of will contests, as with all forms of litigation, are permitted, and indeed encouraged, but this particular settlement will probably not be judicially approved.[18] The distribution of 50% of the estate outright to X is fine, but there is no justification for the provision for the distribution of 50% outright to A and B. X does not care how the other 50% is disposed of; A and B are using the settlement agreement as a means of terminating what remains of the spendthrift trust. Just as A and B could not compel the termination of the spendthrift trust in the absence of a will contest, so A and B could not avoid the spendthrift trust by means of the settlement of the will contest. The court will approve the compromise only with the spendthrift trust intact to the extent of 50% of the net estate.

In our discussion of the right of beneficiaries to compel termination where there is no unfulfilled "material purpose", and termination by agreement of the trustee and beneficiaries in the case of the "material purpose" trust, we have assumed that the beneficiaries were in existence and of age and competent. Frequently, of course, this is not the case. Beneficial interests are frequently in classes of individuals some of whose members are unborn. Beneficiaries often are minors. If such is the case, termination by the beneficiaries is not impossible, but it is cumbersome and impractical. The consent of an unborn cannot be obtained, and the consent of a minor is ineffective. Termination in such circumstances requires the appointment of guardians for the unborn and minors, and judicial approval of the settlement on their behalf.

Obtaining the agreement of all beneficiaries is frequently very difficult also because of the number of individuals or potential individuals involved. The trust frequently has terms as follows: Testator bequeaths in trust to pay the income to A for life, and at A's death, to pay the principal to the issue of A living at his death,

18. Adams v. Link, 145 Conn. 634, 145 A.2d 753 (1958); Estate of Schroeder, 441 N.W.2d 527 (Minn.App.1989); St. Louis Union Trust Co. v. Conant, 499 S.W.2d 761 (Mo.1973); Cahill v. Armatys, 185 Neb. 539, 177 N.W.2d 277 (1970). Contra: Budin v. Levy, 343 Mass. 644, 180 N.E.2d 74 (1962). Uniform Probate Code §§ 3–912, 3–1101, 3–1102 appear to authorize settlements that involve trusts, including "material purpose" trusts. See discussion in Chapter 9, Section 12.

or if there are no such issue, to the issue of testator living at A's death, or if there are no such issue, to the First Baptist Church. Here there are two classes of remaindermen whose membership is open, as well as a third contingent remainderman. Termination in these circumstances is very unlikely, although it is theoretically possible by means of the appointment of guardians, the calculation of probabilities and values, and judicial approval.

We have been discussing termination which is inconsistent with the terms of the trust instrument. There are, of course, various circumstances in which a trust may terminate consistent with the terms of the trust. The terms may provide for the reservation of the power of revocation by the settlor; the trust terminates when the settlor exercises her power to revoke the trust in its entirety. The terms may provide that the trustee may, in her discretion, distribute all or part of the principal at one time or from time to time to the life income beneficiary; the trust terminates when the trustee distributes all the remaining principal to the beneficiary. Of course, the trust which provides for life income to A, and principal to B at A's death, terminates following A's death.

If beneficiaries by unanimous agreement can compel termination of the trust, they can compel modification of the terms of the trust short of termination. If it is a "material purpose" trust, the settlor and beneficiaries can join to effect a modification of the terms of the trust.[19] If all that is desired is a change in a dispositive or administrative provision, it makes no sense to require that they terminate and create a new trust on the same terms except for the modification.

If the settlor retains a power of revocation, he can modify the trust rather than revoke it; it makes no sense to require the revocation and the establishment of a new trust with the modified terms. Also, if the settlor retains a power to modify which entitles him to make himself the sole beneficiary, but does not retain expressly the power to revoke, the settlor can directly revoke; it makes no sense to require first the modification making the settlor sole beneficiary, which entitles the settlor to compel termination.[20]

The situation may arise where the settlor of the irrevocable trust wishes to get his property back. If all the beneficiaries agree, the trustee must reconvey to the settlor. This is similar to the situation in which the beneficiaries can compel termination of a

---

19. Preston v. City National Bank of Miami, 294 So.2d 11 (Fla.Dist.Ct.App. 1974); Mortimer v. Mortimer, 6 Ill. App.3d 217, 285 N.E.2d 542 (1972); In re Trust created by Warner, 263 Minn. 449, 117 N.W.2d 224 (1962); Musick v. Reynolds, 798 S.W.2d 626 (Tex.App. 1990). See Wis.Stat.Ann. 701.12; N.Y.Est. Powers & Trusts Law § 7–1.9.

20. De Lee v. Hicks, 96 Nev. 462, 611 P.2d 211 (1980). See 4 Scott, Law of Trusts §§ 331.1, 331.2 (4th ed., Fratcher, 1989).

"material purpose" trust if the settlor consents, except that here termination is initiated by the settlor for his benefit.

SECTION 3.   DISTRIBUTIVE DEVIATION

The termination we have been discussing involves the premature distribution of principal by agreement of all the beneficiaries, or all the beneficiaries and the trustee, or all the beneficiaries and the settlor, depending upon the nature of the trust and the circumstances.   We define distributive deviation as the distribution of principal to income beneficiaries for whom the income is inadequate, without the consent of the remaindermen who are entitled to receive the entire principal at a later time under the terms of the trust.   Distributive deviation is a principle of judicial construction of settlor intent which has received only limited recognition.

Before we discuss distributive deviation, as we have defined it, it is useful to consider a problem which is, in effect, a halfway house between premature termination and distributive deviation. Testator creates a trust in his will to pay income to A until he is 35, and then to pay principal to A at that age, or to pay principal to A's estate if A dies under 35.   A is 25, unable to work, and in dire need of funds.   The income from the trust is inadequate for his support. A asks the trustee to distribute some principal to him, but trustee declines, citing the "material purpose" principle.   A brings an action to compel distribution of part of the principal.   Despite the fact that this is clearly a "material purpose" trust, the court is likely to direct the trustee in this situation to make distributions from principal to A to the extent necessary for his support.[21]   This constitutes a partial termination.   The testator wished to defer distribution of principal to A until he acquired the maturity to handle the wealth properly, but the beneficiary's need is deemed to be of greater importance than the testator's "material purpose." In this case A is the only person with a beneficial interest in the trust; if principal is distributed prematurely, no one else is harmed. This result constitutes a qualification to the "material purpose" doctrine.   If there were a provision for the distribution of principal to someone other than A in the event A died before reaching 35, and that other person did not consent to the distribution to A, and the court nevertheless ordered the distribution, then distributive deviation, as we have defined it, would have been involved.

Testator dies leaving a will in which he creates a trust to pay the income to his Widow for life, and upon Widow's death, to

21.   First Nat. Bank v. Watters, 220 Ala. 356, 125 So. 222 (1929); Elder v. Elder, 50 Me. 535 (1861); Bennett v. Nashville Trust Co., 127 Tenn. 126, 153 S.W. 840 (1913).   See Whittingham v. California Trust Co., 214 Cal. 128, 4 P.2d 142 (1931); Restatement (Second) of Trusts § 168 (1959).

distribute the principal to testator's descendants then living. There is no provision for distribution of any part of the principal to Widow. Some years later the trust income becomes inadequate to pay Widow's living and medical expenses. Widow is in dire need of additional funds. The consent of all the remaindermen and testator's successors in interest to the distribution of principal to Widow cannot be obtained. Is it conceivable that Widow can obtain a court order directing the trustee to make distributions of the principal to her to cover her expenses? There is some authority that she can.[22] Most of the cases, however, in which this issue has been presented have denied such relief, as one might expect.[23]

The reasoning in support of Widow's claim is that the testator intended that principal should be invaded if income was inadequate to meet Widow's basic needs, although the will did not so provide expressly. The words "income" and "principal" are not to be read literally, but rather are to be construed to allow for the distribution of principal to Widow if necessary to meet her basic needs. The testator was primarily concerned with the needs of his wife, and the language of the will is to be construed in a manner that will provide for her needs. This result extends judicial construction to its limit, if not beyond.

Suppose testator dies leaving a will in which a trust is created to pay $500 per month out of income to X, and upon X's death, to pay the principal, and any undistributed income, to Y. Some years later the income becomes inadequate to cover the specific monthly payment, and the remainderman does not consent to the use of principal to make up the difference. Can X obtain a court order directing the trustee to invade principal to provide the $500 per month? Some courts have so held,[24] reasoning that it was testator's intention to provide $500 per month to X, and that the designation of the source, i.e., income, was not intended as a limitation upon the amount of the monthly payment. Other courts have held that the payment is limited to income.[25]

22. Petition of Wolcott, 95 N.H. 23, 56 A.2d 641 (1948); McAfee v. Thomas, 121 Or. 351, 255 P. 333 (1927). See Restatement (Second) of Trusts § 168, comment d (1959); Cal.Prob.Code § 15409; N.Y.Est. Powers & Trusts Law § 7-1.6(b); Pa.Stat.Ann. tit. 20, § 6102; Wis.Stat.Ann. § 701.13(2).

23. Estate of Van Deusen, 30 Cal.2d 285, 182 P.2d 565 (1947); Staley v. Ligon, 239 Md. 61, 210 A.2d 384 (1965); In re Will of Cosgrave, 225 Minn. 443, 31 N.W.2d 20 (1948); In re Bosler's Estate, 378 Pa. 333, 107 A.2d 443 (1954); Stewart v. Hamilton, 151 Tenn. 396, 270 S.W. 79 (1925); Estate of

Boyle, 252 Wis. 511, 32 N.W.2d 333 (1948).

24. Mitchell v. Wyckoff, 122 Conn. 48, 186 A. 709 (1936); Schloesser v. Schloesser, 329 Ill.App. 604, 70 N.E.2d 346 (1946); Brown v. Berry, 71 N.H. 241, 52 A. 870 (1902); In re Clark's Will, 54 Misc.2d 1015, 284 N.Y.S.2d 244 (1967).

25. Estate of Markham, 28 Cal.2d 69, 168 P.2d 669 (1946); Einbecker v. Einbecker, 162 Ill. 267, 44 N.E. 426 (1896); Wight v. Mason, 134 Me. 52, 180 A. 917 (1935); In re Trusteeship under Will of Whelan, 263 Minn. 476, 116

SECTION 4. ADMINISTRATIVE DEVIATION

The trust instrument, whether it is a living trust agreement or a will which makes provision for a trust, contains dispositive terms, i.e., the beneficiaries and what their interests are, and administrative terms, i.e., what the trustee can and cannot do in the management of the trust assets. For example, the trust may contain a provision which makes it mandatory for the trustee to retain a particular investment, or which forbids the trustee to invest in certain assets. At the time of the creation of the trust, these terms may have made good sense, but years later these directions may be very harmful to the trust, or may even constitute a threat to the viability of the trust. In such circumstances, courts have authorized trustees to disregard such administrative provisions.

Let us assume that a substantial part of the principal of a testamentary trust at its inception consisted of 1000 shares of the common stock of a privately held corporation. The testator had owned these shares for many years, and they had been very profitable for him. The will provided that these shares were to be held in trust for the duration of the trust and were not to be sold by the trustee under any circumstances; such a provision is binding upon the trustee. Some years after the creation of the trust, it becomes clear that the business of this corporation is becoming obsolete and the value of the stock is declining. Because of this the trust is not producing sufficient income for the life beneficiary, and there may not be much left for the remainderman if this stock is retained. In sum, compliance with the directions of the testator threatens the purposes for which the trust was created. The trustee wants to sell this stock and invest the proceeds in securities which have more favorable prospects. In these circumstances, a court will authorize the trustee to disregard the restrictive administrative provision and sell the stock.[26]

It should be emphasized that the trustee is not deemed to possess the power to disregard administrative provisions which are

N.W.2d 811 (1962); Dwight Estate, 389 Pa. 520, 134 A.2d 45 (1957).

A couple of cases have allowed the invasion of principal where the trust instrument provided expressly for "support" out of "income", and the income was inadequate. Longwith v. Riggs, 123 Ill. 258, 14 N.E. 840 (1887); McGill v. Young, 75 N.H. 133, 71 A. 637 (1908).

26. Anderson v. Ryland, 232 Ark. 335, 336 S.W.2d 52 (1960); American State Bank v. Kupfer, 114 Ill.App.3d 760, 70 Ill.Dec. 677, 449 N.E.2d 1024 (1983); In re Estate of Burdon-Muller,

456 A.2d 1266 (Me.1983); Matter of Pulitzer, 139 Misc. 575, 249 N.Y.S. 87 (Sur. Ct.1931), aff'd 237 App.Div. 808, 260 N.Y.S. 975 (1932); Davison v. Duke University, 282 N.C. 676, 194 S.E.2d 761 (1973); Ex parte Guaranty Bank & Trust Co., 255 S.C. 106, 177 S.E.2d 358 (1970). Some states have statutes recognizing the principle of administrative deviation: E.g., Me.Rev.Stat.Ann. tit. 18–A, § 7–404; Pa.Stat.Ann. tit 20, § 7319; Wash.Rev.Code Ann. § 11.100.-040.

damaging to the trust. As a general rule, the trustee must comply with such terms unless a court authorizes her to do otherwise. In an emergency situation, however, where the trustee does not have an opportunity to obtain prior court approval, it seems that the trustee should be permitted to deviate if the circumstances are such that deviation would have been authorized by the court.[27]

Administrative deviation is authorized only where the administrative provision poses a serious threat to the trust. The court will not authorize the trustee to disregard the settlor's direction merely because in the judgment of the court or the trustee the trust would be better off without such provision. For instance, assume the trustee is forbidden to invest in anything except federal, state and municipal bonds. The trustee and the beneficiaries believe that a portion of the assets should be invested in common stocks to protect against inflation. It is generally accepted among investment experts that an investment portfolio should include sound common stocks. The settlor's ultra-conservative investment directions probably will not be disturbed by a court.[28] The investment restriction may be unwise, but it does not threaten the viability of the trust.

If the circumstances are such that the court would, on the petition of the trustee, authorize the trustee to disregard an administrative provision, is the trustee under a duty to apply to the court for such authorization? That is to say, will the trustee be liable to the beneficiaries for consequent losses if she does not apply for authority to deviate? It seems reasonable that the trustee should have such a duty.[29]

In this chapter we have considered various situations in which the provisions of the trust instrument have been disregarded or modified. In Chapter 12, which deals with charitable trusts, we shall discuss the related doctrine of cy pres in which the court supplements the terms of the charitable trust in order that the trust may continue to serve charitable purposes.

27. See 2A Scott, Law of Trusts § 167.1 (4th ed., Fratcher, 1987).

28. Stanton v. Wells Fargo Bank & Union Trust Co., 150 Cal.App.2d 763, 310 P.2d 1010 (1957); Matter of Will of Killin, 703 P.2d 1323 (Colo.App.1985); Troost Avenue Cemetery Co. v. First National Bank, 409 S.W.2d 632 (Mo. 1966); Toledo Trust Co. v. Toledo Hospital, 174 Ohio St. 124, 187 N.E.2d 36 (1962). However, a contrary result was reached in Carlick v. Keiler, 375 S.W.2d 397 (Ky.1964); In re Trusteeship Under Agreement with Mayo, 259 Minn. 91, 105 N.W.2d 900 (1960). See Davison v. Duke University, 282 N.C. 676, 194 S.E.2d 761 (1973).

29. See 2A Scott, Law of Trusts § 167.2 (4th ed., Fratcher, 1987).

Chapter 12

CHARITABLE TRUSTS

SECTION 1. DEFINED AND DISTINGUISHED
FROM THE PRIVATE TRUST

Several preceding chapters of this book have dealt with private trusts, that is to say, trusts created for the benefit of identifiable individuals. The charitable trust is the other category of express trusts. The charitable trust is one whose purpose benefits the community generally. Not every purpose which benefits the community, however, qualifies as a charitable trust purpose. In order for a trust to qualify as a charitable trust, it must have as its purpose the relief of poverty, advancement of education, advancement of religion, promotion of health, advancement of a governmental or municipal purpose, or the promotion of some other purpose beneficial to the community.[1] The last category, if taken literally, would seem to include virtually any form of altruism which is broad enough to benefit a large number of people, but this is not the case, as we shall discuss later.

There are two reasons why it is necessary to distinguish the charitable trust from the private trust. First, the charitable trust does not have to have definite beneficiaries; as we have discussed previously, the private trust is invalid unless the beneficiaries are definite.[2] Second, the charitable trust can have indefinite duration; the duration of the private trust is limited, as a practical matter, by the rule against perpetuities. It is not necessary that the charitable trust have indefinite duration, but it is permissible. It is not necessary that the charitable trust have indefinite beneficiaries, but it is permissible. In all events, however, the charitable trust must serve one of the defined charitable purposes. If the trust does not have definite beneficiaries, it usually fails unless it qualifies as a charitable trust;[3] if the trust has indefinite duration, in most instances it will be invalid, in whole or in part, unless it qualifies as

1. Restatement (Second) of Trusts § 368 (1959).

2. Chapter 5, Section 5.

3. In Section 6 of this chapter we discuss the so-called "honorary trust," which is a category of trust of very limited application in which there are no definite beneficiaries and no charitable purpose, and yet the trust is upheld.

a charitable trust.[4]

The rules concerning the creation of a private trust are applicable to the creation of a charitable trust. As in the case of the private trust, there must be a trustee and trust property. Whereas definite beneficiaries are essential to the private trust, the charitable trust must have a purpose which benefits the community in one of several defined ways. The private trust is enforced by the beneficiaries, whereas usually the only party with standing to enforce the charitable trust is the attorney-general of the state in which the trust is administered.[5] The rules concerning the duties and powers of the trustee of the charitable trust are substantially the same as those applicable to the trustee of the private trust. It should be noted, however, that the Internal Revenue Code specially restricts the powers of trustees of certain tax-exempt charitable trusts with respect to accumulations of income, self-dealing, and investments.

The following would be examples of charitable trusts: trust to establish and operate a hospital in the town of Norwich; trust to establish and operate a college for the study of liberal arts; trust to pay the expenses of maintenance of St. Paul's Church; trust to provide food and lodging for the homeless and destitute in the city of Portsmouth; trust to establish and maintain a public park in the town of Middleburg (governmental purpose); trust to care for stray animals (purpose beneficial to the community). The terms of the charitable trust will provide whether income only is to be used for the trust purpose, or whether principal as well as income may be expended for the trust purpose.

Frequently the person with substantial wealth who wishes to establish a hospital or a college or some other charitable entity will do so by means of a charitable, nonprofit corporation rather than by means of a trust. The corporate form is more common today than the trust form for educational institutions, hospitals, churches, and the like. The modern "foundation" created to subsidize charitable undertakings is more commonly in corporate than trust form. The charitable corporation has indefinite duration as does the charitable trust. The charitable trust is not obsolete, however; it is still used for a variety of charitable purposes as the cases cited in this chapter indicate. We shall see that certain principles governing the charitable trust are also applicable to the charitable corporation.

---

4. It is possible for a private trust to have indefinite duration and be valid: Trust to pay the income to the Men's Club of Middleville, Inc., a noncharity, indefinitely. Needless to say, this is very unusual. The beneficiary is probably entitled to claim the fee outright at any time.

5. See Section 3 below.

Nonprofit corporations may be created for purposes which are charitable under charitable trust criteria, or for purposes which may be considered charitable by the public but do not comply with charitable trust criteria, or for purposes which are not charitable by any measure, such as a country club, all in accordance with the corporation law of the jurisdiction. It should also be noted that whether or not a trust or a corporation is exempt from federal or state taxation because of its charitable or nonprofit character is a matter of federal or state tax law which is independent of charitable trust law and corporation law.

SECTION 2. CHARITABLE PURPOSES; INDEFINITE AND DEFINITE BENEFICIARIES

We have stated that the charitable trust benefits the community, as distinguished from the private trust which has definite beneficiaries, that is, identifiable individuals as beneficiaries. However, the charitable trust may have definite beneficiaries while benefiting the community in a manner required for a charitable trust. Suppose a trust is established to pay the salary of the minister of St. Paul's Church. This is a valid charitable trust because it serves to advance religion.[6] The occupant of the position of minister of St. Paul's Church from time to time is precisely identifiable; there is no question that is a definite class of beneficiaries. In one sense the beneficiaries of this trust are the indefinite group which is affected directly and indirectly by the spiritual leadership of the minister, and in another sense the beneficiaries of this trust consist of the definite class of ministers of this church.

Another example is a trust to pay $500 to the best Latin student in the senior class of Smithtown High School in each year. This is a valid charitable trust because it rewards the study of the classics.[7] Society generally benefits from a trust which encourages educational achievement. In another sense, however, the beneficiaries of this trust are a definite class of individuals, namely, the outstanding Latin scholars in the senior classes of this high school for the indefinite future.

Another example is a trust to pay $10,000 to the research scientist who makes the most significant contribution to the discovery of a cure for cancer, as determined by a panel consisting of the deans of three designated medical schools. This is a valid charita-

6. Simmons v. Reynolds, 183 Kan. 340, 328 P.2d 738 (1958); In re Bell's Will, 141 Misc. 720, 253 N.Y.S. 118 (Sur. Ct.1931); Bode v. Loeffler, 540 S.W.2d 465 (Tex.Civ.App.1976). See Parkersburg National Bank v. United States, 228 F.Supp. 375 (N.D.W.Va.1964).

7. Estate of Puckett, 111 Cal.App.3d 46, 168 Cal.Rptr. 311 (1980); Ashmore v. Newman, 350 Ill. 64, 183 N.E. 1 (1932); Worcester County Trust Co. v. Grand Knight of Knights of Columbus, 325 Mass. 748, 92 N.E.2d 579 (1950).

ble trust under the heading of the promotion of health.[8] Obviously society in general benefits from research of this nature. It is also clear that the outstanding cancer researchers constitute a definite class of beneficiaries.

The definite beneficiaries of the charitable trust sometimes are not as limited in number as in the immediately preceding examples. For instance, a trust to provide necessaries to impoverished members of the First Baptist Church of Amesville is a valid charitable trust. This trust has definite beneficiaries because the membership can always be determined. A trust to pay college scholarships to the children of members of a specific labor union is a valid charitable trust. The children of union members can always be determined. A trust to pay for nursing care for elderly members of a fraternal order is also a valid charitable trust.[9]

A charitable trust may be created to pay the income to Harvard University. In a sense there is one beneficiary, the charitable educational corporation, and in another sense it is the definite class consisting of the students, faculty and other employees of the university, and in still another sense it is society at large which benefits from the existence of an educational institution.

Suppose a person creates a trust with indefinite duration to provide necessaries to his descendants who are impoverished. Clearly this trust relieves poverty, but the problem is whether or not the trust is broad enough in its application to be considered to benefit the community by the standards of charitable trust law. The judicial response has been that it is not of sufficient benefit to the community to qualify as a charitable trust.[10] If a person creates a trust with indefinite duration to provide necessaries to the impoverished descendants of his friend, John Jones, it would not qualify as a charitable trust for the same reason.[11] A trust which is limited to the relations of a particular person will not qualify as a charitable trust. There is authority, however, to the effect that if a charitable trust is otherwise valid, it may provide that preferential consideration be given to descendants or relatives of the settlor or

8. Estate of McKenzie, 227 Cal. App.2d 167, 38 Cal.Rptr. 496 (1964); Pierce v. Tharp, 58 Tenn.App. 362, 430 S.W.2d 787 (1967); Sheen v. Sheen, 126 N.J.Eq. 132, 8 A.2d 136 (1939); In re Judd's Estate, 242 App.Div. 389, 274 N.Y.S. 902 (1934), aff'd 270 N.Y. 516, 200 N.E. 297 (1936). See Estate of Carlson, 187 Kan. 543, 358 P.2d 669 (1961).

9. Quinn v. Peoples Trust & Savings Co., 223 Ind. 317, 60 N.E.2d 281 (1945); Green's Administrators v. Fidelity Trust Co., 134 Ky. 311, 120 S.W. 283 (1909); Roberts v. Corson, 79 N.H. 215, 107 A.

625 (1919); In re Pattberg's Will, 282 App.Div. 770, 123 N.Y.S.2d 564 (1953), aff'd 306 N.Y. 835, 118 N.E.2d 903 (1954).

10. Hardage v. Hardage, 211 Ga. 80, 84 S.E.2d 54 (1954); Kent v. Dunham, 142 Mass. 216, 7 N.E. 730 (1886); Jones v. Webster, 133 Ohio St. 492, 14 N.E.2d 928 (1938).

11. Johnson v. De Pauw University, 116 Ky. 671, 76 S.W. 851 (1903); Ramsey Estate, 7 Pa.D. & C.2d 763 (Orph. 1957).

another person in the disbursement of benefits.[12] A charitable trust may benefit relatives of the settlor or a specific person as long as its purpose is not limited to the benefit of such persons.

The word "benevolent" is sometimes employed as a word of art in the law to describe a purpose which is kind, generous, or altruistic, but not charitable for trust purposes. For instance, a settlor creates a trust to pay one dollar each Christmas to each member of the first grade in the schools of a particular public school district. Clearly this is a kind and generous thing to do, but it does not fall into any of the charitable trust categories, including the "beneficial to the community" category.[13] This type of trust is characterized as benevolent, which means that it is not charitable. A purpose which is "beneficial to the community" must have substantial social benefit.

Some of the purposes which qualify as "beneficial to the community" for charitable trust purposes are the care of animals,[14] improvement of government,[15] assistance of oppressed groups,[16] promotion of temperance.[17] Trusts for the creation of such things as parks, playgrounds, and monuments to public figures may come under this heading or the heading of governmental purposes. A trust was held to be charitable as benefiting the community which provided funds for the care, regardless of financial need, of the children of black people who are imprisoned for crimes of a political nature.[18] Trusts to advance partisan political objectives, however, are not charitable.

What is accepted by the courts as a charitable purpose is likely to be influenced by the prevailing prejudices and conventional wisdom of the period. For instance, it has been held in the past that a trust to assist women in the attainment of equal rights was not a valid charitable trust.[19] There is little doubt that a trust of this nature would be considered charitable today. In the childhood of this author, mental telepathy, clairvoyance, psychokinesis and

---

12. Continental Illinois Nat. Bank v. Harris, 359 Ill. 86, 194 N.E. 250 (1935); In re Butler's Estate, 137 N.J.Eq. 48, 42 A.2d 857 (1945), aff'd 137 N.J.Eq. 457, 45 A.2d 598 (1946); In re MacDowell's Will, 217 N.Y. 454, 112 N.E. 177 (1916); Blackwood Estate, 2 Pa.D. & C.3d 80 (Com.Pl.1977); Gallaher v. Gallaher, 106 W.Va. 588, 146 S.E. 623 (1929).

13. Shenandoah Valley Nat. Bank v. Taylor, 192 Va. 135, 63 S.E.2d 786 (1951).

14. Estate of Goodrich, 271 Wis. 59, 72 N.W.2d 698 (1955).

15. Collier v. Lindley, 203 Cal. 641, 266 P. 526 (1928); Taylor v. Hoag, 273 Pa. 194, 116 A. 826 (1922).

16. Register of Wills v. Cook, 241 Md. 264, 216 A.2d 542 (1966); Jackson v. Phillips, 96 Mass. (14 Allen) 539 (1867).

17. Bowditch v. Attorney General, 241 Mass. 168, 134 N.E. 796 (1922); Lee's Trust, 5 Pa.D. & C.3d 159 (Com. Pl.1974); Harrington v. Pier, 105 Wis. 485, 82 N.W. 345 (1900).

18. Estate of Robbins, 57 Cal.2d 718, 21 Cal.Rptr. 797, 371 P.2d 573 (1962).

19. Jackson v. Phillips, 96 Mass. (14 Allen) 539 (1867).

precognition were in the same category as tea leaf reading; today these subjects are taken seriously by some responsible scientists, or at least they are considered to be worthy of research. Implicit in this discussion of charitable purposes is the premise that a trust for a purpose which purports to advance knowledge or assist social progress, but which most people in the particular day and age would consider to be devoid of any merit, is not likely to qualify as a charitable trust. It is of interest to note that not long ago a trust was held to be charitable the purpose of which was to provide funds for research to discover scientific proof of a soul which leaves the human body at death.[20]

A trust that is created for purposes which are both charitable and noncharitable may be held invalid in toto. For instance, a trust for such "charitable and benevolent" purposes as the trustee shall select, is not a valid charitable trust if the word "benevolent" is construed to denote purposes which are not necessarily charitable.[21] The trust does not have definite beneficiaries, and therefore it can exist only as a charitable trust. The trustee is authorized, however, to use the assets for purposes which are not charitable. That the assets may be applied to noncharitable purposes is enough to prevent its being a charitable trust. There is considerable authority, however, that the use of the word "benevolent" in this context was not intended to mean something different from charitable, and consequently the trust is a valid charitable trust.[22]

SECTION 3. ENFORCEMENT

It is the general rule that the beneficiaries of the private trust are the only parties to have standing to enforce the trust, i.e., enjoin a breach of trust by the trustee, recover for loss resulting from a breach, enjoin the trustee to perform his fiduciary duties, replace the trustee.[23] The general rule, subject to certain exceptions, is that the only party having standing to enforce the charitable trust is the state attorney general, or in some cases the local district attorney.[24] This is consistent with the theory that the

20. Estate of Kidd, 106 Ariz. 554, 479 P.2d 697 (1971).

21. Hegeman's Executors v. Roome, 70 N.J.Eq. 562, 62 A. 392 (1905). See Green v. Austin, 222 Ga. 409, 150 S.E.2d 346 (1966).

22. Smith v. United States Nat. Bank, 120 Colo. 167, 207 P.2d 1194 (1949); Prime v. Harmon, 120 Me. 299, 113 A. 738 (1921); Clark v. Cummings, 83 N.H. 27, 137 A. 660 (1927). See Hight v. United States, 256 F.2d 795 (2d Cir.1958). It should be noted that it is permissible to create a charitable trust in which the trustee is given absolute discretion to distribute the assets "for such charitable purposes as the trustee shall determine."

23. See Chapter 5, Section 7.

24. Attorney General v. Rochester Trust Co., 115 N.H. 74, 333 A.2d 718 (1975); Brown v. Concerned Citizens, 56 Ohio St.2d 85, 382 N.E.2d 1155 (1978); Sarkeys v. Independent School District, 592 P.2d 529 (Okl.1979); Israel v. National Board of Y.M.C.A., 117 R.I. 614,

community in general benefits from the charitable trust; it follows that the legal officer who represents the people's interest is the appropriate party to enforce the charitable trust.

One exception to the general rule is that if there is more than one trustee of a charitable trust, a trustee can bring suit against a breaching trustee to correct a breach of trust.[25] Indeed there may be a duty to do so.[26] This is, of course, as true with respect to the private trust as it is with respect to the charitable trust.

Another exception involves the charitable trust in which the benefit flows to a specific individual or individuals. In such case there is authority that the individual has standing to enforce the trust.[27] An example would be a trust to pay the income as salary to the minister of St. Paul's Church, or to pay scholarships to children of members of a fraternal organization.

The prevailing view is that the settlor of the irrevocable charitable trust has no standing to enforce the trust,[28] which is also true with respect to the settlor of the irrevocable private trust, but there is authority that he does have standing,[29] which is also true with respect to the private trust. The settlor, or his successors in interest, may bring an action to recover the trust property if the charitable trust fails for some reason, but this is not enforcement of the trust but rather the enforcement of a reversionary interest.

SECTION 4. CY PRES

Frequently the charitable trust is established without any provision being made for the disposition of the trust assets in the event the trust purpose cannot be accomplished. For example, the testator bequeaths $200,000 to Bank, in trust, to pay the income as

369 A.2d 646 (1977); Nacol v. State, 792 S.W.2d 810 (Tex.App.1990). Ga.Code Ann. § 53–12–79; Me.Rev.Stat.Ann. tit. 5, § 194; N.Y.Est.Powers & Trusts Law § 8–1.1(f).

25. Holt v. College of Osteopathic Physicians, 61 Cal.2d 750, 40 Cal.Rptr. 244, 394 P.2d 932 (1964); Belcher v. Conway, 179 Conn. 198, 425 A.2d 1254 (1979); Takabuki v. Ching, 67 Hawaii 515, 695 P.2d 319 (1985).

26. See Chapter 13, Section 10.

27. Jones v. Grant, 344 So.2d 1210 (Ala.1977); San Diego County Council v. Escondido, 14 Cal.App.3d 189, 92 Cal. Rptr. 186 (1971); Hooker v. Edes Home, 579 A.2d 608 (D.C.App.1990); German Evangelical St. Marcus Congregation v. Archambault, 404 S.W.2d 705 (Mo. 1966); Alco Gravure, Inc. v. Knapp

Foundation, 64 N.Y.2d 458, 490 N.Y.S.2d 116, 479 N.E.2d 752 (1985); Gray v. St. Matthews Cathedral Endowment Fund, Inc., 544 S.W.2d 488 (Tex. Civ.App.1976). See Restatement (Second) of Trusts § 391 (1959).

28. Amundson v. Kletzing-McLaughlin Memorial Foundation College, 247 Iowa 91, 73 N.W.2d 114 (1955); Hagaman v. Board of Education, 117 N.J.Super. 446, 285 A.2d 63 (1971). See Holden Hospital Corp. v. Southern Illinois Hospital Corp., 22 Ill.2d 150, 174 N.E.2d 793 (1961); Freedman's Aid & Southern Education Soc. v. Scott, 125 Miss. 299, 87 So. 659 (1921).

29. Tate v. Woodyard, 145 Ky. 613, 140 S.W. 1044 (1911). See Hascall and Rogers v. Madison University, 8 Barb. 174 (N.Y.1850).

scholarships for students who are pursuing a Ph.D. degree in religion at Midwest University. Some years later Midwest University does away with its Ph.D. program in religion. The will does not provide for the disposition of the trust assets in the event the purpose of the trust can no longer be accomplished. In the drafting of trusts this type of contingency should be anticipated and provided for, but frequently it is not.

The purpose of the charitable trust may have potentially infinite life, but it may fail at some future time. It seems appropriate to analogize the purpose to an equitable fee simple determinable in land. Following the analogy, the estate of the testator, that is to say, the residuary legatees or heirs, would have an equitable possibility of reverter. This, in turn, would mean that on the failure of the purpose, the trustee holds legal title to the trust property on resulting trust for the residuary legatees or heirs, with the duty to convey such legal title promptly to them. Sometimes this is what happens when the trust purpose fails, but more often that is not what happens. The usual result is that by order of the court the trust assets are applied to a purpose which is similar to the purpose set forth in the trust. This is done pursuant to the doctrine of cy pres (Anglo-French for "as near").[30]

If the trust instrument expressly provides that upon the failure of the trust purpose, the trust is to terminate and the assets pass to the residuary legatees or heirs, then, of course, this direction will be complied with, and if the instrument provides that the assets are to be applied to another specified charitable purpose, or to such other similar charitable purposes as the court shall direct, such directions will be complied with. If, however, the trust instrument is silent, then the court must determine whether it was the intention of the settlor to have the assets pass to the heirs or have the assets applied to another similar charitable purpose pursuant to the doctrine of cy pres. In theory the doctrine of cy pres exists to effect the unstated intent of the settlor. That is to say, the decision of the court to apply cy pres or return the assets to the estate is theoretically based upon its construction of the settlor's intention; in other words, what did the settlor intend, or, more accurately, what would the settlor have intended had he thought about the matter. In most cases it is a matter of construing the intention of a person who never anticipated that this would happen, for if he

---

30. Hardy v. Davis, 16 Ill.App.2d 516, 148 N.E.2d 805 (1958); Anna Jaques Hospital v. Attorney General, 341 Mass. 179, 167 N.E.2d 875 (1960); Knights of Equity Memorial Scholarships Comm. v. University of Detroit, 359 Mich. 235, 102 N.W.2d 463 (1960); In re Farren, 27 Ohio App.2d 31, 272 N.E.2d 162 (1970); Matter of Trust of Gerber, 652 P.2d 937 (Utah 1982); Minn.Stat.Ann. § 501B.31; N.Y.Est. Powers & Trusts Law § 8–1.1; N.C.Gen.Stat. § 36–23.2; Pa.Stat.Ann. tit. 20, § 6110; R.I.Gen.Laws § 18–4–1; Vt.Stat.Ann. tit. 14, § 2328.

had anticipated it, he probably would have made provision for it. It should be noted that cy pres is only applied by the court; the trustee has no authority to make the decision to apply cy pres or not.[31] It is the duty of the trustee to apply to the court for directions.

The issue of whether or not to apply cy pres arises in situations other than the type described in the example discussed above. On occasion a testator will create a trust in his will for a purpose for which the funds are inadequate. For instance, the testator creates a trust to establish a special library for a particular college. The funds are inadequate for the purpose, and the will does not provide for this contingency. The court then must decide if the testator's intention was that the funds should be used for this specific charitable goal and no other, in which case cy pres would not be applied and the trust assets would revert to the residuary legatees or heirs, or whether the funds should be applied cy pres to a related purpose such as the purchase of books for the college.[32]

A charitable trust may be created whose assets exceed what is needed to accomplish the trust purpose. For instance, a trust to pay the income for tuition scholarships for students from a particular community who attend a particular college produces more income than is needed for the purpose. The excess income may revert to the residuary legatees or heirs, or it may be applied cy pres to such a purpose as paying the tuition of students at other colleges from that community.[33]

A testator may make a bequest in his will to a charitable entity which is declined by the charity. For instance, a testator bequeaths $500,000 to Private College, a charitable corporation, to be used only for scholarships for Protestant students. Private College refuses to accept the gift on such religiously restrictive terms. The bequest may fail, or the court may, by applying cy pres, direct that the religious restriction be stricken.[34] It should be noted in this

31. Lockwood v. Killian, 172 Conn. 496, 375 A.2d 998 (1977); Petition of Village of Mount Prospect, 167 Ill. App.3d 1031, 118 Ill.Dec. 667, 522 N.E.2d 122 (1988); Town of Brookline v. Barnes, 327 Mass. 201, 97 N.E.2d 651 (1951); Township of Cinnaminson v. First Camden Nat. Bank, 99 N.J.Super. 115, 238 A.2d 701 (1968); Midkiff v. Kobayashi, 54 Hawaii 299, 507 P.2d 724 (1973). See statutes cited in note 29.

32. In re Estate of Thompson, 414 A.2d 881 (Me.1980); Trustees of Putnam Free School v. Attorney General, 320 Mass. 94, 67 N.E.2d 658 (1946); Knights of Equity Memorial Scholarships Comm. v. University of Detroit,

359 Mich. 235, 102 N.W.2d 463 (1960); Levings v. Danforth, 512 S.W.2d 207 (Mo.App.1974); Fairbanks v. Appleton, 249 Wis. 476, 24 N.W.2d 893 (1946).

33. Estate of Puckett, 111 Cal. App.3d 46, 168 Cal.Rptr. 311 (1980); Quinn v. Peoples Trust & Savings Co., 223 Ind. 317, 60 N.E.2d 281 (1945); Sharpless v. Medford Monthly Meeting, 228 N.J.Super. 68, 548 A.2d 1157 (1988); Union National Bank v. Nuzum, 167 W.Va. 340, 280 S.E.2d 87 (1981).

34. La Fond v. Detroit, 357 Mich. 362, 98 N.W.2d 530 (1959); Howard Savings Institution v. Peep, 34 N.J. 494, 170 A.2d 39 (1961), aff'g 61 N.J.Super. 119, 160 A.2d 177 (1960).

case that the testator did not create a trust, and Private College is a charitable corporation. No charitable trust is involved in the facts, and yet cy pres may be applied. The doctrine of cy pres is applicable to charitable gifts which are not made in trust and which are declined by the charitable entity. As we discuss below, cy pres is also applicable to assets held by charitable corporations.

If the trust has been in existence for a number of years, and then the purpose becomes accomplished or becomes impractical of accomplishment for some reason, the likelihood is very great that cy pres will be applied. If the trust purpose has been accomplished or is impractical of accomplishment at the time the trust is established, which may occur in the case of the testamentary trust where the will is executed a number of years before death, it is less likely that cy pres will be applied, and if a bequest to a charitable corporation is declined, cy pres is less likely to be applied. As we have stated, theoretically the issue is one of the testator's intent, which should not be affected by the time when the purpose fails, but the courts have in fact been more inclined to turn the assets back to private hands where the purpose fails at the outset than where the purpose fails many years later.

The doctrine of cy pres is applicable to charitable corporations as well as to charitable trusts. Gifts to charitable corporations such as colleges and universities, sometimes are made subject to conditions. Testator bequeaths $500,000 to Private University, to be retained and the income from it to be used to pay the salaries of professors of Greek and Latin. At the time the gift was made there were professors in those fields. Private University, as a corporation, holds absolute title to the property received, but it is legally required to abide by the restriction imposed by the donor of the property. In the event the purpose contained in the restriction fails, as would be the case if Latin and Greek were dropped from the curriculum, Private University is not entitled to apply the funds to other purposes unless the court authorizes such use pursuant to the cy pres doctrine.[35] If the court concludes that the testator intended that the funds be used for the stated purpose and no other, the court will order the funds returned to the estate of the testator. Of course, the testator could control the disposition of the assets upon the failure of the purpose by explicit provision in the will.

Cy pres also may be applicable upon the dissolution of the charitable corporation. Some states have statutes which provide

---

35. Dunaway v. First Presbyterian Church, 103 Ariz. 349, 442 P.2d 93 (1968); City of Aurora v. Young Men's Christian Ass'n, 9 Ill.2d 286, 137 N.E.2d 347 (1956); First Universalist Society v. Swett, 148 Me. 142, 90 A.2d 812 (1952); Gordon v. Baltimore, 258 Md. 682, 267 A.2d 98 (1970); St. Joseph's Hospital v. Bennett, 281 N.Y. 115, 22 N.E.2d 305 (1939).

that upon such dissolution the assets are to be distributed to related charitable purposes.[36] In the absence of a statute, a court may do the same under cy pres, or order the return of the assets to the donors if this is practical and the apparent intention of the donors.[37]

There has been litigation in recent years concerning the application of cy pres to racial and religious restrictions. Although the matter is not completely free from doubt, at the present time a racial or religious restriction in a charitable trust or in a gift to a charitable corporation is generally considered to be valid, provided there is no state involvement in the administration of the trust or the corporation and the restriction does not violate any antidiscrimination statute. If a settlor conveys property to Bank, in trust, to pay the income for scholarships for white, Protestant students attending Private College, the trust can probably be administered in accordance with its terms.[38] However, the trustees of certain charitable trusts and corporations have considered such restrictions to be contrary to public policy or impracticable and have been successful in actions to remove the restrictions by application of cy pres.[39] The United States Supreme Court decision holding that educational institutions that practice racial discrimination do not qualify for tax-exempt status under the Internal Revenue Code undoubtedly will accelerate the demise of such racial restrictions.[40]

If the state is involved in the administration of the trust or the corporation, the racial restriction presents a constitutional issue because the state is forbidden to discriminate invidiously under the Fourteenth and Fifth Amendments, except possibly in favor of a minority group to compensate for prior discriminatory treatment.

Shelly v.
Shelly

---

36. E.g., Colo.Rev.Stat. § 7–26–103; Ga.Code Ann. § 14–3–212; Ill.Ann.Stat. ch. 32, § 163a44; Ohio Rev.Code Ann. § 1702.49; Vt.Stat.Ann. tit. 11, § 2602.

37. Stevens Bros. Found. v. Commissioner, 324 F.2d 633 (8th Cir.1963); First Universalist Society v. Swett, 148 Me. 142, 90 A.2d 812 (1952); Allgood v. Bradford, 473 So.2d 402 (Miss.1985). See 4 Scott, Law of Trusts § 397.3 (4th ed., Fratcher, 1989).

38. Moore v. City and County of Denver, 133 Colo. 190, 292 P.2d 986 (1956); Lockwood v. Killian, 172 Conn. 496, 375 A.2d 998 (1977); First National Bank v. Danforth, 523 S.W.2d 808 (Mo. 1975); Weaver Trust, 43 Pa.D. & C.2d 245 (Orph.1967). For a suggestion of a contrary result, see Jackson v. Statler

Foundation, 496 F.2d 623 (2d Cir.1973), cert. denied 420 U.S. 927, 95 S.Ct. 1124, 43 L.Ed.2d 397 (1975).

39. Dunbar v. Board of Trustees of Clayton College, 170 Colo. 327, 461 P.2d 28 (1969); Coffee v. William Marsh Rice University, 408 S.W.2d 269 (Tex.Civ. App.1966); Howard Savings Institution v. Peep, 34 N.J. 494, 170 A.2d 39 (1961); Colin McK. Grant Home v. Medlock, 292 S.C. 466, 349 S.E.2d 655 (App.1986). See Hermitage Methodist Homes v. Dominion Trust Co., 239 Va. 46, 387 S.E.2d 740 (1990); Tinnin v. First United Bank, 570 So.2d 659 (Miss.1987).

40. Bob Jones University v. United States, 461 U.S. 574, 103 S.Ct. 2017, 76 L.Ed.2d 157 (1983).

There is the case in which the testator bequeathed funds to the City of Detroit for the purpose of constructing a playground for white children only. Detroit could not accept the bequest on this condition, and petitioned for the application of cy pres to enable it to receive the funds for the playground purpose without the racial restriction. It was held that the gift failed because the racial restriction was an integral part of the testator's plan.[41] In a case involving a park in Macon, Georgia, which was devised to the city to be used only by white people, and which was operated on that basis for many years, it was similarly held that cy pres was not applicable because the testator's racial restriction was an essential element of the testator's purpose, and the reversion of the land to the heirs was ordered.[42] There have been other decisions, however, involving state action in the administration of charitable funds with racial restrictions in which the courts have held that the trust was to be administered in the future on a color-blind basis.[43]

A gender restriction in a charitable trust or in a gift to a charitable corporation is valid, provided there is no state involvement in the administration of the trust or the corporation and the restriction does not violate any anti-discrimination statute. If a settlor conveys property to Bank, in trust, to pay scholarships to male students at Private College which has students of both sexes, the trust can be administered in accordance with its terms.[44] Cy pres may be applied to expand the beneficiaries to include female students if the restriction becomes impracticable.[45]

If the state is involved in the administration of the trust or the corporation, the gender restriction presents a constitutional issue because the state is forbidden to discriminate on grounds of gender under the Fourteenth and Fifth Amendments except to further some important governmental objective.[46] If the restriction is found to be unconstitutional the gift may remain effective on a

41. La Fond v. Detroit, 357 Mich. 362, 98 N.W.2d 530 (1959).

42. Evans v. Abney, 224 Ga. 826, 165 S.E.2d 160 (1968), aff'd 396 U.S. 435, 90 S.Ct. 628, 24 L.Ed.2d 634 (1970). See Connecticut Bank & Trust Co. v. Cyril and Julia C. Johnson Memorial Hospital, 30 Conn.Sup. 1, 294 A.2d 586 (1972).

43. Commonwealth of Pennsylvania v. Brown, 392 F.2d 120 (3d Cir.1968), cert. denied 391 U.S. 921, 88 S.Ct. 1811, 20 L.Ed.2d 657 (1968); Trammell v. Elliott, 230 Ga. 841, 199 S.E.2d 194 (1973); Wachovia Bank and Trust Co. v. Buchanan, 346 F.Supp. 665 (D.D.C. 1972), aff'd 487 F.2d 1214 (D.C.Cir.

1973); Milford Trust Co. v. Stabler, 301 A.2d 534 (Del.Ch.1973).

44. Shapiro v. Columbia Union National Bank, 576 S.W.2d 310 (Mo.1978), cert. denied 444 U.S. 831, 100 S.Ct. 60, 62 L.Ed.2d 40 (1979); Will of Cram, 186 Mont. 37, 606 P.2d 145 (1980); Matter of Estate of Wilson, 59 N.Y.2d 461, 465 N.Y.S.2d 900, 452 N.E.2d 1228 (1983).

45. Lockwood v. Killian, 172 Conn. 496, 375 A.2d 998 (1977).

46. Mississippi University for Women v. Hogan, 458 U.S. 718, 102 S.Ct. 3331, 73 L.Ed.2d 1090 (1982); Trustees of University of Delaware v. Gebelein, 420 A.2d 1191 (Del.Ch.1980).

nondiscriminatory basis by application of cy pres.[47]

SECTION 5. CHARITABLE TRUSTS AND THE RULE AGAINST PERPETUITIES

We have stated that the charitable trust can have indefinite duration, and that the rule against perpetuities is not applicable to the charitable trust. These statements require some elaboration.

The common law rule against perpetuities provides that, "No interest is good unless it must vest, if at all, not later than twenty-one years after some life in being at the creation of the interest." The interest referred to is, of course, a future interest. The rule does not refer to any limitation upon the duration of a trust. Private trusts seldom have a duration in excess of the period of perpetuities, but it happens, and it would not be violative of the rule against perpetuities if a private trust did have such a duration, as long as every future interest under the trust must vest within the period of the rule. Several states, however, have legislated durational limits for private trusts.[48]

When it is said that there is no limit upon the duration of a charitable trust, this does not constitute an exception to the rule against perpetuities because the rule does not deal with the duration of trusts. However, if there is a future interest under a trust in which all interests are charitable, it is not subject to the rule against perpetuities, and that does constitute an exception to the rule.

Several examples may help to elucidate this discussion. Settlor creates a trust to pay the income to Harvard University in perpetuity. This is a charitable trust, Harvard has a present interest, there is no future interest,[49] the trust has indefinite duration, and the trust is valid in all respects. Suppose settlor creates a trust to use the income for medical research in perpetuity; there is no future interest here, and the trust is valid in accordance with its terms. But suppose a trust is created to pay the income to Harvard University in perpetuity, but if Harvard shall cease to have a graduate school of theology, then the income is to be paid to Yale University in perpetuity. Yale has a future interest, an equitable shifting executory interest to be precise, which interest may not vest within the period of the rule against perpetuities. However, the rule against perpetuities does not apply to a charitable future interest where the preceding interest or interests are also charita-

---

47. In re Certain Scholarship Funds, 133 N.H. 227, 575 A.2d 1325 (1990); Matter of Crichfield, 177 N.J.Super. 258, 426 A.2d 88 (1980).

48. See Chapter 8, Section 9.

49. It may be considered that settlor has a reversionary interest of some kind because Harvard may cease to exist, but reversionary interests are not subject to the rule against perpetuities.

ble.[50] If, however, a trust was created to pay the income to the Men's Club of Middleville, a noncharitable corporation, but if it ever should admit women to membership, then to pay the income to Yale University, Yale's future interest would be invalid because it might vest beyond the period of the rule and the prior interest is not a charity.[51]

It should be noted that a majority of states have legislated modifications of the common law rule against perpetuities, as described in Chapter 8, Section 9.

SECTION 6. HONORARY TRUSTS

The so-called honorary trust is not a charitable trust, but this seems to be the best place to describe and discuss it.

Suppose testator leaves $10,000 to Jones, in trust, for the purpose of caring for testator's pet dog. This cannot be a private trust because there are no human beneficiaries, nor does a trust for one dog qualify as a charitable trust. The courts could well have taken the position that this type of gift is void, but instead the courts have recognized a special type of trust to validate this unusual gift which is neither a private nor a charitable trust. This has been called an "honorary" trust, and the rules of this trust are that the trustee can, if she wishes, hold the funds for the benefit of the dog,[52] but she is not required to do so, and if she chooses not to use the funds for the dog, then the trustee must return the money to the estate.[53] Under no circumstances is Jones, the trustee, to derive any benefit from the fund. The persons who benefit if the trustee does not comply with the terms of the honorary trust are the ones to police its administration. So if Jones spends the $10,000 on herself, the residuary legatees or heirs have a cause of action against her for that amount.

It seems that if the courts are going to go this far in upholding these types of trusts, they may as well go all the way and enforce them on their own motion if necessary. That is to say, if Jones does not care to hold the money for the dog, the court on its own

---

50. Dickenson v. Anna, 310 Ill. 222, 141 N.E. 754 (1923); City of Belfast v. Goodwill Farm, 150 Me. 17, 103 A.2d 517 (1954); Mississippi Children's Home Society v. Jackson, 230 Miss. 546, 93 So.2d 483 (1957); Wilbur v. University of Vermont, 129 Vt. 33, 270 A.2d 889 (1970).

51. Colorado Nat. Bank v. McCabe, 143 Colo. 21, 353 P.2d 385 (1960); Easton v. Hall, 323 Ill. 397, 154 N.E. 216 (1926); Talbot v. Riggs, 287 Mass. 144,

191 N.E. 360 (1934); Farnan v. First Union Nat. Bank, 263 N.C. 106, 139 S.E.2d 14 (1964).

52. Willett v. Willett, 197 Ky. 663, 247 S.W. 739 (1923); In re Searight's Estate, 87 Ohio App. 417, 95 N.E.2d 779 (1950); Stewart Estate, 13 Pa.D. & C.3d 488 (Com.Pl.1979).

53. See 2A Scott, Law of Trusts § 124 (4th ed., Fratcher, 1987).

motion may replace her and appoint a trustee who will. But there is no authority for this.

Honorary trusts have also been upheld for the erection and care of a private monument, tomb or grave, and for the maintenance of a private building.[54] These are not charitable purposes. The honorary trust is upheld only where the purpose, although noncharitable, is very specific, as in the instances we have described. If a trust has a broad purpose, such as the promotion of a partisan political cause, which is noncharitable, it will not qualify as an honorary trust. Also, if the court considers that the purpose, although specific, is frivolous or capricious, it will declare the gift void.[55]

It is often stated that the honorary trust cannot have a potential duration which exceeds the period of the rule against perpetuities,[56] which is lives in being at the creation of the trust plus twenty-one years. However, this limitation is sometimes ignored in the cases upholding honorary trusts.

In 1990 a new "optional" Section 2–907 was added to the Uniform Probate Code which provides that a trust for any noncharitable purpose (other than for pets) may be performed for no longer than 21 years, but in other respects the law as to honorary trusts is unchanged. The Section also contains a provision making valid a trust for "a designated domestic or pet animal and the animal's offspring." The trust must terminate "at the earlier of 21 years after the trust was created or when no living animal is covered by the trust." The trust is enforceable by an individual designated in the trust instrument for the purpose or appointed by the court.

---

54. Leonard v. Haworth, 171 Mass. 496, 51 N.E. 7 (1898); In re Zoller's Estate, 373 Pa. 451, 96 A.2d 321 (1953); St. Stephen's Episcopal Church v. Norris' Administrator, 115 Va. 225, 78 S.E. 622 (1913). There are statutes in some states which make trusts for graves and the like charitable: E.g., Conn.Gen.Stat. Ann. § 47–2; Fla.Stat.Ann. § 689.13; Kan.Stat.Ann. § 12–1419a.

55. Fidelity Title and Trust Co. v. Clyde, 143 Conn. 247, 121 A.2d 625 (1956). See Kelly v. Nichols, 17 R.I. 306, 21 A. 906 (1891).

56. Eaton v. Miller, 250 A.2d 220 (Me.1969); In re Searight's Estate, 87 Ohio App. 417, 95 N.E.2d 779 (1950); Meehan v. Hurley, 51 R.I. 51, 150 A. 819 (1930); Foshee v. Republic National Bank of Dallas, 617 S.W.2d 675 (Tex. 1981). See Union Trust Co. v. Rossi, 180 Ark. 552, 22 S.W.2d 370 (1929); Pope v. Alexander, 194 Tenn. 146, 250 S.W.2d 51 (1952).

Chapter 13

FIDUCIARY ADMINISTRATION

In Chapter 9 we discussed the administration of the decedent's estate. Estate administration consists of the judicial establishment of the validity of the decedent's will if there is one, judicial appointment of a personal representative, and the procedures for the administration of the assets. The personal representative is responsible for the collection of the decedent's assets, the payment of the decedent's debts and taxes and the expenses of administration, and the distribution to the beneficiaries of the estate.

In this chapter we deal with problems of delegation of authority by a fiduciary, conflicts of interest, investments, and the determination of principal and income, among other things. The issues treated in this chapter are generally applicable to both personal representatives and trustees. The personal representative has the short-term function of winding up the decedent's financial affairs; the trustee is a long-term manager of investments. Both are fiduciaries and their responsibilities as such are common. The different nature of their roles, however, means that certain areas of responsibility are more significant for the trustee than for the personal representative. This is certainly the case with respect to investments and the determination of principal and income. In addition, the greater duration of the trustee's function makes the issues discussed in this chapter of greater significance generally to trustees. For these reasons the discussion in this chapter is in terms of the trust and the trustee, but it should be borne in mind that the legal conclusions are usually applicable also to the personal representative.

We have previously stated that the living trust is created by the private transfer of property, without any judicial action. Once the living trust is created, the trustee and the beneficiaries are subject usually to the jurisdiction of the court of general equity jurisdiction. Although the equity court has nothing to do with the assumption of the fiduciary function by the trustee, it may remove the trustee if the trustee fails to perform his function properly. The equity court determines the rights of the beneficiaries and the duties and powers of the trustee, with the benefit of relevant legislation. In some states the trustee of the living trust must submit an accounting of his administration of the trust assets to

270

the court periodically, such as every year or every two or three years.

The testamentary trustee, on the other hand, is the creature of the court having jurisdiction over decedents' estates, which is often a court of special jurisdiction. There is no testamentary trust unless the will is admitted to probate as the valid last will of the testator by the court having probate jurisdiction. The trustee and the beneficiaries are legatees under the will. In many states the party designated in the will as trustee must file an oath that he will properly perform his fiduciary function and sometimes a bond with the probate court, and be approved by the court. The duties and powers of the trustee and the rights of the beneficiaries are enforced usually by the probate court. In many states the testamentary trustee is required to submit an accounting of his administration of the trust assets to the probate court periodically, such as every year or every two or three years.

SECTION 1. DUTY NOT TO DELEGATE

Managing trust assets involves a number of functions. Which of these is the trustee required to perform personally, and which is he permitted to delegate to others? To the extent the trustee is permitted to delegate, what responsibility does the trustee have to oversee what is done? What are the legal consequences of improper delegation?

The broad response to the first question is that the trustee is allowed to delegate ministerial functions except those that he can reasonably be expected to perform personally, and is not allowed to delegate discretionary functions, subject to several qualifications. The trustee is entitled to retain a stockbroker to effect a sale or purchase of stocks and bonds, provided the trustee sets the price, retain a real estate broker in connection with the purchase or sale of land, provided the trustee sets the price, hire a janitor for the apartment building held in trust, hire a plumber to fix the faucets in the building, etc., and pay their charges out of trust funds.[1] These functions come under the ministerial heading. The trustee has a duty to oversee the performance of the delegated ministerial functions in the same manner as a prudent person would oversee such functions with respect to his own property.[2] If the trustee

---

1. Dunbar v. Birmingham Trust Nat. Bank, 286 Ala. 168, 238 So.2d 336 (1970); McLean v. Peyser, 169 Md. 1, 179 A. 58 (1935); Quinn's Estate, 342 Pa. 509, 21 A.2d 78 (1941); Corpus Christi Bank and Trust v. Roberts, 597 S.W.2d 752 (Tex.1980); Patterson v. Old Dominion Trust Co., 156 Va. 763, 159 S.E. 168 (1931).

2. Murdock v. Murdock, 370 So.2d 290 (Ala.1979); McClure v. Middletown Trust Co., 95 Conn. 148, 110 A. 838 (1920); In re Estate of Rosenthal, 189

does not exercise the appropriate oversight with respect to properly delegated functions, he is liable for losses to the trust which result from such breach of trust.

The primary function of the trustee in most trusts is the investment of the assets. This clearly involves a great deal of judgment and discretion. The trustee cannot delegate to another the decisions concerning investments; that is to say, the trustee cannot hire Jones, an investment expert, and authorize him to make whatever investments he thinks proper.[3] But can the trustee pay Jones a fee from trust funds for his investment advice, without delegating the final decision-making authority to him? If the trustee is a bank or an individual who is sophisticated concerning investments, it would be improper to permit the use of trust funds for this purpose.[4] If, however, the trustee is an individual who is not sophisticated concerning investments, it would seem reasonable that he seek such advice and that the expense be payable out of the trust.[5] Whether or not such payment is permissible seems to be a matter of construing the settlor's intent; if he designates a bank as trustee, the settlor assumes that the bank would have no need for soliciting the advice of others, but if he designates his son as trustee whom he knows to be unsophisticated in investment matters, it seems reasonable to conclude that the settlor has impliedly authorized such an expenditure.

It should be emphasized that even if the trustee is permitted to pay for investment advice from trust funds, nevertheless the trustee must not accept the advice blindly, but rather must make an independent decision. This independent decision may be consistent with the advice given. How does one determine whether the trustee who knows little about investments has in fact delegated the investment function by blindly following what purports to be advice, or has made an independent judgment which is the same as the advice given? Obviously this can present a difficult factual question, but realistically the responsible family member who accepts the trusteeship but knows little about investments is likely to receive generous treatment from the court. It follows, in theory at least, that the trustee must have a modicum of investment skill since he has to make an independent judgment with respect to the advice which he receives, and that one who does not possess a

So.2d 507 (Fla.App.1966); In re Webb's Estate, 165 Pa. 330, 30 A. 827 (1895).

3. Washington Loan & Trust Co. v. Colby, 71 App.D.C. 236, 108 F.2d 743 (1939); City of Boston v. Curley, 276 Mass. 549, 177 N.E. 557 (1931); Tavenner v. Baughman, 129 W.Va. 783, 41 S.E.2d 703 (1947).

4. In re Badenhausen's Estate, 38 Misc.2d 698, 237 N.Y.S.2d 928 (Sur.Ct. 1963). See Stillman v. Watkins, 3 Mass. App.Ct. 175, 325 N.E.2d 294 (1975).

5. In re Sellers' Estate, 31 Del.Ch. 158, 67 A.2d 860 (1949); Will of Axe, 132 Misc.2d 137, 502 N.Y.S.2d 943 (Sur. 1986); Thayer Trust, 71 Pa.D. & C.2d 734 (Com.Pl.1975).

modicum of such skill is unqualified and should be removed as trustee. If the trustee is a person who does not possess investment skill, the settlor may provide in the trust instrument that the trustee may retain an investment advisor and rely and act upon his advice; in other words, the settlor may authorize delegation of the investment function. The trustee, however, cannot act on instructions to invest in assets which he has reason to believe are not proper trust investments. This is because the trustee must oversee all actions of those to whom trustee functions are delegated. Also, the trust instrument may name an individual and a bank as co-trustees and provide that exclusive investment authority and responsibility are vested in the bank. The question of investment authority is discussed later in this Chapter.[6]

A bank that uses trust funds to pay an investment expert for his advice commits a breach of trust. The legal consequence of this breach of trust is that the bank must repay the trust for the amount paid for the advice. The legal consequence of the delegation of investment decision-making which is not authorized by the trust instrument is much more serious. If a trustee delegates an investment decision, the trustee is absolutely liable for any decline in the value of the investment.[7] This is true even though the investment is a perfectly sound one and the loss is the result of general stock market or economic conditions. That there would be no liability if the trustee had made the same investment exercising his independent judgment is immaterial. Also, it is immaterial that the person to whom the decision-making was delegated was a recognized investment expert. The breach of trust consists of the delegation of the investment function, and not the lack of due care in the selection of the investment.

To hold the trustee liable for the decline in value of an otherwise proper trust investment because of the manner in which it was selected appears harsh. As we shall see, the rules concerning trustee liability are frequently severe. The reason for such liability is to deter the trustee from committing acts which are not strictly in accordance with his fiduciary responsibility, rather than to correct for economic loss to the trust. The delegation of the investment function can be dangerous; to discourage this, the trustee is held liable for a loss which was not causally related in an economic sense to the delegation of the investment function.

The management of a large trust involves a good deal of bookkeeping. The trustee must keep a record of all receipts, payments and transactions, and submit formal accounts to the

6. See p. 310 below.

7. See In re Estate of Rees, 53 Ohio Law Abs. 385, 85 N.E.2d 563 (App.

1949); In re Kohler's Estate, 348 Pa. 55, 33 A.2d 920 (1943).

court and the beneficiaries at such times as the law requires. Must the trustee do the accounting work himself, or can he hire an accountant to do it for him and pay him out of trust funds? This depends on the nature of the trustee and the trust. If the trustee could be expected to do the accounting itself, then it is improper for the trustee to delegate this function to another.[8] If, on the other hand, the trustee could not reasonably be expected to do the accounting, then delegation of the function is permissible.[9] A bank ordinarily should not be entitled to pay an accountant from trust funds to do the work; an individual trustee who is not an accountant should be entitled to do so unless the trust is small and has no accounting complexities. The issue appears to be that of the settlor's implied intent. That is to say, if the settlor names a bank as trustee, it seems that she anticipates that the accounting will be done by the bank because it is assumed that the bank is staffed to perform that function, whereas if the settlor names an individual who is not an accountant as trustee, it seems that she anticipates that the trustee may have to hire someone to do that work. The settlor may, of course, authorize the payment out of trust funds for accounting services in the trust instrument, regardless of the nature of the trustee.

From time to time in the course of the administration of a trust, the trustee may require legal counseling or representation. It is clear that the trustee who is not a lawyer may retain a lawyer on behalf of the trust where advisable or necessary and pay the lawyer's fee out of trust assets.[10] Obviously the trustee who is not a lawyer cannot be expected to perform legal services for the trust. A lawyer typically exercises considerable discretion in the course of preparing tax returns and handling litigation, as examples, and such delegation of broad discretion by the trustee is permissible. The trustee who is a lawyer is also permitted to retain an attorney for the trust where legal services are required and pay the fee out of trust assets.[11] The reasoning here is that the settlor who chooses a lawyer as trustee presumably does not expect that the lawyer-trustee is to perform legal services in his capacity as trustee.

8. In re Trust of Brown, 213 N.J.Super. 489, 517 A.2d 893 (1986); Matter of Acker, 128 A.D.2d 867, 513 N.Y.S.2d 786 (1987); Hahl Estate, 89 Pa.D. & C. 380 (Orph.1954).

9. Hagedorn v. Arens, 106 N.J.Eq. 377, 150 A. 4 (1930); In re Loeb's Will, 19 Misc.2d 139, 186 N.Y.S.2d 731 (Sur. Ct.1959); Ealer Estate, 17 Pa.D. & C.2d 67 (Orph.1959).

10. In re Corcoran Trusts, 282 A.2d 653 (Del.Ch.1971); In re Estate of Rosenthal, 189 So.2d 507 (Fla.App.1966);

Russell v. Rici, 67 Ill.App.2d 98, 213 N.E.2d 566 (1966); Hanscom v. Malden & Melrose Gaslight Co., 234 Mass. 374, 125 N.E. 626 (1920).

11. Estate of Haviside, 102 Cal. App.3d 365, 162 Cal.Rptr. 393 (1980); Ontjes v. Mac Nider, 234 Iowa 208, 12 N.W.2d 284 (1943); Norris v. Bishop, 207 Ky. 621, 269 S.W. 751 (1925); Rauch Estate, 44 Pa.D. & C.2d 674 (Orph.1968); Swank v. Reherd, 181 Va. 943, 27 S.E.2d 191 (1943).

The lawyer-trustee may, of course, perform legal services for the trust without charge. Whether the lawyer-trustee can retain himself as attorney and pay his fee out of trust funds is a matter which is discussed later in this chapter.[12] Legal expenses incurred by the trustee strictly in his own behalf, such as in connection with a suit by the beneficiaries against him for breach of trust where he is found liable, are not reimbursable from the trust assets.[13]

Although the trustee may delegate substantial discretion to the lawyer in the handling, for example, of a claim, the trustee nevertheless has a duty to oversee the actions of the lawyer.[14] He cannot simply hand the matter over to the lawyer and look the other way. He must check what the lawyer has done from time to time, as a prudent layman would do with respect to a claim which he had against another person.

Trusts frequently provide that the trustee may make payments out of income or principal to a beneficiary in the trustee's discretion without any expressed standard within which the discretion is to be exercised, or may make payments in the trustee's discretion for the support of the beneficiary. Obviously no delegation of the decision-making in this context is permissible.

Returning briefly to investments, there has been litigation over the question of whether the purchase by a trustee of shares of an investment company is a breach of the duty not to delegate. The purchase of such shares is clearly a delegation of the investment function. The purchase of investment company shares also enables the trustee to obtain greater investment diversification than is obtainable by investing the trust assets directly. There is authority permitting this form of investment despite the delegation,[15] and there is legislation in some states which allows it.[16]

We have mentioned the beneficiary's action to recover the loss for the trustee's breach of the duty not to delegate. The beneficiary also can enjoin the trustee from committing such breach if he can catch it in time. And if the improper delegation is extensive it may be the basis for the removal of the trustee.

---

12. See p. 279 below.

13. Public Service Co. of Colorado v. Chase Manhattan Bank, 577 F.Supp. 92 (S.D.N.Y.1983); Epstein v. Epstein, 519 So.2d 1042 (Fla.App.1988); Allard v. Pacific National Bank, 99 Wash.2d 394, 663 P.2d 104 (1983). See Bankers Trust Co. v. Duffy, 295 A.2d 725 (Del.1972); Raszler v. Raszler, 81 N.W.2d 120 (N.D. 1957).

14. McClure v. Middletown Trust Co., 95 Conn. 148, 110 A. 838 (1920).

15. In re Estate of Rees, 53 Ohio Law Abs. 385, 85 N.E.2d 563 (App. 1949).

16. E.g., Colo.Rev.Stat., § 15–1–304; Mich.Stat.Ann. § 26.85; N.H.Rev.Stat. Ann. § 564.18; Ohio Rev.Code Ann. § 2109.371; Pa.Stat.Ann. tit. 20, § 7310.

The Uniform Trustees' Powers Act, which has been legislated in a minority of states, contains a provision which authorizes the trustee as follows:

... to employ persons, including attorneys, auditors, investment advisors, or agents, even if they are associated with the trustee, to advise or assist the trustee in the performance of his administrative duties; to act without independent investigation upon their recommendations; and instead of acting personally, to employ one or more agents to perform any act of administration, whether or not discretionary ...

The Act provides that this power can be exercised only if it is prudent to do so. Uniform Probate Code § 3–715 has substantially the same provision applicable to personal representatives. These are extraordinary authorizations of delegation and greatly modify the common law if applied literally.

SECTION 2. DUTY OF LOYALTY

It is axiomatic that the trustee must not realize any personal gain from the administration of the trust except his fees for serving as trustee.[17] To assure that the fiduciary responsibility is observed, the trustee is also forbidden to place himself in a position in which he could profit from the trusteeship. The trustee is duty-bound to avoid any situation or transaction in which his personal and fiduciary interests conflict.

It is a breach of trust for the trustee to sell trust property to himself individually, or as trustee to buy property from himself individually. It is immaterial that the price is the fair market price, and that the purchase or sale is in all other respects proper and in the best interest of the trust; self-dealing is per se a breach of trust. This is sometimes described as the "no further inquiry" rule. The reason for the rule is to deter trustees from placing themselves in a position in which they could benefit themselves at the expense of the trust, rather than to correct for any economic loss to the trust.

Jones sells certain shares of stock which he owns to himself as trustee for $10,000, which is its fair market value. The stock is a proper trust investment. One year later a beneficiary is advised of the transaction, at which time the value of the shares is $9500. The beneficiary has a cause of action against Jones for rescission, i.e., the return of the stock to Jones in exchange for the $10,000

---

17. There is, however, authority which allows the lawyer-trustee to receive legal fees for his legal services to the trust. See note 31 below.

purchase price.[18] If the value had increased to $10,500, the beneficiary would have his cause of action but probably would not exercise it. Any inordinate delay in bringing the action after the beneficiary is informed of the breach may result in the barring of the action under the doctrine of laches.[19] Also, an expression of approval by the beneficiary of the transaction after it was made may constitute an affirmance which would preclude an action against the trustee, provided the beneficiary is sui juris and there has been full disclosure of all facts bearing on the transaction. It should be noted that the trustee has no reciprocal right to rescind because of the self-dealing; rescission is only available to the beneficiary.

If Jones as trustee sold shares of stock held in trust to himself individually at the fair market value of $10,000, the beneficiaries would similarly have a cause of action for rescission which would probably be exercised if the stock increased in value.[20] If Jones, having purchased the stock from the trust for $10,000, sold it for $10,500 to someone who had no notice of the breach of trust, the beneficiaries would not have a cause of action for the return of the stock, but would have a cause of action against Jones for $500.[21] If the value of the stock was more than $10,500 at the time of the suit, the beneficiaries should be entitled to recover from the trustee the difference between $10,000 and that value; this recovery would be the economic equivalent of rescission which would be available if the property had not been sold.[22]

Let us assume Jones sold ABC stock which he owned to the trust for $10,000, its fair market value, and in another transaction sold XYZ stock he owned to the trust for $20,000, its fair market value. One year later the value of the ABC stock is $9500, and the value of the XYZ stock is $20,500. The beneficiaries are entitled to rescind the ABC stock purchase and retain the XYZ stock.[23] The beneficiaries can pick and choose their causes of action. The trustee does not have a defense that the separate and independent

18. Walding v. Walding, 56 Ala.App. 181, 320 So.2d 687 (1975); Smith v. Tolversen, 190 Minn. 410, 252 N.W. 423 (1934); Tracy v. Central Trust Co., 327 Pa. 77, 192 A. 869 (1937); Wheeler v. Mann, 763 P.2d 758 (Utah 1988).

19. Winn v. Shugart, 112 F.2d 617 (10th Cir.1940).

20. Powell v. Thorsen, 253 Ga. 572, 322 S.E.2d 261 (1984); Home Federal Savings and Loan Association v. Zarkin, 89 Ill.2d 232, 59 Ill.Dec. 897, 432 N.E.2d 841 (1982); Sunter v. Sunter, 190 Mass. 449, 77 N.E. 497 (1906); In re Estate of De Planche, 65 Misc.2d 501, 318 N.Y.S.2d 194 (Sur.Ct.1971).

21. Clay v. Thomas, 178 Ky. 199, 198 S.W. 762 (1917); Schug v. Michael, 310 Minn. 22, 245 N.W.2d 587 (1976); Hartman v. Hartle, 95 N.J.Eq. 123, 122 A. 615 (1923); Pomeroy v. Bushong, 317 Pa. 459, 177 A. 10 (1935).

22. See Matter of Rothko, 43 N.Y.2d 305, 401 N.Y.S.2d 449, 372 N.E.2d 291 (1977).

23. Pennsylvania Co. for Insurance v. Gillmore, 142 N.J.Eq. 27, 59 A.2d 24 (1948); In re Harmon's Trust, 5 Misc.2d 308, 164 N.Y.S.2d 468 (1956).

self-dealing transactions taken as a whole result in no loss to the trust.

Let us assume that Jones as trustee sells stock held in trust to himself individually for $10,000, its fair market value. The stock rises in value to $10,500. Jones as trustee has invested the $10,000 in other stock purchased properly which has risen in value to $10,500. The beneficiaries are entitled to rescind the self-dealing transaction, and Jones has no defense that the proceeds of the self-dealing transaction have been invested to produce a gain which balances the rise in value of the stock sold to himself individually.

The above examples concern dealings between the trustee as fiduciary and the trustee as an individual (or a corporation). The trustee may violate the duty of loyalty in other than a pure self-dealing situation. For example, the trustee violates the duty of loyalty when he sells trust property to a corporation in which he holds 25% of the stock. A conflict of interest exists although there is no self-dealing as such, and liability follows although the transaction is fair to the trust. At some point along the continuum, however, the conflict of interest becomes so attenuated that the "no further inquiry" rule is not to be applied. For example, if the trustee sold trust property to a corporation in which he was a 1% stockholder, there would be no liability unless the transaction was unfair to the trust.[24] It seems, however, that unfairness must be the product of willfulness or negligence, for which the trustee is liable without regard to the question of conflict of interest.

Suppose land is held in trust which for economic reasons should be sold but no reasonable offer has been forthcoming although the property has been on the market for a number of months. The trustee, however, is willing to buy the land at the fair market value. If the trustee obtains court authorization, he can legally purchase the land at its fair value. The court will authorize self-dealing if it is in the interest of the trust.[25]

Self-dealing may be permitted by express provision in the trust instrument. Needless to say, any self-dealing transaction pursuant to such authorization must be fair to the trust in all respects. Also, in the absence of authorization in the trust instrument, the trustee may legally self-deal with the consent of all beneficiaries, provided the price is fair and there has been full disclosure to the beneficia-

24. See 2A Scott, Law of Trusts §§ 170.10, 170.24 (4th ed., Fratcher, 1987).

25. In re Estate of Fiske, 207 Minn. 44, 291 N.W. 289 (1940); Pollack v. Bowman, 140 N.J.Eq. 417, 55 A.2d 8 (1947); In re Scarborough Properties Corp., 25 N.Y.2d 553, 307 N.Y.S.2d 641, 255 N.E.2d 761 (1969); Wheeler v. Mann, 763 P.2d 758 (Utah 1988); Wilkins v. Lasater, 46 Wash.App. 766, 733 P.2d 221 (1987).

ries of all matters which bear on the deal.[26] If the trustee obtains the consent of the beneficiaries to purchase certain stock in the trust at market value, but fails to disclose to the beneficiaries certain private information which he has concerning the stock, the consent would be deemed to have been improperly obtained and the transaction would be a breach of the duty of loyalty. Similarly, if the trustee purchased the stock pursuant to authorization in the trust instrument under the same circumstances, the transaction would not be fair and would be rescindable.[27]

Obtaining the consent of all the beneficiaries is usually very difficult. Frequently there is more than one class of contingent remaindermen; some beneficiaries may be minors; some beneficiaries may be unborn. Guardians would have to be appointed for the minors and the unborn in order for their consent to be obtained. As a practical matter the consent of all beneficiaries will not be sought or obtained in most trusts.[28]

Is it a breach of the duty of loyalty for the bank trustee to purchase property for the trust from a senior officer of the bank? Although the bank is not buying from itself, a conflict of interest exists. Transactions of this nature have been held to be violative of the duty of loyalty.[29]

We have noted that a trustee who is a lawyer is not required to perform legal services for the trust in his capacity as trustee,[30] but he may do so if he wishes. Can the lawyer-trustee retain himself as counsel to the trust and pay himself a fee? This is a form of self-dealing, but the prevailing view is that it is permissible;[31] there is, however, authority to the contrary.[32]

If First National Bank is trustee, and its common stock is a proper trust investment, is it permissible for the bank to purchase

---

26. Steiner v. Hawaiian Trust Co., 47 Hawaii 548, 393 P.2d 96 (1964); Home Federal Savings and Loan Association v. Zarkin, 89 Ill.2d 232, 59 Ill.Dec. 897, 432 N.E.2d 841 (1982); McDaniel v. Hughes, 206 Md. 206, 111 A.2d 204 (1955); Birnbaum v. Birnbaum, 117 A.D.2d 409, 503 N.Y.S.2d 451 (1986).

27. The bank trustee is presented with a legal dilemma when it receives inside information from a corporate borrower whose common stock it holds in trust. For a discussion of the securities and trust law problems presented by this situation, see 9 ABA Real Property, Probate and Trust Journal 292 (1974).

28. Uniform Probate Code § 3–713 makes self-dealing transactions by personal representatives voidable unless permitted by the will, consented to by the beneficiaries, or approved by the court.

29. Steiner v. Hawaiian Trust Co., 47 Hawaii 548, 393 P.2d 96 (1964); Ryan v. Plath, 18 Wash.2d 839, 140 P.2d 968 (1943).

30. See p. 274 above.

31. Norris v. Bishop, 207 Ky. 621, 269 S.W. 751 (1925); Lembo v. Casaly, 5 Mass.App.Ct. 240, 361 N.E.2d 1314 (1977); Rauch Estate, 44 Pa.D. & C.2d 674 (Orph.1968); Swank v. Reherd, 181 Va. 943, 27 S.E.2d 191 (1943). See In re Estate of Tuttle, 4 N.Y.2d 159, 173 N.Y.S.2d 279, 149 N.E.2d 715 (1958).

32. Estate of Haviside, 102 Cal. App.3d 365, 162 Cal.Rptr. 393 (1980); Lightner v. Boone, 221 N.C. 78, 19 S.E.2d 144 (1942).

its own stock for the trust from a third party? It is not self-dealing, but a conflict of interest exists when the bank trustee holds its own stock in trust. The bank may be inclined to retain the stock when it should be sold, because the bank does not wish to depress the price of the stock by placing its holdings on the market for sale. Also, the bank may be inclined to vote the stock to maintain the incumbent management when a change of management may be in the best interest of the trust. The purchase of the bank's stock for the trust is a breach of the duty of loyalty.[33]

Is First National Bank as trustee entitled to deposit trust cash with its own banking department? The deposit is a form of loan to itself, and therefore constitutes self-dealing. Banks live off deposits, and there is the temptation to maintain a large balance rather than invest the funds productively elsewhere. There are statutes in most states, however, permitting deposits in the banking department of the trustee bank.[34]

Finally, there is a common situation which involves a conflict of interest. Testator leaves a portion of her estate to her Daughter and Bank, in trust, to pay the income to Testator's three children in such shares as the trustees shall in their discretion determine from time to time. The discretionary decisions have to be agreed to by both trustees. Daughter has a conflict of interest. It appears that the Testator has authorized the conflict by naming Daughter as trustee. There is no breach of trust as long as distributions to Daughter are made fairly and in all respects in accordance with the trustees' fiduciary obligations.

It should be noted that it is not a breach of the duty of loyalty for a party who is trustee of several trusts to sell the property of one trust to another of its trusts, provided the transaction is in all respects fair to both trusts.[35] The trustee cannot personally profit from the transaction. The result should be different, however, if the trustee has a beneficial interest in one of the trusts.

33. In re Trusteeship of Stone, 138 Ohio St. 293, 34 N.E.2d 755 (1941); Stephan v. Equitable Savings and Loan Association, 268 Or. 544, 522 P.2d 478 (1974); City Bank Farmers Trust Co. v. Taylor, 76 R.I. 129, 69 A.2d 234 (1949); Ind.Code Ann. § 30–4–3–7; Ky.Rev.Stat. Ann. § 386.025; Mo.Ann.Stat. § 362.-550.

34. E.g., Me.Rev.Stat.Ann. tit. 9–B, § 623; Minn.Stat.Ann. § 48.39; Ohio Rev.Code § 1109.12; Vt.Stat.Ann. tit. 8, § 1356; Wis.Stat.Ann. 221.04(6a).

35. In re Binder's Estate, 137 Ohio St. 26, 27 N.E.2d 939 (1940); In re Saeger's Estate, 340 Pa. 73, 16 A.2d 19 (1940). There are statutes, however, to the contrary; E.g., Nev.Rev.Stat. 163.-060; Okla.Stat.Ann. tit. 60, § 175.12; Uniform Trusts Act § 6.

SECTION 3.   DUTY TO KEEP TRUST ASSETS SEPARATE

There is a common law rule that the trustee must hold trust property in the name of the trust.[36] It is a breach of trust for the trustee to hold trust property in the trustee's name individually, or in any name other than that of the trust. The property should be held in the name of "First National Bank, Trustee Under the Will of Robert Smith." This rule, however, has been eroded in certain respects by statute in most states.[37]

One reason for the common law rule is to avoid the temptation of the trustee to manipulate the trust assets and his individual assets to the trustee's personal advantage where there are changes in values. If certain trust property is held in the trustee's individual name, and it increases in value, while certain of the trustee's individual property has declined in value, the trustee is presented with the opportunity to treat the property that has risen as his own and to treat that which has declined as trust property. Another reason for the rule is to avoid the danger that personal creditors of the trustee might attach trust property by mistake. Also, if one is trustee of more than one trust, there could be confusion as to which property belongs to which trust.

The earmarking of trust property as such creates problems when the trustee wishes to sell the property. There is the common law rule that one who knowingly purchases a trust asset from a trustee, or one who participates in the transaction with such knowledge, such as a corporation with respect to changes in stock registration, is bound to make diligent inquiry as to whether the sale was violative of the terms of the trust. If the trustee is forbidden to sell the property under the terms of the trust, and the buyer knows he is buying trust property, the sale may be voidable.[38] This rule has made transactions with trustees very cumbersome and dangerous, and especially impeded commerce in securities which are frequently traded.

To correct the situation, many states enacted statutes to permit bank trustees to hold securities in other than the fiduciary name.[39] It also became the practice to provide in the trust instrument that the trustee could hold trust securities in other than the fiduciary name. The practice developed of registering trust securities in the name of some "company," often a partnership consisting of several bank officers, established solely to hold trust securities for the bank. This is sometimes referred to as registering in the name of a nominee. Securities held in trusts of which a bank is

---

36. Pedigo v. Pedigo's Committee, 247 Ky. 403, 57 S.W.2d 54 (1932); Wolk v. Stefanowicz, 318 Pa. 197, 177 A. 821 (1935).

37. See note 39 below.

38. See Section 12 of this chapter.

39. E.g., Ill.Ann.Stat. ch. 17, § 1676; Ohio Rev.Code Ann. § 1109.26; Pa.Stat. Ann. tit. 20, § 3321; Tenn.Code Ann. § 45-2-1003; Va.Code § 6.1-31.

trustee are usually registered in the name of a nominee. By this means, the purchaser of securities does not know that he is purchasing from a trustee and the risk to the purchaser is avoided.

Most states also have legislation to the effect that the purchaser of securities from a trustee who knows that he is purchasing from a trustee but has no knowledge that the trustee is committing a breach of trust by selling, and the corporation which registers the transfer without any knowledge of a breach, are fully protected from liability.[40] It appears, therefore, that nominee registration of securities is not necessary in such jurisdictions. Nevertheless, nominee registration of securities remains the normal practice everywhere.

The statutes we have described in the preceding two paragraphs do not deal with the fiduciary holding of land. Land normally is held in the name of the trust.

Assuming the situation in which the holding of the asset in other than the name of the trust constitutes a breach of trust, what are the legal consequences to the trustee? Trustee purchases property for $10,000 and holds it in his individual name. The asset is in all respects a proper trust investment. Several years later the trustee sells the asset for $9500. The decline is attributable to general market conditions. There is authority to the effect that the trustee is liable for the $500 loss, although there is no causal relationship between the loss in value and the failure to earmark.[41] Once again, this harsh result is imposed to deter trustees from violating the duty to earmark, and not to correct for economic loss to the trust caused by the trustee's actions. There is, however, contrary authority to the effect that the trustee is liable only for losses caused by the failure to earmark. If this latter rule is adopted, then the trustee is not liable for the $500 loss on these facts.[42] The failure to earmark is a breach of trust in any event, and if assets in the trust are not held in the name of the trust, the trustee can be enjoined to place them in the name of the trust.

It follows from what has just been said that the trustee is forbidden to mingle trust funds and his own funds. It is a breach of trust for the trustee to deposit trust funds in a bank account in his individual name which contains his individual funds as well.[43]

40. See Section 12 of this chapter.

41. In re Gunderson's Estate, 279 Ill.App. 168 (1935). See Wolk v. Stefanowicz, 318 Pa. 197, 177 A. 821 (1935).

42. Miller v. Pender, 93 N.H. 1, 34 A.2d 663 (1943); Buckle v. Marshall, 176 Va. 139, 10 S.E.2d 506 (1940).

43. In re McCabe's Estate, 98 Cal. App.2d 503, 220 P.2d 614 (1950); Smith v. Reddish, 113 Fla. 20, 151 So. 273 (1933); Markus v. Markus, 331 Mass. 394, 119 N.E.2d 415 (1954); Ariz.Rev. Stat.Ann. § 6–862; N.Y.Est. Powers & Trusts Law § 11–1.6; S.D.Comp. Laws Ann. § 55–2–9.

There is also a common law rule to the effect that a trustee must not mingle the funds of separate trusts of which he is trustee. For example, trustee purchases 10,000 shares of ABC Corporation with the funds of three trusts and registers the stock certificate for 10,000 shares in the name of a nominee. Nominee registration is permitted by statute. The trustee records on its books the fractional interests of each trust. The traditional view is that this constitutes a breach of trust.[44] The trustee must have separate certificates representing the interests of the respective trusts. There is authority, however, which permits a trustee to combine the funds of several trusts in one bank deposit in its name as a fiduciary, provided it keeps a record of the interest of each trust on its books.[45] There is also authority which permits a trustee to acquire a single mortgage with the funds of several trusts, provided the trustee keeps a record of the interests of the trusts on its books.[46] Also, there are statutes in many states today which authorize corporate trustees to mingle the funds of their individual trusts into one common trust fund for the purpose of obtaining greater investment diversification than is obtainable from the separate investment of the funds of the individual trusts. The statutory common trust fund is discussed in Section 6 below.

SECTION 4. DUTY TO EXERCISE CARE AND SKILL

The trustee has the pervasive duty to exercise reasonable care and skill in the performance of all the functions of the trusteeship, including the selection of investments, the management of real estate, the selection and oversight of those to whom he has properly delegated, and the safekeeping of trust property. Reasonable care and skill is usually defined as the care and skill that a person of ordinary prudence would exercise in dealing with his own property. The standard is the objective one of the hypothetical person of ordinary prudence; the trustee fails in his duty if he does the best he can but his performance is below that of the hypothesized person.[47]

There is at least one qualification to this definition of the standard. The person of ordinary prudence frequently will take

44. Heaton v. Bartlett, 87 N.H. 357, 180 A. 244 (1935); McCullough's Ex'rs v. McCullough, 44 N.J.Eq. 313, 14 A. 642 (1888).

45. New England Trust Co. v. Triggs, 334 Mass. 324, 135 N.E.2d 541 (1956); Finley v. Exchange Trust Co., 183 Okl. 167, 80 P.2d 296 (1938).

46. First Nat. Bank of Birmingham v. Basham, 238 Ala. 500, 191 So. 873 (1939); Springfield Safe Deposit & Trust Co. v. First Unitarian Society, 293 Mass. 480, 200 N.E. 541 (1936); Bowden v. Citizens' Loan & Trust Co., 194 Minn. 113, 259 N.W. 815 (1935); Ky.Rev.Stat. Ann. § 287.240.

47. Jarvis v. Boatmen's Nat. Bank, 478 S.W.2d 266 (Mo.1972); In re Estate of Lerch, 399 Pa. 59, 159 A.2d 506 (1960); Alderman v. Cooper, 257 S.C. 304, 185 S.E.2d 809 (1971); In re Trust Estate of Higgins, 83 S.D. 535, 162 N.W.2d 768 (1968).

certain risks in the management of his property which the trustee is not entitled to take. The prudent person with a substantial investment portfolio frequently sets aside a small percentage for speculative investment. Such investment speculation would be a breach of trust for the trustee. The trustee is first and foremost a conserver of assets; he is forbidden to invest any portion of the trust in a manner which creates an inordinate risk of loss to the principal of the trust.

There is also substantial authority for another qualification to the definition of the duty of care and skill: If a trustee possesses skills superior to those of the ordinarily prudent person, or represents that he does, then he is held to such higher standard.[48] Banks in many instances have superior skills and usually hold themselves out as having superior skills. It makes good sense that they should be held to a higher standard than the family member with little business experience who reluctantly accepts fiduciary responsibility. The traditional view, however, is that the standard of care and skill remains that of the person of ordinary prudence regardless of the special qualities possessed or represented.[49]

SECTION 5. VARIOUS OTHER DUTIES

The trustee has the duty to collect all the assets which belong to the trust. The testamentary trustee must see to it that the executor of the estate pays over to the trust all that he should when he should.[50] If an asset of the trust is a claim, the trustee must see to it that it is paid and sue to collect it if necessary.

The trustee must make the trust property productive of income, unless it is real estate which is intended for use by a beneficiary. The trustee is excused from this duty only if the settlor has provided in the trust instrument that certain property is to be retained which is not income producing, such as unimproved

---

48. First Alabama Bank of Huntsville v. Spragins, 515 So.2d 962 (Ala. 1987); Matter of Estate of Estes, 134 Ariz. 70, 654 P.2d 4 (App.1982); Estate of Beach, 15 Cal.3d 623, 125 Cal.Rptr. 570, 542 P.2d 994 (1975); Citizens and Southern Nat. Bank v. Haskins, 254 Ga. 131, 327 S.E.2d 192 (1985); Stevens v. Nat. City Bank, 45 Ohio St.3d 276, 544 N.E.2d 612 (1989); In re Estate of Lohm, 440 Pa. 268, 269 A.2d 451 (1970); In re Church's Will, 221 Wis. 472, 266 N.W. 210 (1936).

Uniform Probate Code § 7–302 takes this view, which also applies to personal representatives under § 3–703.

49. Stark v. United States Trust Co., 445 F.Supp. 670 (S.D.N.Y.1978); Estate of Venturelli v. Granville National Bank, 54 Ill.App.3d 997, 12 Ill.Dec. 667, 370 N.E.2d 290 (1977); Security Trust Co. v. Appleton, 303 Ky. 328, 197 S.W.2d 70 (1946); See 2A Scott, Law of Trusts §§ 174, 174.1 (4th ed., Fratcher, 1987).

50. In re Will of Hartzell, 43 Ill. App.2d 118, 192 N.E.2d 697 (1963); In re Rosenfeldt's Will, 185 Minn. 425, 241 N.W. 573 (1932); In re First Nat. Bank of Mansfield, 37 Ohio St.2d 60, 307 N.E.2d 23 (1974); Pepper v. Zions First Nat. Bank, 801 P.2d 144 (Utah 1990).

land or corporate stock on which dividends are not currently being paid. If the trustee receives property in trust from the settlor or the estate which is not income producing, and there is no provision in the trust instrument dispensing with the duty to make trust assets income producing, the trustee must convert it into income producing property within a reasonable period of time.[51]

The trustee must deal impartially with the beneficiaries.[52] Frequently the beneficiaries' interests are economically in conflict. The life income beneficiary is interested in maximizing income, and the remainderman who gets the principal is interested in the preservation of principal. The trustee must invest to produce income without inordinate risk of loss to principal. Sometimes the trustee has the discretion to pay principal to the income beneficiary for support or to pay principal to him in the trustee's discretion without reference to any standard. Here the trustee must act from proper motives and considerations, and is forbidden to act out of partiality or vindictiveness.[53]

The trustee has the duty to keep an accurate record of his management of the trust estate, and to submit accounts to the beneficiaries at their request at reasonable intervals.[54] By statute in many states a testamentary trustee must submit an account to the court periodically, such as every year or every two or three years, and the same is true in some states with respect to inter vivos trustees.[55] The submission to the court may be an ex parte procedure without notice to the beneficiaries, or it may be an inter partes judicial proceeding with notice to the beneficiaries. The legal effect of a judicial accounting proceeding is discussed below.[56] In addition, the trustee has the duty to comply with reasonable requests from the beneficiaries for information about the trust

51. In re McCabe's Estate, 98 Cal. App.2d 503, 220 P.2d 614 (1950); In re Hubbell's Will, 302 N.Y. 246, 97 N.E.2d 888 (1951). See McInnes v. Goldthwaite, 94 N.H. 331, 52 A.2d 795 (1947); In re Estate of Lare, 436 Pa. 1, 257 A.2d 556 (1969).

52. Dupont v. Delaware Trust Co., 320 A.2d 694 (Del.1974); Hurst v. First Kentucky Trust Co., 560 S.W.2d 819 (Ky.1978); Harrison v. Marcus, 396 Mass. 424, 486 N.E.2d 710 (1985); Matter of Estate of Butterfield, 418 Mich. 241, 341 N.W.2d 453 (1983); Sturgis v. Stinson, 241 Va. 531, 404 S.E.2d 56 (1991).

53. See In re Koretzky's Estate, 8 N.J. 506, 86 A.2d 238 (1951); Citizens & Southern Nat. Bank v. Haskins, 254 Ga. 131, 327 S.E.2d 192 (1985); Matter of Jane Bradley Uihlein, 142 Wis.2d 277, 417 N.W.2d 908 (App.1987). See also p. 309 above.

54. Shriners Hospitals v. Robbins, 450 So.2d 798 (Ala.1984); McCormick v. McCormick, 118 Ill.App.3d 455, 74 Ill. Dec. 73, 455 N.E.2d 103 (1983); Briggs v. Crowley, 352 Mass. 194, 224 N.E.2d 417 (1967); Pazdernik v. Stemler, 804 S.W.2d 789 (Mo.App.1990); Bartlett v. Dumaine, 128 N.H. 497, 523 A.2d 1 (1986). Uniform Probate Code § 7–303 so provides.

55. E.g., Conn.Gen.Stat.Ann. § 45a–177; N.H.Rev.Stat.Ann. § 564.19; Ohio Rev.Code § 2109.30.

56. See p. 309 below.

from time to time, short of a formal account of the trustee's management.[57]

SECTION 6.   THE INVESTMENT FUNCTION

The primary function of the modern trustee is the management of investments.   It is the duty of the trustee to produce a reasonable income and to preserve principal.   The hallmark of trustee investment policy is conservatism; significant risk-taking for the purpose of realizing large capital gains is not permissible, in the absence of some specific provision in the trust instrument authorizing or directing speculative investment.

Most states have statutes which establish the standard for the trustee in the performance of his investment function.   Most of the statutes provide, in essence, that the trustee must invest as a prudent person would invest his funds with a view to the preservation of principal and the production of a reasonable income.[58]   These states are referred to as "prudent person rule" jurisdictions.   A few statutes, however, provide that a trustee may invest only in certain specified categories of debt securities, or provide for a maximum percentage that can be invested in corporate stocks and the remainder is to be invested in specified categories of debt securities.[59]   The handful of jurisdictions which limit the trustee to specified categories of investment and specified percentages within categories are called "legal list" states.   The discussion in this section focuses on the prudent person rule for trust investment.

The prudent person rule is something of a misnomer.   Prudent investors frequently invest a small portion of their capital speculatively.   This is forbidden under the prudent person rule.   The following statement explains why:

> In making investments, however, a loss is always possible, since in any investment there is always some risk. The question of the amount of risk, however, is a question of degree.   No man of intelligence would make a disposition of property where in view of the price the risk of loss is out of proportion to the opportunity for gain.   Where, however, the risk is not out of proportion, a man of

---

57. Madden v. Mercantile–Safe Deposit & Trust Co., 27 Md.App. 17, 339 A.2d 340 (1975); Estate of Rosenblum, 459 Pa. 201, 328 A.2d 158 (1974); Shannon v. Frost National Bank, 533 S.W.2d 389 (Tex.Civ.App.1975); Allard v. Pacific National Bank, 99 Wash.2d 394, 663 P.2d 104 (1983).   Uniform Probate Code § 7–303 so provides.

58. E.g.,   Cal.Prob.Code   § 16040; Colo.Rev.Stat.   § 15–1–304;   Conn.Gen. Stat.Ann.   § 45–88;   Del.Code Ann. tit. 12, § 3302;   Ill.Ann.Stat. ch. 17, § 1675; Or.Rev.Stat. § 128.057.

59. E.g., Ala.Const. art. IV, § 74; Ala.Code § 19–3–120; Ky.Rev.Stat.Ann. § 386.020;   Md. Est. & Trusts Code Ann. § 15–106;   Ohio Rev.Code §§ 2109.37, 2109.371;   W.Va.Code § 44–6–2.

intelligence may make a disposition which is speculative in character with a view to increasing his property instead of merely preserving it. Such a disposition is not a proper trust investment, because it is not a disposition which makes the preservation of the fund a primary consideration.[60]

There is great investment latitude under the prudent person rule. Government and corporate bonds, bank certificates of deposit, corporate debentures, and first mortgages are all proper investments, provided, of course, that the governmental unit, the corporation, the bank or the mortgagor is financially sound and the security is adequate. Preferred and common stock of sound, established corporations are within the prudent person rule.

Within the limits of conservative prudence, the trustee must always exercise reasonable care and skill in making investment decisions. The standard of care and skill which must be exercised is an objective, or external standard. That is to say, it makes no difference if the trustee does his best if he does not manage the investments as the reasonably careful and skillful person would. A person not capable of performing in accordance with the objective standard is unfit to be a trustee. As we have discussed previously, however, it is proper for a person of limited investment competence to obtain expert advice, but he must make his own investment decisions, at least in theory.[61] It seems reasonable that if a trustee possesses investment skills which are superior to the objective standard, or represents that he does, such trustee should be held to such higher standard. There is substantial authority to this effect, but traditional trust doctrine would not hold the superior trustee to the higher standard.[62]

The statutory provisions governing trustee investment are subject to the terms of the trust instrument which may be more restrictive or less restrictive. The trust instrument may provide that the trustee is to invest only in certain types of debt securities, which would be more restrictive than the prudent person rule. The will may authorize the trustee to retain certain speculative assets owned by the testator at his death or to make speculative investments which would not be within the prudent person rule. In all events, the terms of the trust instrument control.[63]

60. Restatement (Second) of Trusts § 227, Comment e (1959).

61. See p. 272 above.

62. See p. 284 above.

63. Perling v. Citizens and Southern National Bank, 250 Ga. 674, 300 S.E.2d 649 (1983); In re Estate of Munger, 63 N.J. 514, 309 A.2d 205 (1973); In re Gillingham's Estate, 353 Pa. 493, 46 A.2d 269 (1946); Hoffman v. First Virginia Bank, 220 Va. 834, 263 S.E.2d 402 (1980).

Under the prudent person rule the trustee is not permitted to buy the stock, bonds or debentures of a corporation which does not have an established record of earnings.[64] The trustee is not permitted to carry on a private business.[65] The trustee should not invest in second mortgages.[66] These are all considered to involve too much risk. The trust instrument may, of course, authorize such investments; such authorization, however, would not exculpate the trustee for extremely risky investment in those categories.

Many states have statutes which provide that the trustee may retain property delivered in trust in the case of the living trust, or owned by the testator at his death in the case of the testamentary trust.[67] Does this mean that in a jurisdiction which has the prudent person rule the trustee may retain an investment which it would be imprudent for him to purchase? In such jurisdictions it must expand the trustee's authority to some extent or it is redundant. Frequently the trust instrument contains a provision which authorizes retention of assets delivered in trust or owned by the testator at death. Such a provision has an effect upon the trustee's investment authority similar to that of the comparable statutory provision. In the absence of a statutory provision or provision in the trust instrument authorizing retention, the trustee must dispose of investments which do not conform to the prudent person rule, within a reasonable time.[68] If the trust instrument directs, rather than authorizes, the retention of an asset which is part of the original trust property, the trustee cannot sell unless authorized to do so by the court pursuant to the doctrine of administrative deviation, discussed in Chapter 11, Section 4.

Diversification is a basic investment principle. The prudent investor typically does not put all his eggs in one basket. The investment portfolio should contain different types of investment and should contain a variety of specific investments within each category. The well-diversified large portfolio is likely to contain government bonds, corporate bonds, and common stocks, and a number of different issues within each category. Diversification

---

64. First Alabama Bank of Montgomery v. Martin, 425 So.2d 415 (Ala. 1982); Kimball v. Whitney, 233 Mass. 321, 123 N.E. 665 (1919); Rand v. McKittrick, 346 Mo. 466, 142 S.W.2d 29 (1940); St. Germain's Adm'r v. Tuttle, 114 Vt. 263, 44 A.2d 137 (1945).

65. Donnelly v. Alden, 229 Mass. 109, 118 N.E. 298 (1918); Sebree v. Rosen, 349 S.W.2d 865 (Mo.1961); In re Nagle's Estate, 305 Pa. 36, 156 A. 309 (1931).

66. Matter of Estate of Collins, 72 Cal.App.3d 663, 139 Cal.Rptr. 644

(1977). See 3 Scott, Law of Trusts § 227.7 (3d ed. 1967).

67. E.g., Conn.Gen.Stat.Ann. § 45–89; Del.Code Ann. tit. 12, § 3304; Fla. Stat.Ann. § 737.402; Wash.Rev.Code Ann. § 11.100.060.

68. Citizens' & Southern Nat. Bank v. Clark, 172 Ga. 625, 158 S.E. 297 (1931); McInnes v. Whitman, 313 Mass. 19, 46 N.E.2d 527 (1943); Stevens v. National City Bank, 45 Ohio St.3d 276, 544 N.E.2d 612 (1989).

makes for safety. It avoids the risk of large loss that follows from the concentration of investments that are affected by the same economic factor or factors. The portfolio is less volatile and safer if the investments are spread among a number of different industries and categories of securities which tend to be affected differently by various economic factors. Since the trustee is concerned with the preservation of value, it has generally been held that the trustee has a duty to diversify.[69]

One means of obtaining diversification, particularly for relatively small trusts, is the common trust fund. The bank trustee creates one trust of which it is trustee, consisting of the funds of many of the trusts which it holds. Each contributing trust receives a certificate representing its pro rata interest in the common trust. The funds in the common trust are invested and the income is passed through to the contributing trusts. The value of the principal represented by the certificate, of course, fluctuates with the value of the assets held by the common trust fund. The individual trust may redeem its pro rata interest when necessary at its value at the time of redemption; redemption must take place at the time of distribution of the principal of the trust. Usually a bank will have more than one common trust fund in order to provide for the special investment purposes of the individual trusts. For example, one common trust may emphasize income, another capital appreciation, and another may be balanced between capital appreciation and income. Usually a trustee's investment goal falls into the "balanced" category, but sometimes the trust instrument will indicate a particular concern for the needs of the income beneficiary or for capital appreciation. The individual trust may invest its entire principal in a common trust, or it may invest only a portion of it.

The common trust fund violates the common law duty of the trustee not to mingle the funds of its several trusts. Consequently, legislation has been enacted in most states authorizing banks to establish common trust funds.[70] Usually the bank is authorized under the statute to invest the assets of the individual trusts in a common trust unless the individual trust instrument expressly provides to the contrary.

69. Hamilton v. Nielsen, 678 F.2d 709 (7th Cir.1982); First Alabama Bank v. Spragins, 515 So.2d 962 (Ala.1987); Steiner v. Hawaiian Trust Co., 47 Hawaii 548, 393 P.2d 96 (1964); Chase v. Pevear, 383 Mass. 350, 419 N.E.2d 1358 (1981); In re Trust of Kemske, 305 N.W.2d 755 (Minn.1981); In re Trust of Mueller, 28 Wis.2d 26, 135 N.W.2d 854 (1965). But see Commercial Trust Co. v. Barnard, 27 N.J. 332, 142 A.2d 865 (1958); Matter of Newhoff's Will, 107 Misc.2d 589, 435 N.Y.S.2d 632 (1980), aff'd 107 A.D.2d 417, 486 N.Y.S.2d 956 (1985); Estate of Knipp, 489 Pa. 509, 414 A.2d 1007 (1980).

70. E.g., Ariz.Rev.Stat.Ann. § 6–871; Mo.Ann.Stat. § 362.580; N.M.Stat.Ann. § 46–1–13; N.C.Gen.Stat. § 36A–90; Utah Code Ann. § 7–5–13; Vt.Stat.Ann. tit. 8, § 1357.

The investment of trust assets in shares of an investment company also offers greater diversification to the small or moderate-sized trust than would be available by direct investment. Actually the common trust fund is like an investment company available only to trusts held by one bank. Investing trust funds in an investment company raises the issue of trustee delegation, as we have discussed previously. There is case authority, however, permitting such investment by trustees, and statutes in some states expressly permit it.[71]

If a trustee commits a breach of trust by making an investment in violation of the prudent person rule, she is liable for any decline in value of such investment.[72] The trustee's total investment portfolio may have a value which is substantially above its cost, and the trustee's investment strategy may as a consequence be considered to be successful; nevertheless the trustee is liable for the loss in value of any investment which is not within the prudent person rule. For purposes of liability, each investment is assessed in isolation from the portfolio as a whole. The same result follows, of course, if the trust instrument limits the trustee's investment power to certain categories of investments, and the trustee invests outside such categories.

If the trustee makes two investments which are breaches of trust, and one investment increases in value and the other declines, the trustee cannot use the benefit to the trust which resulted from one breach defensively in a suit by a beneficiary for the breach which caused a loss to the trust. They are independent breaches of trust.[73] The beneficiary can, of course, compel the trustee to sell the improper investment which has risen in value, and the gain inures to the trust.

The action for failure to diversify investments presents a special issue. Let us assume the trustee invests 30% of the trust principal in the common stock of one corporation. The investment is proper except for its size. An investment of 10% of the trust principal in that stock would be proper, let us assume, but anything in excess is a breach of trust for failure to diversify. The value of the stock declines. The trustee is liable not for the loss on the entire purchase, but only for the loss on those shares which made

---

71. See notes 15 and 16 above.

72. Home Savings & Loan Co. v. Strain, 130 Ohio St. 53, 196 N.E. 770 (1935); In re Fouks' Estate, 213 Wis. 550, 252 N.W. 160 (1934). See In re Trusteeship of First Minneapolis Trust Co., 202 Minn. 187, 277 N.W. 899 (1938).

73. Chase v. Pevear, 383 Mass. 350, 419 N.E.2d 1358 (1981); In re Bank of New York, 35 N.Y.2d 512, 364 N.Y.S.2d 164, 323 N.E.2d 700 (1974); State ex rel. Bottcher v. Bartling, 149 Neb. 491, 31 N.W.2d 422 (1948).

the purchase a violation of the duty to diversify, namely, two-thirds of the shares held.[74]

We have emphasized that the trustee is required to invest with a view to the preservation of principal. Stated another way, the trustee is not to take investment risks which could result in serious loss to the trust. In the past, the trustee was not permitted to invest in common stocks under the prudent man rule in some jurisdictions because common stocks involved much greater risk to the preservation of principal than debt securities. The rule we are discussing came about out of fear of the financial collapse of business enterprises. The danger to the preservation of principal arising from monetary inflation over a period of time was not a consideration historically. However, in recent decades it has become apparent that inflation is at least as great a threat to principal as the financial difficulties of business enterprises.

How does the trustee prevent the erosion of the value of the principal as a consequence of inflation? Debt securities, such as government and corporate bonds and bank certificates of deposit, return to the owner the same dollar amount that the issuer received on the original sale. A ten-year $10,000 government bond costs the purchaser $10,000 when she buys at its original issuance, and that is what she gets back ten years later. If the inflation rate during that period averages 5% per year, the value of the principal represented by that security has declined almost 40%. This is a severe loss of purchasing power.

If the trustee had invested the $10,000 in 200 shares of common stock selling at $50 per share at the time of purchase, instead of the $10,000 government bond, the dollar value of that stock ten years later may be the same or less or more, depending on circumstances. These circumstances are business conditions in general, the business conditions of the industry of which the corporation is a part, the business performance of this corporation, and the rate of inflation. The unpredictability of business conditions makes common stock a riskier investment than the bond in one sense. On the other hand, the corporation may be successful and increase its assets and profitability, thereby increasing the value of the stock. The common stock may also rise in value to reflect inflation; as the value of the dollar declines, the corporation's assets and profits should rise in dollar value if all other variables remain constant, which, of course, they never do. It is safe to say that the dollar value of common stock has the potential for keeping pace with or exceeding inflation, thereby preserving or increasing the value of the principal.

74. Steiner v. Hawaiian Trust Co., 47 Hawaii 548, 393 P.2d 96 (1964); Appeal of Dickinson, 152 Mass. 184, 25 N.E. 99 (1890); Baker Boyer Natl. Bank v. Garver, 43 Wash.App. 673, 719 P.2d 583 (1986).

The rate of interest on bonds and certificates of deposit is higher than the rate of dividend return on common stocks. If the interest rate on a high quality $1,000 bond is 8% per year ($80), the dividend on common stock of similar quality having a market value of $1,000 is probably about $40 (4%). Why should this be? If there is inflation, which appears to be a fact of economic life, the bond debtor makes payment at maturity in dollars that are worth less than the dollars it received when it sold the bond. Of course, there is no potential for capital growth in the bond. Responsiveness to inflation and capital growth are potentialities in the case of common stock. These considerations account for the willingness of owners of stock to accept a dividend return which is substantially lower than the interest on a debt security.

The holder of a bond realizes that the dollars she receives at maturity for the bond are going to be worth less than the dollars she paid for the bond when it was issued, because of inflation. The bond investor wants to maintain her principal value and receive a return on that. She attempts to accomplish this by providing for inflation in the interest rate she demands. The interest rate is calculated as projected inflation plus real return; 8% per year is viewed as 5% inflation per year plus 3% real interest return. This is why interest rates usually rise as inflation rises and decline as inflation declines. There are, of course, other factors which affect interest rates, such as the state of the economy and the demand for credit, and governmental fiscal policies.

For the individual investor, the debt security may protect against inflation by means of the interest rate. However, the debt security does not preserve the value of the principal of the trust because bond interest is payable to the income beneficiary. The income beneficiary is getting a large return at the expense of the remainderman who at a later time receives the principal eroded by inflation.

Trustees typically balance their portfolios between debt securities and common stocks. Debt securities are advantageous to the income beneficiary, and except for the erosive effect of inflation, are safer for the remainderman. Common stocks are less desirable for the income beneficiary, and more desirable for the remainderman because of their potential for responsiveness to inflation and for capital growth.

Is there a rule of law that trustees must invest in a manner that protects against the erosive effect of inflation upon principal? There is no such rule as yet, and that is probably sound because no one knows how that is to be done.[75] Common stocks have the

---

75. Restatement (Third) of Trusts § 227, comment e (1992) provides that there is a fiduciary duty to invest with a view to the protection of the purchasing power of the trust assets.

potential for it, and are likely to respond to moderate inflation, but very high inflation is so damaging to the economy that common stocks are likely to fall in value as a result of it. Gold has over history responded well to inflation, but its value tends to be very volatile over the short term, and it is not income-producing. This writer has never understood how gold is valued. It is suggested that the intellectually curious reader continue her pursuit of this question with a member of the economics faculty.

SECTION 7. MODERN PORTFOLIO THEORY

The prudent person rule for investments by trustees has come under attack in recent years as being out of step with contemporary economic learning on investment strategies which would permit greater freedom in the selection of investments by trustees. The prudent person rule requires that every investment be "safe," i.e., not "speculative." Any speculative investment is a breach of trust. Contemporary economic thinking, on the other hand, is concerned with the relationship of the individual investment to the entire investment portfolio. An individual speculative investment may contribute to diversification in a manner that makes the portfolio less, rather than more, volatile. If modern portfolio theory were adopted as the legal standard of prudence, the trustee would be in breach only if the portfolio viewed in its entirety contained risk that was imprudent under the circumstances. The following is a brief description of modern portfolio theory.[76]

All investments have an expected return which varies positively with risk. In this discussion return means total return, i.e., income and increase or decrease of principal. The baseline return is short-term U.S. government debt, which is viewed as riskless and provides the lowest return. Expected returns on other investments are greater in accordance with the degree of risk. Risk is the recognized possibility of performance below the expected return; the greater the potential negative departure from expected return, the greater the risk. The greater the risk, the greater the expected return must be in order to justify or compensate for the risk.

The discussion that follows is concerned with publicly traded common stocks, although the same rules with appropriate adjust-

---

76. The material in this Section appeared in Haskell, The Prudent Person Rule for Trustee Investment and Modern Portfolio Theory, 69 N.C.L.Rev. 87 (1990). For more extended discussions, see Malkiel, A Random Walk Down Wall Street 215–237 (5th ed. 1990); Bines, Modern Portfolio Theory and Investment Management Law: Refinement of Legal Doctrine, 76 Colum.L.Rev. 721 (1976); Langbein and Posner, Market Funds and Trust Investment Law, 1976 Am.B.Found.Res.J. 1; Langbein and Posner, Market Funds and Trust Investment Law: II, 1977 Am.B.Found.Res.J. 1.

ments are considered to be applicable to the entire range of investments. There are two types of risk for investments. One form of risk is that which affects the entire range of securities, such as general economic conditions. This is referred to as "systematic" or "market" risk. Almost all stocks are affected by this risk in the same way, albeit in different degrees. As the market as a whole rises, each stock tends to rise, some in the same degree, some more, some less; and as the market as a whole declines, each stock tends to decline, some in the same degree, some more, some less. Almost all stocks "covary positively" with respect to systematic risk.

The other form of risk is that which peculiarly affects a particular investment or industry, as climate affects an agriculturally related investment, as Japanese imports affect the American auto companies, and as the federal budget affects the aerospace industry. This risk is referred to as "specific," "unsystematic" or "residual" risk. A risk that affects one stock negatively may affect another stock positively, in which case the stocks are said to "covary negatively" with respect to that risk; if they are affected in the same way by the same risk, they "covary positively" with respect to that risk.

A fundamental principle of contemporary economic thinking is that the marketplace compensates the buyer for systematic risk but does not compensate the buyer for specific risk. Systematic risk is unavoidable; almost all stocks covary positively, albeit in different degrees, in relation to that risk. Expected return is the riskless rate (short-term U.S. government debt) plus a rate determined in accordance with the degree of systematic risk.

The marketplace does not compensate the buyer for specific (unsystematic) risk. This is because the investor can balance the specific risk to one stock with the purchase of another stock that is affected positively by the same factor which adversely affects the first stock. In other words, through diversification specific risk can be virtually eliminated. If the investor can avoid the effect of specific risk, there is no reason for the marketplace to compensate him for the risk. The expected return of a stock need not be adjusted upward (i.e., the price of the stock lowered) to reflect specific risk. The expected return is responsive therefore only to systematic risk, which is unavoidable.

If an investor purchases only one stock, she has an expected return that is equal to the riskless rate of return plus the rate of return attributable to the systematic risk of that stock, but the stock also bears its specific risk for which she receives no compensating return. The investor has an expected return which inadequately compensates for the total risk.

An investor holding a substantial portfolio which contains stocks which covary negatively with respect to specific risks has an expected return which adequately reflects the systematic risks of each, and the specific risks of each have substantially cancelled out. The larger the portfolio, the closer the specific risk factor of the portfolio can approach zero. The experts tell us that specific risk can be reduced to a low level with as few as twenty stocks appropriately chosen.

The measurement of systematic risk has been closely quantified. The stock market as a whole is deemed to have a so-called "beta" of 1. All stocks are given a systematic risk figure relating to that standard. A stock with a beta of 1 rises and falls to the same degree on average as the market as a whole. A stock with a beta of 1.5 rises and falls fifty percent more than the market as a whole; a stock with a beta of 2 rises and falls twice as much as the market as a whole; a stock with a beta of .5 rises and falls fifty percent less than the market as a whole, and so on.

Contemporary economic theory supports the position that the investor should maintain a broad portfolio in order to reduce specific risk to a low level. An effective method would be to invest in a so-called "index" or "market" fund which holds the Standard and Poor's 500 stocks, or even broader group of stocks, which substantially replicates the entire market. This investment strategy reduces specific risk to insignificance, and provides a systematic risk of beta 1. If a lower beta is desired, this broad market investment can be mixed with short-term U.S. government securities or other safe short-term debt securities. The riskless investment has the effect of lowering the volatility of the portfolio as a whole. If a higher beta is desired (greater risk in exchange for greater expected return), this can be done by buying more shares of the market fund with borrowed money.

The investor, of course, can establish a portfolio with a beta higher than the market simply by selecting stocks with an average beta greater than the market, or he can establish a portfolio with a beta lower than the market by selecting stocks with an average beta lower than the market. This type of portfolio, however, compromises the diversification that exists with the market fund.

It is apparent that contemporary economic thinking allows for the inclusion of stocks of a speculative nature in a portfolio that is conservatively invested. The speculative stock by definition has high specific risk, and is likely to have high systematic risk as well. It is part of a broad portfolio, however, which cancels the specific risk by diversification and which has a stock beta of 1. The portfolio also has, let us assume, short-term U.S. government securities which reduce the portfolio below the level of beta 1. This is a very conservative portfolio. The speculative stock, however, would be a breach of trust under the prudent person rule. Recent legislation in several states supplements the prudent person principle with language that provides that the trustee's investment decisions are to be judged on the basis of the portfolio as a whole. The language appears to incorporate modern portfolio theory into the prudent person rule to some degree.[77] Illinois recently legislated the principles of modern portfolio theory as expressed in the Restatement (Third) of Trusts described below.[78]

Most economic theorists conclude that the pricing of publicly traded stocks is reasonably efficient, i.e., the price of a stock at any time reflects most, if not all, of the information concerning that stock.[79] If this is accepted, then there is no point in trying to do better than the market as a whole by selecting stocks that are underpriced because there are none, and the cost of research that goes into the selection process is a waste of money. The only way to increase return is to increase risk. There is substantial empirical support for the proposition that institutional investors who are selective with respect to publicly traded stocks do not do any better than the market as a whole over the long term.

If the pricing is reasonably efficient, then a passive strategy of investing broadly in the market without selecting in or out is a prudent and conservative investment policy. This strategy could be implemented by means of a bank common trust fund or by means of investment in a so-called "market" or "index" investment fund. This form of investment by a trustee would be questionable under the prudent person rule because the fund would include "speculative" stocks which are unsuitable for trustee investment. The trust instrument, of course, could authorize such an investment strategy.

Restatement (Third) of Trusts section 227, adopted by the American Law Institute in May 1990, authorizes the trustee to employ modern portfolio theory. It reads, in part, as follows:

§ 227. General Standard of Prudent Investment

The trustee is under a duty to the beneficiaries to invest and manage the funds of the trust as a prudent

---

77. Cal.Prob.Code § 16040(d); Del. Code Ann. tit. 12, § 3302(c); Ga.Code Ann. § 53–8–2(c); Minn.Stat.Ann. § 501B.10; Tenn.Code Ann. § 35–3–117(b); Wash.Rev.Code Ann. § 11.100.-020.

78. Ill.Ann.Stat. ch. 17, § 1675.

79. Lorie, Dodd and Kimpton, The Stock Market: Theories and Evidence 55–77 (2d ed. 1985); Malkiel, A Random Walk Down Wall Street 169–176, 360 (5th ed. 1990); Elton and Gruber, Lessons of Modern Portfolio Theory 180, appearing as Appendix A in Longstreth, Modern Investment Management and the Prudent Man Rule (1986).

investor would, in light of the purposes, terms, distribution requirements and other circumstances of the trust.

(a) This standard requires the exercise of reasonable care, skill and caution, and is to be applied to investments not in isolation but in the context of the trust portfolio and as a part of an overall investment strategy, which should incorporate risk and return objectives reasonably suitable to the trust.

(b) In making and implementing investment decisions, the trustee has a duty to diversify the investments of the trust unless, under the circumstances, it is prudent not to do so.

The introduction, comments and reporter's notes to the section refer to the standard it establishes as the "prudent investor rule." The prudent investor rule radically changes the traditional prudent person rule in several respects.

The section explicitly states that the prudence of an investment is not to be judged in isolation but rather on the basis of its relationship to the portfolio as a whole. An investment which has high specific risk and is "speculative" under the prudent person standard may be permissible under the prudent investor standard if it contributes to diversification of the portfolio and the consequent reduction of total portfolio risk.

The traditional prudent person rule requires a conservative, low-risk investment policy, unless the terms of the trust broaden the trustee's investment powers. Although it is not made explicit in the text of the new section 227, it is clear from the comments to it that the prudent investor standard permits the trustee to adopt an investment strategy that contains more risk than is allowed by the prudent person standard without express authorization in the trust investment, if the objectives, liquidity requirements and risk tolerance of the trust make such a strategy reasonable. There is a recognition, however, that something akin to a presumption of conservatism in investment policy exists even under the prudent investor standard. In sum, the standard of risk and return is a matter of discretionary judgment for the trustee.

Adequate diversification to minimize specific, uncompensated risk is stated to be fundamental under the prudent investor standard, although departure from it may be permissible in special circumstances. The level of suitable risk, therefore, is generally a function of systematic risk.

It should be emphasized that the adoption of portfolio theory is a separate matter from the adoption of a flexible approach to risk-return objectives for trustees. That is to say, the Restatement could have adopted portfolio theory without granting the trustee authority to invest at relatively high levels of risk.

At the same time that Restatement (Third) of Trusts section 227 was adopted, other provisions were adopted including a new section 228 which requires that the trustee conform to the terms of the trust instrument and of course any statute which are not consistent with the prudent investor rule.

SECTION 8. PRINCIPAL AND INCOME

In most trusts the dispositive provisions are stated in terms of income and principal. Consequently it is essential that funds received by the trustee be allocated to the principal account or the income account, and that expenses be allocated to one account or the other. We shall deal first with the allocation of receipts.

Assets delivered in trust by the settlor of a living trust are principal. Assets owned by the testator at the date of death allocable to a testamentary trust are principal. Any gain realized on the sale of principal is principal. If land is held in trust, the net rents are income. If corporate stock is held in trust, the ordinary cash dividends are income. If bonds, debentures, notes, certificates of deposit, or savings accounts are held in trust, the interest received is income.

There is a problem, however, if that which is ordinarily income relates to a period immediately prior to the creation of the living trust, or, in the case of the testamentary trust, the testator's death. Suppose settlor creates a living trust on May 15 consisting of land, bonds and common stock. The rents from the land are payable on the last day of each month for that month. On May 31 the trustee receives the $1,000 rent for May. Approximately half the rent was attributable to the period in May prior to the creation of the trust. That portion appears to have been, in effect, delivered in trust as principal. But that is not the way the common law treated it. At common law, rent did not accrue.[80] That means that it is allocable wholly to principal or wholly to income in accordance with the date on which it was payable. The $1,000 is income because it was payable after the trust was created. By statute in many jurisdictions, however, rent accrues,[81] as described in the next paragraph.

---

80. Rogoski v. McLaughlin, 228 Ark. 1157, 312 S.W.2d 912 (1958); Greene v. Huntington, 73 Conn. 106, 46 A. 883 (1900).

81. Uniform Principal and Income Act § 4; Revised Uniform Principal and Income Act § 4. The Uniform Principal and Income Act is in effect in about 10 states, frequently with modifications.

About 30 states have legislated the Revised Uniform Principal and Income Act, frequently with modifications.

The Uniform Management of Institutional Funds Act allows charitable institutions such as colleges and hospitals, to expend endowment appreciation for operating purposes despite a provision in

Bond interest accrues. Let us assume that a $1,000 bond delivered in trust on May 15 pays 6% annual interest, one-half on February 15 and one-half on August 15. On August 15 the trustee receives the semi-annual interest payment. Is the entire payment allocable to income? It is not. One half is allocable to income and one-half is allocable to principal. The portion attributable to the period from February 15 to May 15 is deemed to have been delivered in trust as principal. The portion attributable to the period following the creation of the trust is allocable to income.[82] Interest on notes, debentures, certificates of deposit and savings accounts accrue in the same manner.

Dividends on corporate stock do not accrue. Suppose 1,000 shares of ABC Corporation common stock was delivered in trust on May 15. On May 1 the board of directors of the corporation declared a dividend of one dollar per share, payable on June 15 to stockholders of record on May 25. The dividend belongs entirely to the trust, and it is wholly allocable to income. Dividends are allocated in accordance with the "stockholder of record" date, regardless of when they are declared or payable. If the dividend was declared on May 1 to stockholders of record on May 14, payable on June 15, the dividend would be paid directly to the settlor because he was the stockholder of record on May 14. If there is no "stockholder of record" date, then the determinative date for these purposes is the date on which the dividend was declared.[83]

The same issue is presented when an income payment is received which relates in part to the period after the death of a life income beneficiary and in part to the period prior thereto. Suppose the life income beneficiary in our previous example dies exactly five years later on May 15, and the remainderman then becomes entitled to the principal. The same assets were held in trust at the life income beneficiary's death, and the same rent, interest and dividend payments were made on the same dates except five years later. Rent payable on May 31 would belong wholly to the remainderman at common law because there is no accrual; under statutes providing for accrual, however, the rent would belong one-half to the life income beneficiary's estate and one-half to the remainderman. The bond interest payment on August 15 would belong one-

the donative instrument limiting disbursements to income. The Act has been enacted in more than half the states.

82. Bridgeport Trust Co. v. Marsh, 87 Conn. 384, 87 A. 865 (1913); Moore v. Downey, 83 N.J.Eq. 428, 91 A. 116 (1914); Horlick v. Sidley, 241 Wis. 81, 3 N.W.2d 710 (1942); Uniform Principal and Income Act § 4; but see Revised Uniform Principal and Income Act § 4.

83. Union Safe Deposit & Trust Co. v. Dudley, 104 Me. 297, 72 A. 166 (1908); In re Northern Cent. Ry. Dividend Cases, 126 Md. 16, 94 A. 338 (1915); Hayward v. Blake, 247 Mass. 430, 142 N.E. 52 (1924); In re Postley's Will, 251 App.Div. 469, 296 N.Y.S. 627 (1937); Uniform Principal and Income Act § 5; Revised Uniform Principal and Income Act § 4.

half to the estate of the income beneficiary and one-half to the remainderman, because bond interest accrues. The dividend payable to stockholders of record on May 25 would belong wholly to the remainderman; a dividend payable to the stockholder of record on May 14, however, would belong wholly to the estate of the income beneficiary. The allocations parallel those which are made at the creation of the trust.[84]

Another problem area has to do with the allocation of income which is received by the executor during the administration of the estate and prior to the distribution to the testamentary trust or trusts. As we have discussed previously,[85] there are three types of testamentary trusts, the specific bequest or devise in trust, the general bequest in trust, and the residuary bequest and devise in trust. If the testator specifically bequeaths 5,000 shares of ABC Corporation common stock in trust, the executor retains the shares during administration and is likely to receive dividends on the shares during the period of administration. Although the trust does not come into existence until the distribution to the trustee, for principal and income purposes the trust is treated as if it came into existence at the date of the testator's death. The dividends received on the shares during administration are distributable to the trustee together with the stock and are payable as income to the income beneficiary.[86] This parallels the treatment of income received during administration on specifically bequeathed property that is not in trust; the specific legatee is entitled to the income earned on the asset during administration.

If the testator makes a general bequest in trust of $200,000, the trust does not come into existence until distribution to the trustee, but for principal and income purposes the trust is treated as if it came into existence at the date of the testator's death. When the executor of the estate distributes the principal to the trustee, he also distributes income which is deemed to have been earned by the $200,000 during the administration of the estate.[87] The principal of the trust is not designated in the will as specific property and is not precisely identifiable during estate administration, and so there is no income that is precisely attributable to the $200,000 that is ultimately transferred to the trustee by the execu-

84. Uniform Principal and Income Act § 4; Revised Uniform Principal and Income Act § 4.

85. See p. 95 above.

86. Bridgeport Trust Co. v. Fowler, 102 Conn. 318, 128 A. 719 (1925); In re Will of DeReu, 293 Minn. 132, 197 N.W.2d 229 (1972); Dennison v. Lilley, 83 N.H. 422, 144 A. 523 (1928); Uniform Principal and Income Act § 3–A; Revised Uniform Principal and Income Act § 5. See Hurt v. Smith 744 S.W.2d 1 (Tex.1987).

87. First Nat. Bank & Trust Co. v. Baker, 124 Conn. 577, 1 A.2d 283 (1938); In re Jackson's Estate, 318 Pa. 256, 178 A. 384 (1935); Uniform Principal and Income Act § 3–A; Revised Uniform Principal and Income Act § 5.

tor. There is allocated, therefore, to the income beneficiary that proportion of the income received on the entire estate, except for specific bequests and devises, that $200,000 bears to such portion of the estate. This is different from the treatment of the $200,000 bequest that is not in trust. The legatee of $200,000 is usually not entitled to interest on the bequest from the date of the testator's death, but in some jurisdictions he is entitled to interest on the bequest at the so-called legal rate after some period of time following the testator's death, such as one year.

If the testator creates a residuary trust, for income purposes the trust is treated as if it came into existence at the testator's death. The executor distributes the residue of the estate to the trustee, including the income earned on the estate other than that which is allocated to specific and general bequests. The income is payable by the trustee to the residuary trust income beneficiary.[88] This parallels the treatment of the residuary bequest which is not in trust, where the legatee receives all that is not otherwise distributed including income received during administration.

We have stated previously that ordinary cash dividends are income. Cash dividends, however, which are in partial or total liquidation of the assets of the corporation are usually allocated to principal.[89] There is authority, however, that liquidating cash dividends are to be apportioned between principal and income on the basis of the source of the distribution; that is to say, to the extent that the distribution appears to have been paid out of earnings accrued since the creation of the trust, the distribution is allocated to income, and the rest is allocated to principal.[90] In most states, stock dividends are always principal,[91] but there is limited authority that they are apportioned between principal and income in accordance with the source of the earnings capitalized in connection with the issuance of the stock dividend.[92] Capital gains dividends of investment companies are principal.[93]

88. In re Estate of Huber, 31 Cal. App.3d 126, 107 Cal.Rptr. 89 (1973); Wachovia Bank & Trust Co. v. Grubb, 233 N.C. 22, 62 S.E.2d 719 (1950); Uniform Principal and Income Act § 3–A; Revised Uniform Principal and Income Act § 5.

89. Revised Uniform Principal and Income Act § 6; Uniform Principal and Income Act § 5.

90. See 3A Scott, Law of Trusts § 236.10 (4th ed., Fratcher, 1988).

91. First Nat. Bank of Tuskaloosa v. Hill, 241 Ala. 606, 4 So.2d 170 (1941);

Powell v. Madison Safe Deposit & Trust Co., 208 Ind. 432, 196 N.E. 324 (1935); Flynn v. Brownell, 371 Mich. 19, 123 N.W.2d 153 (1963); Uniform Principal and Income Act § 5; Revised Uniform Principal and Income Act § 6.

92. See 3A Scott, Law of Trusts § 236.3 (4th ed., Fratcher, 1988).

93. Tait v. Peck, 346 Mass. 521, 194 N.E.2d 707 (1963); In re LaTour's Estate, 110 N.H. 50, 260 A.2d 123 (1969); In re Estate of Rosenbloom, 306 Pa.Super. 131, 452 A.2d 249 (1982); Revised Uniform Principal and Income Act § 6.

Wasting assets also present a principal and income issue. Copyrights and patents are wasting assets because of their limited life. When the period of the copyright or patent expires, there no longer is any value. Copyrights and patents constitute monopolies for a period of time, and during such period revenue is derived because of the monopoly. The copyright or the patent when it is received in trust is principal, and in order to prevent the wasting of that principal, a portion of the revenue received on account of the monopoly during its life should be allocated to principal to maintain its value. The copyright or the patent has a market value at the time it is received in trust, and it is this value which the law attempts to maintain out of the revenues; the income beneficiary is entitled to a reasonable return on that amount which also comes out of the revenues. In other words, the revenues should be allocated in a manner which would produce substantially the same result as if the copyright or patent were immediately sold by the trustee upon receiving it and the proceeds invested in a nonwasting asset such as a bond. Accordingly, from the revenues of the monopoly as received from time to time, an allocation is made between principal and income which provides for a reasonable rate of return, such as 5% per annum, on the market value of the copyright or patent at the time of the creation of the trust.[94]

Mining land is, of course, a wasting asset also. The common law concerning the allocation of revenues between principal and income for trust purposes is rather surprising. If prior to the creation of the trust, a mine or mines were opened, the revenues from such mine or mines during the period of the trust are entirely allocable to income.[95] Revenues derived from mines opened during the period of the trust by the trustee are entirely allocable to principal;[96] the income earned on the revenues derived from the newly opened mines, however, is allocable to the income account. This follows the law of waste as between legal life tenants and remaindermen of mining property, which provides that the life tenant is entitled to exploit previously opened mines for his own benefit, but is forbidden to open any new mines. The Revised Uniform Principal and Income Act § 9 provides for an apportionment between income and principal of the revenues of mining

94. Union County Trust Co. v. Gray, 110 N.J.Eq. 270, 159 A. 625 (1932); In re Estate of Pryor, 51 Misc.2d 993, 274 N.Y.S.2d 427 (Sur.Ct.1966); Revised Uniform Principal and Income Act § 11. But see Uniform Principal and Income Act § 10. See also Donohue Estate, 41 Pa.D. & C.2d 133 (Orph.1966).

95. See Millikin Trust Co. v. Jarvis, 34 Ill.App.2d 180, 180 N.E.2d 759 (1962); McGill v. Johnson, 775 S.W.2d 826 (Tex.App.1989), reversed in part 799 S.W.2d 826 (Tex.1990).

96. Mitchell v. Mitchell, 151 Tex. 1, 244 S.W.2d 803 (1951); Mairs v. Cent.

property in certain circumstances.[97]

There is also the issue as to whether there should be an allocation to principal from the rents derived from buildings held in trust on account of depreciation. A building is a wasting asset although it usually "wastes" much more gradually than the mining property or the patent. There is authority that with respect to buildings which form a part of the original trust estate, the trustee is not required to allocate a fraction of the rents to a depreciation account for the benefit of the principal beneficiaries.[98] If, however, the trustee purchases a building for the trust, there should be a provision for depreciation out of the rents.[99] The Revised Uniform Principal and Income Act § 13 appears to provide for an allocation to principal out of rental income on account of depreciation, regardless of whether the building was part of the original trust estate or was purchased by the trustee.[1]

A bond purchased by the trustee at a premium, that is, at a price in excess of its face value, such as $1100 for a $1000 bond, is a form of wasting asset because the debtor will pay only $1000 to the holder at maturity. The price is $1100 because the interest paid on the bond is higher than the current interest rate in the market for the same quality of security. The value returns to $1000, however, on maturity. The income return calculated on the premium price will be slightly higher than the money market calls for to compensate for the inevitable decline of the value of the bond to $1000 at maturity. In effect, the income beneficiary benefits at the expense of the principal beneficiary. With respect to bonds purchased by the trustee at a premium, there is authority that the trustee should allocate a small fraction of the interest received to the principal account to compensate for the wasting nature of the bond,[2] but there are statutes to the contrary.[3] If a bond was part of the original trust estate and had a value above its face value at the establishment of the trust, there is authority that the trustee is not

Trust Co., 127 W.Va. 795, 34 S.E.2d 742 (1945).

97. See also Uniform Principal and Income Act § 9, which does not provide for apportionment.

98. New England Merchants National Bank v. Koufman, 363 Mass. 454, 295 N.E.2d 388 (1973); In re Roth's Estate, 139 N.J.Eq. 588, 52 A.2d 811 (1947); Matter of Will of Diamond, 137 Misc.2d 43, 519 N.Y.S.2d 788 (Sur.Ct.1987); Chapin v. Collard, 29 Wash.2d 788, 189 P.2d 642 (1948).

99. Harris Trust & Savings Bank v. MacLeod, 4 Ill.App.3d 542, 281 N.E.2d 457 (1972); Thaxter v. Fry, 222 A.2d 686 (Me.1966); In re Trust by Warner,

263 Minn. 449, 117 N.W.2d 224 (1962). Contra: Moore v. Cavett, 368 P.2d 224 (Okl.1961).

1. See Uniform Principal and Income Act § 12.

2. In re Gartenlaub's Estate, 185 Cal. 648, 198 P. 209 (1921); Old Colony Trust Co. v. Comstock, 290 Mass. 377, 195 N.E. 389 (1935); Mercantile-Commerce Bank & Trust Co. v. Morse, 356 Mo. 336, 201 S.W.2d 915 (1947); In re Wells' Estate, 156 Wis. 294, 144 N.W. 174 (1913).

3. Uniform Principal and Income Act § 6; Revised Uniform Principal and Income Act § 7.

to make any allocation to the principal account out of the interest received.[4]

It should be emphasized that the rules concerning principal and income we have been discussing are all subject to the terms of the trust instrument which may define principal and income differently in one or more respects. For instance, the trust instrument may provide that stock dividends are to be considered income for purposes of the trust, or that bond interest payments payable after the death of the life income beneficiary shall belong to the remainderman regardless of any accrual prior to the death.

Now a few words about the allocation of trust expenses to the principal and income accounts. Interest on mortgage debt, income taxes on ordinary income, and where real estate is held in trust, repairs, insurance and land taxes, are usually charged to income. Payments on the principal of mortgage debt, taxes on capital gains, capital improvements on real estate, and expenses incurred in the acquisition and sale of investments are usually charged to principal. Trustees' fees, expenses of accountings, and expenses of litigation are often split between principal and income.[5] The trust instrument is, of course, controlling if it provides for the charging of a particular expense to income or principal contrary to the rules of law which are otherwise applicable.

SECTION 9. POWERS OF THE TRUSTEE

We have discussed the duties of the trustee. Duties are what the trustee must do or must not do. Powers are what the trustee is permitted to do within the limits of his duties. A duty is mandatory, but a power is not. The trustee has the duty to make the trust property productive, i.e., to invest, and the trustee has many proper investments from which he may choose. The trustee has the power to invest in all of them, but obviously he will exercise the power only with respect to relatively few. The trustee cannot have a power that is in violation of a duty;[6] the trustee has a duty not to

4. Higgins v. Beck, 116 Me. 127, 100 A. 553 (1917); Boston Safe Deposit & Trust Co. v. Williams, 290 Mass. 385, 195 N.E. 393 (1935); In re Kilmer's Will, 18 Misc.2d 60, 186 N.Y.S.2d 120 (Sur.Ct.1959).

5. See Uniform Principal and Income Act § 12; Revised Uniform Principal and Income Act § 13; 3 Scott, Law of Trusts §§ 233.2, 233.3 (3d ed. 1967). The statutes cited in this note also provide for apportioning between income and principal regularly recurring expenses normally payable out of income

whenever the expense covers a period which in part is prior to and in part is subsequent to the beginning of the trust, or in part is prior to and in part is subsequent to the termination of an income interest.

6. It is true that a trustee has the "power" to transfer good title to trust property to a bona fide purchaser, although the transfer constitutes a breach of trust by the trustee, as discussed in Section 11 of this chapter. This is a different use of the term "power" from its use in this section.

invest speculatively, and consequently he has no power to invest speculatively. The trustee has the duty to take control of trust assets, including the collection of claims held in trust. The trustee has the power to sue on the claim, or to enter into a settlement of the claim if that seems the better course of action for the trust. The trustee has the duty to act from proper motives in deciding whether or not to make a discretionary payment of principal to an income beneficiary. The trustee has the power to make the principal payment, as well as the power not to make the payment, as long as he complies with his duty.

Duties are imposed by law, but they can be modified by provisions of the trust instrument. On the other hand, at common law powers had to be found in the trust instrument, expressly or by implication, or they did not exist. In most jurisdictions today, however, there is legislation which provides that trustees have certain specified powers.[7] Such legislation, of course, is subject to contrary provisions in the trust instrument. Also, courts find powers to be implied in the trust instrument if they are useful to the administration of the trust. Consequently the difference between the source of duties and the source of powers is largely conceptual without much practical significance.

We have mentioned the powers which a trustee normally has in connection with the performance of his investment function, as well as the power to delegate certain functions in the administration of the trust, to make or not to make certain discretionary payments, to compromise claims, and the like. The trust instrument frequently will contain a detailed list of trustee powers. If it does not, most of the powers which are necessary to the conservative management of property will be deemed to be implied.

There are, however, certain commonplace business actions which the courts have held not to be among the powers possessed by a trustee. Except for government bonds and corporate debentures, the trustee is not empowered to lend on an unsecured basis. Accordingly, there is authority that the trustee is not empowered to sell on credit.[8] The trustee does have the power, however, to sell on credit if it is secured by a purchase money first mortgage and

---

7. E.g., power to sell—La.Rev.Stat. Ann. § 9:2119; Mass.Gen.Laws Ann. c. 203, § 19; N.Y. Est. Powers & Trusts Law § 11–1.1; power to grant options—Ill.Ann.Stat. ch. 17, § 1655; N.Y. Est. Powers & Trusts Law § 11–1.1; power to sell on credit—R.I.Gen.Laws § 18–4–2; Wash.Rev.Code Ann. § 11.98.070; power to mortgage—Minn.Stat.Ann. § 501B.81; Wis.Stat.Ann. § 701.19; power to lease beyond term of trust—N.Y. Est. Powers & Trusts Law § 11–

1.1. Many states have broad trustees' powers legislation, e.g., Illinois, Minnesota, New York, Texas, Washington, and the states which have legislated the Uniform Trustees' Powers Act.

8. Durkin v. Connelly, 84 N.J.Eq. 66, 92 A. 906 (1914); In re Estate of Gould, 17 A.D.2d 401, 234 N.Y.S.2d 825 (1962). See statutes cited in note 3 above, and Uniform Trustees' Powers Act § 3(c)(7), which grant this power.

the security is adequate. Lending on an unsecured basis is considered to be too risky. The trustee is usually not empowered to borrow money or mortgage trust property.[9] The trustee is not empowered to give an option for the purchase of trust property.[10] These limitations reflect the conservatism that is associated with trust administration. Needless to say, the trust instrument controls if it empowers the trustee to lend unsecured, borrow, or grant options. Also, as we have indicated, there are statutes in some jurisdictions which authorize the trustee to borrow, mortgage trust property, and grant options. The Uniform Trustees' Powers Act grants the trustee the power to do all things in the management of the trust that a person of ordinary prudence and judgment would do, and, without limiting the "prudent person" powers as a generality, the Act specifies a number of powers which a trustee shall have, including the power to grant options, borrow money, sell on credit, mortgage trust property, and to engage in considerable self-dealing and delegation of fiduciary functions.[11]

SECTION 10.　LIABILITY OF TRUSTEE TO BENEFICIARIES

The trustee is not an insurer against loss to the trust estate. The trustee is liable to the beneficiaries for loss to the trust estate only if the loss is related to a breach of trust. The trustee commits a breach of trust when he violates one of his duties. The breach may consist of a violation of the pervasive duty to exercise due care, such as the failure to carry casualty insurance on a building held in trust. Or it may consist of a breach of a duty which involves no failure to exercise care, such as the unauthorized purchase of property for the trust from the trustee individually at market value, which property would be a proper investment if purchased from another party. Or it may involve profiting at the expense of the trust, such as the purchase by the trustee individually of trust assets at a price which is below market value. Although there are several beneficiaries, any one of them may bring an action to correct for the breach even though the interests of others may be thereby benefited or protected.

9. Postal v. Home State Bank for Savings, 284 Mich. 220, 279 N.W. 488 (1938); King v. Pelkofski, 24 A.D.2d 1003, 266 N.Y.S.2d 61 (1965), appeal dism'd 18 N.Y.2d 688, 273 N.Y.S.2d 438, 219 N.E.2d 884 (1966), aff'd and modified 20 N.Y.2d 326, 282 N.Y.S.2d 753, 229 N.E.2d 435 (1967); Wilkerson v. Everett, 32 Tenn.App. 11, 221 S.W.2d 537 (1948). See statutes cited in note 3 above, and Uniform Trustees' Powers Act § 3(c)(7) and (18), which grant these powers.

10. Equitable Trust Co. v. Delaware Trust Co., 30 Del.Ch. 118, 54 A.2d 733 (1947); Phillips v. Sexton, 243 Ga. 501, 255 S.E.2d 15 (1979); Moore v. Trainer, 252 Pa. 367, 97 A. 462 (1916). See statutes cited in note 3 above, and Uniform Trustees' Powers Act § 3(c)(12), which grant this power.

11. The Uniform Trustees' Powers Act has been legislated in about fifteen states.

A trustee is not liable for a breach of trust to a beneficiary who has given his consent to it, provided the consenting beneficiary was sui juris and informed of all relevant facts and considerations and of his legal rights.[12] In sum, the consent is effective if it was in all respects fairly obtained. The consent is a transaction between the trustee and the beneficiary and such dealings are closely scrutinized by the courts for fairness. If all the beneficiaries consent to the conduct that would constitute a breach of trust, and if all consents were properly obtained, the trustee is free of any liability. If, however, one beneficiary has consented and another has not, the trustee is not liable to the consenting beneficiary but he is liable to the non-consenting beneficiary for any loss to him. For instance, the life income beneficiary gives his consent to an improper trust investment, but the principal remainderman does not give his consent, and the investment declines in value. The remainderman can compel the trustee to dispose of the investment and restore, from the trustee's personal pocket, the loss to the trust, which constitutes principal, but the life income beneficiary is not entitled to the income from that principal because he consented to the improper investment. The trustee is entitled to the income from what he has restored to the trust during the life of the life beneficiary. If, on the other hand, the principal remainderman consented but the life income beneficiary did not, the trustee would have to restore the loss to the trust, but in this case the life beneficiary would be entitled to the income on what was restored and the trustee would be allowed to withdraw for himself the restored principal at the death of the life beneficiary.[13]

If a beneficiary is dilatory in bringing suit after having obtained knowledge of a breach of trust, the action may be barred by the equitable doctrine of laches.[14] Some states also have statutes of limitations for actions against trustees,[15] but an action may be barred by laches prior to the time the statute of limitations has run.[16] The statute of limitations does not run until the beneficiary has knowledge of the breach or reason to know of it,[17] and, of

12. Heller v. First National Bank of Denver, 657 P.2d 992 (Colo.App.1982); Lambos v. Lambos, 9 Ill.App.3d 530, 292 N.E.2d 587 (1972); Reynolds v. Remick, 333 Mass. 1, 127 N.E.2d 653 (1955); Matter of Estate of Lange, 75 N.J. 464, 383 A.2d 1130 (1978).

13. In re Davenport's Will, 104 N.Y.S.2d 433 (Sur.Ct.1951); Steel's Estate, 32 Pa.D. & C. 55 (Orph.1938).

14. Harvey v. Leonard, 268 N.W.2d 504 (Iowa 1978); McKenney v. McKenney, 214 Md. 397, 135 A.2d 423 (1957); Stevens v. National City Bank, 45 Ohio

St.3d 276, 544 N.E.2d 612 (1989); Murphy v. Emery, 629 S.W.2d 895 (Tenn. 1981); In re Pettee's Will, 266 Wis. 347, 63 N.W.2d 715 (1954).

15. E.g., Ind.Code Ann. § 30–4–6–12; Minn.Stat.Ann. § 541.05(7); Miss. Code Ann. § 15–1–39.

16. McClintock, Handbook of the Principles of Equity § 28 (2d ed. 1948).

17. Jennings v. Jennings, 211 Kan. 515, 507 P.2d 241 (1973); St. Louis Union Trust Co. v. Hunt, 169 S.W.2d 433 (Mo.App.1943); O'Hayer v. De St. Au-

course, laches does not apply unless there has been disclosure of the breach to the beneficiaries.[18] After the breach of trust is committed, such as an improper investment, a beneficiary may express approval of the action. This may constitute an affirmance, i.e., a consent after the fact, and preclude suit by the beneficiary.

It has been held that the trustee is not exculpated from liability for breach of trust because he has relied on erroneous advice from an attorney with respect to the nature of his duties and powers; [19] the trustee is out of luck if his lawyer tells him that a certain stock dividend should be distributed as income when the law provides that it is principal, or that he may sell his property to the trust and it declines in value. There is contrary authority, however, that reliance on advice of counsel on an abstruse legal question affords a defense to an action for breach of trust.[20]

Trust instruments sometimes contain clauses which purport to exculpate the trustee from liability arising out of the administration of the trust. Such clauses may not have the intended effect. A trustee cannot be exculpated from liability for profiting personally at the expense of the trust, such as selling trust property to himself individually for less than its value, even if it is done innocently. In addition, a trustee cannot be exculpated from liability for willful misconduct or gross negligence in the performance of his function. It is contrary to public policy for a trustee to act in this fashion and not be accountable. It is permissible, however, for a trustee to be exculpated from liability for conduct which is less blameworthy, such as ordinary negligence.[21]

The trustee may force the resolution of the issue of his liability for the management of the trust property by an action for the settlement of his accounts to which all beneficiaries are made parties. In this proceeding the trustee presents his account which sets forth what was held at the commencement of the period which

bin, 30 A.D.2d 419, 293 N.Y.S.2d 147 (1968); Condon v. Bank of California, N.A., 92 Or.App. 691, 759 P.2d 1137 (1988); Oak Cliff Bank & Trust Co. v. Steenbergen, 497 S.W.2d 489 (Tex.Civ. App.1973).

18. Harvey v. Leonard, 268 N.W.2d 504 (Iowa 1978); Sloan v. Silberstein, 2 Mich.App. 660, 141 N.W.2d 332 (1966); Murphy v. Emery, 629 S.W.2d 895 (Tenn.1981); Acott v. Tomlinson, 9 Utah 2d 71, 337 P.2d 720 (1959); Skok v. Snyder, 46 Wash.App. 836, 733 P.2d 547 (1987).

19. In re Macky's Estate, 73 Colo. 1, 213 P. 131 (1922); In re Skinner's Estate, 215 Iowa 1021, 247 N.W. 484 (1933); Matter of Rothko, 43 N.Y.2d

305, 401 N.Y.S.2d 449, 372 N.E.2d 291 (1977); Lohm Estate, 440 Pa. 268, 269 A.2d 451 (1970).

20. Richards v. Midkiff, 48 Hawaii 32, 396 P.2d 49 (1964); In re Kohler's Estate, 348 Pa. 55, 33 A.2d 920 (1943). See 3 Scott, Law of Trusts § 201 (3d ed. 1967).

21. Perling v. Citizens and Southern National Bank, 250 Ga. 674, 300 S.E.2d 649 (1983); Axelrod v. Giambalvo, 129 Ill.App.3d 512, 84 Ill.Dec. 703, 472 N.E.2d 840 (1984); Sullivan v. Mosner, 266 Md. 479, 295 A.2d 482 (1972); Boston Safe Deposit and Trust v. Boone, 21 Mass.App. 637, 489 N.E.2d 209 (1986); Jarvis v. Boatmen's Nat. Bank, 478 S.W.2d 266 (Mo.1972).

the account covers, all receipts and transactions for the period, and what is held at the end of the period. The account may be a final account, i.e., one for a period ending at the termination of the trust, or an intermediate account, i.e., one for a period ending prior to the termination of the trust. Frequently the trustee chooses to bring several intermediate accounting proceedings, as well as a final accounting proceeding, during the course of the trust. If there are minor or unborn beneficiaries, the court appoints a guardian ad litem to represent them in accounting proceedings. If the beneficiaries make no objection to the account, or if they do and it is resolved in favor of the trustee by the court, the judgment approving the account is res judicata with respect to all matters disclosed in the account.[22] With respect to matters not disclosed in the account, or misrepresented in the account, the judgment has no effect. As we have indicated elsewhere, the beneficiary is entitled to information from time to time from the trustee concerning the trust upon request, and can compel the trustee to submit a formal account to him at reasonable intervals; also, in many states the trustee is required to submit an account to the court at regular intervals, such as every year or two or three years, but these frequently may be ex parte submissions.[23]

Trusts frequently have two trustees, and occasionally more. In the case of private trusts, all significant action must be taken by all trustees, unless the trust instrument provides otherwise. Trustee action must be unanimous.[24] Trustees of charitable trusts, however, may act by majority decision. It is a breach of trust for one trustee to delegate the performance of trust duties to the other trustee or trustees.[25]

If one trustee commits a breach of trust, the other trustee is not per se liable for the breach. However, if a trustee delegates the performance of a trust function to the other trustee who commits a breach of trust in the course of performing the delegated function, the first trustee is liable for the loss. For instance, if one trustee

---

22. Fraser v. Southeast First Bank of Jacksonville, 417 So.2d 707 (Fla.Dist. Ct.App.1982); In re Peck's Estate, 323 Mich. 11, 34 N.W.2d 533 (1948); In re Shea's Will, 309 N.Y. 605, 132 N.E.2d 864 (1956); Matter of George Massad Trust, 277 N.W.2d 269 (N.D.1979); In re Estate of Sharp, 63 Wis.2d 254, 217 N.W.2d 258 (1974).

23. Uniform Probate Code §§ 7-303 and 7-307 provide for the submission of accounts on request of beneficiaries, and the barring of claims six months after the submission of a final account to the beneficiaries, without judicial proceedings.

24. In re Will of Spilka, 250 Iowa 1021, 97 N.W.2d 625 (1959); Sokol v. Nattans, 23 Md.App. 600, 329 A.2d 115 (1974); Nichols v. Pospiech, 289 Mich. 324, 286 N.W. 633 (1939); Scullin v. Clark, 242 S.W.2d 542 (Mo.1951). Uniform Trustees' Powers Act § 6 provides that a majority of trustees may act.

25. Caldwell v. Graham, 115 Md. 122, 80 A. 839 (1911); Brown v. Phelan, 223 App.Div. 393, 228 N.Y.S. 466 (1928); In re Trust by Mueller, 28 Wis.2d 26, 135 N.W.2d 854 (1965).

delegates the investment function to the other trustee without any authorization to do so in the trust instrument, and the second trustee makes an improper investment, the delegating trustee is liable for any loss.[26]

Each co-trustee is required to keep an eye on the other. If one trustee commits a breach of trust which could have been prevented if the other trustee had been exercising reasonable care over the management of the trust, the second trustee is liable for the resulting loss as well.[27] Also, if one co-trustee commits a breach of trust, the other trustee has a duty to do what is necessary to compel the breaching trustee to restore any loss to the trust, including bringing suit.[28] Sometimes the trust instrument provides that one of two trustees shall have exclusive authority with respect to one aspect of trust administration, such as investments. Such a provision is effective. However, if the other trustee knows or has reason to know that the trust assets are being improperly invested, he has the duty to take action to correct the situation, including bringing suit.[29]

The trust instrument sometimes provides that the trustee is to invest in accordance with the directions of a person possessing investment skill who is not a trustee or otherwise connected with the trust. Such a provision is effective. It is an authorization or direction to delegate the investment function. However, the trustee cannot act on directions to invest in assets which he has reason to believe are not proper trust investments.[30] This is because the trustee must oversee all actions of those to whom trustee functions are properly delegated, as discussed in Section 1 of this chapter. This can, of course, place the trustee in a most difficult position, and the trustee may be required to petition the court for instructions in case there is doubt about the legality of a directed investment, or if the directions are consistently improper. In this situation, although the person with the investment authority is not a trustee, he is still considered to have a duty to exercise his power properly and may be liable to the beneficiaries, together with the

26. Ashley v. Winkley, 209 Mass. 509, 95 N.E. 932 (1911); Walker v. James, 337 Mo. 750, 85 S.W.2d 876 (1935); Matter of Newhoff's Will, 107 Misc.2d 589, 435 N.Y.S.2d 632 (1980), aff'd 107 A.D.2d 417, 486 N.Y.S.2d 956 (1985).

27. Shriners Hospitals v. Robbins, 450 So.2d 798 (Ala.1984); Klatt v. Keuthan, 185 Mo.App. 306, 170 S.W. 374 (1914); In re Koretzky's Estate, 8 N.J. 506, 86 A.2d 238 (1951); In re Adams' Estate, 221 Pa. 77, 70 A. 436 (1908).

28. In re Estate of Hensel, 144 Cal. App.2d 429, 301 P.2d 105 (1956); Richards v. Midkiff, 48 Hawaii 32, 396 P.2d 49 (1964); Harvey v. Leonard, 268 N.W.2d 504 (Iowa 1978).

29. See 2A Scott, Law of Trusts § 185 (4th ed., Fratcher, 1987).

30. Steiner v. Hawaiian Trust Co., 47 Hawaii 548, 393 P.2d 96 (1964); Matter of Will of Rubin, 143 Misc.2d 303, 540 N.Y.S.2d 944 (Sur.Ct.1989). See 2A Scott, Law of Trusts § 185 (4th ed., Fratcher, 1987).

trustee, for highly speculative or otherwise improper trust investments.[31]

On occasion the settlor of a living trust will reserve the power to direct the trustee concerning investments. If the trust is revocable, it seems that the settlor should have no duty of care concerning investments, and the trustee should be permitted to comply with the directions with impunity, because the settlor is, in effect, investing for himself. If, however, the trust is irrevocable, the settlor may have a duty of care, as would the trustee.[32]

If there are two trustees, and both are liable for a breach of trust, they are jointly and severally liable to the beneficiaries for the loss. If one wholly restores the loss to the trust, whether pursuant to a judgment or voluntarily, he is usually entitled to indemnification from the other trustee of one-half the liability.[33] The right of indemnification is different, however, if one trustee is "more guilty" than the other, although they are jointly and severally liable to the beneficiaries. For example, if one trustee appropriates trust funds to his own use, and the other trustee is also liable because he was not exercising due care with respect to the handling of the trust funds, the negligent trustee is entitled to be totally indemnified by the larcenous trustee for anything he restores to the trust on account of the loss, and, of course, the larcenous trustee is not entitled to an indemnification from the negligent trustee for anything he restores to the trust.[34]

If both trustees have committed a breach of trust by, let us say, joining in the making of an improper investment, but no personal gain or other form of moral turpitude is involved, each is entitled to be indemnified by the other to the extent that he has restored more than half the loss to the trust. If, however, both trustees have joined in a breach which involves moral turpitude, the equity court is disinclined to grant relief by way of indemnification to one of the trustees who pays into the trust more than one-half the loss.[35] The equity court will not assist the evil fellow, even though it means that the other evil fellow does not pay his share of the loss.

31. Gathright's Trustee v. Gaut, 276 Ky. 562, 124 S.W.2d 782 (1939); United States Nat. Bank v. First Nat. Bank, 172 Or. 683, 142 P.2d 785 (1943).

32. Steiner v. Hawaiian Trust Co., 47 Hawaii 548, 393 P.2d 96 (1964); Application of Esty, 75 N.Y.S.2d 905 (Sup. Ct.1947).

33. Gbur v. Cohen, 93 Cal.App.3d 296, 155 Cal.Rptr. 507 (1979); Reyburn's Estate, 43 Pa.D. & C. 85 (Orph.

1942); In re Trust by Mueller, 28 Wis.2d 26, 135 N.W.2d 854 (1965).

34. Gbur v. Cohen, 93 Cal.App.3d 296, 155 Cal.Rptr. 507 (1979); In re Rosenfeld's Estate, 180 Misc. 452, 40 N.Y.S.2d 114 (Sur.Ct.1943); In re Trust by Mueller, 28 Wis.2d 26, 135 N.W.2d 854 (1965).

35. 3A Scott, Law of Trusts § 258.3 (4th ed., Fratcher, 1988).

SECTION 11. LIABILITY OF TRUSTEE
TO THIRD PERSONS

In the course of the administration of the trust, the trustee may enter into contracts with third parties or commit torts against third parties or employ agents who commit torts. Is the trustee liable personally on such contracts and for such torts? If the trustee is personally liable, is he entitled to indemnification from the trust assets? Can the trust assets be reached by third parties on account of such liabilities?

Jones, as trustee, is not considered to be the agent of the trust estate as principal. Jones, as trustee, is not a different legal personality from Jones, the individual. The trust assets, however, are not considered to be the property of Jones, the individual, as far as the claims of third parties are concerned. The relationship among Jones, the trustee, and Jones, the individual, and the trust property, with respect to the claims of third parties, is difficult to summarize intelligibly in abstract terms, and no attempt will be made to do so. However, a description of the legal consequences of several transactions should cast some light on the subject.

Suppose that in the course of the administration of the trust, Trustee enters into a contract with Smith for Smith's services at a price of $50,000, which contract is a proper exercise of Trustee's fiduciary powers. Smith knows that the contract was made in the course of the administration of the trust. Nevertheless, Trustee is personally liable on the contract, unless the contract expressly provides that Trustee shall not be personally liable.[36] The fact that it is clear on the face of the contract that it is being made for the trust does not change the result. If Trustee's personal assets are used to satisfy Smith's claim, Trustee is entitled to reimbursement from the trust assets; Trustee may also pay the claim directly from trust assets in the first instance.[37] Smith also can reach the trust property, as well as Trustee's personal assets, to obtain satisfaction of his judgment on the contract. If the contract is proper, the trust assets are answerable, as well as Trustee's personal assets.[38] If, however, the contract expressly provides that Trustee shall not be personally liable, then only the trust assets are available to satisfy Smith's claim.[39]

36. Oberdorfer v. Smith, 102 Ga. App. 336, 116 S.E.2d 308 (1960); Just Pants v. Bank of Ravenswood, 136 Ill. App.3d 543, 91 Ill.Dec. 49, 483 N.E.2d 331 (1985); Onanian v. Leggat, 2 Mass. App.Ct. 623, 317 N.E.2d 823 (1974); Corpus Christi Bank & Trust v. Cross, 586 S.W.2d 664 (Tex.Civ.App.1979).

37. Conley v. Waite, 134 Cal.App. 505, 25 P.2d 496 (1933); Stewart v. Harrison, 210 Miss. 750, 50 So.2d 624 (1951); Matter of Estate of Burke, 129 Misc.2d 145, 492 N.Y.S.2d 892 (Sur.Ct. 1985); In re Estate of Fisher, 461 Pa. 696, 337 A.2d 834 (1975).

38. Faulk v. Smith, 168 Ga. 448, 148 S.E. 100 (1929); King v. Stowell, 211 Mass. 246, 98 N.E. 91 (1912); Ranzau v. Davis, 85 Or. 26, 165 P. 1180 (1917); In re Estate of Fisher, 461 Pa. 696, 337 A.2d 834 (1975).

39. Limouze v. M.M. & P. Maritime Advancement, Training, Educ. and Safety Program, 397 F.Supp. 784 (D.Md.

The trust instrument may provide that Trustee shall not be personally liable on any contracts entered into in the proper administration of the trust. If Smith was on notice of that provision, there is authority that Trustee is not personally liable, whether or not the contract expressly states that Trustee is not to be personally liable.[40] If Smith was not on notice of the provision in the trust instrument, Trustee is personally liable, absent a clause in the contract negating such liability.

Suppose Trustee made the contract with Smith purportedly in the course of administration of the trust, but in fact the contract was not within his trust powers. Smith knew that the contract was made purportedly in the course of the administration of the trust, but he had no knowledge that it was beyond Trustee's powers. There was no clause in the contract barring Trustee's personal liability, nor was there any clause in the trust instrument barring Trustee's personal liability. Trustee is personally liable to Smith,[41] but he is not entitled to indemnification from the trust assets,[42] and Smith cannot reach the trust assets to satisfy his claim.[43] If the contract is not proper, the trust assets are not answerable, but Trustee's personal assets are. If the contract expressly provided that Trustee was not to be held personally liable, Smith would nevertheless have a cause of action against Trustee based on his implied or express representation that the contract was within his powers as trustee and that the trust assets would be available to satisfy Smith's claim.[44]

It seems a bit harsh that the trust assets are not available to satisfy a claim under a contract that is beyond Trustee's powers where Smith has no knowledge of this fact. There is, however, a qualification to the unavailability of trust assets in these circumstances: To the extent that the trust has received some tangible benefit from the performance of the contract by Smith, Smith can reach the trust assets in that amount to satisfy his claim, and Trustee is entitled to reimbursement from trust assets to the same

1975); Kessler, Merci, and Lochner, Inc. v. Pioneer Bank & Trust Co., 101 Ill. App.3d 502, 57 Ill.Dec. 58, 428 N.E.2d 608 (1981); Corpus Christi Bank & Trust v. Cross, 586 S.W.2d 664 (Tex.Civ. App.1979).

40. Brockob Construction Co. v. Trust Co. of Chicago, 6 Ill.App.2d 565, 128 N.E.2d 620 (1955); Baker v. James, 280 Mass. 43, 181 N.E. 861 (1932).

41. Brown v. Churchill, 89 N.H. 441, 200 A. 393 (1938); Kincaid v. Hensel, 185 Wash. 503, 55 P.2d 1050 (1936).

42. Grayson v. Hughes, 166 Ark. 173, 265 S.W. 836 (1924); In re Estate of Fisher, 461 Pa. 696, 337 A.2d 834 (1975).

43. Getty v. Getty, 205 Cal.App.3d 134, 252 Cal.Rptr. 342 (1988); Kerner v. George, 321 Ill.App. 150, 52 N.E.2d 300 (1943); Farmers' and Traders' Bank v. Fidelity & Deposit Co., 108 Ky. 384, 56 S.W. 671 (1900).

44. Restatement (Second) of Trusts § 263 (1959).

extent if payment has been made to Smith from the personal assets of Trustee.[45]

Uniform Probate Code §§ 3–808 and 7–306, legislated in a number of states, change the common law by providing that the personal representative or trustee is not personally liable on contracts properly entered into in his fiduciary capacity unless he fails to reveal his representative capacity and identify the estate in the contract.

Now we move to a consideration of the relationship among Jones, the trustee, and Jones, the individual, and the trust property, with respect to liability to third parties in tort. The conventional trust of stocks and bonds is not likely to produce any torts, but a trust of real estate may do so. If in the course of administering the trust, Trustee negligently injures Smith, Trustee is personally liable.[46] Trustee's negligence also means that his action is in breach of trust; consequently Trustee is not entitled to indemnification from the trust assets,[47] and the prevailing view is that the trust assets cannot be reached by Smith to satisfy his claim,[48] although there is authority that allows Smith to reach the trust assets in these circumstances.[49]

Suppose Trustee employs Green in the course of administering the trust, which is within his trust powers, and Green negligently injures Smith while acting within the scope of his employment. Trustee is personally liable under the doctrine of respondeat superior. Trustee has not committed a breach of trust, despite his liability, because his employment of Green was proper, and Trustee has not violated his duty of care. Consequently, Trustee is entitled to indemnification from the trust assets if his personal assets are used to pay the claim, or Trustee can pay the claim directly from trust assets in the first instance,[50] and Smith can reach the trust

45. Estate of Rainone, 33 A.D.2d 1048, 309 N.Y.S.2d 529 (1970); Matter of Guardianship of Kordecki, 95 Wis.2d 275, 290 N.W.2d 693 (1980); Johnston v. Rothwell, 54 Wyo. 99, 87 P.2d 13 (1939); Restatement (Second) of Trusts § 269 (1959).

46. Colorado Springs Cablevision, Inc. v. Lively, 579 F.Supp. 252 (D.Colo. 1984); Cook v. Holland, 575 S.W.2d 468 (Ky.App.1978); Martin v. Talcott, 1 A.D.2d 679, 146 N.Y.S.2d 784 (1955).

47. Smith v. Rizzuto, 133 Neb. 655, 276 N.W. 406 (1937); In re Lathers' Will, 137 Misc. 226, 243 N.Y.S. 366 (Sur. Ct.1930).

48. Matter of Estate of Shugart, 81 Ill.App.3d 538, 36 Ill.Dec. 770, 401 N.E.2d 611 (1980); In re Estate of Fisher, 461 Pa. 696, 337 A.2d 834 (1975). See 3A Scott, Law of Trusts § 268.2 (4th ed., Fratcher, 1988).

49. Vance v. Estate of Myers, 494 P.2d 816 (Alaska 1972); Smith v. Coleman, 100 Fla. 1707, 132 So. 198 (1931); Miller v. Smythe, 92 Ga. 154, 18 S.E. 46 (1893); Birdsong v. Jones, 222 Mo.App. 768, 8 S.W.2d 98 (1928).

50. See 3A Scott, Law of Trusts § 264 (4th ed., Fratcher, 1988).

assets to satisfy his claim.[51] If Trustee's conduct is proper, the trust assets are answerable, as well as Trustee's personal assets.

Uniform Probate Code §§ 3–808 and 7–306, legislated in a number of states, change the common law by providing that the personal representative or trustee is personally liable for torts in the course of administration of the estate only if he is personally at fault.

A trustee may be liable to a third party by virtue of his title, without regard to contract or tort responsibility. For example, the holder of legal title to real estate may be personally liable for real estate taxes. If the trustee pays the tax from his personal assets, he is entitled to reimbursement from trust assets, or he can pay the tax from trust property in the first instance.[52] The tax collector can, of course, reach the trust property for payment of the taxes. The trustee or personal representative would not be personally liable for the taxes under Uniform Probate Code §§ 3–808 and 7–306.

It should be noted that as a general rule beneficiaries of a trust are not personally liable for the contracts or torts of the trustee, or for assessments upon trust property. One qualification to this rule involves the situation in which the trustee has made a contract or is liable in tort for which the trust assets are answerable and the trustee has made a distribution of trust property to the beneficiaries and not retained sufficient assets to satisfy the claim. In such circumstances, if the trustee pays the claim from his personal assets, he is entitled to reimbursement from the beneficiaries to the extent of what they have received, and the claimant is entitled to recover from the beneficiaries to the extent of what they have received if he is not paid by the trustee from his personal assets or from the assets retained in trust.[53]

SECTION 12. LIABILITY OF THIRD PERSONS

The purpose of the trusts portion of this book is to present the legal framework of private and charitable trusts as vehicles for the donative disposition of accumulated wealth. The subject of third party liability to the trustee or the beneficiaries, or both, is tangential to our purpose, and accordingly only a brief outline is presented here.

If a third party breaches a contract with the trustee, or converts trust property, or damages or wrongfully occupies trust

---

51. Johnston v. Long, 30 Cal.2d 54, 181 P.2d 645 (1947); Cook v. Holland, 575 S.W.2d 468 (Ky.App.1978). It should be noted that charitable immunity from tort liability, if it exists in the jurisdiction, applies to the charitable trust. See 4A Scott, Law of Trusts § 402.2 (4th ed., Fratcher, 1988).

52. 3A Scott, Law of Trusts § 248 (4th ed., Fratcher, 1988).

53. 3A Scott, Law of Trusts § 279 (4th ed., Fratcher, 1988).

property, it is the trustee who normally has the cause of action against the third party, and not the beneficiaries. The trustee is the one in whom is vested the responsibility for the protection of the trust property. If, however, the trustee fails to bring suit when he should have done so, the beneficiaries may bring an action against the trustee to compel him to perform his duty, or bring an action against the third party on behalf of the trust, joining the trustee as a party defendant.[54] If jurisdiction cannot be obtained over the trustee, the beneficiary may maintain an action against the third party without the joinder of the trustee.[55]

Where the trustee transfers trust property to a third party in breach of trust, the property or its value or the proceeds of resale by the third party are recoverable from the third party unless the third party is a bona fide purchaser. If the third party is a bona fide purchaser, and the transfer is in breach of trust, the third party has good title, and the beneficiaries' recourse is only against the trustee for his breach of trust.[56] An example of a transfer in breach of trust would be where the trust instrument directed the trustee to retain the property. Obviously if the trustee makes a transfer of trust property to a third party which is not a breach of trust, the third party gets good title.

In the situation in which the trustee transfers to a third party in breach of trust, the trustee has participated in the conduct which is in conflict with the interest of the trust, as contrasted with the situation in which the third party breaches his contract with the trustee or converts trust property without the participation of the trustee. In the case of the transfer in breach of trust to a third party who is not a bona fide purchaser, the beneficiary may sue the third party on behalf of the trust if the trustee fails to do so.[57] The trustee also may maintain the action against the third party, despite the fact that he participated in the wrong.[58] Whatever is recovered in the action, the property or its value or the proceeds of resale by the third party, passes, of course, to the trust. If the price that was paid by the third party was placed in trust, the third

54. Triplett v. Williams, 269 Cal. App.2d 135, 74 Cal.Rptr. 594 (1969); Apollinari v. Johnson, 104 Mich.App. 673, 305 N.W.2d 565 (1981); Levy v. Carver Federal Savings & Loan, 18 A.D.2d 1062, 239 N.Y.S.2d 384 (1963); Epworth Orphanage v. Long, 199 S.C. 385, 19 S.E.2d 481 (1942).

55. Ettlinger v. Schumacher, 142 N.Y. 189, 36 N.E. 1055 (1894). See 4 Scott, Law of Trusts § 282.2 (3d ed. 1967).

56. Kline v. Orebaugh, 214 Kan. 207, 519 P.2d 691 (1974); Love v. Fauquet,

184 Neb. 250, 166 N.W.2d 742 (1969); Estate of Rothko, 84 Misc.2d 830, 379 N.Y.S.2d 923 (1975), modified 56 A.D.2d 499, 392 N.Y.S.2d 870 (1977), aff'd 43 N.Y.2d 305, 401 N.Y.S.2d 449, 372 N.E.2d 291 (1977); Croak v. Witteman, 73 N.D. 592, 17 N.W.2d 542 (1945).

57. Jones v. Jones, 297 Mass. 198, 7 N.E.2d 1015 (1937); Bonham v. Coe, 249 App.Div. 428, 292 N.Y.S. 423 (1937), aff'd 276 N.Y. 540, 12 N.E.2d 566 (1937).

58. Wetmore v. Porter, 92 N.Y. 76 (1883).

party is entitled to reimbursement from the trust estate; if the trustee did not place it in trust, then the trustee is answerable.

The purchaser of trust property from a trustee who commits a breach of trust in making the transfer, takes good title free of the trust if he paid "value" and did not have "notice" of the breach of trust. If he did not pay "value," or did have "notice" of the breach, he is liable to return the property or its value or the proceeds of resale if he has sold it.

The purchaser can have "notice" of the breach without having actual knowledge of the breach. If the purchaser does not have actual knowledge that he is purchasing from a trustee but has knowledge of facts which would lead a reasonable person to inquire as to whether he was purchasing from a trustee, and if in all likelihood the fact that he was purchasing from a trustee would have been discovered upon a reasonable inquiry, then the purchaser will be held to the knowledge that he is purchasing from a trustee.[59] If the purchaser knows that he is purchasing from a trustee, or is held to such knowledge, then he is also obligated to make diligent inquiry concerning the contents of the trust instrument, and will be held to the knowledge of the terms of the trust which a diligent inquiry would produce, whether or not he has such knowledge. If he is held to the knowledge of the trust terms, he is also held to the knowledge of their legal effect.[60] In most situations the purchaser who is held to the knowledge that he is purchasing from a trustee will also be held to the knowledge of the terms of the trust and their legal effect. If the trust is not in writing, however, the inquiry may not produce the fact that a provision of the trust has been violated. In the case of land, the trust terms are usually a matter of public record, and the routine title search will disclose the terms of the trust.

With respect to transfers of negotiable instruments and investment securities by trustees in breach of trust, statutes offer greater protection to the purchaser than the rule we have been discussing. In effect, the purchaser for value from a person he knows to be a trustee takes good title unless he has actual knowledge or reason to believe that the transfer is in breach of trust. The inquiry principle is not applied.[61] Since most transactions involve land or securities, this problem area is not as complicated as may appear on the surface.

59. See Clark v. Judge, 84 N.J.Super. 35, 200 A.2d 801 (1964); Jackson v. Greenhow, 155 Va. 758, 156 S.E. 377 (1931).

60. Hastings Potato Growers Association v. Pomar, 296 So.2d 55 (Fla.Dist. Ct.App.1974); Hughes v. Spence, 409 S.W.2d 701 (Mo.1966); McKinnon v. Bradley, 178 Or. 45, 165 P.2d 286 (1946).

61. See Uniform Commercial Code §§ 3–304, 8–304; Uniform Fiduciaries Act §§ 4, 6.

The purchaser who is not on notice of the breach by the trustee receives good title if he has paid "value." The purchaser may pay less than the fair market value and still be deemed to have paid "value." [62] If the price is very low, however, the purchaser may be deemed to be on notice that a breach of trust is involved. [63] If the consideration given in exchange for the trust property is nominal, the purchaser will be deemed to be a donee and not to have paid value. [64]

There are a variety of other issues involved in connection with the definition of value and notice in this context, such as whether the satisfaction of an antecedent debt is value, whether the purchaser is protected when he receives notice of the trust or breach after the making of the promise to pay but before payment, whether the purchaser is protected when he receives notice after he has paid the purchase price but before the trustee has transferred the title, what the result is if the purchaser receives notice after he has received title and paid only one-half the purchase price, whether a judgment creditor is a bona fide purchaser, among many others. This area of the law is treated in detail elsewhere. [65]

Trustees maintain fiduciary bank accounts, and consequently banks have regular dealings with trustees. The law, however, concerning bank liability in connection with breaches of trust developed differently from the law concerning the liability of purchasers of land, chattels, and choses in action from trustees. The bank is generally not liable for honoring checks drawn by the trustee on the fiduciary account in breach of trust, including checks payable to the trustee personally, unless the bank knows or has reason to know that a breach is being committed. That is to say, the bank has no duty to inquire concerning the propriety of the trustee's management of the fiduciary account. If the bank actually has no information which would suggest impropriety, it cannot be liable. [66] This is very different from the responsibility of the person who purchases from the trustee who transfers in breach of trust.

A qualification to this generality, however, is where the bank is a creditor of the trustee individually, and receives payment of the

---

62. Kanall v. 318 Lounge, Inc., 1 Mass.App.Ct. 5, 294 N.E.2d 429 (1972).

63. Gaines v. Saunders, 50 Ark. 322, 7 S.W. 301 (1888). See Beall v. Dingman, 227 Ill. 294, 81 N.E. 366 (1907); Kanall v. 318 Lounge, Inc., 1 Mass.App. Ct. 5, 294 N.E.2d 429 (1972).

64. De Everett v. Texas-Mexican Railway, 67 Tex. 430, 3 S.W. 678 (1887). See Kanall v. 318 Lounge, Inc., 1 Mass. App.Ct. 5, 294 N.E.2d 429 (1972).

For definitions of value which protect the good faith purchaser of negotiable instruments and investment securities, see Uniform Commercial Code §§ 3–303, 8–302, 1–201.

65. See 4 Scott, Law of Trusts §§ 297A–312 (4th ed., Fratcher, 1989).

66. See 4 Scott, Law of Trusts §§ 324–324.3 (4th ed., Fratcher, 1989).

debt by a check drawn on the fiduciary account. If this check is a breach of trust, the bank is liable to the trust. The bank is on notice of the breach where it knows that fiduciary funds are being used to pay a personal debt of the trustee to the bank.[67] There is also authority that if the trustee maintains an individual account with the bank, makes deposits to the account by checks drawn on a fiduciary account, and then, in breach of trust, pays his debt to the bank from fiduciary funds in the personal account, the bank is liable.[68]

Trustees sometimes hold corporate stocks and bonds in their fiduciary names. The common law position was that the corporation was bound to inquire concerning the legality of the changes in registration from the name of the trustee to another party. If the corporation knew that a transfer was being made by a trustee, it had a duty to inquire as to whether the transfer constituted a breach of trust. The responsibility of the corporation with respect to transfers was similar to the responsibility of the purchaser of property from the trustee who sold in breach of trust. However, statutes provide that the corporation is not liable for transfers in breach of trust unless it has knowledge of the breach, or has reason to believe that a breach is being committed,[69] as is the case by statute with respect to purchasers of stocks and bonds. The statutes have done away with the duty to inquire.

A great variety of people may have dealings with trustees in the context of a breach of trust, such as those who sell their property to the trustee, lawyers, brokers, and agents of various kinds. As a general proposition, such parties are not liable for participation in the breach unless they know the breach was being committed or had good reason to know of it. They are not required to inquire as to the legality of the trustee's actions.[70] To impose a duty of inquiry as to the legality of the trustee's actions upon one who knowingly deals with a trustee comes close to strict liability, and today such duty is sparingly applied.

67. Schofield v. Cleveland Trust Co., 149 Ohio St. 133, 78 N.E.2d 167 (1948); Pennsylvania Co. for Ins. v. Ninth Bank & Trust Co., 306 Pa. 148, 158 A. 251 (1932); Continental National Bank v. Great American Management & Investment, Inc., 606 S.W.2d 346 (Tex.Civ. App.1980); Uniform Fiduciaries Act § 7.

68. Gluth Bros. Construction, Inc. v. Union Natl. Bank, 166 Ill.App.3d 18, 116 Ill.Dec. 365, 518 N.E.2d 1345 (1988); Grace v. Corn Exchange Bank Trust Co., 287 N.Y. 94, 38 N.E.2d 449 (1941); Commercial State Bank v. Algeo, 331 S.W.2d 84 (Tex.Civ.App.1959); United States Fidelity & Guaranty Co. v. Hood, 122 W.Va. 157, 7 S.E.2d 872 (1940). See, however, Uniform Fiduciaries Act § 9.

69. See Uniform Commercial Code § 8–403; Uniform Fiduciaries Act § 3; Uniform Act for the Simplification of Fiduciary Security Transfers.

70. See 4 Scott, Law of Trusts §§ 326–326.5 (4th ed., Fratcher, 1989); Uniform Trustees Power Act § 7.

SECTION 13.   A WORD ABOUT CONFLICT OF LAWS

In most cases the settlor of the living trust creates the trust in the jurisdiction of his domicile, provides impliedly or expressly that it is to be administered in that jurisdiction, and does not state any preference in the trust instrument for the application of the law of any other jurisdiction.   If land is included in the trust, which is the exception, it is likely to be located in the domiciliary jurisdiction. No conflict of laws question arises in this situation.   In most cases the testator who creates a trust under his will executes his will in his domicile, dies domiciled in the same jurisdiction, provides impliedly or expressly for administration of the trust in the same jurisdiction, and does not state in the will any preference for the application of the law of any other jurisdiction.   If land is included in the trust, it is likely to be located in the domiciliary state.   No conflict of laws question arises in this situation.   If, however, the living trust is created in the settlor's domicile, to be administered in another jurisdiction, or if the trust which is created in the settlor's domicile contains land in another state, or if the settlor expresses in the trust instrument a preference for the application of the law of another state, to name several complicating factors, conflict of laws problems arise.   If the testator creating a testamentary trust executes his last will in the jurisdiction which is then his domicile, dies domiciled in another jurisdiction leaving that same will, and provides for administration in a third jurisdiction or leaves land in the trust situated in another jurisdiction, conflict of laws problems arise.

The subject of conflict of laws as it pertains to trusts is important and very extensive.   The law is fluid and inconclusive in many respects.   It is appropriately considered in instruction in conflict of laws.   The function of this brief section is to apprise the reader of the existence of this problem area.[71]

Issues may arise concerning the applicable law with respect to the formal requirements for the creation of a living trust or the execution of a will, the capacity of the settlor, the validity of the trust in general or of specific provisions, the administration of the trust including the duties and powers of the trustee and the determination of principal and income, and the construction and interpretation of the trust terms, to name the most significant legal problem areas.   The conflict of laws principles concerning living trusts differ in certain respects from those concerning testamentary trusts, and the conflict of laws principles also vary depending upon

---

71.   For thorough discussions of this topic, see Scoles and Hay, Conflict of Laws §§ 21.1–21.7 (2d ed. 1992); Restatement (Second) of Conflict of Laws §§ 267–282 (1971).

will not prevail. The action is frivolous, however, if the client desires to have the action taken primarily for the purpose of harassing or maliciously injuring a person or if the lawyer is unable either to make a good faith argument on the merits of the action taken or to support the action taken by good faith argument for an extension, modification or reversal of existing law.

The language of the Model Rules gives the lawyer a great deal of room to maneuver, but there are limits. The Model Code provisions are substantially the same.

Closely related to the frivolous claim is the issue of the preparation of witnesses. Assisting the witness to present his testimony in an orderly and convincing manner is obviously permissible. Counseling the witness to commit perjury is obviously impermissible. The problematic area is where counseling the witness with respect to the significance or consequences of certain testimony becomes akin to suggesting or advising that the client commit perjury.

Model Rule 1.2(d) provides in part:

A lawyer shall not counsel a client to engage, or assist a client, in conduct that the lawyer knows is criminal or fraudulent. . . .

Model Rule 3.3(a)(4) provides in part:

(a) A lawyer shall not knowingly:

* * *

(4) offer evidence that the lawyer knows to be false. . . .

Model Rule 3.4(b) provides in part:

A lawyer shall not

* * *

(b) falsify evidence, counsel or assist a witness to testify falsely. . . . [8]

Suppose the disappointed heir who is considering contesting the will begins his conversation with the lawyer by asking for the definition of testamentary capacity and undue influence. The lawyer complies with the request. The lawyer has provided the client with information which enables him to tailor his testimony (and maybe that of others) in his interest. The sophisticated client knows that it is dangerous to tell the lawyer something that is damaging to his case, and then change his story; the lawyer may be

---

8. See Model Code DR 7–102, DR 1–102, for comparable provisions.

precluded from presenting the favorable story. Has the lawyer done anything improper by providing the client with the definitions of capacity and undue influence? The client certainly is entitled to be told what the law is. Must the lawyer tell the client that he'll tell him what the law is after the client answers some factual questions? It seems not, although the matter is not free from doubt.

The sophisticated client may know the law already, or may ask for the law before he gives factual responses. The unsophisticated client doesn't know the law, nor is he likely to ask for the law before he answers factual questions. Is it permissible for the lawyer first to tell the client the law of capacity and undue influence without being asked, and then ask the client factual questions? Is this an implied suggestion that the client tailor the facts to serve his interest? Or is the lawyer entitled to provide the unsophisticated client the information that the sophisticated client already knows or knows enough to ask for? It seems that the lawyer should be permitted to do this, but once again the matter is not free from doubt.[9] Suppose the lawyer, after having described the law without having asked any factual questions, invites the client to reflect on the matter for a day or two before he responds to the lawyer's questions about the facts. Does this cross the line?

Suppose the lawyer does not volunteer the definition of capacity and undue influence, but instead begins the conversation by telling the client that if the elderly testator was lucid and alert the day he executed the will, testamentary capacity probably would not succeed as a ground for contest, and that if the elderly testator was a strong-willed person, undue influence would be very difficult to establish. These are statements of fact and law which are more likely to be construed as encouraging the tailoring of the client's response than a broad statement of the law in the area. The lawyer may well have crossed the ethical line.

The last topic in this section is negotiations. It is assumed that in the give-and-take of negotiations people in business puff and bluff, or more bluntly, misrepresent their views of value and what they will be willing to settle for. The morality of such behavior is defended usually on the ground that a willfully false statement is not a lie if the speaker knows that the listener knows that the speaker really doesn't mean it to be a truthful statement. In other words, it is a game and language is not to be taken seriously.

But if it is true that the speaker knows that the listener knows that the speaker really doesn't mean it, then the statement by the speaker would not serve the speaker's end. If the puff or the bluff is understood to be absolutely false, then it would not influence the

9. Wolfram, Modern Legal Ethics
648 (1986).

behavior of the listener. If the speaker knew this to be the case, there would be no point in his making the statement. Although the listener may discount what the speaker is saying, if the speaker's words are to have any effect, the listener must read into them some risk that the speaker means what he says or means what he says to some extent. The speaker necessarily intends this to be the case. If the speaker is saying something that is not true, but the listener thinks that there is a 20% chance that it is true, or some chance that there is a degree of truth in what is said, to that extent the speaker has deceived and the conduct is a lie and is immoral.

In any event, people in business engage in this process and appear to enjoy it. It's a battle of wits and accepted practice. There are degrees of immorality, and this is a minor form of it because all the participants are aware that a game is being played. On the other hand, established practices of this nature do have a tendency to erode standards of trust and confidence in the society; in this sense no form of immorality can be characterized as minor.

The issue here is whether lawyers should engage in settlement negotiations as they are presently conducted. Unquestionably many lawyers do. Lawyers are forbidden to make false statements, but it is done all the time in legal settlement negotiations.

Model Rule 4.1(a) is as follows:

> In the course of representing a client a lawyer shall not knowingly
>
> (a) make a false statement of material fact or law to a third person;

Comment (2) to Model Rule 4.1(a) deals directly with negotiations:

> This rule refers to statements of fact. Whether a particular statement should be regarded as one of fact can depend on the circumstances. Under generally accepted conventions in negotiation, certain types of statements ordinarily are not taken as statements of material fact. Estimates of price or value placed on the subject of a transaction and a party's intentions as to an acceptable settlement of a claim are in this category....

The Comment gives the green light to lawyers to negotiate for settlement of litigation such as the will contest in the same fashion as the layperson. It is a truism that the behavior of people in the professions should be above that of the marketplace. The attempt to justify marketplace standards for lawyers in the Comment to Model Rule 4.1(a) is trade unionism packaged in sophistry.

SECTION 6. THE LAWYER AND THE BANK CLIENT

Lawyers in the trusts and estates area often represent banks as executors and trustees. The corporation is the client, not the directors or officers. The lawyer's duty is to the entity, and she is obligated to serve the interests of the entity exclusively. If the lawyer for the bank as executor or trustee learns that an officer is acting unlawfully, she may be obligated to take action within the corporation to protect the corporate client from the actions of the officer. Such unlawful action by the officer may also place the officer's interest and the corporate client's interest in conflict, in which case the lawyer must make it clear to the officer that she represents the corporation and not the officer, that what is said to the lawyer is available to the corporation, and that any evidentiary attorney-client privilege that exists belongs to the corporation. The lawyer must also advise the officer that he may wish to retain his own attorney.

Model Rule 1.13 deals with this problem:

> (a) A lawyer employed or retained by an organization represents the organization acting through its duly authorized constituents.

> (b) If a lawyer for an organization knows that an officer, employee or other person associated with the organization is engaged in action, intends to act or refuses to act in a matter related to the representation that is a violation of a legal obligation to the organization, or a violation of law which reasonably might be imputed to the organization, and is likely to result in substantial injury to the organization, the lawyer shall proceed as is reasonably necessary in the best interest of the organization. In determining how to proceed, the lawyer shall give due consideration to the seriousness of the violation and its consequences, the scope and nature of the lawyer's representation, the responsibility in the organization and the apparent motivation of the person involved, the policies of the organization concerning such matters and any other relevant considerations. Any measures taken shall be designed to minimize disruption of the organization and the risk of revealing information relating to the representation to persons outside the organization. Such measures may include among others:

> (1) asking reconsideration of the matter;

(2) advising that a separate legal opinion on the matter be sought for presentation to appropriate authority in the organization; and

(3) referring the matter to higher authority in the organization, including, if warranted by the seriousness of the matter, referral to the highest authority that can act in behalf of the organization as determined by applicable law.

(c) If, despite the lawyer's efforts in accordance with paragraph (b), the highest authority that can act on behalf of the organization insists upon action, or a refusal to act, that is clearly a violation of law and is likely to result in substantial injury to the organization, the lawyer may resign in accordance with rule 1.16.

(d) In dealing with an organization's directors, officers, employees, members, shareholders or other constituents, a lawyer shall explain the identity of the client when it is apparent that the organization's interests are adverse to those of the constituents with whom the lawyer is dealing.

The Model Code has no comparable provision, although EC 5–18 recognizes that the lawyer's duty is to the corporation and not the corporate constituents.

Two situations come to mind in the trusts and estates area in which the problem may arise. The bank officer may be investing trust or estate assets in a manner that the lawyer believes to be beyond the powers of the fiduciary. The bank officer may be making discretionary distributive decisions which the lawyer considers to be beyond the powers of the fiduciary. Violation of investment and distributive authority can result in significant liability for the bank and damage to its reputation. The lawyer cannot sit by and let this continue without advising others within the corporation. This also places the officer and the bank in a situation of conflict, of which the lawyer must inform the officer.

SECTION 7. CONFLICTS OF INTEREST:
HUSBAND–WIFE; PARENT–CHILD;
FIDUCIARY–BENEFICIARY

(1) INTRODUCTION

As briefly described in Section 4 above, there are two basic types of conflict of interest: those involving simultaneous representations, and those involving successive representations. The conflicts discussed in this section are primarily of the simultaneous type. In one form of simultaneous conflict the lawyer represents two (or more) clients at the same time with respect to a matter in which the clients' interests are adverse or may come into conflict. In another form of simultaneous conflict the lawyer represents one client in a matter against another client whom the lawyer represents at the same time in another unrelated matter. The simultaneous representations discussed in this section are of the first form.

A typical successive conflict is the lawyer's representation of the disappointed heir in the contest of the will which the lawyer prepared for the testator several years before his death. The lawyer is now representing a client against the interests of a former client in a matter in which the lawyer had previously represented the former client. Model Rule 1.9(a) forbids this form of conflict.

The basic provision of the Model Rules dealing with simultaneous conflicts is Rule 1.7:

(a) A lawyer shall not represent a client if the representation of that client will be directly adverse to another client, unless:

(1) the lawyer reasonably believes the representation will not adversely affect the relationship with the other client; and

(2) each client consents after consultation.

(b) A lawyer shall not represent a client if the representation of that client may be materially limited by the lawyer's responsibilities to another client or to a third person, or by the lawyer's own interests, unless:

(1) the lawyer reasonably believes the representation will not be adversely affected; and

(2) the client consents after consultation. When representation of multiple clients in a single matter is undertaken, the consultation shall include explanation of the implications of the common representation and the advantages and risks involved.

The basic section of the Model Code dealing with simultaneous conflicts is DR 5–105:

(A) A lawyer shall decline proffered employment if the exercise of his independent professional judgment in behalf of a client will be or is likely to be adversely affected by the acceptance of the proffered employment, or if it would be likely to involve him in representing differing interests, except to the extent permitted under DR 5–105(C).

(B) A lawyer shall not continue multiple employment if the exercise of his independent professional judgment in behalf of a client will be or is likely to be adversely affected by his representation of another client, or if it would be likely to involve him in representing differing interests, except to the extent permitted under DR 5–105(C).

(C) In the situations covered by DR 5–105(A) and (B), a lawyer may represent multiple clients if it is obvious that he can adequately represent the interest of each and if each consents to the representation after full disclosure of the possible effect of such representation on the exercise of his independent professional judgment on behalf of each.

There is an additional Model Rule 2.2 which deals with simultaneous conflicts in which the lawyer serves as an "intermediary" between clients:

(a) A lawyer may act as intermediary between clients if:

(1) the lawyer consults with each client concerning the implications of the common representation, including the advantages and risks involved, and the effect on the attorney-client privileges, and obtains each client's consent to the common representation;

(2) the lawyer reasonably believes that the matter can be resolved on terms compatible with the clients' best interests, that each client will be able to make adequately informed decisions in the matter and that there is little risk of material prejudice to the interest of any of the clients if the contemplated resolution is unsuccessful; and

(3) the lawyer reasonably believes that the common representation can be undertaken impartially and without improper effect on other responsibilities the lawyer has to any of the clients.

(b) While acting as intermediary, the lawyer shall consult with each client concerning the decisions to be made and the considerations relevant in making them, so that each client can make adequately informed decisions.

(c) A lawyer shall withdraw as intermediary if any of the clients so request, or if any of the conditions stated in paragraph (a) is no longer satisfied. Upon withdrawal, the lawyer shall not continue to represent any of the clients in the matter that was the subject of the intermediation.

The Model Code has no counterpart to Model Rule 2.2.

Model Rule 1.10(a) deals with imputed disqualification:

> While lawyers are associated in a firm, none of them shall knowingly represent a client when any one of them practicing alone would be prohibited from doing so....

Model Code DR 5–105(D) is to the same effect as Model Rule 1.10(a).

The discussion in this section is in terms of the Model Rules because of their greater comprehensiveness and broader acceptance.

It is obvious that the lawyer cannot represent the plaintiff and the defendant in litigation; the interests of the plaintiff and defendant are directly adverse. Even if the parties consented to the conflicting representations after consultation with the lawyer and full disclosure of the consequences, it would be impermissible to represent both because the lawyer could not reasonably believe that the representation of one would not adversely affect the representation of the other. The lawyer could not possibly be a vigorous trial advocate for the plaintiff against the defendant and vice-versa. The lawyer is required to be a zealous advocate on behalf of his client.[10]

It should be emphasized that the clients' consent to a conflict, however informed, is never sufficient. The lawyer must also be convinced that neither representation will be adversely affected. In other words, the client cannot authorize inadequate professional representation.

It is obvious that the lawyer cannot represent opposing parties in contentious contract negotiations or other adversarial nonlitigious relationships, for the same reason that the lawyer cannot represent opposing parties in litigation. The interests of the negotiating parties are directly adverse. The lawyer cannot satisfy his obligation of zealous advocacy for both clients in this situation, and the fact that the clients consent to the representation of both does not make it permissible.

It is possible, however, that the lawyer could represent one client against another client in a matter in which she is not representing the second client, if the clients consent after consultation with the lawyer. Assume that the lawyer represents one client against another client in a contract negotiation in which she is not representing the second client; she represents the second client in his tax matters. These two matters are unrelated. The lawyer is representing the first client in a directly adverse relationship to the second client, but the interests which the lawyer is representing are not directly adverse. There is a Model Rule 1.7(a) conflict, but the lawyer may believe that she can represent both properly. Assum-

10. Model Rule 1.3; Model Code DR 7–101.

ing informed consent by the clients, these conflicting representations may be permissible.

Suppose codefendants in a civil suit request the lawyer to represent both of them. They have a common defense to the action. They do not anticipate that their interests will conflict at any point with respect to liability or damages or both. The potential for such division inheres in the situation of codefendants. The interests of the codefendants are not now "directly adverse" under Model Rule 1.7(a). The lawyer should anticipate, however, that her representation of one client "may be materially limited by the lawyer's responsibilities to another client ..." under Model Rule 1.7(b). Assuming informed consent by the parties, can the lawyer represent them? To do so, the lawyer must believe that the representation of each party at the present time will not be adversely affected by the representation of the other party. In addition, the lawyer must believe that the likelihood of conflict between the parties is remote. If both conditions are satisfied, the lawyer is permitted to represent both at the same time. Before the consent of the parties to the common representation is obtained, the lawyer must inform the parties that if a conflict does arise, she will no longer be able to represent them together or represent either of them. She will not be able to represent one of them against the other after the conflict appears because this would constitute the representation of a client against a former client in the same matter (a successive representation conflict) which is prohibited under Model Rule 1.9. The hiring of a new lawyer by each client down the road would be cumbersome and expensive. The parties should know about that at the outset before they consent to the common representation.

Another situation similar to the case of the codefendants is that of two or more individuals who wish to construct a business enterprise in which each will make a different contribution, such as management, scientific skill, and finance. They have some understanding of how they wish to structure their relationship but they need the assistance of a lawyer to put their enterprise together properly. Their relationship is harmonious and accommodative. Significant differences, however, may develop as the negotiations proceed, and the lawyer should realize that down the road his representation of one client "may be materially limited by the lawyer's responsibilities to another client ..." under Model Rule 1.7(b). Assuming informed consent, however, the lawyer can represent the parties if he believes that the representation of each party at the present time will not be adversely affected by the representation of the other party or parties. In addition, the lawyer must believe that the likelihood of conflict among the parties is remote. If both conditions are satisfied, the lawyer is permitted to represent all the parties at the same time. Before the parties consent to the common representation the lawyer must inform them that if conflict does arise, he will no longer be able to represent any one of them, for the reasons set forth above. The hiring of another lawyer by each party at a later time would be cumbersome and expensive; the parties should know that before they consent.

There is another important point to bear in mind. After consent has been given to a common representation, either client can withdraw his consent for any reason without regard to the existence of a conflict. If that happens the lawyer can no longer represent either party in the matter.

Model Rule 1.7(b) is the basic conflict of interest section dealing with the situation of the friendly parties whose relationship has the potential for conflict in the future. It is made clear in the Comment to the Rule that the Rule applies both to codefendants or coplaintiffs in litigation, and to friendly parties with the potential for conflict in the nonlitigious situation, such as estate planning and estate administration.

Model Rule 2.2 deals also with the friendly parties who have the potential for conflict in the nonlitigious situation. The Rule is entitled "Intermediary." The title and the Comment imply that the Rule does not apply to codefendants or coplaintiffs. Whether the Rule would apply to the representation of husband and wife in the friendly divorce setting who wish to arrange property and custodial rights is not clear; the friendly divorce is a form of litigation. Model Rule 2.2 requires that the friendly parties with the potential for conflict consent to the common representation, that the lawyer believes that he can properly represent both parties, and that the likelihood of conflict is remote. If conflict arises, the lawyer must withdraw from the common representation and cannot represent one of the parties against the other.

The Model Rules do not state the relationship between Rule 1.7(b) and Rule 2.2. It appears that both rules deal with the friendly parties with the potential for conflict in the nonlitigious setting. The Comment to Model Rule 1.7 states that it may apply to parties in negotiations, to husband-wife estate planning, and to estate administration. The Comment to Model Rule 2.2 states that it applies to parties organizing a business enterprise and to estate administration, among other situations. Rule 2.2 is more explicit and detailed than Rule 1.7(b). The only reasonable conclusion one can draw is that in situations such as estate planning or estate administration, to which both Rules apply, both must be kept in mind but Rule 2.2 is a more specific guide.[11]

11. See Hazard and Koniak, Law and Ethics of Lawyering 588 (1990).

There is the ever-present problem of confidentiality in the area of common representation. Confidentiality has two aspects. First, there is the question of the attorney-client evidentiary privilege. The privilege belongs to the client. Most communications between attorney and client relating to the representation are covered by this privilege. What this means is that neither the attorney nor the client can be compelled to testify concerning such privileged communications unless the privilege is waived by the client.

The attorney-client evidentiary privilege is to be distinguished from the lawyer's professional duty of confidentiality. Under Model Rule 1.6 this duty forbids the lawyer from revealing any information, whatever the source may be, relating to the representation unless the client consents or the lawyer is impliedly authorized to reveal in order to carry out the representation adequately. There are several exceptions to this duty of confidentiality, namely, information pertaining to the client's intention to commit certain crimes in the future, and information that is necessary to enable the lawyer to protect his interests in a controversy with the client. The lawyer's professional duty of confidentiality is obviously much broader than the attorney-client evidentiary privilege. It covers all information relating to the representation, not just communications with the client. Certainly anything covered by the privilege is also covered by the professional duty of confidentiality; a great deal covered by the duty of confidentiality, however, is not covered by the privilege.

What is the status of confidentiality in the common representation? The Comment to Model Rule 2.2 provides in part:

> In a common representation the lawyer is still required both to keep each client adequately informed and to maintain confidentiality of information relating to the representation ... Complying with both requirements while acting as intermediary requires a delicate balance. If the balance cannot be maintained, the common representation is improper ...

This position that the duty of confidentiality to each client in the common representation applies is by no means universally accepted, and indeed would appear to be highly impracticable. There is a widely held view that there is no duty of confidentiality between the clients in the common representation; whatever information the lawyer acquires is available to both clients. This view is much more practicable and is consistent with the spirit of the common representation of clients.[12]

12. See Wolfram, Modern Legal Ethics 274–276 (1986); Hazard, Triangular Lawyer Relationships: An Exploratory Analysis, 1 Georgetown Journal of Legal Ethics 15, 27 (1987); New York State Bar Association, Committee on Profes-

Assume that the lawyer is representing several business people who are putting together an enterprise. In the course of the representation of one of them the lawyer learns that he is in serious personal financial difficulty and is in danger of becoming subject to some form of insolvency proceeding. If the Model Rule 2.2 position is in effect, the lawyer has to keep quiet, but clearly he cannot continue to represent adequately the other clients in this circumstance. The lawyer must withdraw from the representation of all the clients. If the "no confidentiality among common clients" position is in effect, the lawyer has a duty to the other clients to disclose the damaging information. This will probably place the clients in serious conflict, and the lawyer will be required to withdraw from his representation of all. If, however, the information does not split the clients, and the relationship of common purpose and accommodation continues, the lawyer can continue to represent all clients.

When the lawyer undertakes the common representation he should disclose the confidentiality rule that is applicable if the law on the point is established in the jurisdiction. If it is established, it can be changed by agreement. If it is not clear what the rule is, there should be an explicit agreement on the question. It should be also emphasized that damaging information is likely to lead to the lawyer's withdrawal from the representation of all the clients.

In a common representation the evidentiary attorney-client privilege does not apply in any subsequent proceeding between the common clients. The privilege does apply, however, with respect to any proceeding between a common client and a third party.

(2) HUSBAND AND WIFE

(a) A prospective husband and wife may ask a lawyer to represent both of them with respect to a premarital agreement. The parties may have a specific plan in mind with respect to the division of property on divorce, spousal rights in property acquired during the marriage, and the rights of the survivor in the estate of the first to die. The law of premarital agreements is discussed in Chapter 8, Section 5. In the absence of a statute providing otherwise, the courts exercise considerable oversight of such contracts to assure that advantage is not taken of one of the parties. It may appear that there is no reason why the lawyer cannot represent both parties with their informed consent if they have a common goal, know what their rights are, and know what they are giving up, and if the plan appears fair in the circumstances. Even if this is the case, however, it seems to be the prudent course that each party have separate counsel in view of the common law judicial

sional Ethics, Opinion No. 555 (1984); Wortham & Van Liew v. Superior Court, 188 Cal.App.3d 927, 233 Cal.Rptr. 725 (1987).

oversight of such contracts to prevent exploitation. It is arguable that the professional duty of competence would preclude common representation.

If the plan appears to be rather harsh on one of the parties, the lawyer should certainly recommend that the disadvantaged party obtain separate counsel. The disadvantaged party may not fully understand the future consequences, and may be in need of an advocate. The lawyer could not adequately represent both parties in this circumstance, and it may be improper for her to represent one of the parties against the other after consulting with both initially.

The upshot is that the lawyer at the very outset should advise the parties seeking a premarital contract that she can represent only one of them, and that the other party should retain another attorney.

It should be noted that contracts of this nature may be entered into after marriage. The common law rules for such contracts are the same as for premarital contracts. The Uniform Probate Code provisions also apply to both forms of contract, but the Uniform Premarital Agreement Act obviously applies only to premarital contracts.

(b) Husband and Wife may ask the lawyer to prepare their mutual wills in which each leaves his/her entire estate outright to the other if the other survives, or if not, to his/her issue. Will substitute property is to pass in the same way. Neither Husband nor Wife has been previously married; there are two children of their marriage, and neither has had any other children. Their total assets subject to estate tax have a value substantially less than $600,000, so there is no federal estate tax problem. It appears to be a happy relationship. Most lawyers in these circumstances would probably proceed to prepare their wills without raising any problems, and advise them that if their assets increase substantially they may want to consider somewhat different wills to minimize estate taxes.

In fact there are problems that could arise. After the death of the first to die, there is the potential for diversion of the survivor's assets. The survivor may remarry and some of the property may wind up in the hands of the second spouse by living gifts from the survivor, the will of the survivor, or the second spouse's forced share. The lawyer could suggest a contract binding the survivor to dispose of all property to their issue, or a trust for the benefit of the survivor with remainder to issue, to minimize the chances of diversion. For the happily married couple such suggestions could be unpleasant. On the other hand, one of them may take such suggestions seriously, and the other not. If the lawyer raises these questions he may cause trouble where none has existed. Indeed, if it does cause serious conflict, the lawyer would have to withdraw from representing both of them. Does the lawyer's duty of competence require that he raise these issues in this circumstance? Strictly speaking, it does, and the lawyer should obtain the clients' consent to the common representation at the outset.[13] It is safe to say that most lawyers probably would not raise these issues or seek consent.

(c) Husband and Wife come to the lawyer to have her prepare their wills. They are in their late fifties and have been married ten years. Each has been married once before and each has two children by the prior marriage. There are no children of this marriage. Their total assets subject to estate tax have a value of substantially less than $600,000, so there is no federal estate tax problem. Their plan is to have the property of the first to die pass outright to the survivor, and to have the survivor leave all to the four children equally. Will substitute property is to pass in the same way. It appears to be a happy relationship.

As in example (b), there is the potential for diversion by the survivor to a later spouse, and by the later spouse's forced share. In addition, there is the risk that the survivor will favor his/her children over the children of the other. These problems could be obviated, in whole or in part, by a contract between the parties binding the survivor to leave all to the four children equally, or by placing all assets in trust for the survivor for life, with remainder to the children equally. Clearly this situation is more problematic than example (b). It seems that the lawyer would be professionally remiss if she did not raise the problem of the disposition of the assets by the survivor, and obtain consent to the common representation at the outset. Raising the problem may be unpleasant but the duty of competence dictates that it be done in this situation. If one of them wants to create a system of protection and the other does not, the rift may become sufficiently substantial that the lawyer may have to withdraw. On the other hand, the parties may resolve the matter satisfactorily between themselves, and the lawyer may continue the common representation.

(d) Assume the facts of example (b). The lawyer never raises any questions about the plan of mutual wills in which the first to die leaves his/her property to the survivor, and the survivor leaves all to their issue. Between the initial meeting and the date set for the execution of the wills, the lawyer receives a phone call from Wife in which she tells the lawyer that she is very active in her church and makes substantial annual contributions to her church.

13. Restatement of the Law Governing Lawyers § 211, Comment c (Tent. Draft No. 4, April 10, 1991).

She states that if she is the survivor and the children are well off financially, she may be inclined to change her will later and make a substantial bequest for religious purposes; she would leave the rest to the children. She asks if this would be permissible. She makes it clear that she does not want this repeated to Husband.

What is the lawyer to do with this information? The lawyer never discussed the question of confidences with Husband and Wife because there appeared to be no reason under the circumstances to do so. If the view is adopted that the lawyer must not reveal confidences of one client to the other client, then the lawyer must terminate her representation of the clients because she cannot adequately represent Husband so long as she withholds this information, and she cannot continue to represent Wife in her relationship with Husband in this matter because Husband would constitute a former client with respect to this matter.

If the view is adopted that there is no duty of confidentiality between common clients, then the lawyer must disclose the information to Husband. If the parties can agree amicably to a resolution of the problem, the lawyer can continue to represent them; if a serious rift is created, then the lawyer must withdraw from the representation.

(e) The lawyer prepared mutual wills for Husband and Wife in 1990 (first to die leaves all to survivor; at death of survivor, all to their children), and supervised their execution. This was the first time the lawyer had met Husband and Wife. The lawyer told them that if their assets increased significantly they should consider a revision of their wills to minimize estate taxation. The lawyer had no further contact with either of them until she received a phone call from Husband in 1993 in which Husband stated that he wanted to change his will to leave a substantial bequest to his Son if he should predecease Wife, and that if he should survive Wife, to leave a larger share to Son than to the other children. Husband said that he was in business with Son. When the lawyer asked if Wife knew about this, Husband responded that she did not and he did not want it disclosed to her.

Are Husband and Wife still clients of the lawyer? The relationship has been dormant for three years. If they ceased to be clients, then the lawyer must not reveal the information received from a "prospective" client (Husband) to Wife. In addition, the lawyer cannot represent Husband in this matter because it is substantially related to the matter in which the lawyer had represented Wife, a former client, and the Husband's interest is materially adverse to the interest of Wife. Model Rule 1.9 forbids the lawyer from representing Husband against the former client Wife in this circumstance.

If the lawyer-client relationship has continued, however dormant it may be, the lawyer's duties are determined by whether it is assumed that there are no confidences between common clients, or it is assumed that confidences must be maintained between common clients. If there are no confidences, the lawyer must reveal this information to common client Wife. If Husband and Wife cannot work out their differences amicably, the lawyer must withdraw from representation of both of them. If it is assumed that confidences must be maintained between common clients, then the lawyer must not reveal the information but she is precluded from representing both of them. The lawyer cannot adequately represent Wife while withholding such information, and she cannot represent Husband in this matter against Wife, her former client.

It is unclear whether or not Husband and Wife remain clients of the lawyer under these circumstances.[14] It should be noted that in this circumstance the client or the lawyer can terminate whatever lawyer-client relationship exists at any time by notifying the other to this effect.

There is another problem that may arise when the lawyer prepares a will for a client and has no contact with the client for years thereafter. Changes in the estate tax law may occur which call for changes in the party's will. Does the lawyer have an obligation to inform the party of the need for a new will? The issue is whether or not a lawyer-client relationship continues. If it does, then the lawyer's duty of competence requires that the lawyer notify the client. Is the period of time that has passed since the will was executed relevant? There is no clear answer to this problem. To require the lawyer to follow up every person for whom she has prepared a will may be a substantial burden. On the other hand, if the estate tax changes occur within a year of the preparation of the will, it seems reasonable to require the lawyer to notify the party. The lawyer can, of course, cut off any responsibility by a letter to the client terminating the relationship immediately after the will is executed.[15]

(3) PARENT AND CHILD

Sensitive professional questions can arise in the trusts and estates area with respect to parent-child relationships. The following are two such situations.

---

14. See Price, Contemporary Estate Planning 72, 73 (1992); Pennell, Professional Responsibility: Reforms Are Needed To Accommodate Estate Planning and Family Counseling, in U. Miami, 25th Institute on Estate Planning, Chapter 18, page 18–37; Manoir–Electroalloys Corp. v. Amalloy Corp., 711 F.Supp. 188 (D.N.J.1989); Pizel v. Zuspann, 247 Kan. 699, 803 P.2d 205 (1990); Stangland v. Brock, 109 Wash.2d 675, 747 P.2d 464 (1987).

15. For an extended discussion of husband-wife representation, see Collett, And the Two Shall Become As One ... Until the Lawyers Are Done, 7 Notre Dame Journal of Law, Ethics & Public Policy 101 (1993).

Daughter, aged 20, will receive a substantial amount of property outright when she reaches 21, under a trust established by the will of her late maternal grandmother. Daughter's Father does not believe that she has the maturity to handle this wealth properly. Father would like her to establish an irrevocable trust of this property for her benefit, with periodic principal distributions in later years. Father's lawyer represents him in his personal and business matters. Father asks his lawyer to speak to Daughter about creating such a trust. Father will pay the legal fee.

This is a proposal that Daughter become a client of the lawyer. The fact that Father pays the fee has no effect upon the lawyer's responsibility or loyalty to the client.[16] Under Model Rule 7.3 the lawyer cannot solicit Daughter as a client in person or by phone, but he is permitted to solicit by letter provided the letter is labeled as an advertisement. The better course for the lawyer is to tell Father that he must await a call from Daughter.

Once the lawyer-client relationship is properly established with Daughter, the lawyer's duty is to consider only the Daughter's interests. This is not a case of common clients with a common purpose; Father has no interest in this matter in any material or legal respect. Father wants to have Daughter comply with his wishes, and may wish to have a lawyer act as his agent for this purpose, but obviously the lawyer representing Daughter cannot also represent Father for the purpose of furthering Father's purpose. It should be noted that if Father hires another lawyer, under Model Rule 4.2 that lawyer may not speak directly with Daughter without the consent of Daughter's lawyer.

Daughter's lawyer must counsel her as to the advantages and disadvantages of a trust, and the different forms the trust may take. The ultimate decision is Daughter's.

Another situation involves Mother, a very elderly, wealthy person, who has a will in which a substantial fraction of her estate is left to her Son. Son is familiar with the provisions of the will. Mother has a lawyer who handles all her personal matters.

Mother's lawyer also represents Son in his business and personal matters. Recently Son has told the lawyer in her professional capacity that he is in serious financial difficulty, is experiencing episodes of depression, has been using illicit drugs occasionally, and is seeing a psychiatrist. Mother does not know these facts, and Son has made it clear that he doesn't want her to know them.

The lawyer cannot reveal these confidences to Mother, but she can advise Son that he has a moral obligation to tell Mother. Assuming that Son does not tell Mother, the lawyer cannot contin-

---

16. Model Rules 1.8, 5.4; Model Code DR 5–107.

ue to represent Mother in her estate matters because the lawyer has important information that she cannot disclose to Mother. The lawyer must advise Mother that she cannot continue to counsel Mother in her estate matters because of a conflict of interest between Mother and Son.

If Son tells Mother the facts, the lawyer may then counsel Mother in her estate matters and represent Son in that connection as long as the relationship between Mother and Son is open and nonadversarial and the parties consent to the common representation.

(4) FIDUCIARY AND BENEFICIARY

Assume that the lawyer who is retained by the executor to represent him in the administration of the estate, also represents a residuary legatee in her manufacturing business. Does this present a conflict? The executor owes fiduciary duties to the beneficiary; certain conduct of the executor could place him in direct conflict with the beneficiary. This would place the lawyer in the position of representing one client against another client whom he represents in an unrelated matter. The representation of the two clients in that circumstance would be impermissible under Model Rule 1.7(a) without the consent of both clients. Because of the potential for conflict and disruption, the lawyer should advise the executor and the beneficiary of the problem at the outset and under Model Rule 1.7(b) obtain their consents to the current representations. With the consents the representations are permissible.

Assume another situation in which the lawyer retained by the executor is asked by a beneficiary to advise and represent her in connection with her interest in the estate. There is the potential for conflict between the executor and the beneficiary. There is every reason to believe, however, that the executor will comply with his fiduciary duties and that the administration will run its course smoothly. The lawyer is permitted under Model Rule 1.7(b) to represent both parties in this circumstance with their consents. The lawyer must advise them that if the relationship between them becomes adversarial she would have to withdraw as attorney for both.

There is another very important aspect of professional responsibility relating to the fiduciary-beneficiary relationship. In recent years the profession has been focusing on the responsibilities, if any, owed to the beneficiaries by the lawyer who has been retained by an executor or a trustee in connection with his fiduciary function. The estate or trust is not a juridical person or entity as is the corporation. The estate or trust consists of the individual who serves in the capacity of fiduciary with respect to certain property for the benefit of legatees, devisees or trust beneficiaries. When the fiduciary retains the lawyer to represent him in the administration of the estate or trust, certainly the lawyer's client is the person serving in the fiduciary capacity. By virtue of this employment the lawyer does not also represent the "estate" or "trust" as an entity because there is no such entity, and the lawyer does not automatically represent the beneficiaries. It is arguable that the lawyer in this situation should be considered to have as his common clients the fiduciary and the beneficiaries, but the lawyer has not expressly undertaken to represent both, and generally is not considered to have impliedly entered into such a common representation.

A lawyer retained for corporate purposes by the president of a corporation represents the corporation as a juridical entity, and not the president or any other officer or any director. It is the lawyer's duty to serve the interests of the corporation. If the president or other officer acts in an illegal manner to the detriment of the corporation, it is the lawyer's duty to take steps within the corporation to correct the situation. The relationship between the officer and the lawyer may become adversarial. There is no such entity representation in the hiring of the lawyer by the executor or trustee.

The executor or trustee has the fiduciary obligation to act solely in the interests of the beneficiaries. The attorney for the executor or trustee in his fiduciary capacity is being paid from estate or trust funds to perform her professional function. If the fiduciary breaches his duty to the beneficiaries it is at least unseemly that the lawyer should continue to serve at the expense of the estate or trust and remain silent. If the fiduciary's conduct is criminal or fraudulent, the lawyer is forbidden to continue to represent the fiduciary under the provisions of Model Rule 1.2, but the Model Rules do not impose any duty to disclose to the beneficiaries, and indeed Model Rule 1.6 forbids it. If the fiduciary's conduct is illegal but not criminal or fraudulent, the lawyer may continue to assist and counsel the fiduciary under the language of the Model Rules.

Such professional results seem to be very unsatisfactory. As a consequence some courts and commentators have taken the position that although the beneficiaries are not, strictly speaking, clients of the lawyer who is retained by the fiduciary, nevertheless the lawyer owes certain fiduciary duties to the beneficiaries.[17] This

17. See Hazard and Hodes, 1 The Law of Lawyering § 1.3:108 (2d ed. 1992); Price, Contemporary Estate Planning 75, 304 (1992); Hazard, Triangular Lawyer Relationships: An Exploratory Analysis, 1 Georgetown Journal of Legal Ethics 15 (1987); Pennell, Professional Responsibility: Reforms Are Needed To Accommodate Estate Planning and Family Counseling, in U.Miami, 25th Institute on Estate Planning, Chapter 18, page 18–43 (1991); Estate of Gory, 570 So.2d 1381 (Fla.App.1990); Estate of Halas, 159 Ill.App.3d 818, 111

line of thinking is still in its rudimentary stages, and one can only speculate as to appropriate professional responses to specific situations. The thrust, however, seems to be that the lawyer should see to it that the beneficiaries are kept informed concerning the administration, including information involving a breach of trust by the fiduciary. The fiduciary has a duty voluntarily to account to beneficiaries from time to time, and to respond to questions and requests for information. If the fiduciary does not perform this duty satisfactorily, the lawyer should perform it for the fiduciary. The fiduciary is not likely to volunteer information dealing with a breach of trust; it is the lawyer's duty to do so. It goes without saying that the lawyer should counsel against a breach, and should tell the fiduciary to rectify any breach.

How does the obligation to disclose square with the lawyer's duty of confidentiality under Model Rule 1.6? It has been maintained that the disclosure is within the clause which provides that the lawyer may disclose information relating to the representation if the disclosure is "impliedly authorized in order to carry out the representation...." The problem here is that the fiduciary may expressly prohibit the lawyer from such disclosure. The obligation to disclose should be based on some quasi-client relationship with the beneficiaries.

The situation may arise in which the disclosure of breach to the beneficiaries may not be adequate because the beneficiaries may not be able to protect themselves due to their youth or advanced age or lack of sophistication. In such a situation it may be incumbent upon the lawyer to inform the court of the circumstances.[18]

There is an oblique reference to the lawyer's duty to beneficiaries in Comment 8 to Model Rule 1.2. After discussing the lawyer's duty to withdraw if the client engages in criminal or fraudulent conduct, there is the following statement: "Where the client is a fiduciary, the lawyer may be charged with special obligations in dealings with a beneficiary."

Assume that the lawyer informs the beneficiaries of facts which indicate that a breach of trust may have occurred. The fiduciary denies wrongdoing. The beneficiaries hire a lawyer and threaten suit. Can the lawyer continue to represent the fiduciary in the negotiations and in the litigation? Or does the relationship preclude this on the basis that the lawyer would be representing a client (fiduciary) against a "former client" (beneficiaries) whom he

Ill.Dec. 639, 512 N.E.2d 1276 (1987); Charleson v. Hardesty, 108 Nev. 878, 839 P.2d 1303 (1992); Estate of Larson, 103 Wash.2d 517, 694 P.2d 1051 (1985).

18. Estate of Minsky, 59 Ill.App.3d 974, 17 Ill.Dec. 501, 376 N.E.2d 647 (1978).

had represented previously in the same matter? Certainly the lawyer who has been engaged in this "dual representation" of sorts should be precluded if he had received confidential information from the beneficiaries which relates to the negotiations or the litigation. If no such information has been received, then probably the lawyer should not be precluded from continuing her representation of the fiduciary.

The existence of some professional duty to the beneficiaries is in an early stage of development. Most jurisdictions have not dealt with this issue adequately or at all. It may be that in a given jurisdiction a lawyer will have no professional duty to the beneficiaries and must serve the fiduciary exclusively.

Unless the law in the jurisdiction is clearly to the contrary, it seems that the prudent and proper course for the lawyer is to inform the fiduciary and the beneficiaries at the outset that she considers that she has a professional duty to the beneficiaries to inform them concerning any and all matters of administration. The lawyer should also inform the beneficiaries that she is not their lawyer.

It seems that the answer to this general problem should be that due to the nature of the subject matter, the lawyer necessarily represents the fiduciary and the beneficiaries as common clients, with a duty of full disclosure and no confidences. If the clients come into serious conflict, the lawyer must withdraw from representing both sides.

Chapter 15

RESULTING TRUSTS AND CONSTRUCTIVE TRUSTS

The purpose of the trusts portion of this book is to present the legal framework of private and charitable trusts as vehicles for the donative disposition of accumulated wealth. The purchase money resulting trust, discussed in Section 2 of this chapter, is not strictly within our purpose, but it seems advisable to deal with it, in view of the discussion of the other form of resulting trust in Section 1 which clearly is within our purpose. The topic of constructive trusts is a broad one that forms a part of the subject of restitution which is beyond the scope of this book, but it is necessary to deal with a piece of it in Section 3 of this chapter which is concerned with the unenforceable oral express trust. The constructive trust is also discussed in Chapter 3, Section 7, in connection with fraud in the execution of wills.

SECTION 1. THE RESULTING TRUST: WHERE AN EXPRESS TRUST FAILS OR ITS BENEFICIAL PROVISIONS ARE INCOMPLETE

There is a variety of circumstances in which an express trust may fail or its beneficial provisions may be incomplete. The settlor transfers property to Bank, in trust, to pay the income to Jones for his life. There is no remainder interest stated, and no express provision that the trustee is to pay over the principal upon Jones' death to the settlor. Bank holds the legal fee interest, and Jones has an equitable life estate. The beneficial provisions are incomplete. Who has the beneficial (equitable) interest upon Jones' death, Bank or the settlor? The presumption is that it was not intended that the trustee should have any beneficial interest. While Jones is alive, the settlor has a future interest, namely, an equitable reversion in fee. When Jones dies, the settlor's interest is a present equitable fee interest, and it is the Bank's duty to convey its legal fee to the settlor. Upon Jones' death, the language of the law is that the Bank holds on resulting trust for the settlor. It is simply a way of recognizing the existence of an equitable reversion which has not been expressly provided for. Just as the legal reversion in land is usually implied rather than expressed, so the equitable reversion is usually implied. When there are no more express beneficiaries and the trustee becomes obligated to return the assets to the settlor as holder of an implied equitable reversion, it is said that the trustee holds on resulting trust for the settlor. It should be noted that if the trust instrument in our example expressly provided that the trustee was to pay over to the settlor upon Jones' death, the legal result would be the same but it would not be referred to as a resulting trust because the trust relationship between the trustee and the settlor would be an express trust.

It is possible, of course, that the settlor's intention was that the trustee should be the beneficial owner upon Jones' death. If the trustee can convince the court that this is so, then the trustee has it all. The presumption, however, is strongly in favor of the resulting trust for the settlor. If the trustee is a bank, it is virtually inconceivable that a gift to the bank was intended. If the trustee is a person, however, it is possible, but most unlikely, that a gift to the trustee was intended.

It is possible, but unlikely, that the Bank in our example would not receive the legal fee but rather a legal life estate for the life of Jones. As we have indicated previously, the trustee usually holds the legal fee.[1] If, however, the trustee has a legal life estate for the life of Jones, then there is no resulting trust. The settlor has the legal and equitable reversion while Jones lives, and has the present legal and equitable fee automatically upon Jones' death. There is nothing for the Bank to transfer on Jones' death.

There are, of course, other circumstances in which an express trust fails and a resulting trust arises. Settlor transfers to Bank, in trust, to pay the income to Jones for life, and to pay the principal to Jones' descendants who survive him. At Jones' death he has no descendants who survive him; Bank holds on resulting trust for the settlor because the trust instrument did not provide for an alternative remainder, and did not expressly provide for the return to the settlor.

Another example: Testator in his will creates a trust to pay the income to his children for their lives, and upon the death of the survivor to pay the income to his grandchildren for their lives and upon the death of the survivor to pay the principal to his great-grandchildren then living. The remainder to the great-grandchildren violates the rule against perpetuities, and under the traditional application of this rule, the remainder fails; upon the death of the last surviving grandchild the trustee will hold on resulting trust for the estate of the testator (residuary legatees or heirs).[2]

In our discussion of charitable trusts we noted that if the trust purpose became accomplished or could not be served by the trust for other reasons, the court of equity would determine whether the

---

1. See Chapter 5, Section 8.

2. See Chapter 8, Section 9, for discussion of the rule against perpetuities.

trust assets should be applied to another related charitable purpose pursuant to the doctrine of cy pres, or should be held on resulting trust for the settlor or his estate.[3]

It should be noted that there is no statute of frauds issue with respect to the resulting trust. Such statutes usually except the resulting trust and the constructive trust from the requirement of a writing. By definition the resulting trust arises by implication, and consequently it could not be subject to such a requirement.

SECTION 2. THE PURCHASE MONEY RESULTING TRUST

This sub-topic is tangential to the purposes of this book, but a brief treatment is called for to complete the circle with respect to resulting trusts.

In the feudal period a gratuitous transfer of legal title to land by A to B without any reference to a use was presumed to mean that B held legal title to the use of A. This rule developed because feoffments to uses were so common that a gratuitous feoffment without reference to a use was thought probably to have been intended to be to the use of the grantor rather than to have been intended as a gift. The use that was presumed in this circumstance was called a resulting use. The presumption would be rebutted by showing that consideration was given, or by the recital of nominal consideration in the feoffment, or by evidence that a gift was intended, in which cases the grantee would receive an absolute fee. This presumption of a resulting use or trust in the case of a gratuitous conveyance of land is no part of our modern law.

In the feudal period, if A paid the purchase price to X for a conveyance of legal title to land by X to B, B would be presumed to hold legal title on a resulting use for A. This was deemed to reflect A's unexpressed intention. This presumption has been retained in the modern law. Indeed, it has been extended to include transactions in personal property of the same nature. A recitation in the deed to B that B paid consideration for the transfer does not affect the presumption if in fact A establishes that he paid the purchase price. In most states today, if A can demonstrate that he paid the purchase price, a presumption arises that B holds on resulting trust for A, and the burden then is upon B to come forth with evidence that a gift to him was intended;[4] provided, however, that if B is related to A in such a way that a gift would be a reasonable

---

3. See Chapter 12, Section 4.

4. Gabitzsch v. Cole, 95 Ariz. 15, 386 P.2d 23 (1963); Prassa v. Corcoran, 24 Ill.2d 288, 181 N.E.2d 138 (1962); Slo-cum v. Hammond, 346 N.W.2d 485 (Iowa 1984); Medders v. Ryle, 458 So.2d 685 (Miss.1984); Leonard v. Counts, 221 Va. 582, 272 S.E.2d 190 (1980).

inference from the transaction, the presumption of a resulting trust for A does not arise. It should be emphasized that for the purpose of the presumption there is no need for A to demonstrate any understanding with B that he is to hold in trust; the presumption arises merely upon A's establishing that he paid the purchase price. Several states have statutes which completely do away with the presumption of a resulting trust in the purchase money situation.[5]

If the grantee in the deed is the spouse or child of the person who pays the purchase price, the grantee is presumed to hold title free of any trust because a gift is a reasonable inference in these circumstances.[6] If the grantor-spouse or parent can establish that a gift was not intended, however, then the presumption of a gift is rebutted and the grantee holds on resulting trust for the grantor-spouse or parent.[7]

The factual setting of the purchase money resulting trust is very different from that of the resulting trust which arises upon the failure of an express trust. In each case, however, a person has caused legal title to be vested in one person and presumptively intends to retain the beneficial interest for himself. It is this common element which defines the resulting trust.

In the purchase money resulting trust, the trustee holds the legal fee and the person paying the purchase price holds the equitable fee. It is the trustee's duty to transfer the legal fee to the equitable title holder whenever the latter requests, and all income earned on the trust property belongs beneficially to the equitable owner.

The person who pays the purchase price, intends to be the beneficial owner, and has title taken in the name of another person, does this obviously to conceal the fact of his ownership. The secrecy may be completely legitimate. Some people simply do not want the world to know what they own. Also, a person accumulating land for development in a certain area may not want the sellers to know this, for if they do the price of the individual parcels might rise. The secrecy, however, may be for an illegitimate purpose, such as the defrauding of creditors or the tax collector. If the purpose is illegal, the resulting trust may not be enforceable; that

---

5. E.g., Ky.Rev.Stat.Ann. § 381.170; Mich.Stat.Ann. § 26.57; Minn.Stat.Ann. § 501.07; N.Y.Est.Powers & Trusts Law § 7–1.3.

6. Walker v. Hooker, 282 Ark. 61, 667 S.W.2d 637 (1984); Walter v. Home Nat. Bank and Trust Co., 148 Conn. 635, 173 A.2d 503 (1961); Underwood v. Otwell, 269 N.C. 571, 153 S.E.2d 40 (1967); Dodd v. Hinton, 173 W.Va. 69, 312 S.E.2d 293 (1984).

7. Whitlock v. Hause, 694 F.2d 861 (1st Cir.1982); Walker v. Hooker, 282 Ark. 61, 667 S.W.2d 637 (1984); Whitney v. Whitney, 171 Conn. 23, 368 A.2d 96 (1976); Ashbaugh v. Ashbaugh, 222 Ga. 811, 152 S.E.2d 888 (1966); Estate of Spadoni, 71 Wash.2d 820, 430 P.2d 965 (1967).

is to say, the equity court may choose to permit the holder of legal title to have beneficial ownership as well, rather than enforce a resulting trust for the person who initiates the wrong.

The person who pays the purchase price and has title taken in the name of another may, of course, intend to make a gift to the person. In some situations, as we have mentioned, a gift is presumed. In other situations a gift may well have been intended although the presumption is otherwise. Whether the presumption of the resulting trust in the purchase money situation reflects intention more often than not is questionable. It may be that the presumption is a feudal anachronism.

Where A pays X the purchase price for the transfer to B, there may be an express oral agreement between A and B that B holds in trust for A. If the trust property is land, the express trust is unenforceable under the statute of frauds unless there is the requisite written memorandum. A may recover, however, under the resulting trust doctrine. If the statute of frauds is complied with, there is no need to rely on the purchase money resulting trust doctrine. If the trust property is personalty, the statute of frauds is not applicable and the parol evidence rule seldom presents any problem with respect to proving the oral trust. If A proves the existence of the oral trust, then, of course, the purchase money resulting trust doctrine need not be relied upon. If there is some difficulty in establishing the oral trust, A may recover under the purchase money resulting trust doctrine.

SECTION 3. CONSTRUCTIVE TRUSTS: THE UNENFORCEABLE ORAL TRUST

The subject of constructive trusts is a part of the law of restitution. The constructive trust is a remedial device that is employed to correct unjust enrichment. It has the effect of taking title to property from one person whose title unjustly enriches him, and transferring it to another person who has been unjustly deprived of it. The unjust enrichment usually comes about as a result of mistake, fraud, duress, undue influence, or abuse of a fiduciary or confidential relationship. To correct the injustice, the court of equity declares that the unjustly enriched person shall be a constructive trustee for the benefit of the unjustly deprived person, and the court directs that legal title be transferred by the unjustly enriched person to the unjustly deprived person. The constructive trustee is not regarded as a fiduciary with respect to the constructive trust property; his only function is to act to place the title where it belongs. The equity court merely uses the trust analogy to achieve a restitutional result.

The constructive trust remedy is employed in many different situations in which a transfer of property has been made under mistake or is the result of the abuse of a fiduciary or confidential relationship or has been induced by fraud, duress, or undue influence. As we indicated above, the subject of constructive trusts in general is beyond the scope of this book. It is discussed in Chapter 3, Section 7, in connection with fraud in the execution of wills. Here we discuss the remedy as it pertains to the failure of a "trustee" to perform an unenforceable express oral trust.

Suppose O transfers legal title to land to T in fee by deed, and T contemporaneously agrees orally that he will manage the property for O's benefit and reconvey the title to O on request. At the time the transfer and agreement were made, T never intended to perform the oral agreement. O would not have conveyed the title had he known T's intentions. T has induced the transfer by fraudulently misrepresenting his state of mind. The agreement purports to create a trust for O, but it is unenforceable under the statute of frauds. Does T have absolute title to the land, or does O have a remedy to recover title? In this situation it is held that T is a constructive trustee of the land for O, and must reconvey the legal title to O.[8] The express oral trust is not enforceable, but O may prove the existence of the oral trust for the purpose of preventing T from unjustly enriching himself at O's expense. The result is substantially the same as enforcement of the express trust, but it is rationalized in terms of a restitutional remedy.

The oral agreement in these circumstances is often phrased in terms of a simple promise to reconvey the title rather than in terms of a trust with a duty to restore legal title to the grantor on request. The oral contract to reconvey the land is unenforceable because it too violates the statute of frauds, and the constructive trust remedy is available to correct the injustice. It makes no difference whether it is a trust or a contract as far as the constructive trust remedy is concerned. The oral arrangement may be merely the product of ignorance concerning the law, or it may be employed to conceal the grantor's interest for the reasons discussed in connection with the purchase money resulting trust in the preceding section.

Suppose we change the facts of the example in the second preceding paragraph to this extent: T intended to carry out the trust when the agreement was made but subsequently changed his mind. T is not guilty of fraud because he did not induce the transfer by misrepresenting his state of mind. T simply changed his mind later. There is authority for imposing a constructive trust

8. Cohen v. Cohen, 195 Md. 520, 73 A.2d 872 (1950); March v. Gerstenschlager, 436 S.W.2d 6 (Mo.1969); Ferguson v. Ferguson, 55 N.C.App. 341, 285 S.E.2d 288 (1982); Lawrence v. Andrews, 84 R.I. 133, 122 A.2d 132 (1956).

in this situation as well,[9] but the prevailing view is that T is permitted to retain the title.[10] It seems that the moral turpitude is not considered sufficient to move the court to bypass the statute of frauds in this situation by the imposition of a constructive trust.

Suppose the facts of the example were as follows: T intended to carry out the oral agreement at the time he entered into it and later changed his mind, and T was in a confidential relationship with O. Let us assume that T was a child of O whom O trusted implicitly and T was aware of the confidence reposed in him. In this situation, despite the absence of fraud, it is held that T holds the title as constructive trustee for O.[11] One may ask whether O will ever transfer title to T on an oral trust unless there is a relationship of confidence. It appears that a relationship of confidence inheres in the situation. Nevertheless, there are cases in which the rule described in this paragraph has been recognized and yet the court has not found the necessary confidential relationship and has allowed T to retain title because T did not misrepresent his state of mind.[12]

Let us assume that O transfers title to personal property to T in fee by written instrument, and T contemporaneously agrees orally that he will hold the property for O's benefit and reconvey the title to O on request. The statute of frauds does not apply to personal property. There is the possibility that the trust cannot be proved because of the parol evidence rule, but as we have discussed, the parol evidence rule seldom precludes the proof of an oral trust.[13] In most cases the oral trust is enforceable. If it is not enforceable, then a constructive trust may be imposed in accordance with the principles just discussed with respect to the oral trust of land.

Suppose O transfers title to land to T in fee by deed, with the contemporaneous oral agreement that T will hold the property in trust for X (not for O, as in the previous discussion) and will convey

9. Grissom v. Bunch, 227 Ark. 696, 301 S.W.2d 462 (1957); Hertz v. Klavan, 374 A.2d 871 (D.C.App.1977); Austin v. Austin, 135 Me. 155, 191 A. 276 (1937); Miller v. Belville, 98 Vt. 243, 126 A. 590 (1924).

10. Parks v. Parks, 240 Ga. 1, 239 S.E.2d 334 (1977); Meskell v. Meskell, 355 Mass. 148, 243 N.E.2d 804 (1969); Schultz v. Curson, 421 S.W.2d 205 (Mo. 1967); Rosen v. Rosen, 384 Pa. 547, 121 A.2d 89 (1956); Dowgialla v. Knevage, 48 Wash.2d 326, 294 P.2d 393 (1956).

11. Cole v. Adkins, 358 So.2d 447 (Ala.1978); Bramlett v. Selman, 268 Ark. 457, 597 S.W.2d 80 (1980); Cohen v. Cohen, 182 Conn. 193, 438 A.2d 55 (1980); Kam Oi Lee v. Fong Wong, 57 Hawaii 137, 552 P.2d 635 (1976); Clooney v. Clooney, 118 N.H. 754, 394 A.2d 313 (1978).

12. Guerrieri v. Guerrieri, 13 Ill. App.3d 1043, 301 N.E.2d 603 (1973); Meskell v. Meskell, 355 Mass. 148, 243 N.E.2d 804 (1969); Beelman v. Beelman, 121 Ill.App.3d 684, 77 Ill.Dec. 196, 460 N.E.2d 55 (1984); Rosen v. Rosen, 384 Pa. 547, 121 A.2d 89 (1956); Mattes v. Olearain, 759 P.2d 1177 (Utah App. 1988).

13. Chapter 5, Section 2.

the legal title to X upon his request. At the time the oral agreement was made, T intended to abide by it. Subsequently he changes his mind and refuses to convey to X on request. In this situation, as in the corresponding situation where T agreed to hold in trust for O and changed his mind, the prevailing view is that T is permitted to retain the title, and no constructive trust is imposed.[14] If, however, T did not intend to perform the trust at the time he agreed to do so, then a constructive trust is imposed for the benefit of X.[15] One might expect that the constructive trust would be for the benefit of O, because this would do less violence to the statute of frauds, but instead the law gives it to X. A constructive trust for O would prevent T from being unjustly enriched and would not constitute a de facto enforcement of the oral trust rationalized in terms of a restitutional remedy. If T did not fraudulently induce the transfer of the title but was in a confidential relationship with O, T would similarly be deemed to hold title on a constructive trust for X.[16] It should be noted parenthetically that the results are the same if the agreement between O and T is contractual in form, rather than in the form of a trust, as discussed above in connection with the commitment of T to reconvey to O.

(h) If O transfers title to personalty to T in fee by written instrument, with a contemporaneous oral agreement that T will hold the property in trust for X and convey legal title to X on his request, the express oral trust is usually enforceable because the statute of frauds is not applicable and the parol evidence rule normally does not preclude proof of the oral trust.[17] If the oral trust cannot be proved because of the parol evidence rule, then a constructive trust may be imposed in accordance with the principles discussed with respect to the same situation involving land.

The trust property originally may be land which is sold and replaced by personalty, or vice-versa. The applicability of the statute of frauds is determined, of course, by the nature of the property originally transferred in trust. Also, an oral trust may be created consisting originally of both real property and personal property, in which case the statute of frauds would be applicable in part; that is to say, the oral express trust may be enforceable as to the personal property, but not as to the real property. A construc-

---

14. Robertson v. Robertson, 229 Ark. 649, 317 S.W.2d 272 (1958); Ampuero v. Luce, 68 Cal.App.2d 811, 157 P.2d 899 (1945); Kay v. Kay, 763 S.W.2d 712 (Mo.App.1989); Johnson v. Larson, 79 N.D. 409, 56 N.W.2d 750 (1953).

15. Bennett v. Bennett, 83 F.Supp. 19 (D.D.C.1949); Finch v. York, 294 Ala. 382, 318 So.2d 249 (1975); Wellman v. Wellman, 206 Iowa 445, 220 N.W. 82 (1928).

16. Bremer v. Bremer, 411 Ill. 454, 104 N.E.2d 299 (1952); Sojourner v. Sojourner, 247 Miss. 342, 153 So.2d 803 (1963); Garcia v. Marquez, 101 N.M. 427, 684 P.2d 513 (1984); Simpson v. Dailey, 496 A.2d 126 (R.I.1985).

17. See Chapter 5, Section 2.

tive trust may, of course, be enforced with respect to the real property.

To this point we have been discussing oral living trusts of land and personalty. Similar problems can arise under a will. O informs T that he intends to bequeath (or devise) certain property to him outright in his will, provided T agrees to hold the property in trust for X and to convey title to X on request. T agrees to do so and intends to perform the trust. O dies leaving a will which includes the outright bequest to T. The will is admitted to probate. After O's death, T changes his mind and decides to keep the bequest for himself. The oral trust is not enforceable because it does not comply with the formalities required for a valid will. The prevailing view is that T is permitted to retain title,[18] as in the case of the oral living trust, but there is authority that T holds as constructive trustee for X.[19] If T did not intend to perform the trust when he agreed to it, or if T intended to perform the trust when he agreed to it but changed his mind prior to O's death without advising O, or if T was in a confidential relationship with O, T would be a constructive trustee for X.[20] Both personalty and realty are subject to the statutory will requirements, and therefore the legal consequences of the oral testamentary trust are the same regardless of the character of the property. It should be noted parenthetically that the results are the same if the agreement between O and T is in the form of a promise to convey rather than in the form of a trust.

The courts would do less violence to the statutory requirements for a will if they held that the constructive trust was for the benefit of O's estate, that is to say, the residuary legatees or heirs of O. The courts, however, have seen fit not only to prevent T's unjust enrichment but also effectively to enforce the oral testamentary trust.

We have been discussing the typical oral trust situation where the trustee holds for one beneficiary presumably for a short period of time. It is very unusual to have an oral trust of land which

---

18. Kauzlarich v. Landrum, 2 Ill. App.3d 591, 274 N.E.2d 915 (1971); Vance v. Grow, 206 Ind. 614, 190 N.E. 747 (1934); Haack v. Burmeister, 289 Mich. 418, 286 N.W. 666 (1939); In re Weir's Estate, 134 Wash. 560, 236 P. 285 (1925). In 1A Scott, Law of Trusts § 55.1 (4th ed., Fratcher, 1987), it is stated that the devisee or legatee holds on constructive trust regardless of fraud or confidential relationship, but it is not clear that the case law supports this view.

19. Kramer v. Freedman, 272 So.2d 195 (Fla.Dist.Ct.App.1973), aff'd 295

So.2d 97 (Fla.1973); Cickyj (Mykola) v. Skeltinska, 93 Ill.App.3d 556, 49 Ill.Dec. 9, 417 N.E.2d 699 (1981); Teuscher v. Gragg, 136 Okl. 129, 276 P. 753 (1929).

20. See 1A Scott, Law of Trusts § 55.1 (4th ed., Fratcher, 1987).

If T intends to perform the trust when he agrees with O, but later changes his mind prior to O's death without advising O, this is a form of fraud because if O is advised of the change of heart O can revise his will.

provides for the payment of income to A for life, remainder to B. It has been maintained, however, that in such a situation the transferee of legal title who is deemed a constructive trustee should hold on a constructive trust to transfer legal title to another party appointed by the court to serve as trustee to pay the income to A for life, and remainder to B.[21] The unenforceable express trust would thereby be fully enforced in the guise of a restitutional remedy.

---

21. 1A Scott, Law of Trusts § 55.1 (4th ed., Fratcher, 1987). See Risley v. Kirkman, 56 N.J. 464, 267 A.2d 50 (1970); O'Boyle v. Brenner, 273 App. Div. 683, 79 N.Y.S.2d 84 (1948).

APPENDIX

Set forth below are examples of a will and a living trust. Their terms are relatively simple. The purpose is to show the reader what the documents we have been talking about may look like.

WILL

I, John R. Jones, of Hometown, Nameastate, hereby make, publish and declare this as my last will and testament, and revoke my prior wills and codicils.

ARTICLE ONE. I direct my Executor to pay my debts, funeral expenses, and costs of administration.

ARTICLE TWO. I give and devise my cottage property in Woodsville, Vacationstate, to my daughter, Mary Jones, if she survives me, or if she does not survive me, to her children, Susan and Sandra, as joint tenants with right of survivorship, if both of them survive me, or if both of them do not survive me, to the survivor of them who survives me.

ARTICLE THREE. I give and bequeath the horses which I own at the time of my death to my son, Robert Jones, if he survives me.

ARTICLE FOUR. I give and bequeath $25,000 to my son, Carl Jones, if he survives me.

ARTICLE FIVE. I give and bequeath $10,000 to Mercy Hospital of Hometown, and $10,000 to The Baptist Church of Hometown.

ARTICLE SIX. All the rest and residue of my property, real and personal, hereinafter referred to as my "residuary estate," I give, bequeath and devise to my wife, Wilma Jones, if she survives me.

ARTICLE SEVEN. If my wife, Wilma Jones, does not survive me, and I am survived by one or more descendants, I direct that my residuary estate be divided into as many equal shares as there are children of mine who survive me and children of mine who predeceased me who have descendants who survive me, and I give, bequeath and devise one such share to each of my children who survives me, and one such share to the descendants who survive me of each child of mine who predeceased me, such descendants to take by representation.

ARTICLE EIGHT. If my wife, Wilma Jones, does not survive me, and I am not survived by any descendant, I give, bequeath and devise my residuary estate as follows:

1. One-half of my residuary estate to those persons who would be entitled to receive my estate if I had died intestate not survived by a spouse, and in the shares to which they would be so entitled.

2. One-half of my residuary estate to those persons who would be entitled to receive the estate of my wife, Wilma Jones, if she had died intestate on the date of my death not survived by a spouse, under the laws of my domiciliary state at the time of my death, and in the shares to which they would be so entitled.

ARTICLE NINE. Notwithstanding the provisions of Articles Seven and Eight hereof, if any part of my residuary estate becomes payable to a person under 25 years of age, I direct that the property so payable to said person be distributed to the Trustee hereunder and held by the Trustee, in a separate trust, until said person arrives at age 25 or dies prior to that age or the property in trust is fully distributed prior to those dates. I authorize the Trustee, in his or her discretion, to apply any principal and income, in whole or in part, for the comfortable maintenance, education and support of said person, without regard to the other resources of said person or the resources of the parents of said person, by paying the same to a parent or guardian of said person or to the individual with whom said person resides, or by paying any bill incurred by or on behalf of said person, or by making payment directly to said person. The Trustee shall pay any remaining principal and income to said person when he or she reaches age 25, or to the estate of said person if he or she dies prior to age 25.

ARTICLE TEN. I appoint my wife, Wilma Jones, to be the Executor of this will, or if she does not become or ceases to be the Executor, I appoint my son, Robert Jones, to be the Executor of this will, or if he does not become or ceases to be the Executor of this will, I appoint my daughter, Mary Jones, to be the Executor of this will, or if she does not become or ceases to be the Executor, I appoint my son, Carl Jones, to be the Executor of this will.

If any part or parts of my residuary estate are held in trust pursuant to Article Nine, I appoint my son, Robert Jones, to be Trustee of such trust or trusts, or if he does not become or ceases to be such Trustee, I appoint my daughter, Mary Jones, to be such Trustee, or if she does not become or ceases to be such Trustee, I appoint my son, Carl Jones, to be such Trustee.

I direct that no bond is to be required of any Executor or Trustee under this will. I authorize the Executor and the Trustee to administer the estate and trusts without the intervention of any court to the maximum extent permitted by applicable law.

ARTICLE ELEVEN. I direct that no interest of any beneficiary of the income or the principal of any trust created under this will may be anticipated, assigned, transferred or encumbered, or be subject to any creditor's claim or legal process prior to its actual distribution to the beneficiary.

ARTICLE TWELVE. A legatee or devisee under this will is deemed to have survived me only if he or she is living on the sixtieth day following my death.

ARTICLE THIRTEEN. The term "descendants" includes persons who answer that description by virtue of adoption.

ARTICLE FOURTEEN. In addition to powers conferred by law and other provisions of this will, I confer upon the Executor and Trustee, without the necessity of any application to or approval of any court, the following powers: to retain any property owned by me at my death; to invest in common stocks, preferred stocks, bonds, evidences of indebtedness, securities, other forms of personal property, and real property, in the exercise of prudent judgment, notwithstanding any statutory limitations upon investments by fiduciaries; to sell any real or personal property, at private or public sale, for cash or on credit; to lease, mortgage, repair and improve any real or personal property; to borrow money with or without security; to hold a security in the name of a nominee without disclosure of the interest of the estate or trust, but the fiduciary shall be liable for any act of the nominee; to settle, arbitrate or release any claim held by or against the estate or the trust; to distribute the residuary estate or trust property in cash or in kind, or partly in cash and partly in kind.

IN WITNESS WHEREOF, I, John R. Jones, have hereunto set my hand and seal this ___ day of March, 1987.

_____ (Seal)

On the   day of March, 1987, John R. Jones published and declared to us, the undersigned, that the foregoing instrument was his last will, and he requested us to act as witnesses to it and to his signature thereon. He then signed the will in our presence, we being present at the same time. We now, at his request, in his presence, and in the presence of each other, hereunto subscribe our names as witnesses, and each of us declares that in his or her opinion the testator is of sound mind.

_____ residing at _____

_____ residing at _____

———————————————————— residing at ————————

(The statutory affidavit and acknowledgment to make the will self-proved may follow here. Alternatively the will may be executed, attested, and made self-proved simultaneously. See the discussion at page 35 above.)

LIVING TRUST

Bruce Brown, of Smalltown, Nameastate (hereinafter called the "Settlor"), hereby transfers to Smith County Bank (hereinafter called the "Trustee"), the property set forth in Schedule A attached hereto, the receipt of which property Trustee hereby acknowledges, and at the request of the Settlor, the Trustee agrees to hold such property in trust in accordance with the following terms:

I. Settlor reserves the right to amend this trust from time to time, and to revoke this trust wholly at any time or in part from time to time, by a writing signed by the Settlor and delivered to the Trustee in the lifetime of the Settlor. Settlor may, during his life or by his will, add to this trust other property acceptable to the Trustee.

II. During the life of the Settlor, the Trustee shall dispose of the income and principal of the trust as the Settlor may direct from time to time by a writing signed by the Settlor and delivered to the Trustee. If, in the opinion of the Trustee, the Settlor is incapacitated because of illness, age or other cause, the Trustee may, in its discretion, from time to time, apply all or any part of the income and principal toward the support, care and benefit of the Settlor, in such amounts as it may determine without regard to the Settlor's other means. Any income not disposed of in any year shall be added to the principal of the trust at the end of such year.

III. After the death of the Settlor, if the Settlor's son, Robert Brown, survives the Settlor, the Trustee shall dispose of income and principal as follows:

1. During the life of Robert Brown, the Trustee shall pay the entire income quarter-annually or at more frequent intervals to, or for the benefit of, Robert Brown and any living descendants of Robert Brown, in such shares as the Trustee shall in its discretion from time to time determine. The Trustee, in its discretion, may pay the entire income to one or more of the beneficiaries and not pay any income to one or more of them.

2. During the life of Robert Brown, the Trustee is authorized to pay to, or for the benefit of, Robert Brown or any of his descendants, such amounts from principal as the Trustee in its discretion from time to time considers necessary for the support, education or medical needs of any such beneficiary. The Trustee shall consider the income of a beneficiary from all sources and any

other property of a beneficiary in its discretionary decision to make or not to make a payment.

3. At the death of Robert Brown, if Robert Brown is survived by descendants, the Trustee is to divide the trust property then remaining into as many equal shares as there are children of Robert Brown then living and children of Robert Brown then deceased who have descendants then living. The Trustee shall distribute one such share to each living child of Robert Brown, and one such share to the living descendants of each deceased child, the descendants of each deceased child to take such share by representation. Such distributions are subject to Article VI.

4. At the death of Robert Brown, if Robert Brown is not survived by a descendant, the Trustee shall pay over the trust property to the personal representative of Robert Brown's estate, to be administered as part of his estate.

IV. If the Settlor is not survived by his son, Robert Brown, but is survived by a descendant or descendants of Robert Brown, at the death of the Settlor the Trustee is to divide the trust property then remaining into as many equal shares as there are children of Robert Brown then living and children of Robert Brown then deceased who have descendants then living. The Trustee shall distribute one such share to each living child of Robert Brown, and one such share to the living descendants of each deceased child, the descendants of each deceased child to take such share by representation. Such distributions are subject to Article VI.

V. If the Settlor is not survived by his son, Robert Brown, or any descendant of Robert Brown, the Trustee shall pay over the remaining trust property to the personal representative of the Settlor's estate, to be administered as part of the Settlor's estate.

VI. If any trust property becomes distributable to a person under 25 years of age pursuant to Article III(3) or Article IV, the property so payable to said person is to be held by the Trustee, in a separate trust, until said person arrives at age 25 or dies prior to that age or the property in trust is fully distributed prior to those dates. The Trustee is authorized, in its discretion, to apply any principal and income in whole or in part, for the comfortable maintenance, education and support of said person, without regard to the other resources of said person or the resources of the parents of said person, by paying the same to a parent or guardian of said person or to the individual with whom said person resides, or by paying any bill incurred by or on behalf of said person, or by making payment directly to said person. The Trustee shall pay any remaining principal and income to said person when he or she reaches ages 25, or to the estate of said person if he or she dies prior to age 25. Notwithstanding the above provisions of this

Article VI, any separate trust under this Article VI of property distributed pursuant to Article III(3), shall terminate and the property be distributed to the beneficiary thereunder twenty-one years after the death of the Settlor's son, Robert Brown, if the trust has not already terminated.

VII. If Smith County Bank shall cease to be Trustee, State Bank and Trust Company is appointed as Trustee. The Trustee hereunder shall not be required to furnish a bond.

VIII. No interest of any beneficiary of the income or the principal of any trust hereunder may be anticipated, assigned, transferred or encumbered, or be subject to any creditor's claim or legal process prior to its actual distribution to the beneficiary.

IX. The terms "descendants," "child," and "children" include persons who answer that description by virtue of adoption.

X. The Trustee shall not be required to file any periodic or final accounting with respect to any trust hereunder with any court, but it shall file annual accounts of receipts and disbursements and property held with each adult beneficiary and the guardian or person having custody of any minor or incompetent beneficiary.

XI. The Trustee shall receive, and is authorized to charge against the trust, compensation for its services which shall not exceed the compensation it usually receives for similar services at the time the services hereunder are rendered.

XII. In addition to powers conferred by law and other provisions of this instrument, the Trustee shall have the following powers: to retain any property transferred by the Settlor to the Trustee; to invest in common stocks, preferred stocks, bonds, evidences of indebtedness, securities, other forms of personal property, and real property, in the exercise of prudent judgment; to sell any property at public or private sale, for cash or on credit; to lease, mortgage, repair and improve any real or personal property; to borrow money with or without security; to hold a security in the name of a nominee without disclosure of the interest of the trust, but the Trustee shall be liable for any act of the nominee; to settle, arbitrate or release any claim held by or against the trust; to effect distribution of trust property in cash or in kind, or partly in cash and partly in kind.

IN WITNESS WHEREOF, Bruce Brown, as Settlor, and Smith County Bank, as Trustee, hereby sign and seal this instrument, on this   day of March, 1987.

_____ (Seal)
Bruce Brown, Settlor
Smith County Bank, Trustee

(Seal)   By _____
         .   Vice President

(Notarial acknowledgments by Settlor and Trustee follow below)

*

TABLE OF CASES

References are to Pages

Haskell Wills 2E -- 13

INDEX

†